Foreword

This anthology, which includes all the poems prescribed for the Higher and Ordinary Level English Leaving Certificate Examinations of 2013, has been prepared by three experienced teachers of English. Each of the contributors has been able to concentrate on a limited number of the prescribed poets and their work, thus facilitating a high standard of research and presentation.

Guidelines are given which set each poem in context. In addition, each poem is accompanied by a glossary and appropriate explorations, designed to allow the student to find his/her authentic response to the material. Relevant biographical details are provided for each poet. A list of examination-style questions is provided for each prescribed poet at Higher Level along with a snapshot of the poet's work and a sample examination-style essay to aid revision.

Guidelines are included for students on approaching the Unseen Poetry section of the course. There is also advice on approaching the prescribed question in the examination. Students will also find the glossary of poetic terms a valuable resource in reading and responding to poetry.

The poetry course for Leaving Certificate English demands a personal and active engagement from the student reader. We hope that this anthology makes that engagement possible and encourages students to explore the wider world of poetry for themselves. Further discussion of the issues raised in the guidelines can be found in Edco's Leaving Certificate Poetry Notes, 2013. In accordance with the poet's wishes, we have not included guidelines or questions with the poetry of Adrienne Rich.

Teachers can access the New Discovery for Leaving Certificate Higher and Ordinary Level e-book by registering on www.edcodigital.ie

Patrick Murray
Kevin McDermott
Mary Slattery

New
Discovery

Leaving Certificate Poetry Anthology
for Higher and Ordinary Level 2013

Edco
The Educational Company of Ireland

First published 2011

The Educational Company of Ireland
Ballymount Road
Walkinstown
Dublin 12

www.edco.ie

A member of the Smurfit Kappa Group plc

© Patrick Murray, Kevin McDermott,
Mary Slattery, 2011

ISBN 978-1-84536-384-0

QUALITY
I.S. EN ISO 9001:2008
NSAI Certified

Editor: Jennifer Armstrong
Design and layout: Design Image
Cover photographs: Topfoto, Corbis
Printed by W&G Baird

Contents

Acknowledgements

The poems in this book have been reproduced with the kind permission of their publishers, agents, authors or their estates as follows:

'The Armadillo', 'At The Fishhouses', 'The Bight', 'Filling Station', 'First Death in Nova Scotia', 'The Fish', 'In the Waiting Room', 'The Prodigal', 'Questions of Travel', 'Sestina' by Elizabeth Bishop from *The Complete Poems 1927-1979*. © 1979, 1983 by Alice Helen Methfessel. Reprinted by permission of Farrar, Straus and Giroux LLC.

'Thinking of Mr D.', 'Dick King', 'Mirror in February', Chrysalides', from 'Glenmacnass VI Littlebody', 'Tear', 'Hen Woman', 'His Father's Hands', from 'Settings: Model School, Inchicore', from 'The Familiar VII' and 'Belief and Unbelief: Echo' by Thomas Kinsella from *Collected Poems* (2001) by Carcanet Press Limited, reproduced by kind permission of the poet and Carcanet Press.

'Grandfather', 'Day Trip to Donegal', 'Ecclesiastes', 'After the Titanic', 'At it Should Be', 'A Disused Shed in Co Wexford', 'Rathlin', 'The Chinese Restaurant in Portrush', 'Kinsale', 'Antarctica' by Derek Mahon from *Collected Poems* (1999) by kind permission of the author and The Gallery Press, Loughcrew, Oldcastle, Co Meath.

'Pheasant', 'Finisterre', 'Mirror', 'Child', 'Morning Song', 'Elm', 'The Arrival of the Bee Box', 'Poppies in July', 'Black Rook in Rainy Weather', 'The Times are Tidy' by Sylvia Plath from *Collected Poems* (1981) published by Faber and Faber Ltd.

'The Uncle Speaks in the Drawing Room', 'Our Whole Life', from *Collected Early Poems: 1950-1970* by Adrienne Rich. © 1993 by Adrienne Rich. © 1967, 1963, 1962, 1961, 1960, 1959, 1958, 1957, 1956, 1955, 1954, 1953, 1952, 1951 by Adrienne Rich. © 1984, 1975, 1971, 1969, 1966 by W. W. Norton & Company, Inc. Used by permission of the author and W. W. Norton & Company, Inc.

'Storm Warnings', 'Aunt Jennifer's Tigers', 'Living in Sin', 'The Roofwalker', 'Trying to Talk with a Man', 'Diving Into the Wreck', 'From a Survivor', 'Power' by Adrienne Rich from *The Fact of a Doorframe: Selected Poems 1950-2001* by Adrienne Rich. © 2002 by Adrienne Rich. © 2001, 1999, 1995, 1991, 1989, 1986, 1984, 1981, 1967, 1963, 1962, 1961, 1960, 1959, 1958, 1957, 1956, 1955, 1954, 1953, 1952, 1951 by Adrienne Rich. © 1978, 1975, 1973, 1971, 1969, 1966 by W W Norton & Company Inc. Used by permission of the author and W. W. Norton & Company, Inc.

'For Heidi with Blue Hair' by Fleur Adcock from *Poems 1960-2000*, Bloodaxe Books 2000. Reprinted by permission of the publisher.

'The Hug' by Tess Gallagher from *Amplitude: New and Selected Poems* © 1984, 1987. Reprinted with the permission of Graywolf Press, Minneapolis, Minnesota. www.graywolfpress.org.

'Daniel's Duck' by Kerry Hardie from *The Sky Didn't Fall* © 2003. By kind permission of the author and The Gallery Press, Loughcrew, Oldcastle, Co Meath.

'Night Drive' by Brendan Kennelly from *Familiar Strangers: New and Selected Poems 1960-2004*, Bloodaxe Books 2004, reprinted by permission of the publisher.

'Badger' by Michael Longley from *Collected Poems*, published by Jonathan Cape. Reprinted by permission of the Random House Group Ltd.

'Anseo' by Paul Muldoon from *Why Brownlee Left* published by Faber and Faber Ltd.

'Problems' by Julie O'Callaghan from *Tell Me This is Normal: New and Selected Poems*, Bloodaxe Books 2008, reprinted by permission of the publisher.

'The Sun' by Mary Oliver is reprinted by permission of Beacon Press.

'Will we work together?' by Marge Piercy, © 1977, 1980 by Marge Piercy and Middlemarsh, Inc. From *The Moon Is Always Female*, Alfred A. Knopf, 1980. Used with permission of the Wallace Literary Agency, Inc.

'Jungian Cows' by Penelope Shuttle, from *Adventures With My Horse*, published by The Poetry Book Society. Reproduced by kind permission of the poet and David Higham Associates.

'Madly Singing in the City' by Peter Sirr from *Bring Everything* © 2000. By kind permission of the author and The Gallery Press, Loughcrew, Oldcastle, Co Meath.

'Traveling Through The Dark' by William Stafford from *The Way It Is: New and Selected Poems*. © 1962, 1998 by William Stafford and the Estate of William Stafford. Reprinted with the permission of Graywolf Press, Minneapolis, Minnesota. www.graywolfpress.org.

'Do Not Go Gentle into That Good Night' by Dylan Thomas from *Collected Poems* published by Orion. Used by permission of the author.

'Chronicle' by David Wheatley from *Misery Hill* © 2000. By kind permission of the author and The Gallery Press, Loughcrew, Oldcastle, Co Meath.

'A Summer Morning' by Richard Wilbur from *New and Collected Poems* published by Faber and Faber Ltd.

Elizabeth Bishop

1911–79

Biography

Elizabeth Bishop was born on 8 February 1911, in Worcester, Massachusetts. She was the only child of William T. Bishop and Gertrude May Bulmer Bishop. William, who was vice-president of his father's successful building firm, died of Bright's disease when Elizabeth was eight months old. Gertrude was so traumatised by her husband's death that it led to a mental breakdown that resulted in her being hospitalised five years later. Elizabeth never saw her mother again, although she lived until 1934.

Although Elizabeth left published accounts of only two memories of her life with her mother – one of them a short reference in her poem 'First Death in Nova Scotia' – it is clear that the experience left an indelible impression on her, influencing her emotional life and possibly accounting for her later struggles with depression and alcoholism.

Elizabeth was cared for initially by her maternal grandparents at Great Village, a tiny town in Nova Scotia, a time she recollected later with affection. Her grandparents were simple and loving people, and there was a family of aunts and uncles who were caring and kind to her. In 1917, however, her paternal grandparents, the wealthy Bishops, arrived in Great Village by train to take the six-year-old Elizabeth back to live with them in Worcester. Her departure was so sudden that she recalled it as a 'kidnapping' from the happy home she knew to a much more austere environment, a violent change that seems to have created a sense of loss in the child, a sense which remained with her as an adult.

Her unhappiness showed itself in the many illnesses she suffered from – asthma, bronchitis, eczema. The Bishops felt unable to cope with her after only nine months and her mother's older sister, Aunt Maude, rescued the ill and nervous child by taking her to live with her and her husband in the upstairs apartment of a run-down tenement in an impoverished neighbourhood in Revere, Massachusetts. Bishop later said that Aunt Maude had saved her life.

Education

Ill health meant that Bishop had very little formal schooling before the age of fourteen. Her formal education began at Walnut Hill School for Girls. Academically she made great progress. Her literary gifts were apparent and she wrote fiction and poetry for the school magazine. By the time she attended the exclusive all-girls' college at Vassar in New York, where she majored in English literature, she was already considered to have great talent. She was also an accomplished musician and painter. Following graduation Bishop remained in New York, writing poems for small magazines and using money from her inheritance to travel to France, England, North Africa, Spain and Italy. In 1938 she moved to Key West, Florida. In 1946 her first collection of poems, *North & South*, the fruit of ten years' work, received the Houghton Mifflin Poetry Award. Awarded a Guggenheim Fellowship in 1947, she became consultant in poetry at the Library of Congress.

Brazil

Bishop's life changed again in 1951 when, on a visit to Brazil, she met Lota de Macedo Soares. The two women settled together near Rio de Janeiro in a lesbian relationship that was to last until Lota's death in 1967. Bishop described this period as the happiest time of her life: for the first time she had a home and a sense of family with Lota's adopted children. She also continued her travels, visiting Mexico and Europe, and in 1961 she took a trip up the Amazon river to see Indian tribes.

Her second collection, *A Cold Spring*, was published in 1955. Combined with *North & South*, it won the Pulitzer Prize for poetry. Her literary reputation was recognised by the Fellowship of the Academy of American Poets awarded in 1964. In 1965 her third collection, *Questions of Travel*, appeared.

After Lota's death in 1967 Bishop lived for a year in San Francisco, then taught for a number of years at Harvard University, Cambridge, Massachusetts. In 1976, maintaining her pattern of producing a book of poems roughly every ten years, she published *Geography III*. Numerous prizes and awards followed until her death in Boston in 1979. Her *Complete Poems* was published in 1991.

Social and Cultural Context

Bishop is now recognised as one of the best American poets of the twentieth century, although she published only four small volumes of poems over a span of forty years. During her lifetime she was by no means a well-known writer, even though her work was praised by many critics as it appeared. One of the possible reasons for this may be that she was not identified with any particular school or movement in poetry.

Although Bishop's copious letters to her friends and acquaintances reveal her awareness of most of the important cultural movements of her day, she retained to the end a sense of her own independence and integrity. In her work with students at New York and Harvard, she stressed the importance of poetry and observed that it must be worked at if it is to be rewarding – a philosophy that could be said to underlie her considerable poetic achievement.

Literary and artistic influences

Bishop was, however, influenced by many major literary movements. Her earliest published work, which explores imaginary worlds, shows her interest in the ideas of the Symbolist poets of the late nineteenth and early twentieth centuries. She was also influenced by the theories of the early twentieth-century poetic movement Imagism, in which the image is central to a poem's meaning. Her mastery of these techniques is clear in her mature work, but she moved above and beyond them in forging her own distinctive style.

She assimilated other important literary and artistic ideas of the twentieth century. Critics have remarked on the extent to which her poems share the Surrealists' fascination with perspective and vision, for instance, which is not surprising for a poet who was also a painter. (Surrealism, popular in the 1920s and 1930s, seeks to break down the boundaries between rationality and irrationality, to liberate the imagination from reality.)

Child psychology

In her poems about childhood, Bishop is seen to have absorbed the teachings of famous child psychologists of her time such as Melanie Klein and Benjamin Spock. Both of these psychologists emphasised the importance of recognising the child as an individual whose experience in childhood was crucial for healthy development in later life.

In turn, Bishop is acknowledged to have influenced many contemporary and younger poets, in particular Robert Lowell and John Ashbery.

Travel

Bishop's lifelong interest in travel presented her with one of her most important poetic themes. Her desire to see things afresh and her sense of curiosity combined to create in her work an impression of a poet who wishes to engage with other cultures and ways of life. As many critics have remarked, she is a poet who is more interested in geography than history, so that although she lived through World War II, and through turbulent times in Brazil, these are not subjects that engage her poetic attention.

Feminism

Nor was Bishop interested, as a poet, in being part of the feminist movement of the 1960s and 1970s. Although she described herself as having been a feminist from about the age of six – her poem 'In the Waiting Room' would suggest this – she rarely engaged with the issue directly in her work. **She preferred to think of art as being outside gender.**

Bishop was reluctant to be pigeon-holed as a woman poet, believing it would limit her power to reach a wider audience. Throughout her life she refused to allow her poems to be included in all-women anthologies. She was the sort of feminist who believed that a talented woman could compete successfully in any area of life. She regarded overtly feminist poetry as propaganda and disapproved of the new 'confessional' type of poetry in which personal relationships were laid bare. Her own lesbian relationship, with Lota de Macedo Soares, never featured directly in her work.

Timeline

1911	Born on 8 February in Massachusetts; father dies
1916	Mother hospitalised
1917	Lives with grandparents and later Aunt Maude
1930–34	Attends Vassar College, New York
1938	Moves to Key West, Florida
1946	Publishes her first collection of poems, *North & South*; wins Houghton Mifflin Poetry Award
1951	Meets partner, Lota de Macedo Soares; settles in Brazil
1955	Publishes her second collection, *A Cold Spring*; wins Pulitzer Prize for poetry
1964	Awarded Fellowship of the Academy of American Poets
1965	Publishes her third collection, *Questions of Travel*
1967	Lota dies; Elizabeth lives in San Francisco for a year
1970	Poet-in-residence at Harvard University, Massachusetts
1976	Publishes her fourth collection, *Geography III*
1979	Dies in Boston
1991	*Complete Poems* published

The Fish

I caught a tremendous fish
and held him beside the boat
half out of water, with my hook
fast in a corner of his mouth.
He didn't fight.   5
He hadn't fought at all.
He hung a grunting weight,
battered and venerable
and homely. Here and there
his brown skin hung in strips   10
like ancient wallpaper,
and its pattern of darker brown
was like wallpaper:
shapes like full-blown roses
stained and lost through age.   15
He was speckled with barnacles,
fine rosettes of lime,
and infested
with tiny white sea-lice,
and underneath two or three   20
rags of green weed hung down.
While his gills were breathing in
the terrible oxygen
– the frightening gills,
fresh and crisp with blood,   25
that can cut so badly –
I thought of the coarse white flesh
packed in like feathers,
the big bones and the little bones,
the dramatic reds and blacks   30
of his shiny entrails,
and the pink swim-bladder
like a big peony.
I looked into his eyes
which were far larger than mine   35
but shallower, and yellowed,
the irises backed and packed

with tarnished tinfoil
seen through the lenses
of old scratched isinglass. 40
They shifted a little, but not
to return my stare.
– It was more like the tipping
of an object toward the light.
I admired his sullen face, 45
the mechanism of his jaw,
and then I saw
that from his lower lip
– if you could call it a lip –
grim, wet, and weaponlike, 50
hung five old pieces of fish-line,
or four and a wire leader
with the swivel still attached,
with all their five big hooks
grown firmly in his mouth. 55
A green line, frayed at the end
where he broke it, two heavier lines,
and a fine black thread
still crimped from the strain and snap
when it broke and he got away. 60
Like medals with their ribbons
frayed and wavering,
a five-haired beard of wisdom
trailing from his aching jaw.
I stared and stared 65
and victory filled up
the little rented boat,
from the pool of bilge
where oil had spread a rainbow
around the rusted engine 70
to the bailer rusted orange,
the sun-cracked thwarts,
the oarlocks on their strings,
the gunnels – until everything
was rainbow, rainbow, rainbow! 75
And I let the fish go.

Glossary

8	*venerable*:	worthy of respect on account of age, character, position, etc.
16	*barnacles*:	crustaceans or shellfish that cling to rocks, large fish, etc.
31	*entrails*:	inner parts of the fish
33	*peony*:	a large, showy flower
40	*isinglass*:	a whitish, semi-transparent gelatinous substance
52	*wire leader*:	a short piece of wire connecting fish-hook and fish-line
53	*swivel*:	a ring or link that turns round on a pin or neck
59	*crimped*:	curled, wavy
68	*bilge*:	filth that collects in the bottom of a boat
71	*bailer*:	a bucket for ladling water out of a boat
72	*thwarts*:	seats or benches that the rowers sit on
73	*oarlocks*:	devices for holding and balancing the oars on the side of a boat
74	*gunnels*:	gunwale, the upper edge of a boat's side

Guidelines

'The Fish' was written when Bishop lived in Florida in the 1930s. It is included in her first collection, *North & South*. As with so many of her poems, it is based on a real experience that she had of catching a large Caribbean jewfish at Key West.

Commentary

Lines 1–20

In the first few lines of the poem the speaker tells us that she caught a 'tremendous fish' (line 1) that did not resist capture at all, probably because, as she says, he was 'battered and venerable' (line 8). 'Battered' suggests that he has suffered. 'Venerable' is a word often applied to elderly people and hints at the respect Bishop feels for him from the beginning. It also suggests that she is giving the fish some of the attributes of a human being.

She then describes in detail what the fish looked like, using some unusual and original images that appeal to our senses of sight and touch. His skin is compared to 'ancient wallpaper' (line 11), complete with patterns and stains. Vivid colours enable us to visualise the fish: 'brown' and 'darker brown' skin (lines 10 and 12) speckled with lime green and white (lines 16 to 19), as well as suggestions of pink in 'roses' (line 14). She gives us a realistic picture of the fish, seeing him not only in imaginative terms

but also taking care to present him as he really is, his fishy texture and physical characteristics. He is covered in barnacles and infested with sea-lice. From underneath him hang 'rags of green weed' (line 21), seaweed of course, but somehow suggesting the beard of a 'venerable' old man.

Lines 22–33

In these lines Bishop focuses on the fish as an alien creature, leaving aside for a time any human characteristics he might have. The 'frightening gills / fresh and crisp with blood' (lines 24–25) and the 'coarse white flesh' (line 27) appeal to our sense of touch, while we can see the 'dramatic reds and blacks / of his shiny entrails' (lines 30–31). The pattern of flower imagery is continued as his pink swim-bladder is compared to a 'big peony' (line 33).

Lines 34–65

Despite the barrier between animal and human, **Bishop begins to empathise with the fish**: 'I looked into his eyes' (line 34). She describes the eyes with great care. **Details are important to her,** such as whether the fish's eyes are larger and shallower than those of humans, and how the irises seem 'backed and packed / with tarnished tinfoil' (lines 37–38). As is part of her characteristic method of description, she clarifies this last image: not just any tinfoil but tinfoil 'seen through the lenses / of old scratched isinglass' (lines 39–40). (Isinglass is a gelatinous substance that causes an object viewed through it to seem somewhat hazy.) The adjectives 'tarnished' and 'old' continue the notion of age that has been introduced from the beginning.

The narrator is under no illusion that the creature responds to her, but she certainly responds to him. She admires 'his sullen face / the mechanism of his jaw' – the features belong to humans, as does the 'lip' and 'mouth' she mentions with the pieces of fish-line hanging from it (lines 45 to 55). She describes the hooks and fish-lines as 'weaponlike' (line 50), and sees that the fish has struggled many times to escape capture. Words such as 'strain and snap' (line 59) emphasise how difficult it must have been for him.

The achievement of the fish in escaping capture becomes like that of a war hero who has endured conflict and is now honoured for it. We visualise a battle-scarred general, decorated for bravery: the fish-lines are 'like medals with their ribbons / frayed and wavering' (lines 61–62). Now the fish seems really to have earned the adjective 'venerable' used earlier in the poem.

Lines 65–76

For the remainder of the poem Bishop is concerned with her own response to capturing the fish. When she says that she 'stared and stared' (line 65), it suggests

that she has an important moment of recognition that influences what she now does. She is recording her admiration for the uniqueness of the fish. She also sees the fish as a creature with rights within his own environment, the sea. He has a right to an existence that is independent of humans.

There are a number of aspects to her sense of 'victory' (line 66). It was a great achievement to have caught such a 'tremendous fish'. There is also her victory in achieving an insight into the experience of the fish, how he has struggled and overcome difficulties. Given the circumstances of Bishop's life, it is possible that she sees in the fish a fellow creature, suffering and struggling like herself.

For all these reasons, Bishop is overjoyed at this moment of recognition. She expresses her joy in a lovely metaphor of beauty and hope, a rainbow. The metaphor has its origin in the oil that had spread around a 'pool of bilge' (line 68) that lay at the bottom of the boat. With her usual eye for details she describes parts of the boat as 'rusted' (line 70) and 'sun-cracked' (line 72), creating a link between the well-used boat and the 'venerable' fish. It seems appropriate that even the boat shares in the 'victory' that finally belongs to the fish: 'And I let the fish go' (line 76).

Tone of the poem

The tone of the poem goes beyond any conventional delight a person might feel at having 'caught a tremendous fish' (line 1). Bishop reveals her growing interest and emotional involvement in the fish and his struggle, past and present. The admiring tone of the language used to describe him suggests that she recognises the difficulties he has had, and his achievements in overcoming them.

She also recognises that he is a creature from another element far removed from that of humans. She is full of wonder at the difference between them. Finally, she is humble in her recognition that the fish has a right to his own freedom. There is no regret in the last line: 'And I let the fish go.'

Fable

The poem can be read as a fable (a poem with a message or a moral). In many traditional fables there is an encounter between a human and an animal in which the human learns an important lesson. From the beginning of the poem the fish seems more than just a creature of nature. Bishop gives him some human characteristics, as in a traditional fable. He is a 'venerable' (well-respected) and aged general, who has received awards for his bravery in battle. He has struggled and has gained 'wisdom' from those struggles. It may be that the lesson of the poem (the reason why she finally let the fish go) is connected with her awareness that the fish has a moral right to his own survival. Such an interpretation would indicate that Bishop recognised the complex relationship human beings have with the natural world. Writing in the 1930s, she would have been ahead of her time in having such a modern, ecologically aware attitude to nature.

Form of the poem

The poem is written as one long narrative with a clear beginning, progression and ending. It is unrhymed, which helps to give the impression of the speaking voice, with the exception of the last two lines, where a rhyming couplet gives a sense of closure. The metre Bishop chooses is dimeter, with two stresses per line (as in 'He didn't fight') or trimeter with three stresses ('He hadn't fought at all'). This form of metre echoes speech rhythms and is particularly suitable for telling a story.

Sound patterns in the poem

Although the poem does not rhyme, Bishop makes use of sound patterns such as assonance, consonance and alliteration. For example, you may notice the repeated 'u' sound in 'hung a grunting', 'i' sound in 'skin . . . strips' (assonance); alliteration in 'big bones' and 'tarnished tinfoil'; and consonance in the phrase 'speckled with barnacles'. Such sound patterns are to be found throughout the poem and contribute to its harmonious effect.

Thinking about the poem

1   'I caught a tremendous fish'. In lines 1 to 9 of the poem, how does Bishop show that the fish was 'tremendous'?

2   How does Bishop describe the fish in lines 16 to 21?

3   Choose the word that in your view best defines Bishop's description of the fish: attractive, imaginative or realistic. Explain your choice.

4   Where in the poem does Bishop present the fish as having human characteristics?

5   Where in the poem, however, are we made aware that this is an illusion?

6   'I stared and stared' (line 65). Why is this a significant moment in the poem?

7   How do Bishop's feelings about the fish change as the poem progresses?

8   Why, in your opinion, does she release the fish? Who has had the 'victory' here, in your opinion?

9   What sort of person do you imagine Bishop to be, from reading this poem?

10 Bishop once said, 'I simply try to see things afresh.' Does she achieve this in 'The Fish'? Support your answer by reference to the poem.

Taking a closer look

1   The fish is compared to wallpaper (lines 10 to 15) and to an old army general (lines 61 to 64). Which of the comparisons do you find most convincing? Give a reason for your view.

2   Choose two more examples of similes (comparisons) used in the poem and say whether you liked them or not. Give reasons.

3   Comment on Bishop's use of colour in describing the fish.

Imagining

1   You wish to include 'The Fish' in an anthology entitled *Nature*. Give reasons why this poem would be suitable for the anthology.

2   You wish to make a short film or video of this poem. Describe how you would use lighting and music to create atmosphere.

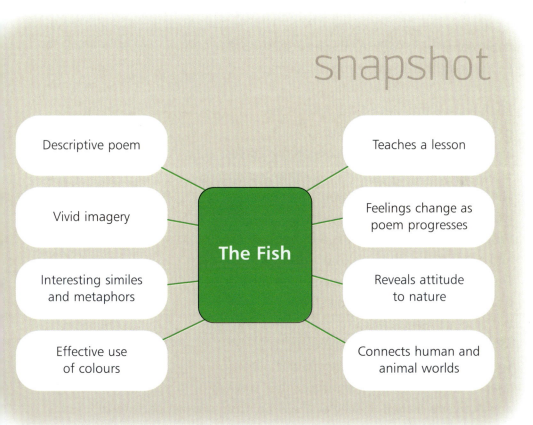

snapshot

Descriptive poem

Vivid imagery

Interesting similes and metaphors

Effective use of colours

The Fish

Teaches a lesson

Feelings change as poem progresses

Reveals attitude to nature

Connects human and animal worlds

The Bight

(On my birthday)

At low tide like this how sheer the water is.
White, crumbling ribs of marl protrude and glare
and the boats are dry, the pilings dry as matches.
Absorbing, rather than being absorbed,
the water in the bight doesn't wet anything,   5
the color of the gas flame turned as low as possible.
One can smell it turning to gas; if one were Baudelaire
one could probably hear it turning to marimba music.
The little ocher dredge at work off the end of the dock
already plays the dry perfectly off-beat claves.   10
The birds are outsize. Pelicans crash
into this peculiar gas unnecessarily hard,
it seems to me, like pickaxes,
rarely coming up with anything to show for it,
and going off with humorous elbowings.   15

Black-and-white man-of-war birds soar
on impalpable drafts
and open their tails like scissors on the curves
or tense them like wishbones, till they tremble.
The frowsy sponge boats keep coming in   20
with the obliging air of retrievers,
bristling with jackstraw gaffs and hooks
and decorated with bobbles of sponges.
There is a fence of chicken wire along the dock
where, glinting like little plowshares,   25
the blue-gray shark tails are hung up to dry
for the Chinese-restaurant trade.
Some of the little white boats are still piled up
against each other, or lie on their sides, stove in,
and not yet salvaged, if they ever will be, from the last bad storm,   30
like torn-open, unanswered letters.
The bight is littered with old correspondences.

Click. Click. Goes the dredge,
and brings up a dripping jawful of marl.
All the untidy activity continues, 35
awful but cheerful.

Glossary

Title	*Bight*: a wide bay
2	*marl*: a thick, clay-like soil
3	*pilings*: timber posts driven into the ground to make a foundation
7	*Baudelaire*: Charles Baudelaire, a French Symbolist poet (1821–67)
8	*marimba music*: African xylophone music played by jazz musicians
9	*ocher dredge*: orange-brown-coloured machine for clearing mud
10	*claves*: musical keys
16	*man-of-war birds*: large tropical seabirds
20	*frowsy*: ill-smelling, untidy
21	*retrievers*: dogs trained to find and fetch things
22	*jackstraw gaffs*: splinters of wood used as hooks to land large fish
24	*chicken wire*: wire netting
25	*plowshares*: the detachable part of a plough that cuts and turns the soil
29	*stove in*: broken

Guidelines

'The Bight' was probably written in 1948 and is found in the collection *A Cold Spring* (1955).

Some of the details in this poem appeared first in a letter Bishop wrote when she lived in Key West, Florida, to her friend and fellow poet Robert Lowell. Excavations being carried out at Garrison Bight, Key West, left the harbour, as she describes it, 'always in a mess . . . it reminds me a little of my desk'. This remark might help us to appreciate her reference to Baudelaire, and indirectly to his 'theory of correspondences'. This Symbolist poet believed that there was a connection between the spiritual and physical worlds, so that one could express one's thoughts and feelings by describing objects and scenes.

It could be said that this is what the poem does. **It moves from description of ordinary activity (the dredging of the harbour) – what it looks and sounds like – to discovery of a more private world.** What Bishop sees and hears as the bight is excavated seems to lead her to contemplate the connections ('correspondences', line 32) between what is going on there and her work as a creative artist searching for material and trying to put shape on it.

Commentary

Stanza 1

The poem begins by describing the scene at low tide in the bight (or bay). Although the objects she sees are ordinary – the clay deposits (marl), the boats and the wooden posts (pilings) – she describes them in unusual metaphors and similes. The marl is shaped like 'ribs' that stick out from a body; with the adjectives 'white' and 'crumbling' the image she creates is surreal and a little menacing (line 2). The boats are dry, as are the wooden posts.

The water that 'doesn't wet anything' is 'the color of the gas flame turned as low as possible' (lines 5 and 6). She develops this image further when she says, 'One can smell it turning to gas' (line 7). Taken together with the phrase 'dry as matches' (line 3) there may be an underlying sense of anxiety about the scene, a fear of fire or a gas explosion.

At this stage Bishop introduces the name of Baudelaire, the French Symbolist poet mentioned in the overview above. If she were he, she says, perhaps she could make even more connections – not only see and smell the gas but also hear it turning to something completely different, like music. (In his poetry Baudelaire frequently used synaesthesia, or combination of senses in one image.) Despite sounding slightly dismissive here, we should be aware that Bishop is in fact making such connections right though the poem.

Lines 9 to 15 show Bishop's remarkable ability to observe ordinary reality and present it in a new way through unusual metaphors and similes. The dredge that is carrying out the excavation sounds as if is playing music (ironically recalling the reference to Baudelaire). She describes the pelicans as if they are machines rather than creatures. They are 'like pickaxes' in the way they 'crash' into the gas-like water, coming up with nothing to show for it.

Stanza 2

In lines 16 to 19 she describes large 'man-of-war birds' in similarly mechanised terms, with their tails open 'like scissors' but ending in a 'tremble'. Like the pelicans, they cannot find any food in the shallow water. Other objects, too, are seen as ineffective:

the ill-smelling boats, compared to 'retrievers', that keep coming in with useless things such as bits of fishing line (lines 20 to 24).

The whole impression is one of pointlessness and is continued when she describes other random objects that catch her attention. Once again the comparisons she makes are unusual. The 'blue-gray shark tails' (line 26) bound for Chinese restaurants that are drying on the chicken-wire fence along the dock are 'like plowshares' (line 25) – another word depicting a machine. The little boats that were damaged during the last storm still have their sides broken and may never now be salvaged; she compares them to 'torn-open, unanswered letters' (line 31).

Significantly, she comments, 'The bight is littered with old correspondences' (line 32). This line has interesting connotations. It echoes the French word used by Baudelaire (*correspondances*, meaning connections), but it is also of course a play on the idea of letter writing. Perhaps this is why she noted that the bight reminded her of her desk. The last four lines bring us back to the sound of the dredge as it digs up more and more mud. The activity goes on, not beautiful, not uplifting, but nevertheless 'cheerful' (line 36).

Interpreting the poem

As in many poems, the last lines offer a clue to the central idea of the poem. Might Bishop be saying that life itself, like the activity in the bight, is not always beautiful, and sometimes seems fruitless, but still has its own energy and purpose?

The subtitle '*(On my birthday)*' is revealing. (As it was not actually Bishop's birthday, it is perhaps even more significant in drawing attention to itself.) A birthday is a time of celebration, but also a time to take stock, to look at the past as well as the future and to think about one's life and work. Although she hardly appears in the poem directly, it is possible that the poet is reviewing her life and achievements by exploring the activity in the bight. From this point of view, the last line would suggest a hopeful if realistic attitude that reveals a great deal about Bishop as a person.

A poet's imagination

Bishop's unusual choice of images and similes, the seemingly random objects she mentions, may also reflect the untidiness of the subconscious that is the basis of a poet's imagination. Sometimes the work of the imagination yields nothing that is useful or beautiful, as the images of ineffectiveness and waste that are found in the poem suggest. There is no attempt to make the bight picturesque. In fact the opposite is true. The emphasis seems to be on the untidiness or even ugliness of the scene.

Yet, we should be aware of the irony, for this poet at least, that despite the struggle of artistic creation, a poem has been written. She has produced a clear and precise description of the activity going on in the bight, including the many details and technical terms that make the scene realistic. Almost all of the senses have been used to describe the sounds, textures and visual impact of what she sees before her.

Sound patterns in the poem

Appropriately for a poem that describes the dredging of a bay, the language the poet uses emphasises the untidiness and even ugliness of the scene. This lack of harmony is reflected in the sounds of the words, which are anything but harmonious. You will notice this if you try saying the lines aloud. Polysyllabic words and harsh consonants add to the effect. For example, the hard 'c' and 'k' sounds used in lines 9 to 13, echoing the harsh sounds of hard work.

Thinking about the poem

1   Look at the ways Bishop uses to describe the bight – sensuous images, similes and metaphors – and discuss her ability to really 'see' her surroundings.

2   Would you agree that her description is extremely individual, even unusual? Which images strike you as being particularly so?

3   Most poets love to use the sounds of words to create atmosphere. Point out where Bishop does this most effectively.

4   Bishop was an accomplished painter. How is this indicated, if at all, in this poem?

5   How would you describe the poet's mood in the poem: depressed, optimistic, humorous or celebratory? Perhaps you would suggest another word?

6   Do you like the way the poet has used language in this poem? Explain your answer.

7   Can 'The Bight' give us an insight into Bishop's personality and her attitude to her work? Explain your answer.

8   You wish to include 'The Bight' in a talk entitled 'Introducing Elizabeth Bishop'. Write out what you would say in your talk. You might consider such aspects as her powerful descriptions, her unusual use of language, and how you responded to the poem.

At the Fishhouses

Although it is a cold evening,
down by one of the fishhouses
an old man sits netting,
his net, in the gloaming almost invisible,
a dark purple-brown,   5
and his shuttle worn and polished.
The air smells so strong of codfish
it makes one's nose run and one's eyes water.
The five fishhouses have steeply peaked roofs
and narrow, cleated gangplanks slant up   10
to storerooms in the gables
for the wheelbarrows to be pushed up and down on.
All is silver: the heavy surface of the sea,
swelling slowly as if considering spilling over,
is opaque, but the silver of the benches,   15
the lobster pots, and masts, scattered
among the wild jagged rocks,
is of an apparent translucence
like the small old buildings with an emerald moss
growing on their shoreward walls.   20
The big fish tubs are completely lined
with layers of beautiful herring scales
and the wheelbarrows are similarly plastered
with creamy iridescent coats of mail,
with small iridescent flies crawling on them.   25
Up on the little slope behind the houses,
set in the sparse bright sprinkle of grass,
is an ancient wooden capstan,
cracked, with two long bleached handles
and some melancholy stains, like dried blood,   30
where the ironwork has rusted.
The old man accepts a Lucky Strike.
He was a friend of my grandfather.
We talk of the decline in the population
and of codfish and herring   35

Elizabeth Bishop

while he waits for a herring boat to come in.
There are sequins on his vest and on his thumb.
He has scraped the scales, the principal beauty,
from unnumbered fish with that black old knife,
the blade of which is almost worn away.   40

Down at the water's edge, at the place
where they haul up the boats, up the long ramp
descending into the water, thin silver
tree trunks are laid horizontally
across the gray stones, down and down   45
at intervals of four or five feet.

Cold dark deep and absolutely clear,
element bearable to no mortal,
to fish and to seals . . . One seal particularly
I have seen here evening after evening.   50
He was curious about me. He was interested in music;
like me a believer in total immersion,
so I used to sing to him Baptist hymns.
I also sang 'A Mighty Fortress Is Our God.'
He stood up in the water and regarded me   55
steadily, moving his head a little.
Then he would disappear, then suddenly emerge
almost in the same spot, with a sort of shrug
as if it were against his better judgment.
Cold dark deep and absolutely clear,   60
the clear gray icy water . . . Back, behind us,
the dignified tall firs begin.
Bluish, associating with their shadows,
a million Christmas trees stand
waiting for Christmas. The water seems suspended   65
above the rounded gray and blue-gray stones.
I have seen it over and over, the same sea, the same,
slightly, indifferently swinging above the stones,
icily free above the stones,
above the stones and then the world.   70

If you should dip your hand in,
your wrist would ache immediately,
your bones would begin to ache and your hand would burn
as if the water were a transmutation of fire
that feeds on stones and burns with a dark gray flame.   75
If you tasted it, it would first taste bitter,
then briny, then surely burn your tongue.
It is like what we imagine knowledge to be:
dark, salt, clear, moving, utterly free,
drawn from the cold hard mouth   80
of the world, derived from the rocky breasts
forever, flowing and drawn, and since
our knowledge is historical, flowing, and flown.

Glossary

4	*gloaming*: twilight
6	*shuttle*: tool used to repair fishing nets
10	*cleated*: strips of wood have been nailed on to prevent slipping
10	*gangplanks*: narrow movable walkways
15	*opaque*: not transparent
18	*translucence*: light shining through
24	*iridescent*: coloured like the rainbow
24	*coats of mail*: pieces of armour
28	*capstan*: revolving cylinder used for winding cable
32	*Lucky Strike*: a brand of cigarette
52	*total immersion*: form of baptism practised by some Christians
74	*transmutation*: change from one form into another
77	*briny*: very salty

Guidelines

'At the Fishhouses' comes from *A Cold Spring* (1955).

In 1946 Bishop paid a visit to the place of her childhood, Nova Scotia. It was her first time to go there since her mother's death in 1934. For a time she stayed in Halifax, across the bay from Dartmouth where her mother had lived and eventually died. Bishop's letters suggest that she was depressed during this visit, possibly due to the resurfacing of painful memories. 'At the Fishhouses' contains some echoes of notes she made while there. She wrote that other parts of the poem came to her in a dream.

Commentary

Lines 1–12

Like many of Bishop's poems, it opens with an objective description, in this case of the fishhouses and the old man who sits there, mending his nets. **The atmosphere of the place is conveyed vividly in images that engage almost all our senses.** Images of light and colour appeal to our visual sense. 'The air smells so strong of codfish / it makes one's nose run and one's eyes water' (lines 7–8) combines the sense of smell and touch, making us feel as if we are there in person. The fishhouses are carefully described in everyday, conversational language as places where ordinary business is conducted.

Lines 13–25

The phrase 'All is silver' in line 13 introduces a change in atmosphere and language. **The poem moves from the concrete world of the senses – the place itself, what can be seen and heard – to the world of the imagination.**

The sea symbolises the depth of this world: it is opaque and mysterious, an idea that is followed through as the poem progresses. In contrast, the silver light that shines on 'the benches / the lobster pots, and masts' is clear (lines 15–16). It is caused by a covering of fish scales and moss, signs of age and mortality. The detailed description in lines 21 to 25 shows the effects of light on the wheelbarrows and the fish scales. The language transforms them from ordinary objects into romanticised images. In this light even the flies are 'iridescent' or rainbow-coloured (line 24).

Lines 26–40

Now the poet directs her attention to what is behind the fishhouses, where there is a capstan (a machine used for winding cable) that has fallen into disuse. This 'ancient' device has 'some melancholy stains' on it, 'like dried blood', which reminds us that this is a place of death, if only for the fish (lines 28 to 30).

She encounters the old fisherman, 'a friend of my grandfather' (line 33); the personal reference suggests the importance of this place for Bishop as memories of her childhood resurface. The old man's way of life is fast disappearing, but, like the rest of the scene, he is given a strange sort of glamour, transformed by the poet's imagination.

Lines 41–46

This short section seems to form a bridge between the two longer parts of the poem. The ramp where boats are hauled down into the sea is made of 'thin silver / tree trunks' (lines 43–44) that descend further and further into the water, just as Bishop is also leading the reader into an imaginative experience with the sea and the seal she sees there. Images of light and colour, and the sense of depth created by the repetition of the word 'down', add to the atmosphere of romance and mystery.

Lines 47–66

From these lines on Bishop enters imaginatively into the sea as part of elemental nature, 'Cold dark deep and absolutely clear' (line 47). This image of icy beauty emphasises the otherness of the sea. It implies an utter contrast with the decaying human world as represented by the fisherman and the fishhouses.

Bishop's encounter with the seal and her interpretation of it gives us another insight into how we can perceive the world in an imaginative way. As in 'The Fish', the seal seems to communicate with her at some, almost religious, level, so that she (humorously) sings Baptist hymns to him. But he does not leave his natural element of water for a moment, and the poet cannot enter it ('total immersion' is impossible), and so any communication she establishes with him is ultimately an illusion. She had, however, experienced a sort of communication with him, in contrast with the sea, which is absolutely separate from the human world.

As she does throughout the poem, Bishop now switches her attention from the sea back to the land behind her, focusing on the fir trees that stand waiting to be cut down for Christmas, before returning to contemplate the mystery of the sea.

Lines 67–77

'I have seen it over and over' – these words introduce a richly evocative description of the sea. Repetition, alliteration of 's' sounds and assonance combine to create an almost hypnotic effect. Sensuous images evoke the power and mystery of the sea. There are images of touch ('If you should dip your hand in', line 71) and taste ('it would first taste bitter', line 76), visual images and similes ('as if the water were a transmutation of fire', line 74). The overall impression is that Bishop is trying to understand the sea through the senses, which is the way we experience the world, but the images are all qualified with the word 'if'. Might this suggest that it is impossible to have a perfect understanding of the sea?

Lines 78–83

The poem ends in a beautiful lyrical passage, when Bishop compares the sea to human knowledge and contemplates the complex nature of that knowledge. The language she uses suggests that she has had a moment of vision. The sea is not the source of all knowledge, but it is like what 'we imagine knowledge to be' (line 78). It is both sensory and abstract. We can know the world through our senses. It is 'dark, salt, clear, moving' (line 79). These sensuous words are placed alongside abstract ideas of time, such as 'forever' and 'historical' (lines 82 and 83). Thus knowledge is both sensory and abstract.

The poet earlier described the sensations we would experience if we were to dip our hands into the sea. In the same way, knowledge may be painful. It may even be unbearable. Bishop's insight in these final lines is that knowledge may even be disillusioning, as the images of 'cold hard mouth' and 'rocky breasts' imply (lines 80 and 81). Knowledge, like the sea, is 'utterly free' (line 79); it can never be static but must instead constantly change and move. And like the sea, knowledge may be utterly indifferent to human beings with their preoccupations with death and loss.

Interpreting the poem

It could be said that the poem has as its underlying theme questions not only of what we know about the world, but also of how we know the world. Does our perspective shift constantly, as the sea does? Is knowledge (by which Bishop seems to mean understanding rather than reason or external facts) dependent upon a particular time and place (historical)? Is it merely temporary, ongoing (flowing), soon to become flown, or past, since we will take our understanding with us when we die? These are complex questions that have occupied philosophers for centuries.

How the poem is organised

To an extent Bishop has answered the question of how we know the world through how she has organised her poem. For instance, her perspective is constantly shifting, from the concrete world of the senses (what she sees and hears around her), to the transforming power of the imagination (the light and beauty of the scene) to the world of contemplation of the sea. She seems to suggest that we 'know' the world in many ways.

We should also take into account that Bishop does not actually equate the sea with knowledge. Rather, the sea 'is like what we imagine knowledge to be' (line 78). Here it is the poet herself who is making the comparison rather than discovering an absolute meaning that was already there. The distinction is significant because, as the critic Robert Dale Parker points out, 'First she sees . . . then wonders if she is wrong'.

Personal experience

Brett Millier comments on the possible personal basis of the poem. He suggests that the 'chill maternal image' at the end of the poem – 'the cold hard mouth' and 'the rocky breasts' (lines 80 and 81) – remind us that Bishop is returning to her motherland, the place of her disturbed and disturbing childhood. He goes on to say:

> Having spent a good part of the previous two years working with Dr. Ruth Foster on the origins of her depression and alcoholism, Elizabeth must have felt that her inheritance from her mother, what she 'derived' from that troubled relationship – her 'knowledge' of herself and her Nova Scotia past – was indeed 'flowing and drawn' and hopelessly temporal and irremediable, 'historical, flowing and flown'.

Perhaps, from this point of view, 'knowledge' of her mother and of her own past was indeed unbearable.

Bishop and nature

Bishop's early reputation as a poet was as a meticulous observer of the world around her. The critic Randall Jarrell claims that each of her poems should have written about it: 'I have seen it.' Others have recognised that what interests her is more complex. It is what her biographer, David Kalstone, describes as the mysterious relation between what she observes in nature and what it 'spiritually' signifies. So her encounter with the fish in 'The Fish' and her description of the activity in 'The Bight', as well as her descriptions in 'At the Fishhouses', have their spiritual side as metaphors of a deeper meaning to be found in nature than appreciation of it for its own sake.

Thinking about the poem

1   Discuss the descriptions of the five fishhouses and the old fisherman mending his nets. Would you agree that Bishop makes us feel as if we are actually there?
2   From the beginning we are made aware of the sea. How is it presented at first? What characteristics is it given?
3   Why, in your opinion, does the poet introduce the character of the old fisherman, whom she describes as 'a friend of my grandfather' (line 33), into the poem?

What atmosphere does she create by the language she uses to describe him and his work?

4   Explore the second section of the poem (lines 40 to 46). Do you detect a change of tone in these lines? Why is the word 'down' repeated? Might it be interpreted metaphorically as a comment on the poet's changing perspective?

5   How do you respond to the poet's encounter with the seal? What kind of relationship does she have with him?

6   There are a number of religious references in the poem. Give possible reasons for this.

7   How does her sense of being able to communicate with the seal differ from her attitude to the sea?

8   What does she learn from the sea? Comment on the language she uses to describe it.

9   Would you agree with the view that the sea becomes a metaphor for human knowledge? If so, what might her description suggest about Bishop's understanding of what human knowledge may be?

10   Do you like this poem? Would you include it in an anthology of Bishop's best poems?

The Prodigal

The brown enormous odor he lived by
was too close, with its breathing and thick hair,
for him to judge. The floor was rotten; the sty
was plastered halfway up with glass-smooth dung.
Light-lashed, self-righteous, above moving snouts,   5
the pigs' eyes followed him, a cheerful stare –
even to the sow that always ate her young –
till, sickening, he leaned to scratch her head.
But sometimes mornings after drinking bouts
(he hid the pints behind a two-by-four),   10
the sunrise glazed the barnyard mud with red;
the burning puddles seemed to reassure.
And then he thought he almost might endure
his exile yet another year or more.

But evenings the first star came to warn. 15
The farmer whom he worked for came at dark
to shut the cows and horses in the barn
beneath their overhanging clouds of hay,
with pitchforks, faint forked lightnings, catching light,
safe and companionable as in the Ark. 20
The pigs stuck out their little feet and snored.
The lantern – like the sun, going away –
laid on the mud a pacing aureole.
Carrying a bucket along a slimy board,
he felt the bats' uncertain staggering flight, 25
his shuddering insights, beyond his control,
touching him. But it took him a long time
finally to make his mind up to go home.

Elizabeth Bishop

Glossary	
Title	*Prodigal*: wasteful, spendthrift
10	*two-by-four*: a length of timber with a cross-section measuring two inches by four inches
20	*companionable*: sociable, suitable as a companion
23	*aureole*: a halo of light around a blessed figure or saint

Guidelines

The poem was written in 1951 and is included in the collection *A Cold Spring* (1955). Bishop began to drink destructively during her college days and by 1939 she was an alcoholic. As she had no real family and no permanent home, her drinking often led to her leaving embarrassing situations and making herself effectively homeless. Her drinking may have had a genetic basis as her father, grandfather and three uncles all drank heavily. Furthermore, the circumstances of her life led to depression, which in turn she tried to alleviate by drinking. She tells us that 'The Prodigal' sprang from an experience in Nova Scotia in 1946 when 'one of my aunt's stepsons offered me a drink of rum, in the pig sties at about nine in the morning'. In the same letter, she speaks of the poem as having resulted from her experience of undergoing psychoanalysis.

The poem, a double sonnet, is based on the story of the prodigal son told in the gospel of St Luke, chapter 15, verse 15. The parable describes how the younger son of a rich man claims his inheritance early and leaves home. He squanders all his money and is forced to work as a swineherd, living with the pigs he tends. Eventually he returns home, where he is welcomed and forgiven by his father, who is so delighted to see him that he prepares a feast of a fatted calf. This leads to resentment on the part of the elder son, who had remained at home and helped his father.

Commentary

Stanza 1

Bishop dramatises the time before the prodigal returns home rather than the homecoming itself. She does not flinch from describing the squalor in which the prodigal lives among the pigs in the pigsty, with their 'brown enormous odor', 'breathing' and 'thick hair' (lines 1 and 2). We can almost smell and hear the animals among which the prodigal lives. We can see the rotten floor and 'glass-smooth dung' (line 4) that plasters the walls. His life has been degraded, so much so that he does not even know how far he has fallen: he lives too close to the animals 'for him to judge' (line 3).

Bishop describes the pigs in a non-judgemental, almost approving, way. They offer the prodigal some comfort and companionship. Their eyes follow him with 'a cheerful stare – / even the sow that always ate her young' (lines 6–7). Such a realistic detail makes us realise how low the prodigal has sunk, especially since he scratches the sow's head in spite of being sickened at what he sees. It is a measure of his self-deception that he has come almost to accept his living conditions.

He also deceives himself (and perhaps others too) about his drinking: 'he hid the pints behind a two-by-four' (timber plank; line 10). But the poem also suggests that he is still capable of seeing beauty and hope in his surroundings. He appreciates the sunrise that 'glazed the barnyard mud with red' and the 'burning puddles' (lines 11 and 12). However, his self-deception also allows him to think that 'he almost might endure / his exile' (lines 13–14) for some time longer. Clearly he is not yet ready to face his problems and change his life.

Lines 15–23

The second stanza, in effect a second sonnet, opens with the word 'but', which signals another perspective on the situation. There may be a possibility of hope, as the imagery of light used throughout the stanza suggests: the 'star' (line 15) the 'faint forked lightnings' (line 19), the 'lantern' and the 'sun' (line 22) and a 'pacing aureole' (halo of light; line 23) on the mud. The image of the star is particularly appropriate in a poem that carries biblical echoes. But there is also a sense of isolation in the image of the farmer going about his business, shutting up the cows and horses in the barn. They may have been 'safe and companionable as in the Ark' (line 20), but there is no indication of any human contact between the farmer and the prodigal.

Lines 24–28

The prodigal's moment of truth occurs when he becomes aware of 'the bats' uncertain staggering flight', which gives him 'shuddering insights' (lines 25 and 26). He does not want to recognise the truth, but at last he realises his terrible isolation. The bats terrify him because their blind flight resembles his stumbling through life and his uncertain future.

But the decision 'to go home' is not an easy or inevitable one: it takes him 'a long time' to make it (lines 27 and 28). The implication is that the idea of 'home' is not without problems for the prodigal. Home may be seen as the last resort rather than the first place of refuge.

Personal experience

The last line recalls Bishop's circumstances as someone for whom 'home' did not truly exist. Home often signifies the notion of parental love and support, which Bishop lacked throughout her childhood due to her father's early death and her mother's mental illness. Home may be a difficult place if you do not feel loved there. On the other hand, in accepting love at home you make yourself vulnerable. These underlying concerns, and our awareness of Bishop's struggles with alcoholism, make 'The Prodigal' one of her most revealing poems.

Form of the poem

'The Prodigal' is a double sonnet, twenty-eight lines in length. It does not conform to a regular rhyme scheme.(Its rhyme scheme is *abacdbcedfeggf* in the first sonnet, *abacdbecfedfgh* in the second.) It has been pointed out that the last word, 'home', does not have a true rhyme and this has the effect of isolating the word (and the idea) within the poem.

Thinking about the poem

1 Which words and phrases best convey the squalor and degradation of the prodigal's living conditions, in your view?

2 Do you like Bishop's description of the pigs? Give a reason for your view.

3 Does the poem show an understanding of the prodigal's behaviour and state of mind? Give a reason for your opinion.

4 Which one of the following words best describes Bishop's attitude to the prodigal: sympathetic, compassionate or judgemental? Explain your choice.

5 'The second sonnet gives the reader a different perspective from the first.' Would you agree with this statement? Give a reason for your opinion.

6 What role does the farmer play in the story told in the poem?

7 Why, in your opinion, does the prodigal make the decision he does at the end of the poem?

8 The poem has been said to be full of 'pain, alienation and bitterness'. Would you agree with this view? Give a reason for your opinion.

9 On the other hand, others have found the poem to be 'optimistic'. Would you agree with this? Give a reason for your opinion.

10 Would you agree that this poem reveals a great deal about Bishop, although it is not written in the first person? Refer to the poem in your answer.

Taking a closer look

1 'The floor was rotten; the sty / was plastered halfway up with glass-smooth dung' (lines 3–4). What do you find interesting about the sounds in this line?

2 'And then he thought he almost might endure / his exile yet another year or more' (lines 13–14). Can you explain why the prodigal thought he could go on living as he did?

3 'But it took him a long time / finally to make his mind up to go home' (lines 27–28). What might Bishop means to convey by this final line of the poem?

Imagining

1 Imagine you are the prodigal. In a series of three diary entries, describe the life you lead and how you feel about it.

2 You have been asked to make a short film to accompany a reading of the poem. Explain how you would use music, sound effects, images, colour, etc. to capture the atmosphere.

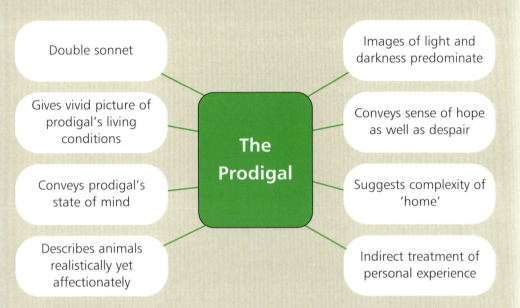

The Prodigal

- Double sonnet
- Gives vivid picture of prodigal's living conditions
- Conveys prodigal's state of mind
- Describes animals realistically yet affectionately
- Images of light and darkness predominate
- Conveys sense of hope as well as despair
- Suggests complexity of 'home'
- Indirect treatment of personal experience

Elizabeth Bishop

Questions of Travel

There are too many waterfalls here; the crowded streams
hurry too rapidly down to the sea,
and the pressure of so many clouds on the mountaintops
makes them spill over the sides in soft slow-motion,
turning to waterfalls under our very eyes.   5
– For if those streaks, those mile-long, shiny, tearstains,
aren't waterfalls yet,
in a quick age or so, as ages go here,
they probably will be.
But if the streams and clouds keep travelling, travelling,   10
the mountains look like the hulls of capsized ships,
slime-hung and barnacled.

Think of the long trip home.
Should we have stayed at home and thought of here?
Where should we be today?   15
Is it right to be watching strangers in a play
in this strangest of theatres?
What childishness is it that while there's a breath of life
in our bodies, we are determined to rush
to see the sun the other way around?   20
The tiniest green hummingbird in the world?
To stare at some inexplicable old stonework,
inexplicable and impenetrable,
at any view,
instantly seen and always, always delightful?   25
Oh, must we dream our dreams
and have them, too?
And have we room
for one more folded sunset, still quite warm?

But surely it would have been a pity   30
not to have seen the trees along this road,
really exaggerated in their beauty,
not to have seen them gesturing
like noble pantomimists, robed in pink.
– Not to have had to stop for gas and heard   35
the sad, two-noted, wooden tune
of disparate wooden clogs
carelessly clacking over
a grease-stained filling-station floor.
(In another country the clogs would all be tested.   40
Each pair there would have identical pitch.)
– A pity not to have heard
the other, less primitive music of the fat brown bird
who sings above the broken gasoline pump
in a bamboo church of Jesuit baroque: 45
three towers, five silver crosses.
– Yes, a pity not to have pondered,
blurr'dly and inconclusively,

on what connection can exist for centuries
between the crudest wooden footwear   50
and, careful and finicky,
the whittled fantasies of wooden cages.
– Never to have studied history in
the weak calligraphy of songbirds' cages.
– And never to have had to listen to rain   55
so much like politicians' speeches:
two hours of unrelenting oratory
and then a sudden golden silence
in which the traveller takes a notebook, writes:

'Is it lack of imagination that makes us come   60
to imagined places, not just stay at home?
Or could Pascal have been not entirely right
about just sitting quietly in one's room?

Continent, city, country, society:
the choice is never wide and never free.   65
And here, or there . . . No. Should we have stayed at home,
wherever that may be?'

Glossary		
1	*here*: Brazil
11	*hull*: outer body or frame
12	*barnacled*: covered with crustaceans
20	*the other way around*: seen from the southern hemisphere
34	*pantomimists*: people taking part in a pantomime
37	*disparate*: dissimilar, completely different
45	*Jesuit baroque*: ornate seventeenth-century architectural style often found in churches in Brazil
51	*finicky*: overdone, fussy
52	*fantasies*: fanciful designs
54	*calligraphy*: the art of handwriting; refers here to the design of the cages
57	*oratory*: public speaking
62	*Pascal*: Blaise Pascal, French mathematician and philosopher (1623–62)

Elizabeth Bishop

Guidelines

This poem is the title poem of the collection *Questions of Travel* (1965).

Bishop travelled a great deal throughout her life, visiting, among other places, Europe, various parts of the United States and Mexico before her trip to Brazil in 1952. Although she remained in Brazil for many years with her partner, Lota de Macedo Soares, she continued to be interested in travel.

The poem takes a quizzical look at the notion of travel and why we feel the need to do it. It also questions our ability to understand other people's cultures.

Commentary

Stanza 1

The poem is set in Brazil. At the beginning there is a slight touch of travel-weariness, as if the speaker has seen and done too much. Everything seems excessive and crowded, but beautiful too, as the language she uses suggests. Similes and metaphors help the reader to visualise the landscape, while sound effects such as sibilance ('soft slow-motion', line 4) and alliteration ('travelling, travelling', line 10) help create a harmonious aural effect.

Stanza 2

In the second stanza Bishop raises some of the 'questions of travel' that she would like to ask. In line 14, she wonders whether it would have been better to have stayed at 'home' (in her case, the United States) and 'thought of here' (Brazil). In other words, would imagining some place be as good as travelling to it?

Other questions occur to her. What ethical right do tourists have to watch the people of other cultures, as if they are watching a play? The metaphor of theatre emphasises the unreality of travel as opposed to living in a place. The question also touches on what has become a modern concern, the notion of 'ethical tourism'.

Possibly addressing the poem to herself as an enthusiastic traveller, Bishop wonders why people feel compelled to seek out different and strange sights. Is it childishness? Her tone is wryly humorous as she describes the usual tourist experience of staring 'at some inexplicable old stonework, / inexplicable and impenetrable' (lines 22–23). Here she implies the limitations we all have in understanding the culture of others. She also comments on the clichéd response most tourists make to the sights that are 'instantly seen and always, always delightful' (line 25).

Stanza 3

Bishop said that she was always interested in her poems showing the mind in action instead of in repose. Characteristically, then, the third stanza shows her working out some of the answers to the questions she has asked. But she continues to recognise uncertainty in her own mind, while at the same time delighting herself and the reader with her quirky observations of Brazilian life and culture. The details she chooses bring this world alive to us by appealing to our senses and focusing on the aspects of culture that make Brazil unique. She suggests that the claims of reality are more pressing than those of the imagination. It would surely 'have been a pity / not to have seen the trees along this road' (lines 30–31). These are particular trees, 'gesturing / like noble pantomimists' (lines 33–34) and not just any generalised view. In lines 35 to 39 she recalls hearing 'the sad, two-noted, wooden tune' of clogs 'carelessly clacking' over the floor of a petrol station. This, too, is a specific sound, peculiar to the footwear of Brazil and therefore part of its unique culture. Another example she chooses is the 'fat brown bird' (line 43) that sings in its elaborately designed birdcage, a kind seen throughout South America. Her conclusion is that by studying such artefacts as the wooden clogs and the birdcage, one can understand the culture of a people.

Her final observation about the rain in Brazil has a slightly humorous tone: it is 'unrelenting' as she says, 'like politicians' speeches' (lines 55 to 57). When it stops, the traveller may ask some final questions in a typical traveller's log or diary.

Stanzas 4 and 5

The last two stanzas are presented in italics, signifying the handwritten notes of a traveller's diary. Once again Bishop returns to the idea of the competing claims of the imagination versus reality. Does the act of travelling imply a lack of imagination, since one can imagine places even if one has not visited them? On the other hand, she questions the belief of the great French philosopher Blaise Pascal, who stated, 'I have discovered that all the unhappiness of men arises from one single fact, that they cannot stay quietly in their own chamber.'

Bishop suggests that the 'question of travel' is more complex. We may not be as free as we think to choose our destinations or to decide not to travel: for some people, staying at home may be impossible. Similarly, the notion of 'home' that we leave behind may not be as simple as it seems. We could take into account here the ambivalent attitude to 'home' expressed in 'The Prodigal'.

Personal experience

As in so many of her poems Bishop reveals a great deal about herself in this poem. As always, she shows her ability to describe the world around her, in this case some of the Brazilian landscape and culture. Underlying the 'questions of travel' that she raises are also questions relating to the opposite, to staying at home. Due to her disrupted childhood, Bishop had no experience of what a stable and happy home life might be like. So her last question about home, 'wherever that may be' (line 67) is a poignant reminder of the deep loneliness at the heart of so many of her poems.

Language of the poem

The language Bishop uses here is a blend of the poetic and the conversational, which seems appropriate to convey the notion of someone thinking aloud. She handles many variations of tone, including being speculative, tentative, humorous and lyrical.

Thinking about the poem

1   How would you describe the poet's attitude to the landscape suggested in the first stanza? How does she communicate her feelings?

2   Which of the questions about travel raised by Bishop in the second stanza do you find the most interesting? Write a short note in response to the question.

3   Explore the details of her travel experiences that Bishop focuses on in the third stanza. Do you find them revealing, unusual, eccentric? Perhaps you can suggest another term?

4   Comment on the variations of tone in the poem. What effect is created?

5   Examine the sound effects Bishop uses in the poem and say how they contribute to its meaning.

6   Would you agree that Bishop gives the impression in this poem of someone thinking aloud? Comment further on this view.

7   From your reading of the poem, did Bishop approve of travel and travellers?

8   Why, in your opinion, did Bishop write 'Questions of Travel'?

9   Compare the poem with any two of Bishop's other poems under the following headings:

   The poet's attitude to nature.

   The poet's use of striking images.

   The poet's interest in cultures other than her own

   What the poem reveals about the poet as a person.

10   Although written half a century ago, would readers nowadays respond to the issues raised in the poem?

The Armadillo

for Robert Lowell

This is the time of year
when almost every night
the frail, illegal fire balloons appear.
Climbing the mountain height,

rising toward a saint   5
still honored in these parts,
the paper chambers flush and fill with light
that comes and goes, like hearts.

Once up against the sky it's hard
to tell them from the stars –   10
planets, that is – the tinted ones:
Venus going down, or Mars,

or the pale green one. With a wind,
they flare and falter, wobble and toss;
but if it's still they steer between   15
the kite sticks of the Southern Cross,

receding, dwindling, solemnly
and steadily forsaking us,
or, in the downdraft from a peak,
suddenly turning dangerous.   20

Last night another big one fell.
It splattered like an egg of fire
against the cliff behind the house.
The flame ran down. We saw the pair

of owls who nest there flying up   25
and up, their whirling black-and-white
stained bright pink underneath, until
they shrieked up out of sight.

The ancient owls' nest must have burned.
Hastily, all alone,   30
a glistening armadillo left the scene,
rose-flecked, head down, tail down,

and then a baby rabbit jumped out,
short-eared, to our surprise.
So soft! – a handful of intangible ash   35
with fixed, ignited eyes.

Too pretty, dreamlike mimicry!
O falling fire and piercing cry
and panic, and a weak mailed fist
clenched ignorant against the sky!   40

Glossary

Title	*Armadillo*: a burrowing mammal found mainly in South America; it rolls up into a ball inside its bony armour if it is in danger
Dedication	*Robert Lowell*: American poet and friend of Bishop; in response he dedicated 'Skunk Hour' to Bishop
1	*time of year*: 24 June
5	*saint*: San Juan (St John); his feast day, 24 June, is celebrated in Brazil
16	*Southern Cross*: constellation in the southern hemisphere; its four major stars form the shape of a cross
35	*intangible*: cannot be touched
36	*ignited*: on fire
37	*mimicry*: imitation
39	*weak mailed fist*: the armadillo rolled up into a ball looks like a fist made of armour (coat of mail), however, it is weak

Guidelines

First published in *The New Yorker* magazine in 1957, 'The Armadillo' is found in the collection *Questions of Travel* (1965). It is dedicated to the poet Robert Lowell, Bishop's friend, who considered the poem to be among her best work.

St John's day, 24 June, is the winter solstice (the shortest day of the year) in

Brazil, which is in the southern hemisphere. In order to honour the saint, it was the custom of the local people to send up fire balloons into the sky. These helium-filled balloons carried paper boxes, which then self-ignited. The idea was to let them drift towards the shrine of St John in the mountains. If the balloons fell into the forest before the fire was extinguished, they caused a forest fire. For this reason, and because of the damage done to the ecosystem and the animals, the practice was declared illegal, although it still occurred widely.

Bishop wrote to a friend in 1955 that she was in two minds about the fire balloons. She admired them as they lit up the sky, but she was horrified at the damage they caused. The poem expresses her feelings about the custom.

Commentary

Stanzas 1 to 4

As in many of Bishop's poems, she begins with a short narrative ('This is the time of year') that sets the poem in context. She writes as an observer rather than a participant in the custom. When you read the poem you can trace the differing attitudes she has to the balloons.

You can almost hear her thinking aloud as she describes the balloons as precisely as possible: what they look like, how they move through the sky. The tone at this stage is admiring. She sees the balloons as 'hearts' (line 8), as 'stars' (line 10), responding to their charm and recognising the loving reason for their existence.

In the fourth stanza the tone is still admiring as she describes how the balloons float upwards towards the major constellation in the southern hemisphere, the Southern Cross.

Change of tone

The balloons are described as 'steadily forsaking us' mere mortals looking up (line 18). There is a suggestion that they have a higher-bound purpose as they make their way towards the heavens. But quite soon we are made aware of the dreadful consequences when the balloons drop into the forest. The word 'dangerous' (line 20) takes the reader aback somewhat.

Images of suffering birds and animals, presented without comment, have an emotive effect on the reader: the owls that are burnt out of their nest and that 'shrieked up out of sight' (line 28) in pain and terror. The armadillo, having no defences against fire, is forced out into the open.

In the ninth stanza a 'baby rabbit' ('soft' and 'short-eared') is seen in a horrifying image as 'a handful of intangible ash', its eyes 'ignited', destroyed by fire.

Final stanza

In the final stanza, placed in italics for emphasis, Bishop's indignation finally breaks through. It is not entirely clear to whom she is addressing the accusation '*Too pretty, dreamlike mimicry!*', but there are a number of possibilities.

Is she accusing the balloons of being deceptively pretty, as she had described them earlier? Unlike the stars that they resemble, they are dangerous to the animals on earth.

Or, as has been suggested, might she be addressing herself as a poet, criticising her depiction of the whole scene as too beautiful, too obviously poetic, when what is really happening is horrific? If we reread the poem in the light of the final stanza, we become aware of the poetic devices she has used – simile, metaphor, sound effects such as alliteration and rhyme and above all powerful imagery. The poet's art has been exposed for what it is – an act of pretty mimicry.

There is no mistaking the angry tone, however. The speaker is in complete sympathy with the natural world here. The armadillo, as depicted in the last two lines, is ignorant of evil and powerless to protect itself in the face of human cruelty.

Allegory

We might also take into account a possible allegorical reading of the last image of the armadillo. It may show Bishop's awareness of the links between all the elements of nature, including human beings, as they suffer from oppression and wrong. The mailed fist recalls human responses to oppression, past and present. This might lead us to reinterpret the fire balloons as instruments of war and destruction, set in motion by the forces of superstition. This is a pessimistic reading of the poem.

Thinking about the poem

1 Would you agree that this poem shows Bishop's remarkable gift for precise description? Comment on the techniques she uses in order to make us share in her experience of the event.

2 Is there a sudden change of tone as the poem progresses? Where precisely would you locate the change?

3 What consequences do the balloons have for the natural world? How does the poet convey these consequences?

4 How would you interpret the line '*Too pretty, dreamlike mimicry!*' in the last stanza? Justify your answer.

5 Comment on Bishop's use of language in the last stanza.

6 Why did Bishop choose the title 'The Armadillo' for her poem, in your view?

7 Compare Bishop's attitude to nature in 'The Fish' with the attitude she expresses here.

8 From your reading of this poem, what does it reveal about Bishop as a person?

9 Would you agree with Robert Lowell's opinion that 'The Armadillo' is one of Bishop's best poems?

Sestina

September rain falls on the house.
In the failing light, the old grandmother
sits in the kitchen with the child
beside the Little Marvel Stove,
reading the jokes from the almanac,   5
laughing and talking to hide her tears.

She thinks that her equinoctial tears
and the rain that beats on the roof of the house
were both foretold by the almanac,
but only known to a grandmother.   10
The iron kettle sings on the stove.
She cuts some bread and says to the child,

It's time for tea now; but the child
is watching the teakettle's small hard tears
dance like mad on the hot black stove,   15
the way the rain must dance on the house.
Tidying up, the old grandmother
hangs up the clever almanac

on its string. Birdlike, the almanac
hovers half open above the child,   20
hovers above the old grandmother
and her teacup full of dark brown tears.
She shivers and says she thinks the house
feels chilly, and puts more wood in the stove.

It was to be, says the Marvel Stove.   25
I know what I know, says the almanac.
With crayons the child draws a rigid house
and a winding pathway. Then the child
puts in a man with buttons like tears
and shows it proudly to the grandmother.   30

But secretly, while the grandmother
busies herself about the stove,
the little moons fall down like tears
from between the pages of the almanac
into the flower bed the child   35
has carefully placed in the front of the house.

Time to plant tears, says the almanac.
The grandmother sings to the marvellous stove
and the child draws another inscrutable house.

Glossary

Title	*Sestina*: a poetic form (see guidelines)
4	*Little Marvel Stove*: a brand of solid-fuel stove
5	*almanac*: a calendar that gives details of weather predictions, tides, phases of the moon and other events on the basis of astrological calculations; for this reason, it was sometimes thought to have magic powers. Many of these annual publications feature other material such as jokes
7	*equinoctial*: at the time of the autumn equinox (i.e. September)
39	*inscrutable*: cannot be understood, mysterious

Guidelines

'Sestina' is included in the collection *Questions of Travel* (1965). It was originally given the title 'Early Sorrow', which offers us an insight into the origin of the poem and the nature of the experience depicted in it. It was among the first poems that Bishop wrote about her childhood. She was in her fifties, living in Brazil, before she was able to write about her traumatic experiences as a child in Nova Scotia, just before and after her mother's final departure for the psychiatric institution in which she was to spend her life. It is thought that psychoanalysis helped Bishop to retrieve buried memories of that time.

Commentary

Stanza 1

The domestic scene painted at the beginning of the poem seems cosy at first, in contrast to the wet and darkening conditions outside the house. We can picture the child and the grandmother reading from the almanac, surrounded by familiar and comforting objects. But as the poem progresses we become aware that all is not well. The grandmother is 'laughing and talking to hide her tears' (line 6).

Stanza 2

In the second stanza Bishop enters into the child's mind as she tries to make sense of what is taking place. She has no idea why her grandmother is crying, but thinks in her childish way that the almanac had foretold her tears, as it had the weather. As children do, she focuses on the familiar objects around her: the kettle, the stove. The rain is beating on the roof. This image is bleak and rather threatening. Again, it contradicts the apparent cosiness of the scene.

Stanza 3

From a child's perspective, objects often have a personality and a life. To the young Elizabeth, 'the teakettle's small hard tears' (overflow of water) seem to 'dance like mad on the hot black stove' (lines 14 and 15). This is a revealing image. The stove that seemed so cheerful, almost toy-like in the first stanza now appears threatening. The drops of water that dance 'like mad' jolts us into remembering that Bishop's mother was institutionalised for mental illness when Bishop was a young child. The phrase suggests something out of control that contrasts with the grandmother's actions in tidying the place and hanging up the almanac.

Stanza 4

The grandmother is clearly suffering grief at what has happened to her daughter and to her granddaughter, but hides her sorrow by drinking tea and pretending she feels chilly.

To the child, the almanac that hovers over them on the wall is like a bird – another rather menacing image. The cup in line 22 is described as being full of not tea, but 'dark brown tears'. The impression we get is that their grief would overwhelm them if it was expressed.

As in the previous stanzas, the language here is simple and childlike, focusing throughout on objects (linguistically on nouns). Bishop's experience of psychoanalysis and her readings of child psychology taught her that young children tend first of all to name the world, without realising the significance of what it is these names represent. In the poem these objects come to bear the weight of the child's emotions, without her being consciously aware that this is so.

Stanza 5

In the fifth stanza the child makes the stove and the almanac speak. Neither of them says directly what has happened or is happening in the family, since the child was unlikely to have been told exactly what that was. But psychoanalysis made Bishop familiar with the concept of a child's knowing and not knowing at the same time.
The pictures that a child who has been traumatised will draw are often quite revealing. So, for instance, the house, with the figure of a man in it, might be understood by a psychologist to represent the child's awareness of the father she had lost (Bishop's father died when she was a baby). The 'rigid' house with its 'winding pathway' may represent tension and difficulties that the family experienced.

Stanza 6

Although still poignant, the mood seems to lift somewhat in the sixth stanza. In her child's imagination Bishop sees the 'little moons' of the almanac (that denote the phases of the moon over the course of each month) falling 'down like tears' onto the flower bed that she has drawn in her picture. Might the flower bed suggest a sense of hope for the future? At the very least it points to a possibility of beauty and happiness in the future.

Envoy

In the envoy (shorter final stanza) Bishop makes the almanac speak again. It gives a rather cryptic message to the child: '*Time to plant tears*'. We can interpret this message in a number of ways. For some commentators, it suggests that for the adult Bishop it is time to bury tears, to put away the 'early sorrow' that was the first title of the poem. On the other hand, the line may look towards the child-poet's future rather than the adult-poet's past. It may suggest that the child will use her grief creatively, to express it through the medium of poetry and the imagination, as Bishop does here.

The final two lines appear to strengthen the second interpretation. The grandmother seems to have overcome the worst of her grief, and the child continues to draw her picture of an ideal house.

Tone of the poem

What Bishop leaves unsaid in this poem is almost as significant as what she says. No grief or sorrow is directly expressed, but there is an underlying atmosphere that is painfully emotional. While her relationship with her grandmother, who acts as a mother figure, is seen as positive, the poem begs the question as to where her mother and father are. It is another reminder that Bishop's concept of 'home' may not have been entirely happy.

Form of the poem

Bishop chose to deal with these painful memories in the form of a sestina. This is an archaic and difficult form of poetry, highly stylised and formal. In a sestina there are six unrhymed stanzas of six lines and a seventh stanza of three lines, known as an envoy.

Only six words are used at the end of the lines; in Bishop's poem the words are house, grandmother, child, stove, almanac, tears. Each stanza is linked by this intricate pattern of line-endings: the six words are repeated in a different order in each stanza so that the last word in each stanza recurs as the ending of the first line in the next. The word order is as follows: *abcdef, faebdc, cfdabe, ecbfad, deacfb, bdfeca*. The envoy uses all of the six end words, three of them (*ace*) at the ends of the lines and the other three (*bdf*) within the lines.

It can be seen that a sestina is a form that involves great discipline and control of one's material. It allows for ritual repetition, almost as a child's game does. Some critics have seen the form as particularly suited to the theme of the poem, childhood sorrow. Writing a sestina offers a formula within which grief may be repeated and yet contained.

When Bishop changed the title of the poem, she drew attention to the form of the poem, so that effectively it becomes a subject in the poem.

Thinking about the poem

1   Explore the changes of mood and atmosphere throughout the poem. How are they created, in your opinion?

2   What evidence is there to suggest that we are viewing the things in the kitchen – the stove, the kettle, the almanac – as well as the figure of the grandmother, from a child's perspective? In answering, try to imagine yourself as a child again and how you saw the world around you.

3   How would you describe the relationship between the child and the grandmother?

4   Explore the idea of time and the idea of family as they recur throughout the poem. How are they connected with the poem's theme, do you think?

5   Can you explain the significance of the child's drawing in stanza 5?

6   Which of the six key words used in the poem is the most significant in your opinion? Explain your choice.

7   How did you respond to this poem?

8   Compare 'Sestina' and 'First Death in Nova Scotia' as poems about childhood memories. Which poem do you find the more affecting?

9   'Bishop's poems reveal a great deal about her life'. Discuss this statement, referring (among other poems) to 'Sestina'.

First Death in Nova Scotia

In the cold, cold parlor
my mother laid out Arthur
beneath the chromographs:
Edward, Prince of Wales,
with Princess Alexandra,   5
and King George with Queen Mary.
Below them on the table
stood a stuffed loon
shot and stuffed by Uncle
Arthur, Arthur's father.   10

Since Uncle Arthur fired
a bullet into him,
he hadn't said a word.
He kept his own counsel
on his white, frozen lake,   15
the marble-topped table.
His breast was deep and white,
cold and caressable;
his eyes were red glass,
much to be desired.   20

"Come," said my mother,
"Come and say good-bye
to your little cousin Arthur."
I was lifted up and given
one lily of the valley   25
to put in Arthur's hand.
Arthur's coffin was
a little frosted cake,
and the red-eyed loon eyed it
from his white, frozen lake.   30

Arthur was very small.
He was all white, like a doll

Elizabeth Bishop

that hadn't been painted yet.
Jack Frost had started to paint him
the way he always painted   35
the Maple Leaf (Forever).
He had just begun on his hair,
a few red strokes, and then
Jack Frost had dropped the brush
and left him white, forever.   40

The gracious royal couples
were warm in red and ermine;
their feet were well wrapped up
in the ladies' ermine trains.
They invited Arthur to be   45
the smallest page at court.
But how could Arthur go,
clutching his tiny lily,
with his eyes shut up so tight
and the roads deep in snow?   50

Glossary

3	*chromographs*: coloured copies of pictures
4	*Edward, Prince of Wales*: (1841–1910), member of the British royal family, eldest son of Queen Victoria and Prince Albert, later became King Edward VII
5	*Princess Alexandra*: married Edward in 1863
6	*King George*: (1865–1936), British monarch, King George V
6	*Queen Mary*: (1867–1953), wife of King George V
8	*loon*: an aquatic bird, the great crested grebe
14	*kept his own counsel*: kept his thoughts to himself
25	*lily of the valley*: a white flower
34	*Jack Frost*: a childish name given to frost
35	*Maple Leaf*: emblem of Canada; 'Maple Leaf Forever' is a phrase from the Canadian national anthem at the time the poem was written
42	*ermine*: white fur
46	*page*: a boy attendant

Guidelines

This poem follows 'Sestina' in the collection *Questions of Travel* (1965). Like 'Sestina', it is one of the poems Bishop wrote in her fifties in which she recaptures childhood memories. She had recently undergone psychoanalysis to help her recognise the causes of her struggles with depression and alcoholism. As in 'Sestina', the perspective is that of a child.

The poem tells of Bishop's first disturbing encounter with death. It is interesting to note that it contains one of the few direct references to her mother found in Bishop's work, although her presence is implicit in many of Bishop's poems of loss. Set in her childhood home in Nova Scotia, the poem records the death of her cousin, whom she calls Arthur. Bishop was not quite four when he died.

Commentary

Stanza 1

The child-narrator describes the scene in the parlour where Arthur has been laid out, significantly enough by her mother. From the beginning, repetition plays a part in creating atmosphere. The parlour is 'cold, cold' (line 1).

As a child does, Bishop names the objects that she sees in the room where Arthur lies: the coloured pictures of the royal family on the walls, the stuffed bird that had been shot by Arthur's father.

Stanza 2

At first the child's interest appears to lie completely in the stuffed bird. She personifies the bird, saying that 'he hadn't said a word' (line 13) since he was shot. She focuses on the primary colours of the bird and his 'red' glass eyes. **She seems unable to distinguish between what is real and what is imaginary.** But her awareness of his silence and his motionlessness is perhaps a way of skirting around the subject of death rather than articulating it fully.

Stanza 3

Bishop remembers being lifted up by her mother to 'say good-bye' (line 22) to her little cousin. This is a poignant scene, all the more so when we consider that once again Bishop's memory of her mother is bound up with moments of loss. She uses a childlike image to describe Arthur's coffin: 'a little frosted cake' (line 28). In her childish way she imagines the 'red-eyed loon' (is he weeping too?) wanting it for himself (line 29).

Stanza 4

Again, Bishop describes Arthur in his coffin in terms a child might use. The language is simple. The images are appropriate for a little girl. Arthur is 'like a doll' (line 32).

'Jack Frost' is a name children often give to frost; here it allows Bishop to show how aware the child is of the coldness of death. At this point she associates the winter frost of Arthur's pallor with the Canadian flag and by extension the Canadian national anthem (at the time of writing). In her confusion she thinks that Jack Frost had begun to paint the child only to leave him unfinished, but by repeating the word 'forever' she reveals that somehow she knows that Arthur himself is gone forever.

Stanza 5

In this final stanza the child invents a sort of fairy-tale ending for Arthur. He is going to be a 'page at court' (line 46) for the royal family whose pictures are on the walls. They, like the loon, are seen to be in the colours of death: red and ermine (white fur). But as she asks, how could Arthur go out in the snow all alone? This is a terrifying image for a child, and suggests that deep down she knows that it is impossible.

Child's experience of death

As the title suggests, 'First Death in Nova Scotia' describes Bishop's first encounter with death as a child and her confusion about what it really means. As in 'Sestina', the concept of the child's knowing and not knowing is crucial. It is clear that the child has a subconscious awareness of what it is to be dead. Repetition of key words and phrases – 'cold', 'white', 'frozen', 'painted', 'forever' – underline the fact that the child's understanding of death, though naïve and not analysed, is instinctive. Yet it is an imperfect understanding; the poem is psychologically credible when she invents the fairy-tale ending for the little boy, at the same time wondering how this could happen.

Form of the poem

The poem is divided into five ten-line, mostly unrhymed, stanzas. Longer stanzas allow Bishop to give the impression of someone looking about and thinking aloud. The metre chosen by Bishop in this poem, mainly three-stress lines (trimeter), has been regarded as the most speechlike of metres and therefore appropriate to telling a story (see also 'The Fish').

Thinking about the poem

1   The first stanza describes what the child saw in the 'cold, cold parlor'. What significance does each object have for her as the poem progresses?

2   How does she feel about the stuffed loon? What atmosphere is created by her description of the bird?

3   Would you agree that the poet's choice of language is remarkably childlike throughout? Explain your view.

4   How does the poem convey the child's natural confusion and naivety about death? Does she have any idea of what death means?

5   Do you find this poem disturbing, unusual, moving . . . ? Perhaps you would suggest another term?

6   Which of the two poems 'Sestina' or 'First Death in Nova Scotia' best conveys a childhood experience, in your view?

7   If you were to compile your choice of Bishop's poems for an anthology, would you choose this one? Make a case for or against its inclusion.

Filling Station

Oh, but it is dirty!
– this little filling station,
oil-soaked, oil-permeated
to a disturbing, over-all
black translucency.   5
Be careful with that match!

Father wears a dirty,
oil-soaked monkey suit
that cuts him under the arms,
and several quick and saucy   10
and greasy sons assist him
(it's a family filling station),
all quite thoroughly dirty.

Do they live in the station?
It has a cement porch   15
behind the pumps, and on it
a set of crushed and grease-
impregnated wickerwork;
on the wicker sofa
a dirty dog, quite comfy.   20

Some comic books provide
the only note of color –
of certain color. They lie
upon a big dim doily
draping a taboret   25
(part of the set), beside
a big hirsute begonia.

Why the extraneous plant?
Why the taboret?
Why, oh why, the doily?   30
(Embroidered in daisy stitch
with marguerites, I think,
and heavy with gray crochet.)

Somebody embroidered the doily.
Somebody waters the plant,   35
or oils it, maybe. Somebody
arranges the rows of cans
so that they softly say:
ESSO–so–so–so
to high-strung automobiles.   40
Somebody loves us all.

Glossary

3	*oil-permeated*: saturated with oil
5	*translucency*: shine
8	*monkey suit*: dungarees, overalls
10	*saucy*: cheeky
18	*impregnated*: penetrated
24	*doily*: an ornamental cloth
25	*taboret*: a low seat or stool without a back or arms
27	*hirsute*: hairy
27	*begonia*: a flowering plant
28	*extraneous*: not essential
31	*daisy stitch*: a design
32	*marguerites*: daisies
33	*crochet*: a type of knitting done with a small hook
39	*ESSO*: a brand of oil and petrol products
39	*so-so-so*: as explained by Bishop: 'a phrase people used to calm and soothe horses'; here it also refers to the way in which the cans are arranged

Guidelines

'Filling Station' is from the collection *Questions of Travel* (1965). The poem describes a particular petrol station.

Commentary

Stanzas 1 and 2
The poet almost seems to enjoy describing the grease and grime she sees in the petrol station, where presumably she has stopped to fill up her car. Everything she sees appears oily and dirty: 'oil-soaked, oil-permeated' to the extent that it has an 'over-all / black translucency' or shine (lines 3 to 5). Humorously, she warns (herself or someone else) to be careful of a lighted match, as the place could quickly go up in flames.

Stanza 2 describes members of the family who own and work in the station: a father and 'several' (line 10) sons. Like their surroundings, they are 'greasy' (line 11) and 'quite thoroughly dirty' (line13). The tone of voice here is light-hearted.

Stanza 3

With characteristic Bishop curiosity about the world around her, she begins to ask questions about what she sees here. She finds some evidence to answer her question as to whether the family live in the filling station, unlikely as it might seem at first. On the porch she can see a set of wicker chairs, 'crushed and grease- / impregnated' (lines 17–18) like everything else, and there is an equally 'dirty dog, quite comfy' (line 20), lying on the sofa. The colloquial word 'comfy' suggests she finds the scene pleasant despite the dirt. This is certainly not a soulless, alien place. It is a family environment, complete with a dog, though even at this stage we cannot fail to notice that there is no mention of a woman in this all-masculine setting.

Stanzas 4 and 5

In the fourth stanza other objects attract Bishop's attention: 'comic books provide / the only note of color – / of certain color' (lines 21–23). This detail highlights how impossible it is to know what colour anything here really is. She goes on to pick out a 'big dim doily' (decorative cloth) placed over a taboret (a type of seat) as well as a large hairy plant (lines 24–27). Then in stanza 5 she wonders aloud about these objects: 'Why the extraneous plant? / Why the taboret? / Why, oh why, the doily?' (lines 28–30). Although everything is dirty ('doily' even rhymes with 'oily'), these are objects that suggest a desire for a more ordered life. Someone has gone to the trouble of embroidering the doily; it may be 'gray' now but it has been carefully decorated by hand.

Stanza 6

Bishop answers her own questions in the final stanza. **Somebody cares about this place and has tried to improve it, even if their efforts are futile:** the begonia gets more oil than water, she humorously suggests. That same 'somebody' has taken the trouble to arrange the petrol cans in some kind of order, so that they 'softly say: / ESSO–so–so–so' (lines 38–39). Bishop has explained these sounds as those used to soothe restless horses, which accounts for the next witty line: 'to high-strung automobiles' (line 40). The words suggest a soothing, calming presence among the working atmosphere of the filling station.

The final line, 'Somebody loves us all', sums up her conclusion that there is an affectionate presence in the filling station, possibly a maternal figure that completes the family, although she is not visibly present.

Interpreting the poem

Although 'Filling Station' is quite simply written, it can be read on a number of levels. It can be interpreted as an expression of Bishop's optimistic view of life, despite her personal difficulties, especially the lack of a mother in her childhood. She seems to suggest that a mother's presence may be always felt, even if she is not actually there. So the father, in his ill-fitting overalls, and the 'greasy' sons have had at least some experience of feminine care and affection. It does not matter that they are dirty and unattractive as somebody has loved them. By extension, might Bishop herself have benefited from her mother's love in her very earliest years, before illness caused her mother to disappear from her life? And despite her later problems, might 'somebody' have loved her too?

Regret

Some readers feel that the light-hearted tone of the poem is tinged with regret. After all, the filling station has been allowed to become so dirty. The mother is nowhere to be seen. Has she gone away or simply given up the battle against the oil and grease? Might this be an indirect expression of grief for Bishop's deprived childhood? From this point of view, the final line is somewhat ironic as not everyone has 'somebody' to love them.

Allegory

An allegory is a story with a symbolic meaning. Some people have interpreted 'Filling Station' as an allegory of human life. The filling station can be seen as a little world in itself, symbolic of the real world that is full of disorder and sordidness. Efforts to improve it with some kind of decoration (the doily, the begonia, the petrol cans) can be interpreted as a metaphor for our earthly efforts to create beauty out of ugliness and order out of randomness. 'Somebody loves us all' may then imply a divine perspective that oversees our efforts. The poet has placed the word 'Somebody' within the last stanza so that it takes a capital letter, a respect normally given to the word 'God'. The line recalls the phrase often embroidered on samplers (in this case a doily): God loves us all.

Satire

The critic Guy Rotella offers another view of the poem. He sees it as a satire (a poem that mocks or ridicules something) of a certain kind of nature poem in which nature is seen as containing a lesson or moral that the poet can discover. In such poems, details of the natural scene are revealed as part of God's eternal plan, and the poem leaves the reader with a message, as in the last line of this poem. Rotella argues that

Bishop's description of the petrol station corresponds to the descriptive aspects of such nature poems. He suggests that the poem indicates her cynical attitude to such moral lessons or 'truths.' This is a rather bleak reading of the poem, since it implies that the statement in the last line is not at all valid.

Sound patterns in the poem

Bishop makes frequent use of sibilance (repetition of 's' sounds) in the poem – for instance in words such as 'soaked', 'translucency', saucy', 'greasy' and so on. This has an almost onomatopoeic effect as it suits the impression of oiliness and grease that she wants to give. The poem does not rhyme, as is appropriate when the impression is that of a speaking voice, but assonance (repetition of vowel sounds) in 'that match' for instance and alliteration in 'family filling' and 'dim doily' contribute to the harmony of the poem.

Thinking about the poem

1. How does the poet elaborate on her opening exclamation: 'Oh, but it is dirty!'?
2. How would you describe Bishop's attitude to the filling station? Does it change at any point?
3. What puzzles her about the filling station?
4. What conclusion does she come to when she sees the doily and the plant?
5. How does the poem give the impression of someone thinking aloud?
6. What picture of Bishop does the poem reveal to the reader? Do you find the personality revealed attractive?
7. Which one of the following statements is closest to your own view of the theme of the poem?

    Everybody is loved by somebody.

    We shouldn't judge by appearances.

    Life is full of surprises.

    Explain your view.
8. Is 'Filling Station' a serious or a light-hearted poem? Support your answer by reference to the poem.
9. A critic once remarked on the 'deceptive casualness' of Bishop's poems. Would you agree that this view could be applied to 'Filling Station'? Give reasons for your answer.
10. 'Good poetry creates vivid pictures in our minds.' In your view, is this true of 'Filling Station'?

Taking a closer look

1   Give **three** examples of Bishop's descriptive skill and say why you chose them.

2   Comment on the phrase 'high-strung automobiles' in line 40.

3   'Somebody loves us all.' Is this a good ending to the poem? Explain your opinion.

Imagining

1   Imagine you are the 'somebody' who has tried to look after this filling station. Write an entry from your diary explaining how you attempt to keep the place tidy and how you feel about it.

2   You have been asked to speak to your class about this poem. Write out the talk you would give, describing what the poem is about and giving your personal response to it.

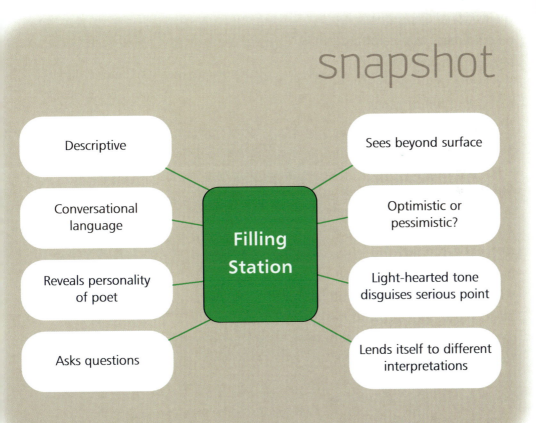

snapshot

Descriptive

Conversational language

Reveals personality of poet

Asks questions

Filling Station

Sees beyond surface

Optimistic or pessimistic?

Light-hearted tone disguises serious point

Lends itself to different interpretations

In the Waiting Room

In Worcester, Massachusetts,
I went with Aunt Consuelo
to keep her dentist's appointment
and sat and waited for her
in the dentist's waiting room.   5
It was winter. It got dark
early. The waiting room
was full of grown-up people,
arctics and overcoats,
lamps and magazines.   10
My aunt was inside
what seemed like a long time
and while I waited I read
the *National Geographic*
(I could read) and carefully   15
studied the photographs:
the inside of a volcano,
black, and full of ashes;
then it was spilling over
in rivulets of fire.   20
Osa and Martin Johnson
dressed in riding breeches,
laced boots, and pith helmets.
A dead man slung on a pole
– "Long Pig," the caption said.   25
Babies with pointed heads
wound round and round with string;
black, naked women with necks
wound round and round with wire
like the necks of light bulbs.   30
Their breasts were horrifying.
I read it right straight through.
I was too shy to stop.
And then I looked at the cover:
the yellow margins, the date.   35

Suddenly, from inside,
came an *oh!* of pain
– Aunt Consuelo's voice –
not very loud or long.
I wasn't at all surprised;   40
even then I knew she was
a foolish, timid woman.
I might have been embarrassed,
but wasn't. What took me
completely by surprise   45
was that it was me:
my voice, in my mouth.
Without thinking at all
I was my foolish aunt,
I – we – were falling, falling,   50
our eyes glued to the cover
of the *National Geographic*,
February, 1918.

I said to myself: three days
and you'll be seven years old.   55
I was saying it to stop
the sensation of falling off
the round, turning world
into cold, blue-black space.
But I felt: you are an *I*,   60
you are an *Elizabeth*,
you are one of *them*.
Why should you be one, too?
I scarcely dared to look
to see what it was I was.   65
I gave a sidelong glance
– I couldn't look any higher –
at shadowy gray knees,
trousers and skirts and boots
and different pairs of hands   70
lying under the lamps.

I knew that nothing stranger
had ever happened, that nothing
stranger could ever happen.

Why should I be my aunt,   75
or me, or anyone?
What similarities –
boots, hands, the family voice
I felt in my throat, or even
the *National Geographic*   80
and those awful hanging breasts –
held us all together
or made us all just one?
How – I didn't know any
word for it – how "unlikely" . . .   85
How had I come to be here,
like them, and overhear
a cry of pain that could have
got loud and worse but hadn't?

The waiting room was bright   90
and too hot. It was sliding
beneath a big black wave,
another, and another.

Then I was back in it.
The War was on. Outside,   95
in Worcester, Massachusetts,
were night and slush and cold,
and it was still the fifth
of February, 1918.

Glossary		
1	*Worcester, Massachusetts*: Bishop lived there with her paternal grandparents; she was very unhappy	
2	*Aunt Consuelo*: this was in fact Bishop's Aunt Florence	
9	*arctics*: overshoes or galoshes	
14	*National Geographic*: magazine of the National Geographic Society, famous for its articles on geography and anthropology and its wonderful photographs	
20	*rivulets*: small streams	
21	*Osa and Martin Johnson*: famous husband and wife team of explorers	
23	*pith helmets*: sun helmets made from pithy swamp plant	
25	*Long Pig*: the dead man is to be roasted by the cannibals like a pig on a spit	
26	*pointed heads*: the babies' heads are bound with string to force them into a point	
28–29	*necks . . . wire*: in certain cultures long necks are considered to be sexually attractive; the women's necks are extended by having metal rings wound around them	

Guidelines

'In the Waiting Room' opens the collection *Geography III* (1976).

Bishop dated many of her adult attitudes back to the age of six, which was the age at which her paternal grandparents 'kidnapped' her and brought her to live with them in Worcester, Massachusetts, where the poem is set. She revealed in a letter to a friend that her memory of the experience she describes in the poem was detailed and vivid.

At the age of six she became aware of herself, for the first time, as a member of the human race and specifically as a female member. In the letter she reveals that other men and women had told her that they had similar moments of realisation in their childhoods.

She wrote the poem, like 'Sestina' and 'First Death in Nova Scotia', when she was in her fifties –almost half a century after the experience it recalls.

Commentary

Lines 1–17

As is typical of a poem by Bishop, the poem begins with a narrative account in a factual tone. In this poem it concerns a visit Bishop made as a child with her Aunt Consuelo (Aunt Florence in real life) to a dentist. The location and the time are described very precisely and with Bishop's usual eye for detail. We can visualise the people waiting, dressed appropriately for that time and place in 'arctics' (overshoes) and 'overcoats' (line 9), later elaborated upon as 'trousers and skirts and boots' (line 69). While she waits for her aunt, the child reads the *National Geographic* magazine and looks at the photographs.

Lines 18–35

The narrator records what she sees in the photographs: pictures of a volcano as it erupts and famous explorers dressed for their expeditions. **But other pictures surprise and disturb her, as visions of a world she hardly knew existed.** There are images of cannibalism (the 'Long Pig', line 25, 'slung on a pole', line 24) as well as babies with seemingly deformed heads and naked women with their necks 'wound round and round with wire / like the necks of light bulbs' (lines 29–30).

The reader may be aware that what she sees are the beautifying rituals and customs of other cultures. But the child has no such frame of reference. She can only stare in alarm at the 'horrifying' breasts of the women (line 31). She is so embarrassed that she is 'too shy to stop' (line 33).

But we can also see how the seemingly random choice of objects she describes may suggest the diversity of the world, as she is about to realise it, in the contrast between the heavily clothed people around her and the people of other cultures who have quite different values and attitudes. The shock of this contrast makes her reassure herself by looking at the cover of the magazine, and the date, wishing perhaps to locate herself once again within the world she knows.

Lines 36–53

Aunt Consuelo's cry of pain from the dentist's room becomes somehow blended with her own involuntary cry of surprise at what she has seen in the magazine, to the extent that she becomes rather disoriented for a short time.

For the first time she has become aware of herself as a human being with her own identity and place in the world. She realises that she and her aunt share the same identity as family, and as women and human beings with the people in the photographs. Her disorientation at this discovery is expressed in images of 'falling, falling' (line 50), almost fainting, trying to hold on to the present: February 1918.

Lines 54–74

The narrator clings to ordinary facts – that her seventh birthday is just three days away – to counteract the bewildering discovery she has made, which she continues to describe as having the 'sensation of falling off / the round, turning world / into cold, blue-black space' (lines 57–59). The image of the globe is revealing. It suggests that she is losing the sense of perspective that allows one to view the world from one's particular vantage point of location and culture.

As a child, of course, she could not have analysed her experiences in this way, and the narrator does not suggest that she does. Instead, she shows us the child coming to realise that she is an individual, and that she is also 'one of *them*' (line 62) – a member of the human race, but specifically, too, a female member. She asks the unanswerable question: '*Why* should you be one, too?' (line 63). She expresses her realisation that she is not unique in the world. Even as a child she senses how important this discovery is.

Lines 75–89

The child's questions continue. She wonders about the similarities between herself and her aunt and between them and the women in the photographs. How could human beings all be individuals and yet so similar? And how and why was she here in that particular place, at that particular moment, listening to the patient cry out in the dentist's room, when meanwhile others were elsewhere being mutilated (as she saw it)? These are fundamental, unanswerable questions, and Bishop does not attempt to answer them.

Lines 90–99

In the final two stanzas we see Bishop's characteristic ability to accept uncertainty. After the feelings of shock – she is still 'sliding / beneath a big black wave' (lines 91–92) – she is 'back in it' (line 94), that is, the world she knows, Worcester, Massachusetts, in February 1918, with seasonal weather outside and ordinary men and women in the dentist's waiting room.

Interpreting the poem

You will notice how many questions are asked in the poem. They are phrased simply, but they are nonetheless profoundly philosophical. They speculate about the nature of existence and how extraordinary it is to be one's self as well as a part of the human race. They hint at how arbitrary location is, and culture and custom may be.

Aunt Consuelo allows 'an *oh!* of pain' (line 37) to escape, and in that culture it 'could have / got loud and worse but hadn't' (lines 88–89). This may be an implicit recognition of how repressed and inhibiting this society is. Yet in other parts of the world women allow themselves to be mutilated in order to be sexually attractive to men. Women's bodies are exposed in some parts of the world; here, they are muffled up. These questions of the relative nature of human culture were of great interest to Bishop. We saw her touch on them in 'Questions of Travel' and 'The Armadillo'.

The title of the poem may also be interpreted as metaphorical. The child is 'in the waiting room', waiting to take her place as a conscious member of the human race with all its complexity.

Thinking about the poem

1   Examine how the poet conveys the atmosphere in the waiting room.
2   What contrast is suggested between the people in the waiting room and the people in the magazine?
3   What is the child's response to the articles she read and the photographs she saw?
4   Where would you locate the central moment of realisation or discovery in the poem?
5   What questions does her discovery cause her to ask? How did you respond to these questions?
6   Why does she call her aunt 'a foolish, timid woman' (line 42)? Support your answer by reference to the poem.
7   Does she get across her feelings well in lines 55 to 74? Explain your answer.
8   The final lines of the poem bring us back to the waiting room. But does the child see the world as she saw it previously?
9   Was the 'moment of truth' strange or incredible for a child? Have you ever shared in such a realisation, or wondered about similar issues?
10   Compare the poem, as a memory poem, with 'Sestina' and 'First Death in Nova Scotia'. Which poem do you prefer?
11   Can you see, from this description of her childhood experience, any connection between the young Bishop and the poet she will later become?
12   Write out the talk you would give on the poems of Elizabeth Bishop, using this poem as an example of her style and concerns.

General Questions

1   You have been asked to give a short presentation entitled 'Introducing Elizabeth Bishop'. Write out the text of the talk you would give.

Here are some possible areas that you might focus on in your presentation:

● Bishop's poems reveal a great deal about her life, especially her childhood, and her personality.

● Her descriptions are always vivid and fresh, in line with her desire to see things in a new way.

● You can see how, as a painter as well as a poet, she was interested in the shape, colour and texture of things around her, and this is reflected in her use of language.

● Her poems are hardly ever purely descriptive, there is almost always a deeper theme.

2   Bishop once said, 'I simply try to see things afresh.' To what extent, do you think, does she achieve this in her poems?

3   'Bishop's poems are rarely simply descriptive. They always have a deeper theme.' Would you agree with this view of Bishop's work? Explain your answer.

4   A critic once remarked on the 'deceptive casualness' of Bishop's poems. Would you agree with this assessment of her tone and poetic methods? Explain your answer.

5   'Bishop has a remarkable ability to understand how a child's mind works.' Would you agree with this view of Bishop's work? Explain your answer.

6   'Elizabeth Bishop: a personal response'. Write your response, which could include discussion of how you respond to the following aspects:

● Her choice of themes – childhood experience, travel, the natural world, the creative imagination – do they appeal to you?

● The speculative nature of her poems, the questions they raise and sometimes answer.

● Her use of language, her striking imagery, the sounds of her poems, etc.

● Her personality and outlook as revealed in her work.

● The emotions her poems evoke.

Remember to support your points with reference to or quotation from the poems on the course.

7   'The poetry of Elizabeth Bishop appeals to the modern reader for many reasons.' Discuss. (Leaving Certificate exam, 2002.)

Possible reasons include:

● Her themes are varied – childhood memories, relationship with the natural world, family situations, travel, etc. The modern reader can identify with these themes and the issues she raises.

- Her powers of description (the sensuous imagery and painterly qualities in her poems) allow the reader to enter into her experiences.
- Her use of language – how she conveys both thought and emotion – is striking.
- The sounds and shapes of her poems (the varied forms in which she writes: sestina, sonnet, longer narrative poems) are interesting.

You must always support your points by reference to or quotation from the poems on the course.

8   'A sense of homelessness and not belonging is a central theme in the poetry of Elizabeth Bishop'. Discuss this statement.

9   'Bishop's narrative style and her use of conversational language make her poems accessible to the reader.' Would you agree with this view? Explain your answer.

10   'Bishop has written some deeply moving poems.' Write an essay in which you agree or disagree with this view.

Sample Essay

Elizabeth Bishop poses interesting questions delivered by means of a unique style. Do you agree with this assessment of her poetry? Your answer should focus on both themes and stylistic features. Support your points with the aid of suitable reference to the poems you have studied.

I would agree that the questions Elizabeth Bishop poses in her poems are wide-ranging and interesting. She often creates the impression of someone thinking aloud, reflecting on the world about her, on her own experience and the issues it raises. She is preoccupied with what it means to be human in a world that she sees as uncertain and constantly changing. These questions – about identity, about death, about travel, about human beings' relationship with nature, about the experience of love and loss – are expressed in a unique and attractive style.

[Introductory paragraph refers to question asked and indicates areas that will be developed]

Bishop has frequently been praised for her ability to describe situations and objects clearly and precisely. This descriptive power extends also to emotions and abstract ideas. We can see her gift at work in 'In the Waiting Room'. The setting is described with her usual vivid detail. We are told the date (February 1918), the place (Worcester, Massachusetts), the name of her companion (Aunt Consuelo). The patients in the dentist's waiting room are described in terms of their clothes, 'arctics and overcoats', and later 'gray knees / trousers and skirts and boots'. She remembers her childish horror at seeing photographs in the *National Geographic* of 'Babies with pointed heads / wound round and round with string', 'naked women' with their necks 'wound round and round with wire / like the necks of light bulbs'. They had 'horrifying' breasts. Repetition of 'round and round' and the light bulb simile contribute to the impact of the descriptions.

As we read on further, we continue to identify with the young Elizabeth's growing disturbance at what she has seen. It causes her to consider fundamental human questions: Who am I? Why am I here rather than anywhere else? Although only seven years old, she experiences a moment of truth: 'But I felt: you are an *I*, / you are an *Elizabeth*, / you are one of *them*'. Her awareness of who she is – not only a particular person but also a woman, like the women in the magazine – leads her to a further question: 'Why should I be my aunt, / or me, or anyone?' That these deep philosophical questions are expressed in simple childlike language adds to the impact they have on the reader.

[Discussion of poem refers to themes (questions posed) and features of style]

In 'Questions of Travel' Bishop poses a series of questions about the human desire to leave home and seek out new experiences. The tone in this poem is more detached than that in 'In the Waiting Room'. She is clearly amused at the tendency of travellers to be impressed at 'any view, / instantly seen and always, always delightful?' and the clichéd description of 'one more folded sunset'. She wonders why people feel the need to see the 'tiniest green hummingbird in the world' or travel to 'stare at some inexplicable old stonework'. Unlike 'In the Waiting Room', she suggests answers to these questions.

We see her great love of Brazil, where she lived for many years, in the painterly way she evokes its trees 'like noble pantomimists, robed in pink'. She describes in precise detail some of the unique cultural artefacts of that country: the wooden clogs worn by the people and the ornate birdcages they make. The images she creates include sound effects: the clogs 'carelessly clacking' is onomatopoeic; as well as vivid visual metaphors: the birdcage is a 'bamboo church of Jesuit baroque'. When she compares the heavy rain of Brazil to 'politicians' speeches' we respond to her sense of humour as well as to the freshness of the description. Her conclusion is that it would have been 'a pity' not to have had such experiences.

In characteristic Bishop manner, however, she leaves her readers not with a definite conclusion but with an invitation to think for themselves. The eminent philosopher Blaise Pascal came to the conclusion a long time ago that travel was the source of much unhappiness. But Bishop appears to dispute this idea when she raises the question, in the last line, of where exactly 'home' may be, and why we should have stayed there. In so doing she touches once again on one of her most enduring themes: the nature of home. It may seem to be a simple idea for many people, but for a poet whose childhood was so unstable it is a legitimate question to consider. By ending her poem with a question mark Bishop leaves the question open.

[Discussion of second poem also includes references to themes and stylistic features; note how quotations and references are incorporated into sentences]

Another poem in which we see Bishop thinking aloud about a human problem is 'First Death in Nova Scotia.' In this poem, as in 'In the Waiting Room', the speaker is the child Elizabeth coming to terms with her first experience of death, of her 'little cousin Arthur'. Her surroundings, her interpretation of her cousin's death, her inability to distinguish between what is real and what is imaginary are all characteristic of a child's view of the world. The language she uses is simple, with lots of primary colours such as red and white, and the images are also childish: Arthur's coffin is a 'little frosted cake'.

As a child Bishop would have had endless questions about death, as we are aware as we read through the poem, but she invents a sort of fairy-tale ending for Arthur that is psychologically credible for a child. He is going to be a page in a royal court, like the picture she sees on the wall. But by her final question: 'But how could Arthur go . . . ?' the speaker shows that she knows that this cannot really happen. Although this is a child's confusion about the permanence of death, it has a moving effect on the reader.

[Personal response to issues in poem]

In a number of her poems Bishop is preoccupied with the relationship of human beings to nature. In poems such as 'The Fish' and 'The Armadillo' she shows that she understood how human beings and nature are inextricably linked in a moral chain. As usual, her style is not to lecture or to find fault but to allow her descriptions of the natural world to speak for themselves. By doing this she leaves the reader with questions relating to human responsibility towards other creatures.

In 'The Armadillo', for instance, she describes the custom in Brazil of sending fire balloons up into the sky to celebrate St John's Day in June. Her tone of admiration is clear in the beautiful images she creates: 'the paper chambers flush and fill with light / that comes and goes, like hearts'. She compares them to the stars and to planets like Venus and Mars. But she also sees the damage the fire balloons do to the birds and animals when they fall into the forest. Images of suffering are presented to the reader without comment. Visual details such as 'stained bright pink' and the onomatopoeic word 'shrieked' leave us in no doubt as to the destruction that is caused by the custom. The armadillo, forced out into the open and rolled up into a ball, looks like a fist made of armour ('mailed') but is merely a weak, defenceless creature. No one could fail to be moved by her picture of the 'baby rabbit' that becomes a 'handful of intangible ash'.

Once again Bishop is dealing with an important question. Why should human activities and culture bring about suffering in the natural world? This is the underlying theme of the poem. In her poem 'The Fish', she also implicitly questions the right of a human being to conquer such a majestic creature, 'battered and venerable' as he was. Her sense of respect, as well as sympathy, for the fish's struggles leads her to release the fish: 'And I let the fish go.'

[Theme of nature discussed; based mainly on one poem but reference to another to support the argument]

In conclusion it must be said that these questions of existence and death, of how we should live and be responsible in life, are only a few of the selection of interesting questions that Bishop raises in her poems. In posing them and in attempting to answer some of them we see her capacity for close observation, her ability to create vivid images and her emotional involvement. Her style is always appropriate to her theme, whether she is speaking in the voice of a child or as a well-travelled adult. Above all we respond to the humanity of the questions she poses.

[Conclusion refers to both themes and style, as terms of question required]

Elizabeth Bishop

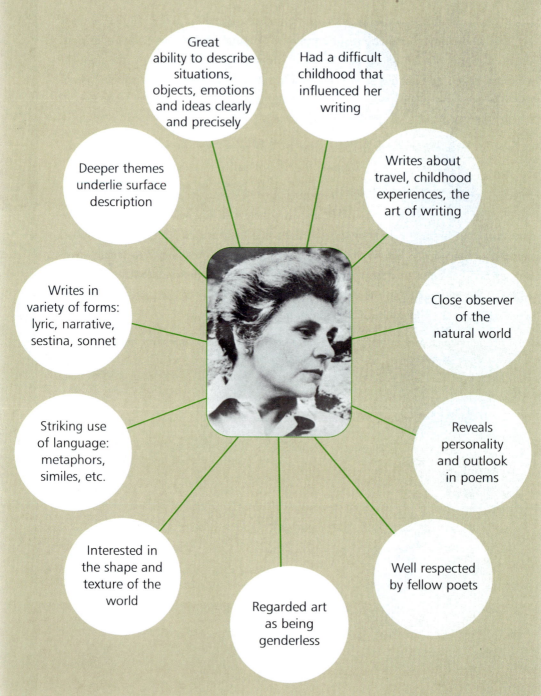

Great ability to describe situations, objects, emotions and ideas clearly and precisely

Had a difficult childhood that influenced her writing

Deeper themes underlie surface description

Writes about travel, childhood experiences, the art of writing

Writes in variety of forms: lyric, narrative, sestina, sonnet

Close observer of the natural world

Striking use of language: metaphors, similes, etc.

Reveals personality and outlook in poems

Interested in the shape and texture of the world

Well respected by fellow poets

Regarded art as being genderless

Gerard Manley Hopkins

1844–49

GOD'S GRANDEUR
SPRING*
AS KINGFISHERS CATCH FIRE
THE WINDHOVER
PIED BEAUTY
INVERSNAID*
FELIX RANDAL
NO WORST THERE IS NONE
I WAKE AND FEEL THE FELL OF DARK
THOU ART INDEED JUST, LORD

Biography

Gerard Manley Hopkins was born at Stratford, Essex, in 1844. He was the eldest child of a prosperous, middle-class family. In 1863 he won a scholarship to Oxford, where he came under the influence of John Henry Newman, the most brilliant religious thinker of his age. Hopkins had the best education available to an Englishman of his class and in 1867 he completed an outstanding academic career at Oxford.

Catholic priest

Hopkins had enjoyed a privileged life of scholarship and dignified leisure at Oxford. However, he reached a turning point in 1866, when, at the age of twenty-two, he converted from the Church of England to Catholicism, under the influence of Newman, who had also converted to Catholicism.

In 1868 Hopkins joined the Society of Jesus and he was ordained a priest in 1877. He was an exemplary priest, devout and conscientious. He served in a number of parishes, including one in a slum district in Liverpool, which he called 'a hellhole'. He was depressed by the poverty and squalor of the industrial towns in which he ministered. In 1882 he was appointed Classics master at Stonyhurst College, a Jesuit public school. The final appointment of his life came in 1884, when he became professor of Greek at University College Dublin, which was managed by the Society of Jesus. Hopkins was not happy in Ireland. He was a patriotic Englishman who found it difficult to understand the hostility of Irish nationalists to his native country. He also found that the great quantity of scripts he had to examine weighed upon his spirit.

Poet

When Hopkins joined the Jesuits he decided to burn all the poems he had written and to write no more unless ordered otherwise. He believed, for reasons good or bad, that he should devote himself exclusively to the service of God, and that this meant not exercising his talent as a poet. For seven years, at an age when most poets would be developing and perfecting their techniques, Hopkins denied himself the opportunity to do this.

Sacrificing his one outstanding talent put a great strain on him. Eventually, a kind and understanding Jesuit superior, conscious that Hopkins was making himself suffer without good reason, suggested that there was no contradiction between serving God and writing poetry, since poetry could be written in the service of God. In response, Hopkins decided to write a long poem with a religious theme. The subject was the shipwreck of the *SS Deutschland*, with five nuns on board, at the mouth of the River

Thames in December 1875. 'The Wreck of the Deutschland' (1876), a magnificent statement of religious faith, featured new rhythms, new rhymes, new syntax and a vocabulary new to the English poetry of his day. The editor of the Jesuit publication *The Month* refused to publish it because he found it unreadable. Victorian taste was not ready for Hopkins' innovations.

During his lifetime Hopkins was deprived of an audience for his poetry. Only a few friends were familiar with his poems. His friend and fellow poet Robert Bridges published a selection of his poems in 1918, twenty-nine years after Hopkins' death. The 750 copies took almost ten years to sell. Hopkins' reputation as a poet did not become widespread until the second edition of 1930.

The seeds of his substantial modern reputation were sown by F. R. Leavis in an essay in *New Bearings in English Poetry* (1932). Leavis asserted that Hopkins was 'one of the most remarkable technical innovators who ever wrote, and he was a major poet'. In time he was seen by some critics as one of the greatest of the Victorian poets, and as one of the greatest religious poets in the English language. The first complete edition of his work was published in 1967. His work attracted the admiration of many twentieth-century poets, including Ted Hughes and Seamus Heaney.

Death

A year before his death Hopkins confessed to Robert Bridges that he could give himself 'no sufficient reason for going on'. In 1889 he fell ill with typhoid fever. Having received the last rites of the Catholic Church, he died peacefully. During his final hours he was heard to murmur, 'I am so happy.'

Social and Cultural Context

Hopkins lived in Victorian Britain, which was experiencing a massive growth in prosperity. This was largely based on conquests abroad as the British empire became the largest in the world. The industrial revolution was also rapidly changing the face of the British countryside.

Poverty

Prosperity had its darker side, as Hopkins was to discover when he ministered in wretched industrial cities where masses of poor and unemployed people, as well as workers who were underpaid, overworked and underfed, existed in filthy cramped conditions. Large numbers of destitute people lived in workhouses on public charity. This side of Victorian life is memorably described by Charles Dickens in such novels as *Oliver Twist* and *Hard Times*.

Some of Hopkins' poems reflect his experience of poverty and squalor in the towns where he served as a priest, among them 'God's Grandeur'. His concern for the spiritual well-being of his parishioners is seen in 'Felix Randal'.

Religion

It was also a time notable for intense debate on the place of religion in public and private life. For many British people, Christian belief seemed to be undermined by the scientific work of Charles Darwin, whose *Origin of Species* (1859) and *Descent of Man* (1871) explained the origin of mankind in terms of gradual evolution rather than direct creation by a divine power.

Hopkins remained unaffected by the turmoil caused by Darwin's theory. He found assurance and certainty in the Catholic religion, which is reflected throughout his poetry. **All his work is shaped by a deep sense of God's presence in the natural world and in everything from the human being to the humblest thing in nature.**

Poetic influences

Hopkins' poetry was ahead of its time and therefore his unusual poems were not published in his lifetime. However, his poetry and his outlook cannot be divorced from his Victorian background. He was a Victorian gentleman and a British patriot. Like many others, he was indebted to Keats, but adapted that poet's style to religious purposes. All his poetry is religious. It looks back to early seventeenth-century devotional poets such as John Donne and George Herbert and enters into dialogue with God, as they did. Hopkins' experiments with language, rhythm and alliteration were influenced by Old English Poetry. In his response to nature, he looks back to the early nineteenth-century Romantic poets: Wordsworth, Coleridge, Keats and Shelley.

Some leading twentieth-century critics, particularly Leavis, suggested that Hopkins anticipated Pound, Eliot, Yeats and other twentieth-century poets in his adventurous treatment of poetic language and in freeing poetry from its conventional decorative baggage. In this sense, at least, Hopkins is a 'modern' poet.

Hopkins and the Language of Poetry

When considering the language of Hopkins' poems, we should bear in mind that **Hopkins reformed the language of Victorian poetry, and in so doing created a new language for English poetry**. That is, the language he used seemed new to his contemporaries. However, it was by no means entirely new as a poetic language. In developing it, he was strongly influenced by early English (Anglo-Saxon), which belongs to the Germanic family of languages.

English as we now have it is a compound of Anglo-Saxon, Classical Greek and Latin, Norman French and other European languages, together with Scandinavian elements. Many of the simple, basic, everyday words in English derive from Anglo-Saxon. Hopkins favoured these at the expense of the more learned polysyllabic vocabulary derived from Greek, Latin, French and Italian.

Alongside vocabulary, another important element is syntax (word order). Hopkins often inverts the normal order of the words he uses. For example, 'Selfyeast of spirit a dull dough sours' (in 'I Wake and Feel the Fell of Dark'). Sometimes he omits connectives and relative pronouns. In 'No Worst, There Is None', for example, 'Wretch, under a comfort serves in a whirlwind' may seem puzzling until we supply the relative pronoun 'that' after 'comfort'. The effect of such omissions is to make each single word carry considerable weight.

In addition, Hopkins tried to strengthen the language by using good strong monosyllables of Anglo-Saxon origin ('God's Grandeur' is dominated by these) and by his continuous use of vigorous alliteration (accented syllables close to each other beginning with the same consonantal sound) as in 'Felix Randal': 'Fatal four disorders', 'great grey drayhorse . . . bright and battering'.

Hopkins also used internal rhyme, a traditional feature of Irish poetry. The following three lines from 'As Kingfishers Catch Fire' illustrate this feature.

> Stones ring; like each tucked string tells, each hung bell's
> Bow swung finds tongue to fling out broad its name;
> Each mortal thing does one thing and the same

Here we have a complex pattern of internal rhyme. In the first of the three lines, 'ring' rhymes with 'string', while 'tells' rhymes with 'bell's'. The internal rhyming is continued in the next two lines. In the third of the lines, 'thing' and 'thing' rhyme with each other and with 'fling', 'ring' and 'string' in the previous two lines.

Hopkins felt the need to devise new and specialised terms to describe his poetic practice. The most important of these terms are sprung rhythm, inscape, and instress.

Sprung rhythm

The metre of many of Hopkins' poems is based on a fixed number of stressed syllables, surrounded by a variable number of unstressed ones. Thus, in 'The Windhover', the first two lines each have five strong beats, on which the emphasis of the voice is placed:

> I caught this morning morning's minion, king-
> dom of daylight's dauphin, dapple-dawn-drawn Falcon, in his riding

The first line has ten syllables, while the second has sixteen. As we read the poem, we realise that what the lines have in common is the sequence of five major stresses or beats in each. It is important to note that sprung rhythm is speech-based rhythm: that is, it is based on the way in which the stresses on strong beats might occur in natural speech.

One advantage of using sprung rhythm is that the poet can get nearer to the natural, and sometimes more flexible, rhythms of everyday speech. Another advantage is that since the poet is not bound by a fixed metre (for example the iambic pentameter that Shakespeare uses in his sonnets – five weak syllables and five strong ones), he has far greater freedom to make his words and phrases enhance his logical meaning.

Hopkins used sprung rhythm because he wanted to bring out the beauty that lies in the spoken language. To explain this he said, 'Poetry is speech framed to be heard for its own sake and interest, even over and above the interest of meaning.'

Inscape

Hopkins was passionately conscious of the distinctive individuality of everything, from the humblest objects in creation (rocks, stones, trees, birds) to the mind of man, the most individual of all things. For Hopkins, each thing had its own inscape, which expressed itself in some design or pattern.

He coined the term 'inscape', which he did not explicitly define, to describe the unified set of qualities in an object that belong inseparably to it, or are typical of it. The idea is that by being thoroughly familiar with these qualities we may grasp the individual essence of each object.

Hopkins saw it as the poet's duty to observe things with the concentration necessary to grasp their uniqueness and so to inscape them. His interest in the inscape or distinct individuality of all things had strongly religious overtones; the more conscious he became of the uniqueness of each object, the more deeply he was aware of its ultimate source.

In order to express the inscapes or distinctive qualities of things, Hopkins was obliged to use language in an entirely new way. The inscape of every given object is, by definition, unique, so Hopkins was driven to the invention of new compound words in an attempt to express the essence of things as he contemplated them. This is why we find so many apparently monstrous adjectival groups in front of nouns. For example, in 'The Windhover', we find the 'dapple-dawn-drawn Falcon'. In this phrase he isolates one aspect of the bird to express what he thinks is its individual essence or inscape. For him, at the moment of writing, the essential thing about the windhover was that it was riding the dawn as if it were on a charger.

Sometimes the inscape of a thing can be expressed in a single word, for example 'the fell of dark' in the sonnet 'I Wake and Feel the Fell of Dark'. The dark's inscape is found here in the terrifying qualities suggested by the word 'fell' (malevolence).

Instress

A term related to inscape is 'instress', which for Hopkins meant the force or energy that keeps a thing in existence and makes it strive after continued existence. While inscape stands for the inherent individuality of a thing, instress stands for the inherent energy or instinctive force that animates it.

Since the instress is a force, it must be expressed in terms of the impression an object makes on a person. To take an example, an object displaying great activity often recalls, for Hopkins, the flames of fire; he also associates the sound of bells with the flames of fire (See 'As Kingfishers Catch Fire'). In 'The Windhover', we have an association of activity with the flames of fire and the pealing of bells to express the instress or distinctive force animating the windhover.

In a 'Meditation', written in 1881, Hopkins interpreted this force in spiritual terms: 'All things therefore are charged with love, are charged with God and if we know how to touch them give off sparks and take fire, yield drops and flow, ring and tell of him.'

Timeline

1844	Born on 28 July in Stratford, Essex, to prosperous parents
1863	Attends Balliol College, Oxford
1866	Follows John Henry Newman into the Catholic Church
1867	Graduates with a first-class degree in Classics
1868	Becomes a Jesuit novice
1874–7	Studies theology and learns Welsh in north Wales
1876	His major poem 'The Wreck of the Deutschland' is rejected by a Jesuit journal
1877	Ordained a priest. Writes some of his best poems, including 'Pied Beauty' and 'The Windhover'
1884	Appointed professor of Greek at University College Dublin
1885	Writes his 'terrible sonnets'
1889	Dies in Dublin of typhoid fever
1918	Robert Bridges, poet and friend of Hopkins, publishes an edition of Hopkins' poems
1967	First complete edition of Hopkins' works was published

God's Grandeur

The world is charged with the grandeur of God.
It will flame out, like shining from shook foil;
It gathers to a greatness, like the ooze of oil
Crushed. Why do men then now not reck his rod?
Generations have trod, have trod, have trod;   5
And all is seared with trade; bleared, smeared with toil;
And wears man's smudge and shares man's smell: the soil
Is bare now, nor can foot feel, being shod.

And for all this, nature is never spent;
There lives the dearest freshness deep down things;   10
And though the last lights off the black West went
Oh, morning, at the brown brink eastward, springs –
Because the Holy Ghost over the bent
World broods with warm breast and with ah! bright wings.

Gerard Manley Hopkins

Glossary		
1	*charged with*: filled with the energy of; the image is of an electric battery
2	*foil*: gold-leaf or tinsel
3	*oil*: oil from crushed olives
4	*reck his rod*: care about God's anger and the punishment it may bring
8	*being shod*: wearing shoes
11	*last lights*: setting sun
13	*bent*: sleeping

Guidelines

This sonnet was completed by Hopkins in 1877. It deals with one of the poet's favourite themes: the contrast between the eternal freshness of nature and the damage done to the face of the earth by human activity.

Commentary

There are two worlds in this poem: the world of nature and the world of human activity.

The natural world

The world of nature is first. This is God's creation. The first line recalls Psalm 19: 'The heavens declare the glory of God'. The natural world is shot through with the splendour of its creator. It is charged, as an electric battery might be, with the divine energy (line 1) that constantly sustains and renews it (lines 9 and 10). God's grandeur flames out like the light given out by gold leaf (line 2).

The next image of the traces of God's splendour throughout the natural world – 'like the ooze of oil' (line 3) – is based on the Bible. In the Old Testament, oil was a symbol of power, kingship and priesthood. The image of crushed olives suggests the crushing of human selfishness for the glory of God.

In lines 9 to 14 the speaker expresses deep faith in the power of nature to renew itself in spite of the immense damage done to the earth by the activities of human beings. Already, in line 4, he has wondered why people ignore God's law and do not fear the consequences of this ('Why do men then now not reck his rod?'). **Hopkins' religious faith leads him to believe that nature will triumph.** The renewal of nature, as Hopkins sees it, is presided over by the Holy Ghost, who broods over the earth as a life-giving presence (lines 13 and 14) and ensures its fruitfulness. It is because of this that 'nature is never spent' (line 9).

The human world

The world created by human activity is contrasted with the world created by God, whose law human beings ignore. The human world is depicted in lines 5 to 8. The emphasis here is on the harm done to the natural world by the activity of generations of human beings: 'And all is seared with trade; bleared, smeared with toil' (line 6). The beauty of nature has been effaced by the industrial activities of human beings.

Hopkins was thinking here of such places as St Helen's, Lancashire, which he later described as 'probably the most repulsive place in Lancashire', where 'the stench of sulphuretted hydrogen rolls in the air'.

Hopkins observes that people have lost their immediate contact with nature: by wearing shoes, they no longer feel the soil (lines 7 and 8).

Language of the poem

As you read the poem aloud, you will notice that Hopkins chooses plain, simple words, mostly of one syllable, rather than unfamiliar or learned ones. The following words from the poem all have their origin in Old English or in the Anglo-Saxon elements in Middle English: world, God, will, shook, gathers, greatness, ooze, reck, rod, trod, smeared, smell, bare, foot, shod, spent, dearest, freshness, deep, down, things, though, last, lights, black, west, went, morning, brown, brink, eastward, springs, Holy Ghost, broods, warm breast, bright, wings.

Hopkins uses alliteration in every line of this poem. For example the first three lines contain: 'grandeur of God', 'shining from shook foil'; 'gathers to a greatness' and 'ooze of oil'. This gives vigour and emphasis to what he has to say.

Another common feature of Hopkins' style is his use of internal rhyme. For example, 'rod' at the end of line 4 rhymes with the treble 'trod' in line 5.

Thinking about the poem

1   'God's Grandeur' is based on a contrast. Identify this contrast and explain how Hopkins develops it.
2   How, according to the poet, does nature reflect God?
3   What, as the poet sees it, are the effects of human activity on the state of the planet?
4   Hopkins complains that human beings do not care about God's anger. Why is God angry?
5   Hopkins is hopeful that nature is destined to triumph in the face of man's destructiveness. Refer to the poem for evidence of this.
6   What kind of God is contemplated in the poem?
7   'God's Grandeur' has much in common with 'Spring' and 'Pied Beauty'. Develop this idea.
8   'God's Grandeur' reads like a very modern poem. What 'modern' issue does it raise?
9   On the evidence of this poem, how does Hopkins think that human beings should live? What kind of world would he like?
10   In the first eight lines of the poem there are various images of oil. What do these images signify?
11   Hopkins believed that, as a result of original sin, both mankind and nature are corrupted. How does the poem reflect this belief?
12   Describe the impact the language of the poem has on you.

Spring

Nothing is so beautiful as spring –
When weeds, in wheels, shoot long and lovely and lush;
Thrush's eggs look little low heavens, and thrush
Through the echoing timber does so rinse and wring
The ear, it strikes like lightnings to hear him sing;   5
The glassy peartree leaves and blooms, they brush
The descending blue; that blue is all in a rush.
With richness; the racing lambs too have fair their fling.

What is all this juice and all this joy?
A strain of the earth's sweet being in the beginning   10
In Eden garden – Have, get, before it cloy,
Before it cloud, Christ, Lord, and sour with sinning
Innocent mind and Mayday in girl and boy,
Most, O maid's child, thy choice and worthy the winning.

Glossary		
2	*weeds, in wheels*: the weeds that 'shoot' in wheels may be blackberry stems
10	*strain*: a melody
11	*it*: the sweet pleasures of spring
11	*cloy*: becomes tasteless; or induces a feeling of disgust or nausea as a result of over-indulgence
14	*maid's child*: Christ, the son of the Virgin Mary

Guidelines

As in almost all of Hopkins' poems, the impulse behind this sonnet is mainly religious. The springtime of the year reminds Hopkins of the springtime of the world before the sin of Adam and Eve caused them to be expelled from the Garden of Eden and lose their original innocence.

Commentary

The structure of the poem is simple. The first eight lines (the octave) are descriptive, while the final six lines (the sestet) are reflective.

The descriptive part

The first eight lines inscape (express the essence of) various features of spring that strike Hopkins as expressing its characteristic notes. These lines also inscape individual natural objects. Weeds, for example, are viewed in a natural way: 'When weeds, in wheels, shoot long and lovely and lush' (line 2). The thrush is said to 'rinse and wring / The ear' (lines 4–5). This carries strong religious overtones: 'rinse' suggests purification by Holy Water; 'wring' is a play on words that conveys the strong impact of the thrush's song and the clear, bell-like quality of its sound. For an explanation of 'inscape' see section on 'Hopkins and the Language of Poetry' above.

The reflective part

In lines 9 and 10 Hopkins asks a question and answers it: the joyful fertility of spring is an echo, or 'strain', of the beauty of the earth when it was first created. The beautiful picture of spring in the first eight lines reminds Hopkins of the beauty 'in the beginning / In Eden garden' (lines 10–11). He reflects on the parallel between the beauty and innocence of the world at the beginning and the beauty and innocence of young people in the springtime of their lives, before innocence is turned 'sour with sinning' (line 12).

At the end of the sonnet three themes come together in a powerful statement of the divine purpose in creation. These themes are: the unspoiled beauty of the spring, the innocence of youth and the sinless nature of Christ and his mother (he is the 'maid's child').

As in many of his sonnets, Hopkins uses his last six lines to introduce a religious reflection arising from what has gone before. Notice that in these six lines spring is associated with the youthful freedom from sin in girls and boys. There is a second Fall (like that of Adam and Eve in the Garden of Eden) when sin takes away youthful innocence. This is why Hopkins pleads with Christ to protect the innocence of children still in the springtime of their lives.

Lines 11 to 14 are a prayer to Christ to claim the minds of young, innocent girls and boys before they overindulge and fall victim to sin.

Language of the poem

In this poem Hopkins employs many of the features identified in the section on 'Hopkins and the Language of Poetry' above. Weeds are inscaped in line 2, as are thrush's eggs in line 3 and the peartree leaves in lines 6 and 7. As in 'God's Grandeur', the vocabulary here consists mainly of plain, everyday words. Hopkins makes generous use of alliteration. For example, 'When weeds, in wheels, shoot long and lovely and lush' (line 2). In some places the lines run on to give the effect of the liveliness associated with spring. Lines 7 and 8 provide a good example: 'that blue is all in a rush / With richness; the racing lambs too have fair their fling'.

Some of the imagery of the poem is quite novel. The eggs of the thrush are imagined as 'little low heavens' (line 3). The song of the thrush 'does so rinse and wring / The ear (lines 4–5). The season of spring recalls 'Eden Garden' (line 11).

Thinking about the poem

1   In 'Spring' Hopkins is concerned with innocence. How does the poem reflect this concern?

2   Hopkins gives his subject a specifically religious context. Show how he does this.

3   Does this sonnet betray anxiety or fear for the future? How does Hopkins suggest that an earthly paradise may be lost?

4   Does the sonnet suggest that Hopkins is suspicious of the natural world?

5   The reference in the last line to Christ as a 'maid's child' is central to the meaning of the poem. In what way?

6   Describe the impact the poem has on you as a reader.

7   This poem was written over a century ago. Is it still worth reading? Give reasons for your answer.

8   The poem contains many images associated with spring, either directly or indirectly. Choose two images that appeal to you and say why you find them appealing.

Taking a closer look

1   The sonnet has two distinct parts. The first, consisting of eight lines, has the poet looking at a scene. The second, consisting of six lines, places the scene in a context and draws a lesson from it. How are the scenes and the lesson related?

2   It has been said that 'Spring' encourages readers to look at the season with fresh eyes. How does it do this?

3 One critic distinguishes two voices in the poem, the second one being heard from line 9 onwards. The same critic believes that the second voice is not in harmony with the first. Comment on the two voices, and explain why you agree or disagree with the critic.

4 Can you suggest why Hopkins associates beauty, innocence and freedom from sin with 'Eden Garden' (line 11)?

5 Hopkins is notable for his original use of language. Mention some examples from this poem.

6 'Spring' and 'God's Grandeur' both deal in different ways with the notion of an ideal world that has long since vanished and given way to the present troubled one. Comment on the poet's treatment of this theme in the two poems. Which one do you prefer and why?

7 The subject of this poem clearly arouses strong emotions in the speaker. Discuss the ways in which the poem captures these emotions.

Imagining

1 If you were asked to provide music to accompany a reading of this poem, what kind of music would you choose? Describe and explain your choice with reference to the poem.

2 Imagine you are Hopkins. Write a letter to a friend giving your reasons for writing this sonnet.

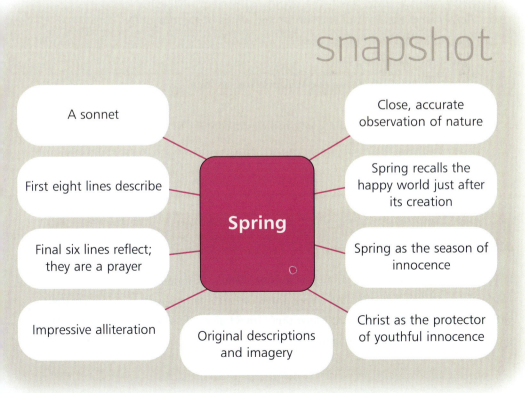

snapshot

- A sonnet
- First eight lines describe
- Final six lines reflect; they are a prayer
- Impressive alliteration
- Original descriptions and imagery

Spring

- Close, accurate observation of nature
- Spring recalls the happy world just after its creation
- Spring as the season of innocence
- Christ as the protector of youthful innocence

As Kingfishers Catch Fire

As kingfishers catch fire, dragonflies draw flame;
As tumbled over rim in roundy wells
Stones ring; like each tucked string tells, each hung bell's
Bow swung finds tongue to fling out broad its name;
Each mortal thing does one thing and the same: 5
Deals out that being indoors each one dwells;
Selves – goes itself; myself it speaks and spells,
Crying What I do is me; for that I came.

I say more: the just man justices;
Keeps grace: that keeps all his goings graces;   10
Acts in God's eye what in God's eye he is –
Christ. For Christ plays in ten thousand places,
Lovely in limbs, and lovely in eyes not his
To the Father through the features of men's faces.

Glossary

1	*catch fire*: the flash of the sun on the wings of the kingfisher
1	*draw flame*: the flash of the sun on the wings of the dragonfly
3	*tucked*: an old form of 'plucked'
4	*bow*: the clapper of a bell
7	*Selves*: becomes its distinctive self, acts out its identity
9	*justices*: acts justly
10	*Keeps grace*: observes God's will, behaves according to God's law

Guidelines

It is worth considering this sonnet alongside 'God's Grandeur'. Compare also the following remark by Hopkins: 'All things therefore are charged with love, are charged with God, and if we know how to touch them [they] give off sparks and take fire, yield drops and flow, ring and tell of him.'

Commentary

Like Hopkins's other sonnets, this one has a two-part structure. In the octave (lines 1 to 8) he deals with the non-human creation. In the second part, the sestet (lines 9 to 14), he deals with human beings. The idea that every created thing, from stones and dragonflies to human beings, has a unique identity unites the two parts of the poem.

The octave

In the first eight lines Hopkins depicts the efforts of every non-human thing in the natural world to proclaim its identity. This identity is inscaped (has its essence expressed) by Hopkins. An example is his account of the impact of water on stones: 'As tumbled over rim in roundy wells / Stones ring' (lines 2–3). In this example, 'tumbled over rim in roundy wells' is an adjectival phrase qualifying 'stones' and thus catching the essence of the moment of impact. Similarly, the ringing of the bell tells the world of its inner nature or essence. Each natural thing does the same as the bell and tells the world of the essence that dwells inside it.

Everything proclaims its individual character, as if it were saying: I am myself and nobody or nothing else (line 7). Each thing in nature is conscious that its uniqueness is the reason for its existence (line 8). Hopkins is echoing Christ's words as recorded in the Bible: 'Pilate therefore said to him: Art thou a king then? Jesus answered: Thou sayest that I am a king; for this was I born, and for this came I into the world: that I should give testimony to the truth. Everyone that is of the truth, heareth my voice' (John, chapter 18, verse 37).

The sestet

In the final six lines of the sonnet Hopkins considers the uniqueness of human beings, whom he regarded as 'more selved and distinctive than anything in the world'. In this poem the most important attribute of a human being is freedom of choice. This makes humans unique among creatures. They can choose, or refuse, to give glory to God.

As Hopkins explains, humans express their true individuality, their inner essence, by obeying God's commandments. This idea is conveyed in the lines: 'I say more: the just man justices; / Keeps grace: that keeps all his goings graces' (lines 9–10). By thus keeping close to God's will, human beings make Christ present in the world. They act out the past that God has chosen for them as an expression of their identity. As Hopkins puts it, the person who behaves justly 'Acts in God's eye what in God's eye he is — / Christ' (lines 11–12): those who freely give God glory by living according to God's plan for them fulfil the purpose of their being.

The final two lines claim that the beauty of Christ is revealed to God (the Father) through the beauty of those who live good Christian lives.

Thinking about the poem

1. In the first eight lines of the sonnet Hopkins is suggesting that each created thing tries to proclaim its individual identity. List the examples he gives to illustrate this point. Comment on the effectiveness of each example.

2. In the final six lines of the sonnet Hopkins introduces a new theme, related to the theme of the first eight lines. What is this theme? How does he develop it?

3. According to Hopkins, human beings differ from the rest of creation in one significant way. What is this?

4. What is the role of Christ in the sonnet?

5. Comment on the resemblances between this sonnet and 'Pied Beauty'. What differences can you discover between the two sonnets?

6. Discuss the theme of celebration in the poem.

7. How would you describe the mood of the poem? Refer to the text.

8. What, according to Hopkins, is the true role of human beings? Why, does he think, were human beings created? How can people achieve true happiness?

9. The first eight lines of the poem offer a contrast to the final six lines in two significant ways. Identify the contrast by reference to the text.

10. Hopkins uses language in an original way in this poem. Write about the poem from this point of view, giving examples of words and phrases that strike you as original.

11. Many early readers found this poem difficult to understand. Can you suggest why? Give examples to illustrate your answer.

The Windhover

To Christ our Lord

I caught this morning morning's minion, king-
dom of daylight's dauphin, dapple-dawn-drawn Falcon, in his riding
Of the rolling level underneath him steady air, and striding
High there, how he rung upon the rein of a wimpling wing,
In his ecstasy! then off, off forth on swing,   5
As a skate's heel sweeps smooth on a bow-bend: the hurl and gliding
Rebuffed the big wind. My heart in hiding
Stirred for a bird, – the achieve of, the mastery of the thing!

Brute beauty and valour and act, oh, air, pride, plume here
Buckle! AND the fire that breaks from thee then, a billion   10
Times told lovelier, more dangerous, O my chevalier!
No wonder of it: sheer plod makes plough down sillion
Shine, and blue-bleak embers, ah my dear,
Fall, gall themselves, and gash gold-vermillion.

Glossary		
Title	*Windhover*: a kestrel, distinguished by the habit of hunting its prey by sustained hovering	
1	*caught*: saw, caught sight of	
1	*minion*: favourite	
2	*dauphin*: heir	
2	*dapple-dawn-drawn*: attracted from his lair by the dappled dawn	
4	*rung . . . rein*: a technical term from falconry meaning to rise in spirals; there may be a pun on rein/reign, with reference to the bird as a royal horseman riding the wind	
4	*wimpling*: rippling, fluttering	
6	*bow-bend*: wide arc	
7	*Rebuffed*: controlled, mastered	
8	*achieve*: perfection	
10	*Buckle*: the meaning of this word is much disputed, but the context suggests that it means 'collapse', or 'give way under pressure'	

10	*AND*: and as an inevitable result
11	*chevalier*: knight; here Christ
12	*No wonder of it*: it is not surprising
12	*plod*: hard work; sheer plod may be a pun on 'ploughshare'
12	*plough*: ploughed land
12	*sillion*: furrow
13	*ah my dear*: these words are addressed to Christ
14	*vermillion*: the traditional colour of royal blood; the blood here is from the gash in Christ's side

Guidelines

This sonnet, written in 1877, is the most famous, and most analysed, of Hopkins' poems. It has provoked considerable discussion of its local difficulties. There are wide disagreements among critics over the basic meaning of some key words and phrases. Examples are 'rung upon the rein' (line 4) and 'Buckle!' (line 10).

Commentary

The language may be difficult, but the structure of the sonnet is straightforward. **The first eight lines are devoted to the windhover and the final six concern Christ.**

The octave

The first eight lines emphasise the bird's total mastery of the air, which is his element. His activities are presented by means of metaphors. The metaphor, Hopkins' favourite figure of speech, involves describing one thing in terms of another. For example, the depiction of the windhover as a 'dauphin' (line 2): the world of daylight is a kingdom, its heir or crown prince is the windhover, who has been drawn from his habitat by the attractions of the dappled dawn. His splendid movements are observed ('caught') by the speaker of the poem.

The windhover is pictured as a knight on a horse, riding the air. This image is clearly suggested in words such as 'riding', 'underneath him', 'striding high', 'rein' and 'mastery'. Later in the sonnet, Christ, whose splendour is reflected in that of the windhover, also appears as a knight ('my chevalier', line 11).

The words 'rolling level underneath him steady' (line 3) are best understood as a single unit of language, a compound adjective qualifying 'air'. This is how Hopkins inscapes (or conveys the essence of) the air, which resembles a great highway across which the bird makes his journey.

The windhover is described as ringing 'upon the rein of a wimpling wing' (line 4). Here the bird, by means of a mixture of metaphors, seems to become a bell, hanging by its wings in mid-air. 'Wimpling' can mean quick-beating, fluttering or rippling. The image of the bird as a bell seems to be suggested by the phrases 'how he rung' (line 4) and 'off forth on swing' (line 5). Thus, we seem to have an image of the windhover, bell-like, swinging back and forth in a wide arc ('on a bow-bend', line 6), having mastered ('rebuffed') the strong wind.

Given that the subject of the first eight lines is a windhover, it seems preferable to assume that Hopkins is using 'to ring' as a technical term, from falconry, meaning to rise in spirals. However, some critics have been tempted to read 'to ring upon the rein' as a metaphor from horse training, since this term is applied to a horse circling at the end of a long rein held by its trainer. Imaginative interpreters have also suggested that the line evokes ringing bells attached to the reins of a royal charger.

The simile of the skate's heel may suggest that 'bow-bend' (line 6) is to be understood as referring to the 'figure eight' in skating. This would imply that Hopkins sees the windhover's flight in terms of the curve made by the heel of a skater who is skating around the bend of a loop.

The idea of the windhover as a hanging bell, filling the heavens with joyful news ('in his ecstasy', line 5) of his own glory, seems to be confirmed by the sonnet 'As Kingfishers Catch Fire'. In that sonnet, Hopkins tells how 'each hung bell's / Bow swung finds tongue to fling out broad its name'.

The sestet

Hopkins compresses a great density of meaning, or suggestion, into the final six lines, which deal with Christ. The sub-title of the poem, '*To Christ our Lord*', provides an all-important clue that 'my chevalier' (line 11) is Christ.

'Brute beauty' (line 9) describes the merely natural, mortal beauty of the windhover, which does, however, give off flashes of divine beauty, like every natural thing. However glorious the windhover may be, the power and glory of Christ ('the fire that breaks from thee', line 10) is a 'billion' times greater.

The biggest difficulty of interpretation is posed by 'Buckle' (line 10). There are several schools of thought on this. One holds that Hopkins may be using the verb to suggest a fusion or clasping together of the elements of 'beauty', 'valour', 'act', 'air', 'pride' and 'plume' (line 9) into a blessed unity. Another interpretation is that 'Buckle' means break or collapse, and that Hopkins is conveying the idea that the mortal beauty and pride of the windhover collapses into nothingness when confronted by the glory of

Christ, who is a billion times lovelier than all the splendid qualities of the windhover taken together. A third school of thought suggests that both senses of 'Buckle', with the opposite meanings of 'fuse' and 'collapse' are present simultaneously. To accept this is to regard 'The Windhover' as an open text, in which a given word or group of words can mean several things at once, even when these meanings contradict each other.

It is likely that 'sheer plod makes plough down sillion / Shine' (lines 12–13) refers to the gleaming of the earth when it is broken open in the act of ploughing. This is an example of Hopkins' belief that humble actions produce unexpected flashes of beauty. The final lines of the poem convey this idea: dull embers can break open to reveal 'gold-vermillion' fire. The 'blue-bleak embers' (line 13) refer to Christ's crucified body. Hopkins does not find it surprising that the highest spiritual qualities should flash forth from a heart that has been purified by suffering and conflict.

Rhythm of the poem

The sweep of the language in this poem is best considered in relation to Hopkins' use of sprung rhythm (explained above in the section headed 'Hopkins and the Language of Poetry'). Consider lines 1 to 4. It is evident that in these lines both the sense and the metre have to be carried forward from line to line. The effect is to reproduce the continuous swoop and hurl of the windhover's flight. In lines 5 and 6, again, the rhythm of the words suggests the surging, swooping flight.

Thinking about the poem

1   How does Hopkins relate the windhover to Christ? What have they in common? How do they differ?

2   'The poem is less about the windhover than about Christ.' Discuss this idea with reference to the text.

3   How does Hopkins convey his sense of Christ's superiority?

4   What qualities in the windhover does Hopkins admire most?

5   What is the significance of Hopkins' reference to Christ as 'my chevalier' (line 11; meaning 'my knight')? How does this relate to the first eight lines of the sonnet?

6   How do the movement, rhythm and alliteration in the poem help to convey its meaning?

7   Consider the final six lines as a meditation on the Christian way of life, particularly in its emphasis on sacrifice, struggle and the search for perfection.

8　Comment on Hopkins' use of the theme of sacrificial suffering and voluntary sacrifice in the final six lines. What do suffering and sacrifice achieve, according to Hopkins?

9　In this sonnet we encounter the natural speech of a person under the stress of excitement. Mention some of the elements that make the poet's language natural and true to life.

10　Throughout the poem there is an urgent activity, an ongoing life and movement. Give three examples of this.

11　One critic has suggested that in 'The Windhover', Hopkins is addressing Christ, his own heart and the windhover, because the three are inseparable in his mind. Can you find evidence in support of this idea?

12　Hopkins added the dedication, 'To Christ our Lord', some time after he composed the poem. Without this dedication, would you be able to recognise this sonnet as a Christian poem? If so, which words or expressions would allow you to do this?

Pied Beauty

Glory be to God for dappled things –
For skies of couple-colour as a brindled cow;
For rose-moles all in stipple upon trout that swim;
Fresh-firecoal chestnut-falls; finches' wings;
Landscape plotted and pieced – fold, fallow, and plough;　　　　5
And all trades, their gear and tackle and trim.
All things counter; original, spare, strange;
Whatever is fickle, freckled (who knows how?)
With swift, slow; sweet, sour; adazzle, dim;
He fathers-forth whose beauty is past change:　　　　10
Praise him.

Glossary

Title	*Pied*: variegated like a magpie; patches of different colours
1	*dappled*: marked with spots
2	*couple-colour*: of two colours
2	*brindled*: streaked, two-coloured
3	*rose-moles*: red spots that look like moles
4	*firecoal*: coals of fire; Hopkins liked to think of chestnuts being as bright as coals
5	*plotted and pieced*: patchwork effect created by the pattern and variety of fields
5	*fold*: fields devoted to grazing
5	*fallow*: unused fields
5	*plough*: cultivated fields
6	*trades*: occupations
6	*gear and tackle and trim*: equipment appropriate to the trade; 'tackle' suggests rigging for a ship; 'trim' may refer to outfits or fittings
7	*counter*: contrasting
7	*spare*: unique
8	*fickle*: liable to change
9	*adazzle*: glittering, sparkling
10	*He*: God
10	*fathers-forth*: generates, creates

Guidelines

'Pied Beauty' is a hymn of praise to God for the rich, endless variety of nature. It is an example of what Hopkins called a 'Curtal sonnet'. He explained that it was an experimental form of the sonnet, 'constructed in proportions resembling those of the sonnet proper, namely 6 + 4 instead of 8 + 6, with, however, a half line tailpiece'. The tailpiece consists of two words.

Commentary

Contrast and difference

As in many of his poems, Hopkins is dealing here with the individuality and distinctiveness of natural things (see 'As Kingfishers Catch Fire' for a similar idea). The piedness referred to in the title highlights how many things are similar without being identical. Nature lives in constant movement and change but never repeats itself. No two 'couple-coloured' cows, skies, trout or finches' wings are exactly alike. They are original.

This distinctiveness is indicated particularly in line 7 where 'counter' (contrasting), 'original', 'spare' (unique) and 'strange' (singular) all point to the infinite variety of creation. Hopkins also celebrates anything that is 'fickle' in nature (line 8). This is his way of indicating the endless movement and change of form, shape and colour undergone by everything he observes.

All this emphasis on natural variety, change and contrast is leading up to a point made in line 10 and the tailpiece: 'He fathers-forth whose beauty is past change: / Praise him'. Here Hopkins is making a theological point: God, the cause of movement in everything, is himself unmoved. God is the origin of all change, but God is unchangeable ('past change'). This is the supreme contrast for Hopkins. A world of endless variety and change owes its existence to an unchanging principle: God. God maintains the glorious diversity and individuality of natural things.

The first line, the tenth and the tailpiece indicate the purpose Hopkins had in mind when writing the poem. 'Pied Beauty' is a poem of love and praise for the endlessly interesting variations provided for by a creator whose changeless beauty is their source.

Instress

Hopkins expresses the view that all things are upheld by instress and are meaningless without it. Instress, as Hopkins understood it, was the undercurrent of creative energy that supports and holds together the created world. It gives shape, form and meaning to the eye of the beholder. Without the current of instress that runs through both the world of nature and the minds of those who perceive nature, there would be no link between outward nature and the human mind.

The idea of instress is finely expressed in 'Pied Beauty'. Here Hopkins delights in the endless variety of nature. At the same time, instress organises all this variety into a unified pattern and, since instress also runs through the human mind, it enables the human mind to make sense of the outer world.

'Pied Beauty' makes another point: the hidden energy (instress) that moulds things into distinctive shapes, patterns and colours (inscapes) is the energy of God, the author of nature and of mankind. Nature is the visible sign of God's invisible, unceasing creative energy (instress), which maintains nature's essential unity in diversity: 'He fathers-forth whose beauty is past change' (line 10).

Sound patterns in the poem

The dominant sound pattern in the poem is created by continuous alliteration. This occurs in every line. There are some brilliant examples, such as 'With swift, slow; sweet, sour, adazzle, dim' (line 9). Assonance (the rhyming of vowel sounds without the rhyming of consonants) also contributes to the sound-pattern. For example: 'rose-moles' (line 3); 'knows', 'slow', 'forth' (lines 8 to 10).

Thinking about the poem

1   Would you agree that this is more than a descriptive poem?

2   What feature has this poem in common with 'The Windhover', 'Spring', 'God's Grandeur' and 'As Kingfishers Catch Fire'?

3   The poet mentions many different natural features. What do they all have in common? How do they give unity to the poem?

4   How does the poem convey the idea that God is the beginning and the end of all things?

5   The poem moves with quickening pace from air to earth to water and fire to the varied activities of human beings, finally returning to God. Comment on the details of this movement.

6   In 'Pied Beauty' nature lives in movement and change. How does Hopkins develop this idea?

7   In 'Pied Beauty' there is an elaborate pattern of sound (assonance, alliteration and rhyme), which echoes the meaning of the poem. Comment on the working out of this pattern.

8   Consider the poem as an expression of Hopkins' belief that God is reflected in nature.

9   What does Hopkins mean when he says that God's beauty is 'past change' (line 10)?

10   There is a paradox (a seeming contradiction) in the relationship between Hopkins' God and the created universe. Comment on this.

11   Why might Hopkins admire 'dappled things' so much?

12   'Pied Beauty' has been described as a poem written with a special purpose in mind. Comment on this.

Inversnaid

This darksome burn, horseback brown,
His rollrock highroad roaring down,
In coop and in comb the fleece of his foam
Flutes and low to the lake falls home.

A windpuff-bonnet of fawn-froth   5
Turns and twindles over the broth
Of a pool so pitch-black, fell-frowning
It rounds and rounds Despair to drowning.

Degged with dew, dappled with dew
Are the groins of the braes that the brook treads through,   10
Wiry heathpacks, flitches of fern,
And the beadbonny ash that sits over the burn.

What would the world be, once bereft
Of wet and of wildness? Let them be left,
O let them be left, wildness and wet;   15
Long live the weeds and the wilderness yet.

Glossary	
Title	*Inversnaid*: a tiny settlement in the Scottish Highlands that Hopkins visited in August 1881
1	*burn*: a small stream
2	*rollrock highroad*: the rocky bed that the water flows over
3	*coop*: an enclosed space where the water is hemmed in by rocks
3	*comb*: the ribbed fanlike effect of fast-running water striking a stone and flowing over it
4	*flutes*: forms grooves
5	*windpuff-bonnet of fawn-froth*: the windblown vapour that rises from a pool at the foot of a waterfall
6	*twindles*: coined by Hopkins, this word probably combines 'twists', 'dwindles' and 'twitches'; another possible meaning is 'dwindling into twins' (i.e. dividing itself in half)

6	*broth*: disturbed water
7	*fell-frowning*: frowning in a sinister way; a fell is also a mountain
9	*degged*: sprinkled
9	*dappled*: marked with spots of light and dark
10	*groins of the braes*: the point at which folds of land join, giving a sinewy-type appearance to the hillsides
10	*brook*: a stream
11	*wiry heathpacks*: clumps of heather
11	*flitches*: bunches, clumps, russet tufts
12	*beadbonny ash*: the rowan tree, or mountain ash, with its pleasing (bonny) red berries (looking like beads)
12	*sits over*: overhangs
13	*bereft*: deprived

Guidelines

The inspiration for this poem came from the poet's longing for the wildness, peace and beauty of the Scottish Highlands. The poem was composed in 1881 after he had visited Inversnaid for a few hours. It celebrates the wild splendour of the Scottish Highlands, a welcome contrast to the ugliness of cities such as Liverpool and Glasgow, in which Hopkins served as a priest. 'Inversnaid' is also a display of the poet's considerable verbal skills.

Hopkins catches the distinctiveness of what he is describing by inscaping it. His pictures of details of the landscape are fresh, original and accurate. He made careful observations of flora and fauna with scientific accuracy, recording them in his notebooks. The results of this painstaking work are evident in such poems as 'Inversnaid'.

Commentary

Stanza 1

Sound, rhythm, movement and description work together to achieve striking effects in the first stanza. The rapid, powerful surge of the dark stream (the 'burn') is perfectly suggested in the elaborate alliteration and lively rhythm of the first two lines ('burn, horseback brown' and 'rollrock highroad roaring'). The lines also convey the excitement of the journey made by the stream over its rocky road.

Hopkins' skills of close observation are reflected in lines 3 and 4, which also show his inventive use of words. 'Coop' suggests both enclosed space and water cooped up, while the activity depicted in 'comb' is the ribbed effect of water running swiftly as it strikes and flows over a stone. The foam produced by the stream reminds Hopkins of the fleece of a sheep.

Stanzas 2 and 3

These stanzas continue the description of the stream's progress through the Scottish landscape. In lines 5 and 6 Hopkins again displays his verbal ingenuity. To achieve the distinctive impression he is looking for, he invents a verb ('twindles') to describe the movement of the windblown vapour rising from a pool at the foot of the waterfall. 'Twindles' is a portmanteau word (one that combines other words to form a new one). It telescopes 'twists', 'twitches' and 'dwindles'.

He also makes use of the occasional dialect word. For example 'Degged' in line 9 is a Lancashire dialect word for 'sprinkled'.

Stanza 4

Whereas the first three stanzas are purely descriptive, the final stanza reflects on the value of what the poet has seen at Inversnaid. A lover of nature, Hopkins pleads that such areas 'Of wet and of wildness . . . be left' (line 14), noting that the world needs 'the weeds and the wilderness yet' (line 16).

Hopkins was always able to find spiritual meanings in nature, although this is one of the few poems in which God is not mentioned. However, the flowing stream in the Highland wilderness has biblical overtones. For Hopkins, it signifies the waters of spiritual healing and rebirth so often mentioned in both Old and New Testaments.

Thinking about the poem

1 Consider 'Inversnaid' as an example of Hopkins' descriptive power.

2 What does the scene depicted in the poem mean to Hopkins?

3 Show how rhythm and movement contribute to the meaning of the poem.

4 'Hopkins' descriptive language is never static: it is full of urgency, excited activity, of ongoing life.' Comment on this view with reference to 'Inversnaid'.

5 Hopkins had a deep longing for solitude away from the haunts of men. How does this poem reflect that longing?

Taking a closer look

1 The language used in this poem is unusual. Give some examples and say what you think of these.

2 In what ways is this a clever poem?

3 There is much use of alliteration in this, as in other poems by Hopkins. What effect does Hopkins achieve by beginning so many successive words with the same sound?

4 Comment on Hopkins' use of internal rhyme. Give examples.

5 'Inversnaid' is a poem about nature. In what way does the treatment of nature here differ from Hopkins' treatment of it in 'God's Grandeur', 'Spring' and 'Pied Beauty'? What do these poems have that 'Inversnaid' lacks?

6 Describe the feeling you get from reading this poem. Illustrate your answer from the text.

Imagining

1 Hopkins kept a diary and recorded his visit to Inversnaid. Write the diary entry for this visit.

2 If you were asked to provide music to accompany a reading of this poem, what kind of music would you choose? Describe and explain your choice by referring to the words and music of the poem.

3 You have been asked by the local tourist board to write a short piece for a holiday brochure promoting short breaks in the vicinity of Inversnaid. Your piece should make use of some details from the poem.

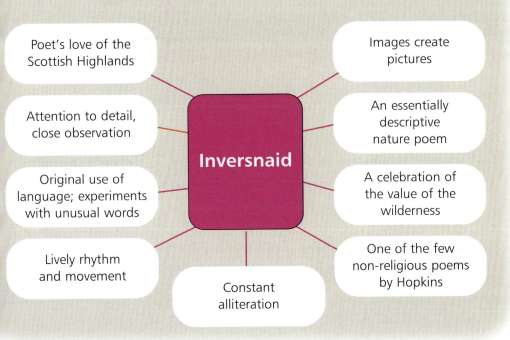

Poet's love of the Scottish Highlands

Attention to detail, close observation

Inversnaid

Original use of language; experiments with unusual words

Lively rhythm and movement

Constant alliteration

Images create pictures

An essentially descriptive nature poem

A celebration of the value of the wilderness

One of the few non-religious poems by Hopkins

Felix Randal

Felix Randal the farrier, O is he dead then? my duty all ended,
Who have watched his mould of man, big-boned and hardy-handsome
Pining, pining, till time when reason rambled in it and some
Fatal four disorders, fleshed there, all contended?

Sickness broke him. Impatient he cursed at first, but mended   5
Being anointed and all; though a heavenlier heart began some
Months earlier, since I had our sweet reprieve and ransom
Tendered to him. Ah well, God rest him all road ever he offended!

This seeing the sick endears them to us, us too it endears.
My tongue had taught thee comfort, touch had quenched thy tears,   10
Thy tears that touched my heart, child, Felix, poor Felix Randal;

How far from then forethought of, all thy more boisterous years,
When thou at the random grim forge, powerful amidst peers,
Didst fettle for the great grey drayhorse his bright and battering sandal!

Glossary

1	*farrier*:	blacksmith
3	*when reason rambled in it*:	when Felix lost the full use of his mind
4	*disorders*:	illnesses
4	*contended*:	fought (to kill Felix)
6	*anointed*:	given the last rites of the Church
6	*heavenlier heart*:	a more religious outlook, a heart ready to accept God's will
7	*sweet reprieve and ransom*:	Holy Communion
8	*tendered*:	given
8	*all road ever*:	in whatever way
9	*us too it endears*:	sick people grow to love the priests who minister to them in their illnesses
13	*random*:	built of stones of irregular shapes and sizes
13	*peers*:	fellow blacksmiths
14	*fettle*:	fix
14	*sandal*:	shoe

Guidelines

The speaker of the poem is a Catholic priest. One of his parishioners, a blacksmith named Felix Randal, has just died. Felix was a strong, burly man before multiple illnesses destroyed his health and strength. When illness first made him suffer, he cursed his fate. However, his religious belief and the sacraments of the Church consoled him and reconciled him to his suffering. The priest-speaker is happy that he has been able to comfort Felix. He knows that illness brings people closer to their priests. He has been deeply moved by the suffering of Felix.

The location of the poem, 'a smoke-sodden little town in Lancashire', meant a lot to Hopkins. It was a place where he encountered people who needed him desperately, and their need was what he needed.

Commentary

The sonnet follows the usual structural pattern. The first eight lines (the octave) are descriptive: dealing with the circumstances of Felix's illness and death, his character and the priest's response to his suffering. The final six lines (the sestet) are devoted to the speaker's reflections on what Felix has meant to him.

The descriptive part

The speaker has just heard that Felix the blacksmith is dead. This being so, his duty towards Felix has ended (since he has given Felix the last rites of the Church). This opening line shows the lengths to which Hopkins was prepared to go in his technical experiments with language. Within a single line we find an extraordinary correspondence of sound between 'dead then' and 'ended', the last being almost an inverse of the first. In the remainder of the first stanza the priest-speaker describes his experience of seeing the body of a well-built and handsome man attacked by four fatal diseases, until the time came when Felix's mind was enfeebled and disordered by illness.

The onset of illness broke this powerful man's spirit, and he impatiently cursed his God for inflicting this suffering on him. He learned, however, to accept his sufferings when the priest anointed him. Even before this anointing, Felix had shown a more Godly attitude ('a heavenlier heart', line 6) after he had received Holy Communion ('our sweet reprieve and ransom', line 7). Here we have the Christian teaching that Christ's sacrifice on the cross was a ransom offering to God. Because of this offering, God reprieved the human race from its sentence of death. The speaker asks God to pardon Felix for all the ways in which he wandered from the path of virtue.

The reflective part

In lines 9 to 11 the speaker reflects on his relationship with Felix, on the mutual love between priest and parishioner that often develops out of the illness of the latter. He also reflects on the comfort offered by religion and the deep emotional effect of Felix on the heart of the priest. In line 11, Felix is a 'child' in the spiritual sense.

The final three lines of the poem are solemn, splendid and rhetorical. In line 12 Hopkins is saying: In your active days, when you were fit and strong, how far away sickness and death were from your thoughts. Line 13 provides an interesting example of double meaning. Hopkins describes the forge in which Felix worked as 'random grim', suggesting that it was built of stones of irregular shapes and sizes. The phrase may also carry a hint that in his carefree days Felix was essentially an unthinking person, 'random' in his thoughts as well as in his place of work.

In his forge, Felix was a man of rare strength even among his fellow blacksmiths (his 'peers', line 13). The final line, with its resounding alliteration, brings the sonnet to a powerful climax as the speaker imagines Felix fixing a great bright shoe on a magnificent drayhorse.

Language of the poem

The language reflects the essential quality of Felix as a strong and powerfully built blacksmith when he was in his prime and a master of his trade. This is emphasised in the emphatic alliteration: 'big-boned and hardy-handsome' (line 2), 'powerful amidst peers' (line 13), confidently shoeing the 'great grey drayhorse' (line 14). Felix is inscaped in these descriptions. The terrible nature of the illness that brought him low is also emphasised in strong alliteration: 'Pining, pining . . . reason rambled' (line 3), 'Fatal four disorders' (line 4).

Hopkins maintains a continuous flow of sound and meaning, not alone through alliteration, but also by means of internal rhyme. One daring example features an unusual version of this in line 1: ('O is he dead then? my duty all ended') in which we are invited to reverse the order of 'dead then' to rhyme with 'ended'. Another example is 'cursed at first' (line 5).

Thinking about the poem

1   How are the strength, power and simplicity of the early Felix suggested by Hopkins?

2   Show how the poem mingles profound sadness with joy. Where is the source of the joy?

3   On the evidence of the poem, what is the speaker's opinion of Felix?

4   Does this poem make a good case for the value of a priest as a member of his community? Base your answer on a close reading of the text.

5   Imagine you are Felix telling his relatives about his last illness. Write a brief account of what he might say.

6   How would you describe the tone of the poem? Does it vary?

7   Hopkins makes considerable use of alliteration throughout the poem. Choose three particularly good examples, and comment on their effectiveness.

8   How do the final six lines of the poem contrast with the first eight lines?

9   In what ways do the priest and blacksmith benefit each other?

10   In what ways does the outlook of Felix change as his sickness becomes worse?

11   Would you describe Felix as a fundamentally good man? Base your answer on what is revealed in the poem.

12   Write your own response to the poem, referring to aspects you liked/disliked.

The Terrible Sonnets

Hopkins was prone to depression for much of his life. During his time in Dublin he was seldom free of it. He was plagued with anxiety about work still to be done. He expressed his loss of mental and physical well-being in the six sonnets he composed in 1885. These poems – commonly called the 'terrible sonnets', 'dark sonnets' or the 'sonnets of desolation' – include 'No Worst, There Is None' and 'I Wake and Feel the Fell of Dark'. The torments they describe are of a kind often found in the work of deeply spiritual people who explore the desolation and despair they feel when they pass through the experience known as 'the dark night of the soul'.

Written during a prolonged period of psychological and spiritual suffering, Hopkins conveys a strong sense of misery and dejection in his 'terrible sonnets'. His profound unhappiness was partly, though not entirely, due to the circumstances of his life in Dublin. It also had deeper roots in his earlier life. Having become a Catholic and a Jesuit priest, Hopkins found himself in a variety of difficult positions. He was a patriotic Englishman whose Protestant friends regarded him as less than a patriot because of his membership of a 'foreign' church. His life in Ireland was disturbed by the ordeal of having to endure the enthusiasm of Irish Jesuits for Home Rule, which he regarded as unlawful. He considered Ireland as an essential part of Great Britain.

Hopkins' literary talents never found a full outlet at any time in his life. He never commanded an appreciative audience for his poetry, virtually none of which was published until long after his death. His gifts as a preacher were never properly recognised. He was a considerable classical scholar who produced no important work of scholarship. He was a lover of natural beauty who had to spend years working in ugly, industrial slums, among people who could not be expected to share his tastes. His health was never robust, with the result that he often lacked energy and vitality. His academic work in Dublin did not satisfy him. He imposed strict and harsh penances on himself, thinking this would make him spiritually strong and believing that to lead a good Christian life one must endure pain and suffering.

The combination of these factors turned his life into a harsh and weary grind. Hopkins' strict sense of duty suppressed his natural inclinations. His health was made worse by his feeling of being abandoned by God. The attacks of despair described in these sonnets were not unfamiliar to Hopkins. He had experienced them in the past. He knew that the horrors he had experienced before, and was experiencing as he wrote the sonnets, would come again.

No Worst, There Is None

No worst, there is none. Pitched past pitch of grief,
More pangs will, schooled at forepangs, wilder wring,
Comforter, where, where is your comforting?
Mary, mother of us, where is your relief?

My cries heave, herds-long; huddle in a main, a chief-   5
woe, world-sorrow; on an age-old anvil wince and sing –
Then lull, then leave off. Fury had shrieked "No ling-
erring! Let me be fell; force I must be brief".

O the mind, mind has mountains; cliffs of fall
Frightful, sheer, no-man-fathomed. Hold them cheap   10
May who ne'er hung there. Nor does long our small
Durance deal with that steep or deep. Here! creep,
Wretch, under a comfort serves in a whirlwind: all
Life death does end and each day dies with sleep.

Glossary		
1	*Pitched past pitch*: made blacker than black; or thrown farther than grief can throw; or beyond any measurable pitch (a musical analogy)
2	*schooled*: trained, conditioned
2	*at forepangs*: by previous pangs of grief or suffering
3	*Comforter*: the Holy Ghost
5	*cries heave, herds-long*: his cries of distress go on and on like the bellowing of cattle
5–6	*huddle . . . woe*: his sufferings focus on a great universal sorrow, or bunch themselves together like terrified animals
8	*fell*: malevolent, cruel (and swift in the infliction of pain)
10	*Hold them cheap*: dismiss or underestimate them
11	*ne'er*: never
12	*Durance*: the human ability to endure
13	*whirlwind*: mental and emotional turmoil

Guidelines

This sonnet belongs to the period of Hopkins' unhappy residence in Dublin. It is a violent, terrifying cry of spiritual desolation and spiritual torment. It is dense with meaning and profound in its exploration of the depths of horror to which human despair can bring those who are its victims.

Commentary

The structure of the sonnet is clear. The eight lines of the octave (lines 1 to 8) describe the intense mental agony of a man in deep despair or depression. The six lines of the sestet (lines 9 to 14) offer a general reflection on what has been described in the octave.

The octave

The opening sentence of the poem, 'No worst, there is none', means that there is no such thing as 'worst' where human suffering is involved. **As long as people live, even greater suffering may be in store for them.** Hopkins is also suggesting that there is no greater agony than religious despair.

From 'Pitched past' to the end of line 2, Hopkins is picturing the soul (or mind) being flung ('pitched') from one extreme state ('pitch') of misery to another. 'Pitched' and 'pitch' also carry suggestions of blackness. Three distinct meanings may be present in 'Pitched past pitch of grief':

- The speaker is cast away even farther than grief could cast him.
- His unhappy position is staked out beyond the plot ('pitch') allotted to grief to work in.
- His gloom is more pitch-black than the blackness of grief.

The phrase 'schooled at forepangs' (line 2) is an example of the type of verbal shorthand that is typical of Hopkins. He is saying: before moving to the next stage of more extreme pain, the soul has been trained ('schooled') by earlier pain ('forepangs'). The phrase 'wilder wring' means that each torment will be worse than the one before it. In the face of such horror, the speaker asks the Holy Spirit (the 'Comforter') to show him what comfort can be found (line 3). He looks to the Virgin Mary ('mother of us') for relief (line 4). These pleadings remain unanswered.

The principal image of lines 5 and 6 conveys the idea of long, anguished, animal-like calls of distress. These cries are endless, they are as panic-stricken and disordered as a stampeding herd. The 'chief- / woe' is a universal sorrow. The image of the anvil reminds us that God's most dedicated servants can suffer the cruellest blows. Here the speaker is thinking of God as a blacksmith, hammering the soul on an anvil. In line 6 'age-old' suggests that God has been doing this to the souls of his servants through the ages. The phrase 'wince and sing' presents a terrible image of a human being wincing with pain, but at the same time rejoicing in his suffering, the soul singing God's praise, because this shows him to be one of God's chosen ones: the holiest people traditionally endure the greatest suffering.

The 'Fury' of line 7 is both the malignant hellish spirit of classical mythology and the tumult of a mind approaching madness. The terrible cry of fury, echoing in Hopkins' tormented mind, means: I must, of necessity carry out my malevolent ('fell') task quickly (line 8).

The sestet

In the most celebrated part of the poem, 'O the mind . . . hung there' (lines 9 to 11), we have an image of a terrified, despairing mind presented in terms of a mountain climber confronted with the prospect of plunging into an unmeasured abyss. This is a good instance of the way in which Hopkins' language enacts its meaning. He is using the full body and movement of the language: all the words are doing something.

When the mind reaches an intolerable pitch of stress, it can collapse into immeasurable depths of horror. Only those who have never experienced desolation, terror and despair, who have never been plunged beyond comfort, who have never had to struggle to maintain a precarious grip on sanity ('hung there', line 11), can pass these things off with a casual shrug ('Hold them cheap', line 10).

Human beings lack the capacity to cope with such mental collapse. They are unable to endure the experience he has been describing. This is because the realities of the steep cliffs and deep pits of despair are too horrible to bear for more than a short time. The only consolation for people in a depressive agony is that it will end (with death), just as today's agonies end with tonight's sleep. The tone of the final two lines is one of suicidal despair. The reference to a 'wretch' creeping 'under a comfort' (line 10) echoes the plight of the tormented King Lear, houseless in the storm, creeping into a hovel. This 'comfort' cannot 'serve', or fulfil, a useful purpose in this 'whirlwind' of mental and emotional turmoil. This recalls the whirlwind in the Book of Job (chapter 38, verses 1 to 3), out of which God demands that Job answer for his ignorant complaints about his cruel fate. By analogy, God will also demand a similar kind of answer from Hopkins.

Thinking about the poem

1 This is one of the most pessimistic accounts of mental and physical suffering in English poetry. Discuss the nature and source of the suffering depicted here.

2 Is this a poem of total despair? Is there any relief from the condition Hopkins describes?

3 Discuss the effectiveness of the imagery of the poem in conveying the meaning. What do the dominant images suggest?

4 How does Hopkins suggest that the spiritual and mental torments he records are not peculiar to himself?

5 Hopkins was a deeply religious man. What help does he get from his religious faith here?

6 Is this a typical Hopkins poem? In your answer, refer to other Hopkins poems on your course.

7 Why, according to the speaker in this poem, is there no such thing as the 'worst' (line 1)?

8 Who or what is 'Fury' in line 7? What is fury's role?

9 Comment on the image of the mountains and cliffs of the mind in lines 9 and 10. What idea do these convey? Who are those 'who ne'er hung there' (line 11)?

10 What is the 'comfort' (line 13) on which human beings can rely when facing the horrors described in the poem?

11 The poem is about deep personal suffering. Do you feel that the suffering comes from within the speaker, or is due to external factors? You might refer to other Hopkins poems on the subject of suffering: 'Felix Randal' and 'I Wake and Feel the Fell of Dark', for example. Explain your answer.

12 Many commentators have suggested that Hopkins invented a new kind of language to express difficult ideas. Consider this poem as an illustration of this, giving examples of the poet's novel use of words and images.

I Wake and Feel the Fell of Dark

I wake and feel the fell of dark, not day.
What hours, O what black hours we have spent
This night! what sights you, heart, saw; ways you went!
And more must, in yet longer light's delay.

With witness I speak this. But where I say   5
Hours I mean years, mean life. And my lament
Is cries countless, cries like dead letters sent
To dearest him that lives alas! away.

I am gall, I am heartburn. God's most deep decree
Bitter would have me taste: my taste was me;   10
Bones built in me, flesh filled, blood brimmed the curse.

Selfyeast of spirit a dull dough sours. I see
The lost are like this, and their scourge to be
As I am mine, their sweating selves; but worse.

Glossary

1	*fell*: as a noun it means the hairy skin of an animal, as an adjective it means evil or malevolent
2	*black hours*: the hours of darkness and despair before morning
5	*witness*: good reason
7	*dead*: undelivered, unanswered
8	*him*: God
8	*away*: absent, indifferent
9	*gall*: a sore on the skin
9	*decree*: law
10	*my tastes was me*: he has to endure self-hatred and self-disgust

Guidelines

'No Worst, There Is None' ended with a suggestion of closure: sleep will put an end to even the most savage mental suffering. 'I Wake and Feel the Fell of Dark' takes even this limited comfort away. A new, terrifying day follows a short, restless night's sleep. The speaker must face a continuation of countless miseries without the prospect of relief.

Commentary

The octave

The four opening lines of this sonnet describe an experience common to people suffering from depression, many of whom wake long before daybreak and are tormented by despairing thoughts until it is time to rise. **The first three lines describe the horrors endured in a short night of sleep disturbed by nightmares. This is bad enough, but in the waking hours until daybreak, further self-torturing agonies of the mind must be endured.**

The 'fell' of line 1 carries two simultaneous meanings. The dark is fell or malevolent it also resembles the fell or skin of a beast, an image of nightmarish horror. The symbolism of light and darkness used in the first four lines is traditional. Darkness signifies spiritual desolation, while light signifies hope and comfort, which are far away.

Lines 5 to 8 may be paraphrased as: I say this with good reason. I have said that my sufferings extended over hours. I should have said that they have extended over years, even over the whole of my life. My countless cries to heaven for help are like undelivered letters to God, from whom I feel totally separated. Each bout of depression seems like a lifetime of misery.

The sestet

The first sentence of line 9, 'I am gall, I am heartburn', presents an image of the speaker's state, but it is not merely symbolic. **The speaker's whole being is racked by physical, as well as spiritual, suffering.** Indeed the physical discomfort mirrors the spiritual suffering. In speaking this line one should place a strong emphasis on 'am' both times.

The speaker can find no cause for his being chosen to experience such intense bitterness. The only explanation is to be sought in the mysterious providence of God (his 'most deep decree', line 9). The speaker's disgust as he contemplates his condition is expressed in terms of some evil-tasting food ('my tastes was me', line 10). The 'curse' of line 11 is the speaker's unbearable spiritual and mental suffering and his physical distress. He sees the curse as having originated at his birth and as being part of his very nature – his bones, flesh and blood.

In line 12, 'Selfyeast of spirit a dull dough sours', he imagines his spiritual malaise in terms of sodden, indigestible bread. His soul is so oppressed that its most appropriate image is that of clammy, heavy dough.

In his closing sentence the speaker sees a similarity between his condition and that of the lost souls in hell, isolated and alone in their self-centred torments. Hopkins believed that the punishment endured by the damned souls in hell was that they had to confront their own evil selves.

It can scarcely be said that the poem ends on a hopeful note, but there is a slight withdrawal from total despair. While sharing in kind some of the experiences of the damned, the speaker sees a difference in degree between their miseries and his: theirs extend into eternity. **The speaker is not in hell, therefore the damned are worse off than he is because their torment, unlike his, is endless.**

Language of the poem

A central theme of this sonnet is that spiritual and psychological illness is expressed through painful physical symptoms of acute discomfort and nausea. Hopkins' choice of imagery in the final six lines reflects this: 'I am gall, I am heartburn' (line 9), for example. The image of a bitter taste in his mouth, the bitter taste being the taste of himself ('my tastes was me', line 10) indicates self-disgust and self-hatred.

Perhaps the most vivid image of the relationship between spiritual suffering and physical symptoms is: 'Selfyeast of spirit a dull dough sours' (line 12). Here Hopkins is expressing the idea that his sense of spiritual sickness is so overwhelming that something physically clammy, sour and lumpish has settled like a dead weight on both body and soul. The image of the damned souls in hell confronting 'their sweating selves' (line 14) is another example of spiritual and bodily torment combined. These images inscape a tortured soul: the distinctive quality of this particular soul is that it is doomed, by 'God's most deep decree' (line 9), to express its spiritual torment through intense physical pain and self-torture.

The early morning darkness is also inscaped in the opening line. In his depressed state, Hopkins thinks of darkness as fell, or evil. 'Fell' could also refer to the hairy skin of some dangerous animal: the inscape of darkness, its unique quality, is thus conveyed as the danger posed by a wicked, sinister beast.

From beginning to end, alliteration is freely employed (from 'feel the fell of dark, not day' to 'sweating selves'). This adds considerable emphasis to the poet's despair. The vocabulary consists of plain, familiar words.

Thinking about the poem

1   What is the experience described in the first line of the poem?

2   Why is the speaker's lament like 'dead letters' sent to someone who lives 'away' (lines 7 and 8)? Who is this someone?

3   What is the 'curse' referred to in line 11?

4   What does the speaker mean by saying that the bitter taste he experiences is himself (line 10)?

5   In what way does Hopkins compare himself to a damned soul in hell?

6   Where in the poem does Hopkins associate bodily misery with mental and spiritual suffering?

7   Is this poem about self-pity, or does it have a broader dimension?

8   Comment on the symbolism of light and darkness in the poem.

9   In line 2 the speaker refers to 'black hours we have spent'. What is the significance of 'we' here?

10 What kind of intervention would help to ease the speaker's misery?

11 How would you describe the tone of the last line of the poem?

12 The poem becomes more intense as it proceeds. How is this growing intensity created? You might refer to the physical as well as the mental suffering of the poem.

Thou Art Indeed Just, Lord

Justus quidem tu es, Domine, si disputem tecum:
verumtamen justa loquar ad te: Quare via impiorum
prosperatur? &c.

Thou art indeed just, Lord, if I contend
With thee; but, sir, so what I plead is just.
Why do sinners' ways prosper? and why must
Disappointment all I endeavour end?
Wert thou my enemy, O thou my friend,   5
How wouldst thou worse, I wonder, than thou dost
Defeat, thwart me? Oh, the sots and thralls of lust
Do in spare hours more thrive than I that spend,
Sir, life upon thy cause. See, banks and brakes

Now, leavèd how thick! lacèd they are again   10
With fretty chervil, look, and fresh wind shakes
Them; birds build – but not I build; no, but strain,
Time's eunuch, and not breed one work that wakes.
Mine, O thou lord of life, send my roots rain.

Glossary

Epigraph *Justus . . .* : the prophet Jeremiah (chapter 12, verse 1) wonders why
God permits the good to suffer and the wicked to prosper; the Latin is
translated in the first three lines of the poem

1	*contend*: argue, dispute, debate
7	*thwart*: obstruct, frustrate
7	*sots*: drunkards
7	*thralls*: slaves
9	*brakes*: thickets
10	*leavèd how thick*: how thick they are with leaves
11	*fretty chervil*: wild parsley with delicately fringed ('fretty') leaves
13	*Time's eunuch*: the 'time' here is the present, when he feels so unproductive; a eunuch is a man incapable of having children – Hopkins uses the word as a metaphor for his unproductive life
13	*work that wakes*: a living work; Hopkins may be referring to his priestly work or to his poetry

Guidelines

This sonnet was written in Dublin on St Patrick's Day, 1889. In the previous year
Hopkins had begun to feel depressed, 'to enter on that course of loathing and
hopelessness which I have so often felt before, which made me fear madness'. He
asked himself, 'What is my wretched life? Five wasted years almost have passed in
Ireland. I am ashamed of the little I have done, of my waste of time . . . All my
undertakings miscarry . . . I was then for death . . . O my God, look down on me.'
These sentiments are reflected in this sonnet.

Commentary

Note that in this sonnet the octave extends into part of line 9.

The octave

In the opening two lines of the poem, Hopkins recognises the righteousness and justice of God when he complains to him ('if I contend'). However, he also feels that he has justice on his side and therefore good reason to question God's justice in the two respects mentioned in lines 3 and 4. **He cannot understand why God allows sinners to prosper, while good faithful men like himself meet with failure and frustration in everything they attempt.** His key point is that if God, who is his friend, were instead his enemy, God could not treat him any worse than he already does. Those who are debased and enslaved by the sins of the flesh, who are 'the sots and thralls of lust' (line 7), prosper more as a result of the casual work of their spare time than the speaker does, even though he devotes his entire life to God's service. The expression to 'spend . . . life' (lines 8 and 9) means to pass time as well as to wear oneself out.

The sestet

The sestet present a contrast between the luxuriant, creative, productive life of nature and the barrenness, dryness and sterility of the speaker's life. Chervil stands for the rich abundance of nature (line 11). The speaker, in contrast, is 'Time's eunuch' (line 13) because the creative impulse has failed him; he has not brought forth any work that lives ('wakes'). **The final line is a prayer to the God of life to nourish his creative talent, just as rain from heaven causes plants to flourish.**

Thinking about the poem

1   Does there appear to be a contradiction in the first two lines?
2   Summarise the complaints put forward by the speaker. Do you find them convincing?
3   How does Hopkins set himself apart from other people? Does he envy these people? Would he wish to be like them?
4   Is there any sense in which the speaker is being unreasonable?
5   What do the words 'one work that wakes' (line 13) suggest to you?
6   The final six lines of the poem show nature at its most productive and fertile. How do these lines fit in with the earlier section of the poem (lines 1 to 8)? What is their purpose?

7   How would you interpret the final line of the poem? What is its tone?

8   Write a response to the poem, focusing on aspects of it that you liked and/or disliked and making close reference to the text.

General Questions

1   'A distinctive, even eccentric use of language is one of the most obvious things about Hopkins.' Examine his poems from this point of view.

2   Hopkins was deeply conscious of the individuality of each created thing. How is this reflected in his poetry?

3   In his religious poetry Hopkins reveals a profound understanding of some of the dark corners of the human mind. Illustrate this from his 'terrible sonnets'.

4   'Everything in Hopkins is influenced by his belief in God.' Consider his poems in the light of this comment.

5   'The poems of Hopkins alternate between gladness and dejection.' Show how this is so.

6   'Every detail in Hopkins' poetry reveals his passion for careful and accurate observation.' Comment on this in the light of his poems.

7   What kind of personality emerges from the poetry of Hopkins?

8   Discuss the elements of conflict in the poetry of Hopkins.

9   'Hopkins uses startling imagery in the exploration of his themes.' Comment on the poems of Hopkins on your course in the light of this statement.

10   Write an essay in which you explain why you like or dislike Hopkins' poetry. Support your arguments by reference to, or quotation from, the poems on your course.
     Reasons for liking Hopkins' poetry might include:
     ● The poems are original and distinctive.
     ● Hopkins' descriptions make us see what is being described in a new way.
     ● Hopkins is a great nature poet.
     ● The poems deal with great issues in a compelling way: a human's place in the universe, our relationship with God, the reflection of God in nature.
     ● Hopkins is one of the great masters of language.
     The following are reasons you might give for not liking Hopkins' poetry:
     ● The poems are extremely odd.
     ● Many of the poems are baffling, and slow to yield up their meaning.
     ● Hopkins invented a new language, which is difficult to learn.
     ● Hopkins does not deal with subjects that interest me.
     ● The poems seem to have been written for learned adults, not for young students.

Sample Essay

Write an introduction to the poetry of Gerard Manley Hopkins for new readers that concentrates on two aspects:

(a) The things that mattered most to Hopkins

(b) Your own response to his language and imagery.

The two things that mattered most to Hopkins were his fixed belief in the Christian God as the source of the beauty of the natural world, and the distinct individuality of everything, from the humblest objects to the mind of man.

[Addresses terms of question immediately]

For Hopkins, God as revealed by Christ was the source of everything in the world. As he puts it in 'God's Grandeur', 'The world is charged with the grandeur of God'. In spite of man's efforts to spoil this grandeur, the power of God continues to renew it:

Because the Holy Ghost over the bent

World broods with warm breast and with ah! bright wings

It is a mystery to Hopkins that human beings ignore God's law, in spite of God's goodness and kindness in giving them a beautiful world to enjoy: 'Why do men then now not reck his rod?'

[First point illustrated by reference and suitable quotation from the poem]

In 'The Windhover' Hopkins marvels at the gracefulness, beauty and power of the bird as it masters its element, the air. At the same time, he recognises that the beauty and achievements of so splendid a creature are insignificant in comparison with the glory of Christ, who is 'a billion / Times told lovelier, more dangerous'. It is significant that Hopkins dedicated 'The Windhover' to 'Christ our Lord'.

[Second poem referred to in support of first point]

Throughout his nature poems, Hopkins is always conscious that the beauty he finds in the natural world has its source in God. 'Pied Beauty' provides a good example of this. Hopkins finds an endless variety in nature, 'Landscape plotted and pieced – fold, fallow, and plough'. The point of the poem, however, is not all this varied natural beauty. All this leads back to God: 'He fathers-forth whose beauty is past change: / Praise him.' Even in his poems of personal despair, he looks for help, not to human agencies, but to God, as in 'Thou Art Indeed Just, Lord: 'O thou lord of life, send my roots rain'.

[Third and fourth poem cited and quoted to support first point]

Hopkins, apart from being preoccupied with the religious dimension of creation, was also a firm believer in the distinctive individuality of every single thing on earth. He coined a special term, 'inscape', to describe the set of qualities in an object that belong to it and to nothing else, and which therefore define it and express its essence. Each thing has its inscape or selfhood, which is expressed in some design or pattern. In the poetry of Hopkins, we notice that he has observed things with the concentration required to grasp their uniqueness and so to inscape them.

[Second point supported by reference to inscape]

The idea of the uniqueness of each created thing is explored in 'As Kingfishers Catch Fire'. Here, Hopkins depicts a world in which everything he observes, from stones and dragonflies to human beings, tries to assert its identity. Hopkins invents new words and combinations of words in an attempt to express this identity or essence. In the following lines he employs 'selves' as a verb to mean 'acts out its identity':

> Selves — goes itself; *myself* it speaks and spells,
> Crying *What I do is me; for that I came.*

[Poem cited and quoted in support of second point]

The just man defines his identity by acting justly, an idea expressed by Hopkins in 'the just man justices'. The selfhood of each given thing is, by definition, unique, so Hopkins uses compound words to express this. 'The Windhover' has many examples. In that poem we find groups of adjectives in front of nouns. The windhover appears as a knight riding the dawn on a charger; this is the essential thing about the bird as Hopkins sees it. Thus, he describes him as a 'dapple-dawn-drawn Falcon', riding 'the rolling level underneath him steady air'. In the sonnet 'I Wake to Feel the Fell of Dark', the defining feature of the dark is encapsulated in the terrifying qualities suggested by 'fell' (meaning the hairy skin of a wild animal as well as evil).

[Other poems cited and quoted to support second point]

The language and imagery of the poetry of Hopkins appeal to me in various ways. First of all, it is primarily descriptive, but in a most distinctive and original sense. What I admire most is the way in which Hopkins manages to condense so much meaning into relatively few words.

In 'God's Grandeur', for example, the history of human activity on the planet is recorded with admirable economy:

> And all is seared with trade; bleared, smeared with toil;
> And wears man's smudge and shares man's smell: the soil
> Is bare now, nor can foot feel, being shod.

[First point about language and imagery supported by reference to a poem and a suitable quotation]

The freshness and originality of Hopkins' descriptions of natural things is also appealing, making the reader look at the natural world in a new way, as in 'Spring':

When weeds, in wheels, shoot long and lovely and lush;

Thrush's eggs look little low heavens, and thrush

Through the echoing timber does so rinse and wring

The ear, it strikes like lightnings to hear him sing.

[Second point about language and imagery supported by reference to a poem and a quotation]

I also admire the mastery of detail shown in his descriptions. 'Pied Beauty' is remarkable for this, suggesting that Hopkins approached features of his landscapes with the eye of a painter:

For skies of couple-colour as a brindled cow;

For rose-moles all in stipple upon trout that swim;

Fresh-firecoal chestnut-falls . . .

[Third point about language and imagery supported by reference to a poem and a quotation]

My favourite piece of description is that of the younger 'Felix Randal' labouring in his 'random grim forge', strong and powerful as he fettles 'for the great grey drayhorse his bright and battering sandal'. What I most admire here is the use of strong, emphatic alliteration to suggest the power and strength both of the blacksmith and of the magnificent horse he is shoeing, which will batter the roads with his great iron shoes.

[Fourth point about language and imagery supported by reference to a poem and a quotation]

Another great image is found in 'No Worst, There Is None'. Here, what can happen to the human mind in a state of depression is unforgettably described in terms of a mountainous landscape. The collapsing mind is likened to a climber facing a deep abyss, 'frightful, sheer, no-man-fathomed', and having fallen, trying to hold on to a ledge by his fingertips. Time and again, Hopkins uses striking images to bring home to the imagination the full effect of what he is suffering. In 'I Wake and Feel the Fell of Dark', instead of telling us that God does not answer his cries for help, he conveys the same idea in a memorable simile. His cries are 'like dead letters sent / To dearest him that lives alas! away'.

[A further point supported by brief quotation and comment]

Many poets are descriptive, but often their descriptions lead nowhere beyond themselves. This does not happen with Hopkins. He is a descriptive poet with a purpose. All his descriptive passages occur in an overall context. This context is the presence of God in everything, so that what is being described is another example of God's beauty being reflected in his creation.

[Answer rounded off with a concise general comment]

Gerard Manley Hopkins

Religious faith is at the heart of his poetry

An important experimenter and innovator

Sees diversity in nature contained within an overall unity

Reveals his compassion for others

Range of human interest is relatively narrow

Strives to express the essence or 'inscape' of each individual thing

Remarkable descriptive powers

Highly distinctive use of language

A profoundly gifted nature poet

Celebrates the activity of God in the world

'Terrible sonnets' explore tortured states of mind and psychological conflicts

Thomas Kinsella

b. 1928

Biography

Thomas Kinsella was born on 4 May 1928 in the Inchicore/Kilmainham area of Dublin. The eldest child of John and Agnes Kinsella, he was educated at the Inchicore Model School and the Christian Brothers' Secondary School on North Richmond Street. In 1946 he was awarded a scholarship to study at University College Dublin, but when he left to join the Irish civil service as a junior executive officer he began to study as a night student.

It was around this time that he started to write, contributing poems and reviews to student magazines and to the Irish language publication *Comhar*. In 1951 he moved to the Department of Finance as an administrative officer, but his primary interest was in literature and cultural matters.

In 1955 Kinsella married Eleanor Walsh. The couple have three children. His wife's ill health at this period meant that Kinsella had to juggle his domestic responsibilities with an increasingly successful poetic career as well as his work in the Department of Finance.

Literary career

Poems, his first collection, appeared in 1956. However, it was *Another September* (1958) that brought him to wider attention as it won the Guinness Poetry Award. *Moralities* appeared in 1960, followed by *Downstream* in 1962. In 1965 an invitation to be writer-in-residence at Southern Illinois University at Carbondale allowed him to resign from the civil service to pursue a career in literature.

In 1970 he became a professor of English at Temple University, Philadelphia. The family lived in the United States until 1971 when they moved back to Dublin to live in the city centre at Percy Place. Kinsella's link with Temple University was strengthened in 1975 when he established a programme in Irish studies. This allowed him to divide his academic year between Philadelphia and Dublin. *Nightwalker and Other Poems* was published in 1968. *New Poems* appeared in 1973, as well as *Selected Poems 1956–68*.

In 1972 Kinsella established the Peppercanister Press. Named after the nickname of a local church, it operated from Kinsella's home and publishes his poems (with the collaboration since 1981 of John F. Deane's Dedalus Press).

Throughout his career Kinsella has worked to recover the lost tradition of Gaelic literature, through translations, including the great Irish epic the *Táin Bó Cúailgne* (1969) and *An Duanaire: Poetry of the Dispossessed 1600–1900* (1981).

In 1988 Kinsella and his wife moved from Dublin to Co. Wicklow where he still lives. In 1990 he retired from Temple University and the Irish studies programme; however, he still spends part of the year in Philadelphia. His *Collected Poems* appeared in 2001. Kinsella has won numerous awards and honours, including Guggenheim Fellowships, the Denis Devlin Memorial Award, the Irish Arts Council Triennial Book Awards and honorary doctorates from the University of Turin and the National University of Ireland.

Social and Cultural Context

The Ireland into which Kinsella was born and in which he was educated was economically depressed. He grew up during a time of high unemployment and emigration. His family background was urban working class. His father and his grandfather worked in Guinness's brewery and the extended family lived in the Inchicore/Kilmainham area of Dublin.

Secondary and third-level education was available only to those who could afford it. Scholarships enabled the young Kinsella to go to secondary school and to enter UCD, although he soon left to take up a position in the Irish civil service.

The influence of the Catholic Church was strong: he has said that its influence on his upbringing was 'so pervasive that it hardly counted as an influence at all; it was a reality like oxygen'.

Culturally speaking Ireland was in the doldrums during the early 1950s. The two most influential poets of the time were Patrick Kavanagh and Austin Clarke. Poets were dependent upon British companies to publish their work and on British critics to review it. Kinsella's initial association with Liam Miller and the Dolmen Press (founded in 1951) succeeded in breaking Irish writers' dependence upon British publishing houses.

Poetic influences

Kinsella has acknowledged that his early influences included the poets Ezra Pound, W. H. Auden and W. B. Yeats. Although he accepted the status of Yeats as a major Irish poet, and recognised the achievements of Kavanagh and of Clarke, he was not content to confine himself to only Irish concerns in his work. His earlier poems do not deal with Irish social or cultural issues to any great extent. However, he later referred to his earlier work as full of 'pointless elegance' in which he had failed to find his true voice as a poet.

As his career developed he began to confront many of the political issues of his day. Later still he made more use of personal material, exploring family relationships in recognisable settings in Ireland and especially in his native city, Dublin.

For Kinsella, poetry is a form of responsible reaction to the predicament one finds oneself in. When asked in an interview with the critic Donatella Abbate Badin, 'Why do you write?', he replied, 'To try to understand: to make sense. To preserve what I can and give it a longer hold on life.' These statements may enable us to understand the personal, social and cultural values behind a remarkable body of work.

Politics

Kinsella worked in the Department of Finance and was for a time secretary to T. K. Whitaker, who was instrumental in formulating the Irish government's Programme for Economic Development in 1958. Although inevitably involved in the programme, Kinsella saw the downside of emphasising material expansion to the detriment of any other.

He reacted negatively to the greed and what he saw as empty nationalism of Irish society as it developed in the 1960s. In 'Nightwalker' and in the 'Peppercanister One Fond Embrace' he satirised such attitudes and personalities in often savage verse. This disapproval was echoed in a practical way by his involvement in the protests concerning the destruction of the remains of Viking settlements in Dublin's Wood Quay in 1978. After a futile attempt to save the site for archaeological development, Kinsella and others occupied the site in a peaceful protest that came to no avail.

Kinsella was also involved in controversy following the publication of 'The Butcher's Dozen' in 1972. Although he had never espoused the strong nationalist views he encountered at school, he was outraged at the Widgery report on the killings of Bloody Sunday in Derry in January 1972. This was one of the most horrific events of the Northern Ireland conflict known as the Troubles. The Widgery report almost entirely exonerated the British paratroop regiment from culpability for the death of thirteen civilians on that day. Kinsella's nationalist outrage alienated many readers, especially in England. Some critics also reacted negatively, not only to his political views but also to what they saw as the biased nature of their expression.

Literature in Irish

Kinsella's achievement in promoting and fostering the study of Irish literature is well recognised. He has established Irish studies programmes in universities in the United States. In his editing of *The Oxford Book of Irish Verse* (1986) he brought many Irish poems (in translation) to a wider audience. In 1969 he published his translation of the Irish epic the *Táin Bó Cúailgne*, an enormous task that had taken him fifteen years. He saw it as an 'act of responsibility . . . it's ours, Irish, and it deserved a new currency'. For him, it was a way of placing himself within an Irish poetic tradition.

In an interview in 1993 he spoke of the 'dual tradition' in Irish poetry, saying that he came to recognise that it is not necessary to abandon one aspect of Ireland's literature in order to deal with the other. He went on to say: 'We have a dead language with a powerful literature and a colonial language with a powerful literature. The combination is an extremely rich one.' In 1995 he published *The Dual Tradition*, in which he elaborated on these views.

Theories of Carl Jung

Kinsella has made fruitful use of his study of the theories of Carl Jung (1875–1961), one of the most influential of twentieth-century psychologists. For Jung, psychological well-being lay in a person's search for 'individuation', by which he meant personal growth and development. This involved confronting one's unconscious thoughts and feelings. Childhood experiences were crucial to adult development, in his view.

In the 1970s Kinsella's exploration of his childhood memories and his social origins led to more personal and increasingly complex poems. This change of direction caused some readers to see his poems as challenging. The poet Denis O'Driscoll has spoken of the 'lonely and courageous route' that Kinsella took as a poet when he abandoned lyric elegance and traditional form (rhyme, self-contained stanzas, for example) for a more self-focused and complex approach. These poems allow the reader to gain more of a sense of Kinsella's background and to enter more intimately into his experience.

A 'Dublin' poet

Kinsella has been called the 'quintessential Dublin poet'. Memories of his childhood in Dublin have been expressed in poems that meticulously detail his surroundings. Dublin is observed and celebrated in his work. Places are named and recognised – James's Street, Basin Lane, Inchicore.

The prestigious honour of Freedom of the City was awarded to him in 2007 (as well as to his former collaborator, artist Louis le Brocquy) in recognition of their 'enormous contribution to the city, in art and literature'. In his address to Dublin City Council as he accepted the award, Kinsella spoke of his native city: 'Dublin gave many important things their first shape and content for me. I learned to look at the world through the rich reality of the inner city – a living history . . . '.

Timeline

1928	Born on 4 May in Dublin
1934–46	Educated at Inchicore Model School and O'Connell CBS
1946	Joins Irish civil service as junior executive officer
1951	Begins association with Liam Miller, Dolmen Press
1955	Marries Eleanor Walsh
1956	Publishes first collection, *Poems*
1958	*Another September* wins Guinness Poetry Award
1965	Moves to Southern Illinois University as writer-in-residence
1969	Dolmen Press publishes *Táin Bó Cúailgne*
1971	Moves back to Dublin
1972	Establishes Peppercanister Press
1973	*Selected Poems 1956–68* appears
1975	Establishes Irish studies programme in Dublin
2001	Publishes *Collected Poems*
2007	Dublin City Council awards him Freedom of the City

Thinking of Mr D.

A man still light of foot, but ageing, took
An hour to drink his glass, his quiet tongue
Danced to such cheerful slander.

He sipped and swallowed with a scathing smile,
Tapping a polished toe.   5
His sober nod withheld assent.

When he died I saw him twice.
Once as he used retire
On one last murmured stabbing little tale
From the right company, tucking in his scarf.   10

And once down by the river, under wharf-
Lamps that plunged him in and out of light,
A priestlike figure turning, wolfish-slim,
Quickly aside from pain, in a bodily plight,
To note the oiled reflections chime and swim.   15

Thomas Kinsella

Glossary	
Title	*Mr D.*: may be the poet Austin Clarke (see Guidelines)
3	*slander*: gossip or false reports
4	*scathing*: withering, scorching

Guidelines

This poem is from the collection *Another September* (1958). It is one of Kinsella's 'portrait' poems, in which he describes both ordinary and well-known people. According to Donatella Abbate Badin, 'Thinking of Mr D.' is a portrait of the poet Austin Clarke, whom Kinsella admired but whom he considered to have been isolated as a poet in 1950s literary Dublin.

Kinsella wrote about Clarke in similar terms in another poem, 'Brothers in the Craft':

Again and again, in the Fifties, 'we' attended
Austin Clarke. He murmured in mild malice
and directed his knife-glance curiously among us.

Even though he portrays him as somewhat detached and isolated in literary circles, Kinsella is on record as admiring Clarke as a poet. In fact he edited Clarke's *Collected Poems* after the poet's death in 1974.

It has also been suggested that Kinsella had in mind the Italian poet Dante Alighieri as the subject of this portrait. A further interpretation has been that it is a portrait of Stephen Dedalus, the hero of James Joyce's novel *A Portrait of the Artist as a Young Man*, in his later years. However, the poem can be appreciated as a portrait of a complex individual in a literary context, without attempting to make too close a connection with an actual literary character.

Commentary

Stanzas 1 and 2

The poem describes 'Mr D.' as an ageing man who is nevertheless still lively – 'light of foot' (line 1) – and who enjoys being in company, but who remains somewhat detached from his surroundings and his companions. Polite and cheerful, he nonetheless falls short of engaging wholeheartedly in the conversations around him: 'his sober nod withheld assent' (line 6). Yet he is also capable of enjoying – perhaps even instigating – gossip, as suggested by the image of him as he drank, accompanied with a 'scathing smile' and 'tapping a polished toe' (lines 4 and 5).

Stanza 3

After the death of 'Mr D.' the speaker has two further lasting memories of him. One was the way in which he would take his leave of the company 'On one last murmured stabbing little tale' (line 9). Might he himself have told the story? The poem is ambiguous about this, but it adds to the portrait of him as a somewhat cynical man who may have taken pleasure in the downfall of others. There is a sarcastic tone in the phrase 'the right company' (line 10) that depicts neither 'Mr D.' nor his followers in a good light. His gesture as he leaves, 'tucking in his scarf' (line 10), after perhaps ruining someone's reputation, suggests someone who is indifferent. This is not an attractive aspect of the man.

Stanza 4

A second image of 'Mr D.', in the final stanza, is more sympathetic. In remembering 'Mr D.' as a solitary figure, walking down by the river, the speaker shows him to be lonely and sensitive. The adjectives Kinsella uses to describe him hint at the contradictions in his character. 'Priestlike' suggests someone prepared to sacrifice himself for his art, as well as someone who is set apart from others, but 'wolfish' suggests a predatory person, perhaps selfish or even cruel (line 13).

Kinsella also depicts 'Mr D.' as someone who never confronted sorrow or pain directly: he is seen as 'turning . . . quickly aside from pain.'(lines 13–14). What sort of 'pain' (physical or mental) is left unexplored. Yet 'Mr D.' still had the poet's urge to perceive and record his surroundings, the light reflected on the river and the sound of the water: 'the oiled reflections' that 'chime and swim' (line 15). **These contradictory aspects of his personality leave the reader with a sense of a complex, real person.**

'Mr D.' and poetry

Throughout the poem Kinsella has hinted at the poetic values of 'Mr D.'. There are subtle puns in the image of him as 'light of foot' (line 1) and 'tapping a polished toe' (line 5), which relate to poetic metre (feet) and rhythm, as well as his tendency to note the 'oiled reflections' that 'chime' (line 15). (One of the main characteristics of Austin Clarke's poems, arguably, was its musicality.) These are clearly poetic qualities that Kinsella admires. But there may also be an indication that Kinsella saw him as a poet who never truly confronted ugliness or pain in his work.

Another aspect of 'Mr D.'s' career that Kinsella does not fully admire was his role in the literary circle described in the poem. Kinsella recognises his status within the group. His detachment from it at times is also in his favour, although there is a suggestion that he plays a part in spreading literary gossip. He comes across as cynical and indifferent.

Most portrait poems indirectly reveal the values of the poet who writes them. In 'Mr D.' Kinsella conveys his own suspicion of the 'right company' (line 10), the literary group that 'Mr D.' belonged to. He sees it as negative and damaging.
It is in the final lines, however, that Kinsella's poetic values are seen most clearly. He sees that surface beauty and polish are not enough for poetry. It must not avoid difficult themes and unpleasant experiences.

Thinking about the poem

1   From the evidence of the poem, what sort of man was 'Mr D.'?

2   In your view, does the poet like 'Mr D.'?

3   Which detail of 'Mr D.'s' behaviour best conveys his personality to the reader, in your opinion?

4   From the following phrases choose the **one** which, in your opinion, best reveals the poet's attitude towards the literary group that 'Mr D.' belongs to:

> He thinks they are cruel and unfeeling.
>
> He thinks they are interesting.
>
> He dislikes them intensely.

Explain your choice.

5   Would you agree that the poem presents 'Mr D.' as a complex, real person? Give reasons for your answer.

6   Choose **two** images from the poem that appeal to you and give reasons for your choice.

7   Does the poem suggest anything to you about Kinsella's views on the role of a poet in society? Would he like to be like 'Mr D.'? Explain your answer.

Taking a closer look

1   'A man still light of foot' (line 1). 'Tapping a polished toe' (line 5). Comment on the effectiveness of these phrases in describing 'Mr D.'.

2   Kinsella uses the adjectives 'priestlike' and 'wolfish' about 'Mr D.' (line 13). Say what these words suggest to you.

Imagining

1   Imagine that you are 'Mr D.'. Write a short entry in your diary in which you give your honest opinion of the 'right company' you meet.

2   You are one of the members of the literary group described in the poem. Write out (in dialogue form) a conversation you have with another member, or with 'Mr D.'. Base your conversation on the poem.

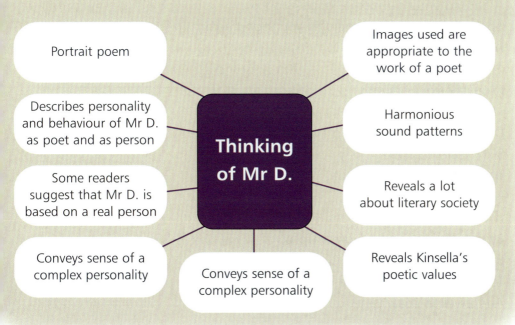

snapshot

Thinking of Mr D.

- Portrait poem
- Describes personality and behaviour of Mr D. as poet and as person
- Some readers suggest that Mr D. is based on a real person
- Conveys sense of a complex personality
- Conveys sense of a complex personality
- Images used are appropriate to the work of a poet
- Harmonious sound patterns
- Reveals a lot about literary society
- Reveals Kinsella's poetic values

Dick King

In your ghost, Dick King, in your phantom vowels I read
That death roves our memories igniting
Love. Kind plague, low voice in a stubbled throat,
You haunt with the taint of age and of vanished good,
Fouling my thought with losses.   5

Clearly now I remember rain on the cobbles,
Ripples in the iron trough, and the horses' dipped
Faces under the Fountain in James's Street,
When I sheltered my nine years against your buttons
And your own dread years were to come: 10

And your voice, in a pause of softness, named the dead,
Hushed as though the city had died by fire,
Bemused, discovering . . . discovering
A gate to enter temperate ghosthood by;
And I squeezed your fingers till you found again   15
My hand hidden in yours.

I squeeze your fingers:

Dick King was an upright man.
Sixty years he trod
The dull stations underfoot.   20
Fifteen he lies with God.

By the salt seaboard he grew up
But left its rock and rain
To bring a dying language east
And dwell in Basin Lane.   25

By the Southern Railway he increased:
His second soul was born
In the clangour of the iron sheds,
The hush of the late horn.

An invalid he took to wife.   30
She prayed her life away;
Her whisper filled the whitewashed yard
Till her dying day.

And season in, season out,
He made his wintry bed.   35
He took the path to the turnstile
Morning and night till he was dead.

He clasped his hands in a Union ward
To hear St James's bell.
I searched his eyes though I was young,   40
The last to wish him well.

Glossary		
2	*igniting*: setting alight	
11	*named the dead*: may be the patriots who had died in the area (e.g. Robert Emmet in 1803)	
13	*Bemused*: confused or lost in thought	
22	*salt seaboard*: Dick King had been born in the west of Ireland	
24	*dying language*: Dick King was an Irish speaker	
25	*Basin Lane*: a street in Inchicore, Dublin	
26	*Southern Railway*: the Great Southern Railway had works at Inchicore	
38	*Union ward*: the workhouse, later a hospital	
39	*St James's bell*: the bell of the foundry in James's Street	

Guidelines

'Dick King' is from the collection *Downstream* (1962). In *A Dublin Documentary* (2006) Kinsella tells us that Dick King was an elderly neighbour who lived in a nearby cottage with his wife:

> He seemed to be always there: a friend of the family, a protector of my unformed feelings . . . I wrote two poems for him, in memory of his importance during those early years. Neither of the poems achieved completeness, but their parts came together.

In this spirit of love and friendship Kinsella addresses Dick King's ghost and remembers incidents from his childhood.

Commentary

'Dick King' links two incomplete poems, written at different times, to form one poem.

Stanzas 1–4
From the beginning there is a sense of loss in the poem. Thinking of Dick King reminds Kinsella of how time has passed. He speaks directly to the man's ghost, calling it 'Kind plague' (line 3) as it seems to 'haunt' him with good memories (line 4), and yet leaves him with a terrible sense of loss (line 5).

Images of his childhood come into his mind. Their Dublin setting – rain on the cobblestones, the horses drinking from the fountain in James's Street – conjure up memories of his childish trust in the elderly man, which he expresses in the lovely image of himself as he 'sheltered my nine years against your buttons' (line 9). Dick King's own 'dread years' were yet 'to come' (line 10).

Dick King had been a link with previous generations as he 'named the dead' (line 11), keeping alive the memory of others who had died, perhaps neighbours and relatives, or even the patriot dead of the past.

Now the poet pays tribute to him. As once, as a nine-year-old boy, he had squeezed King's fingers in a gesture of affection, now he metaphorically does so again by tenderly recalling the details of the man's history.

Stanzas 5–10

The second part of the poem takes on a more jaunty rhythm – like that of a ballad – as it tells Dick King's story. An Irish speaker from the west of Ireland (he brought 'a dying language east', line 24), he had spent sixty years working for the Great Southern Railway at Inchicore. Kinsella portrays him as an uncomplaining, hardworking man, married to a pious wife who suffered from ill health. His admiration for the man is summed up in the compliment he pays him: 'Dick King was an upright man' (line 18).

Nonetheless, the poem also hints at the tragedy of Dick King's life, its unending routine and hardship. The phrase 'he made his wintry bed' (line 35) has connotations of the well-known expression 'he made his bed so he'll have to lie in it' – a rather harsh view of life, but one that is echoed in Kinsella's comment that he endured his routine 'season in, season out' (line 34).

Sadly, Dick King ended his days in what he knew as a workhouse, the Union on James's Street in Dublin. These were the 'dread years' of line 10. But the tone of the final two lines softens the harsh picture to some extent, as Kinsella remembers how as a young boy he 'searched his eyes', wishing him, then as now, nothing but the best.

Elegy

The poem is an elegy (a poem lamenting a dead person). Kinsella mourns Dick King's loss as symbolic of 'vanished good' (line 4), his own childhood relationships. He praises him throughout, directly and indirectly. He finds some consolation in keeping Dick King's memory alive. **He has become part of the 'temperate ghosthood' (line 14) of the past, a symbol of continuity between past and present.**

Thinking about the poem

1. What is the dominant feeling in this poem: love, sorrow or fear? Perhaps you might suggest another emotion?
2. What sort of person was Dick King, as Kinsella suggests in the poem?
3. How would you describe the relationship Kinsella had with the dead man?
4. Would you agree that the poem succeeds in evoking a way of life that is gone? Explain your view.
5. Choose **three** images that appeal to you from the poem and explain your choice.
6. How does Kinsella use sound to convey meaning in the poem (e.g. onomatopoeia, rhyme, alliteration, repetition)? Give examples.
7. Explore the pattern of images of language throughout the poem (e.g. vowels, voice, named). How do they contribute to the meaning of the poem?
8. An elegy is a poem written to commemorate someone who has died. Is 'Dick King' effective as an elegy? Give reasons for your view.
9. Do you think that the two parts of the poem blend successfully? Support your view by reference to the poem.
10. 'Dick King' has been called 'a wonderful Dublin poem'. Do you agree with this view? Support your answer by reference to the poem.

Chrysalides

Our last free summer we mooned about at odd hours
Pedalling slowly through country towns, stopping to eat
Chocolate and fruit, tracing our vagaries on the map.

At night we watched in the barn, to the lurch of melodeon music,
The crunching boots of countrymen – huge and weightless   5
As their shadows – twirling and leaping over the yellow concrete.

Sleeping too little or too much, we awoke at noon
And were received with womanly mockery into the kitchen,
Like calves poking our faces in with enormous hunger.

Daily we strapped our saddlebags and went to experience   10
A tolerance we shall never know again, confusing
For the last time, for example, the licit and the familiar.

Our instincts blurred with change; a strange wakefulness
Sapped our energies and dulled our slow – beating hearts
To the extremes of feeling – insensitive alike   15

To the unique succession of our youthful midnights,
When by a window ablaze softly with the virgin moon
Dry scones and jugs of milk awaited us in the dark,

Or to lasting horror, a wedding flight of ants
Spawning to its death, a mute perspiration   20
Glistening like drops of copper, agonised, in our path

Glossary

Title	*Chrysalides*: plural form of chrysalis (pupa); this is the third, intermediate and transient, stage of development of an ant
1	*mooned about*: wandered about aimlessly
3	*vagaries*: ramblings
14	*sapped*: drained
20	*spawning*: generating or producing spawn

Guidelines

The poem is from the collection *Downstream* (1962). Like many of Kinsella's poems it begins with a vividly described, real experience: a cycling holiday he spent with his friends in his youth – probably the last summer they had before they began to study or work. Hence the significance of the title 'Chrysalides', which is an intermediate and transient stage of development. **The title indicates the theme and prepares us for the analogy from nature in the final lines.**

Kinsella does not say exactly who his companion or companions were, but it has been suggested that it may be a love poem, describing the innocence of young love. In this case it could be read as an awakening to the transient nature of human relationships, symbolised by the ants that die as they mate. On the other hand, the critic Brian John refers to the characters in the poem as

'the young boys' and suggests that it concerns adolescents on the verge of the transition into adulthood. Readers must make up their own mind as to which reading they prefer.

Commentary

Lines 1–12

The poem captures the carefree atmosphere of the time with details of what they ate and what they saw, how they pedalled from place to place with no real purpose, the different places they stayed in and the welcome they were given by the country people they met. The images and metaphors Kinsella uses convey the sense of freedom and wonder they felt. At night they slept in barns, watching the (adult) countrymen dancing to melodeon music, not yet ready to join in themselves.

In these descriptive stanzas Kinsella makes use of the senses to convey the vividness of the experience. There was the taste of 'chocolate and fruit' (line 3), the sound of music and 'crunching boots' (line 5) and the sight of men dancing with their 'shadows' on the 'yellow concrete' (line 6). He compares himself and his companions to 'calves poking our faces in with enormous hunger' (line 9) as they were given food in country kitchens. The effect of the simile is almost tactile if you imagine calves jostling one another at feeding time.

Lines 13–21

The tone of the poem becomes more reflective from the fourth stanza on. Looking back on that 'last free summer' (line 1), Kinsella realises how little experience of life he and his friends had. Caught up in their own world, they had no consciousness of the change that was taking place in their lives.

The daily routine of the holiday seemed to lull them into a false sense of timelessness in which their feelings were suspended, 'insensitive alike' (line 15) to the passage of time and to the horror of death and decay. He suggests that they were immune to the passing of their youth, the happiness and beauty of finding 'dry scones and jugs of milk' (line 18) on a window 'ablaze softly with the virgin moon' (line 17). Regret is the dominant feeling in these lines.

What brought them face to face with reality was their coming across a colony of ants, in which the male ants die even as they mate with the female. The 'wedding flight' is in fact 'spawning to its death' (lines 19 and 20). **This image of horror and death has stayed with Kinsella for the rest of his life.** But the poem suggests that the full implications of the scene, for their own lives, escaped them at that time. This was the realisation that the moment of death (for human beings as well as for ants) is inherent in the moment of birth.

Sound patterns in the poem

Although there is no end-rhyme, internal patterns of sound are established from the beginning. For example, assonance in the first stanza: the 'o' sounds in 'odd', 'stopping' and 'chocolate', and the 'a' sounds in 'tracing' and 'vagaries'. In the second stanza there is repetition of 'u' sounds in 'lurch' and 'crunching'; and in the third stanza 'e' sounds are repeated in 'sleeping' and 'received'. There are further examples throughout the poem.

Other sounds add unobtrusively to the musical quality, for example alliteration in 'melodeon music' (line 4) and consonance in 'experience' and 'tolerance' (lines 10 and 11).

Memories

This is one of Kinsella's poems recounting a memory that took hold in his imagination and fuelled later poems (see also 'Dick King', 'Hen Woman' and 'Tear').

As part of the collection *Downstream*, the poem has been seen by critics as representing Kinsella's intention to move from his earlier formal poems to more personal material that would also confront the disturbing and the horrific in his own experience.

Thinking about the poem

1 Would you agree that there is a sense of loss in the poem? What, precisely, has the poet lost?

2 Does the poem give a good picture of a youthful holiday? Support your answer by reference to the poem.

3 Explore the significance of the 'Like calves' simile (line 9) and 'virgin moon' (line 17) metaphor in the poem and say how they contribute to the poem's theme.

4 Select **three** images that appeal to you from the poem and explain your choice.

5   Comment on the title of the poem, 'Chrysalides'. Is it appropriate?

6   How do you interpret the final images in the poem?

7   How do you respond to these final images?

8   Is the poet critical of his youthful self or is he accepting of it? Give reasons for your answer.

9   Compare the poem with 'Hen Woman' or 'Dick King' as a poem of memory and say which poem you prefer and why.

10   You wish to include this poem in a talk entitled 'Introducing Thomas Kinsella'. Say why the poem is appropriate for the talk.

Mirror in February

The day dawns with scent of must and rain,
Of opened soil, dark trees, dry bedroom air.
Under the fading lamp, half-dressed – my brain
Idling on some compulsive fantasy –
I towel my shaven jaw and stop, and stare,   5
Riveted by a dark exhausted eye,
A dry downturning mouth.

It seems again that it is time to learn,
In this untiring, crumbling place of growth
To which, for the time being, I return.   10
Now plainly in the mirror of my soul
I read that I have looked my last on youth
And little more; for they are not made whole
That reach the age of Christ.

Below my window the awakening trees,   15
Hacked clean for better bearing, stand defaced
Suffering their brute necessities,
And how should the flesh not quail that span for span
Is mutilated more? In slow distaste
I fold my towel with what grace I can,   20
Not young and not renewable, but man.

Glossary		
1	*must*: mould, mustiness	
6	*riveted*: engrossed, attention fixed on	
14	*age of Christ*: Jesus Christ was aged thirty-three when he died	
16	*hacked*: pruned roughly	
16	*better bearing*: providing more fruit	
16	*defaced*: with spoiled looks	
17	*brute necessities*: required harsh treatment	
18	*the flesh*: human beings	
18	*quail*: flinch in fear	
18	*span*: period of time	

Guidelines

'Mirror in February' is from the collection *Downstream* (1962). The speaker catches sight of his face in a mirror and reflects on the ageing process.

Commentary

Title

The title of the poem creates expectations and invites the reader to explore connotations of language and image. By drawing attention to the mirror, Kinsella prepares the reader for a confrontation of some sort. Mirrors have often been used as symbols of revelation or reflectors of the truth. They have been associated with luck and with one's shadow self – a mirror is where we may see ourselves more closely than anywhere else.

February is a transitional time of year. Winter is not yet over and yet there are signs of spring. We may be aware of both death (winter) and life (spring) at the same time. As we read through the poem we see how relevant this may be to Kinsella's moment of realisation.

Stanza 1

The setting of the poem is the speaker's bedroom, where he is shaving before a mirror. The intimate setting (in the next stanza we learn that it is his old bedroom in the house where he grew up) and the act of shaving prepare us for the personal nature of the poem.

From the beginning the speaker's surroundings play an important part. 'Dry bedroom air' (line 2) contrasts with the damp February day outside. He is aware of the sights and smells in the garden outside as the February day dawns. There is the sight of dawn although the trees are still 'dark' (line 2). There are smells of 'must and rain' and 'opened soil' (lines 1 and 2), an image that takes on connotations of death (i.e. a freshly dug grave) as the poem progresses.

Still half-asleep, his 'brain / Idling on some compulsive fantasy' (lines 3–4) – a vivid way of describing the dreamy start to the day – he suddenly catches sight of himself in the mirror. Like an artist's self-portrait, he sees himself in an objective and not very attractive way, looking tired and perhaps disappointed. He has 'a dry downturning mouth' (line 7). Assonance and alliteration help to establish the atmosphere of gloom, e.g. heavy consonantal 'd' sounds in 'day dawns', 'dark' and 'dry' as well as long vowel sounds in 'rain', 'air' and 'brain'.

Stanza 2
In a rather weary tone, the speaker accepts that he must 'learn' something 'again' in this place where he grew up – 'untiring' since it never stops teaching him lessons (lines 8 and 9). Looking into the mirror becomes a metaphor for inspecting the 'mirror of my soul' (line 11). He realises that he is no longer young, having reached the 'age of Christ' (line 14) – traditionally, Christ was thirty-three years old when he died. Even more painfully, he sees that death and decay await him. He will no longer be 'whole' (line 13).

Stanza 3
Once again he turns his attention to the trees outside in the garden. Now 'awakening' (line 15), as he has in the early morning, the trees have been cropped back for renewal in spring. This is part of their 'brute necessities' (line 17), it is what nature requires to be done. Contemplating this, he wonders how should human beings – in particular, himself – not feel afraid ('quail') as they also face ageing and death? Unlike the trees, however, he cannot be pruned in order to grow better. He deliberately uses strong language – 'hacked' (line 16), 'mutilated' (line 19) – to drive the point home. The thought upsets and frightens him.

He maintains a certain dignity in the face of ruin, however, by accepting his future as an inevitable part of his humanity. Although he experiences 'slow distaste' (line 19) for the lesson he has just learned, he proceeds to 'fold my towel with what grace I can' (line 20). The image suggests a possibility of order arising from the chaos of living. Coming after the honesty of the phrase 'not young and not renewable', the word 'man' bears a great deal of weight as an image of consolation and possibility (line 21).

Pathetic fallacy

The poem is one of many poems in which nature provides a means of expressing a sense of time passing and the inevitability of death. Kinsella makes use of what is known as the 'pathetic fallacy' (where natural phenomena are described as if they feel as humans do) in making an analogy between the trees and his situation. Although a relatively young man, he reveals an anxiety about death that is one of the main themes of his poetry.

Form of the poem

The poem is a lyric formally divided into three seven-line stanzas. End-rhyme is used throughout. **The longer stanza allows the poet to establish, develop and meditate on his theme.** In the first stanza the poet sets the scene, establishes his mood and prepares the reader for some revelation. In the second he develops the analogy with nature (the trees) and makes a discovery about his life. The final stanza reflects on this realisation and moves towards a certain closure in the last line.

Thinking about the poem

1   What is the speaker's mood in this poem?
2   How did you respond to the description of the weather and the trees?
3   How does the poem make us aware of death from the beginning?
4   What impression of the speaker do you gain from reading the poem?
5   What exactly has the speaker had to 'learn' from looking in the mirror?
6   The poem has images of suffering and grace. Give **one** example of **each** and explain why you chose it.
7   In this poem, it is clear that the speaker is:
       Afraid of old age and death.
       Hopeful because he is 'man', i.e. a human being.
       Choose the phrase which you think best describes the poet's feelings.
     Explain your choice.
8   Do you like this poem? Give a reason for your opinion.

Taking a closer look

1   Choose **two** of the following words that help to create the atmosphere in the third stanza: 'hacked' (line 16), 'suffering' (line 17), 'mutilated' (line 19). Comment on the impact made by these words in the poem.
2   Suggest a different title for the poem.

1   You wish to make a short film of this poem. Describe what setting, music, lighting, etc. you would use to convey the atmosphere to viewers.

2   Your class is compiling an anthology called *Moments of Truth*. Make a case for including 'Mirror in February' in the anthology.

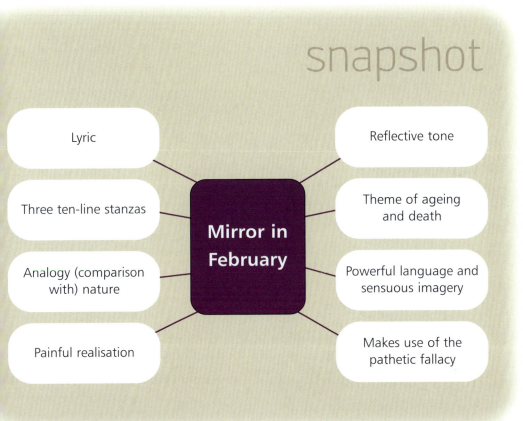

snapshot

Lyric

Three ten-line stanzas

Analogy (comparison with) nature

Painful realisation

Mirror in February

Reflective tone

Theme of ageing and death

Powerful language and sensuous imagery

Makes use of the pathetic fallacy

Thomas Kinsella

Hen Woman

The noon heat in the yard
smelled of stillness and coming thunder.
A hen scratched and picked at the shore.
It stopped, its body crouched and puffed out.
The brooding silence seemed to say 'Hush . . .'   5

The cottage door opened,
a black hole
in a whitewashed wall so bright
the eyes narrowed.
Inside, a clock murmured 'Gong . . .'   10

(I had felt all this before.)

She hurried out in her slippers
muttering, her face dark with anger,
and gathered the hen up jerking
languidly. Her hand fumbled.   15
Too late. Too late.

It fixed me with its pebble eyes
(seeing what mad blur).
A white egg showed in the sphincter;
mouth and beak opened together;   20
and time stood still.

Nothing moved: bird or woman,
fumbled or fumbling – locked there
(as I must have been) gaping.

                        *

There was a tiny movement at my feet,   25
tiny and mechanical; I looked down.
A beetle like a bronze leaf
was inching across the cement,
clasping with small tarsi
a ball of dung bigger than its body.   30

The serrated brow pressed the ground humbly,
lifted in a short stare, bowed again;
the dung-ball advanced minutely,
losing a few fragments,
specks of staleness and freshness.   35

                        *

A mutter of thunder far off
– time not quite stopped.
I saw the egg had moved a fraction:
a tender blank brain
under torsion, a clean a new world.   40

As I watched, the mystery completed.
The black zero of the orifice
closed to a point
and the white zero of the egg hung free,
flecked with greenish brown oils.   45

It fell and turned over slowly.
Dreamlike, fussed by her splayed fingers,
it floated outward, moon-white,
leaving no trace in the air,
and began its drop to the shore.   50

*

I feed upon it still, as you see;
there is no end to that which, not understood,
may yet be hoarded in the imagination,
in the yolk of one's being, so to speak,
there to undergo its (quite animal) growth,   55

dividing blindly, twitching, packed with will,
searching in its own tissue
for the structure in which it may wake.
Something that had – clenched in its cave –
not been now as was: an egg of being.   60

Through what seemed a whole year it fell
– as it still falls, for me, solid and light,
the red gold beating in its silvery womb,
alive as the yolk and white of my eye.
As it will continue to fall, probably, until I die,   65
through the vast indifferent spaces
with which I am empty.

*

It smashed against the grating
and slipped down quickly out of sight.
It was over in a comical flash.   70
The soft mucous shell clung a little longer,
then drained down.

She stood staring, in blank anger.
Then her eyes came to life, and she laughed
and let the bird flap away.   75

'It's all the one.
There's plenty more where that came from!'

Glossary

3	*shore*: a word used in Dublin for a sewer opening
15	*languidly*: listlessly
19	*sphincter*: ring-shaped muscle that opens and closes an orifice
29	*tarsi*: five-jointed foot in insects
31	*serrated*: notched like a saw
40	*torsion*: strain produced by twisting
42	*orifice*: opening
47	*splayed*: spread out
71	*mucous*: slimy
76	*It's all the one*: it makes no difference, it does not matter

Guidelines

'Hen Woman' is from *New Poems* (1973). It is a narrative poem that recalls an incident from Kinsella's childhood, when he saw an old woman pick up a hen just as it was laying an egg. Although the woman tried to catch it, the egg had fallen through the air, smashed through a grating and fallen down into the 'shore' (sewer's opening). The sight of the egg emerging from the hen astonished the child so much that he never forgot it. In *A Dublin Documentary* (2006) Kinsella described it as a 'scene ridiculous in its content, but of a serious early awareness of self and of process: of details insisting on their survival, regardless of any immediate significance'. In the same book he has described the setting of the poem:

> Also the yard outside, a silent square courtyard at the back, off Basin Lane, with a couple of whitewashed cottages in the corners, with half-doors. A separate world, with a few other people, and cats and hens and a feel of the country. A whole place that has long disappeared.

As well as the voice of the child who witnesses the event, we hear the voice of the adult who meditates on its significance.

Commentary

Lines 1–24

The first part of the poem sets the scene and describes what happens from the point of view of the young boy, of the old woman and indeed even that of the hen. Rich sensuous images – the heat of the day, the hint of thunder in the air, the movements of the hen, the sight of the old woman emerging from the darkness of her cottage – seem to suggest that something significant is about to happen.

The old woman, clearly annoyed that the hen is about to lay its egg outside in the street, tries to grab it before it does so. The hen, too, reacts in its own way to the event, while the young boy simply stands there, as he says, 'gaping' (line 24) in surprise at seeing the egg emerge, and close enough to the hen to register its 'pebble eyes' (line 17). It was as if time stood still. The moment is captured in all its drama.

Lines 25–35

The moment is so etched into his consciousness that the speaker's senses are heightened. He becomes acutely aware of what is happening around him, even the movement of a small beetle at his feet as it makes its way across the ground, carrying a ball of dung. (A dung beetle or scarab is a symbol of life in Egyptian mythology, and was considered sacred.)

Lines 36–50

In the third part of the poem his attention returns to the egg as it emerges from the hen. **The event is presented almost in cinematic slow motion.** The egg is realistically described. Like any new-laid egg it is 'flecked with greenish brown oils' (line 45), but it is also given metaphorical significance as a 'clean new world' (line 40).

An egg is a source of life and a symbol of unity. For the watching child, it is a means of having the 'mystery' of the beginnings of life, of birth, 'completed' or finally understood (line 41), having seen the mechanics of how the egg was laid. As in a dream, he watches the woman's fumbling fingers miss the egg as it falls into the 'shore'.

Lines 51–67

The fourth part is the most abstract section of the poem. The adult poet breaks away from the child's point of view to ponder on the significance that the event assumed for him. Kinsella sees that this childhood incident had a greater impact on his imagination than one might have expected.

He makes use of the egg as a metaphor of how the imagination seizes upon an idea and then allows it to develop within the consciousness – just as an egg contains cells that multiply and divide once fertilised, in animals and humans alike. The experience has become part of his being, so that he can say he is able to 'feed upon it still' (line 51) in memory that makes him who he is, and in poems that express his inner consciousness. He expects the experience to be more fruitful yet, even for the rest of his life.

Lines 68–77

The final part of the poem reverts back to the past, to the tale of the old woman and the actual fallen egg as seen by the child. The atmosphere becomes lighter – the scene had its 'comical' side after all (line 70), which the old woman starts to appreciate.

After her initial annoyance at losing the egg she laughs and lets go of the hen, with the good-humoured comment, 'It's all the one. / There's plenty more where that came from!' (lines 76–77). Her words play wittily on eggs as symbols of unity (the yolk, the white, the shell, all in one container, so to speak). This seems to give the story a sense of closure, but it also ironically points toward the endless possibilities of such childhood memories for the poet himself.

Kinsella's change of direction

During the 1960s Kinsella embarked upon a study of the psychology of Carl Jung (1875–1961). Jung placed great emphasis on the importance of childhood experience and memory for the adult who seeks what he called 'individuation' or the realisation of one's own potential in life. According to Jung, in order to achieve personal growth in a psychological sense (individuation) it is necessary to bring to light our unconscious desires, as expressed in our dreams, for example.

Critics have pointed out that exploring these ideas changed the direction of Kinsella's poetry. His poems became more autobiographical and introspective. He became more interested in the origins of his creativity, whether it stemmed from certain specific childhood experiences (such as in 'Hen Woman' or 'Tear') or was part of a genetic and historical inheritance (such as in 'His Father's Hands'). Kinsella, of course, had always used memories as a basis for poems, as we have seen in 'Dick King' and 'Chrysalides'. However, in 'Hen Woman' we can see Jungian ideas applied more closely.

Jung and mythology

Jung placed great importance on the role of mythology in human civilisation. He saw that certain myths and legends occur time and time again in different cultures and eras. This led him to believe that myth is part of the human psyche and, as such, highly significant. For example, the story of the hero who undertakes a dangerous journey, the obstacles encountered on the quest and the opposing villain occurs time and again, so that these figures have come to be archetypes (or original models) of particular human behaviour.

There are many mythical echoes in 'Hen Woman'. The old woman is a neighbour, but as she emerges from the 'black hole' (perhaps connoting the pit of the underworld) of her cottage, muttering angrily, she becomes an archetype of the witch-like figure of the old hag (*cailleach* in Irish). The hag plays an important role in many myths, as a fearsome creature who may yet impart wisdom or teach a lesson.

It is significant that the poem ends with her words of wisdom and that the young boy has never forgotten them. Her light-hearted acceptance of the hen's future laying capacity highlights the potential for life that an egg symbolises. This might also be applied to the creative possibilities of experience for a poet, like Kinsella.

Thinking about the poem

1   Does the poet succeed in conveying the scene of the incident well? Refer to the poem in your answer.

2   'Kinsella makes use of all his senses to re-create the experience in the poem.' Discuss this statement, supporting your answer by reference to the poem.

3   Which section of the poem do you prefer? Give reasons for your view.

4   Explore the imagery of light/darkness and colour throughout the poem and comment on its significance.

5   Would you agree that the poem skilfully combines realistic description with abstract meditation? Support your answer by reference to the poem, paying particular attention to the language the poet uses.

6   Why, do you think, does Kinsella say 'the egg still falls, for me' (line 62)?

7   Why, in your opinion, was the incident such a significant one for the young boy?

8   In line 70 the poet comments, 'It was over in a comical flash.' Did you find the incident to be comical in any way? Explain your response.

9   Does an awareness of the mythological aspects of the poem help or hinder your enjoyment of it? Give reasons for your view.

10 Compare this poem with 'Tear' in its treatment of Kinsella's memories of childhood. Which poem do you prefer and why?

Tear

I was sent in to see her.
A fringe of jet drops
chattered at my ear
as I went in through the hangings.

I swallowed in chambery dusk.   5
My heart shrank
at the smell of disused
organs and sour kidney.

The black aprons I used to
bury my face in   10
were folded at the foot of the bed
in the last watery light from the window

(Go in and say goodbye to her)
and I was carried off
to unfathomable depths.   15
I turned to look at her.

She stared at the ceiling
and puffed at her cheek, distracted,
propped high in the bed
resting for the next attack.   20

The covers were gathered close
up to her mouth,
that the lines of ill-temper still
marked. Her grey hair

was loosened out like a young woman's   25
all over the pillow,
mixed with the shadows
criss-crossing her forehead

and at her mouth and eyes,
like a web of strands tying down her head   30
and tangling down toward the shadow
eating away the floor at my feet.

I couldn't stir at first, nor wished to,
for fear she might turn and tempt me
(my own father's mother)   35
with open mouth

– with some fierce wheedling whisper –
to hide myself one last time
against her, and bury my
self in her dying mud.   40

Was I to kiss her? As soon
kiss the damp that crept
in the flowered walls
of this pit.

Yet I had to kiss.   45
I knelt by the bulk of the death bed
and sank my face in the chill
and smell of her black aprons.

Snuff and musk, the folds against my eyelids,
carried me into a derelict place   50
smelling of ash: unseen walls and roofs
rustled like breathing.

I found myself disturbing
dead ashes for any trace
of warmth, when far off   55
in the vaults a single drop

splashed. And I found
what I was looking for

– not heat nor fire,
not any comfort,   60

but her voice, soft, talking to someone
about my father: 'God help him, he cried
big tears over there by the machine
for the poor little thing.' Bright

drops on the wooden lid   65
for my infant sister.
My own wail of child-animal grief
was soon done, with any early guess

at sad dullness and tedious pain
and lives bitter with hard bondage.   70
How I tasted it now –
her heart beating in my mouth!

She drew an uncertain breath
and pushed at the clothes
and shuddered tiredly.   75
I broke free

and left the room
promising myself
when she was really dead
I would really kiss.   80

My grandfather half looked up
from the fireplace as I came out,
and shrugged and turned back
with a deaf stare to the heat.

I fidgeted beside him for a minute   85
and went out to the stop
It was still bright there
and I felt better able to breathe.

Old age can digest
anything: the commotion
at Heaven's gate – the struggle
in store for you all your life.

How long and hard it is
before you get to Heaven,
unless like little Agnes
you vanish with early tears.

Glossary

5	*chambery*: of a room, a chamber
37	*wheedling*: coaxing
49	*Snuff*: powdered tobacco for sniffing, taken as stimulant or sedative
49	*musk*: strong-smelling perfume
50	*derelict*: in ruins
69	*tedious*: boring
70	*bondage*: captivity
95	*little Agnes*: the poet's infant sister

Guidelines

'Tear' is from *New Poems* (1973). As mentioned in the Guidelines for 'Hen Woman', Kinsella's reading of the psychology of Carl Jung encouraged him to explore childhood experiences and memories in his poems from the 1970s on. He has recalled the important role his grandparents played in his childhood:

> . . . it was in a world dominated by these people that I remember many things of importance happening to me for the first time. And it is in their world that I came to terms with these things as best I could, and later set my attempts at understanding.

In this poem the young Thomas is sent to visit his grandmother Kinsella, his father's mother, as she lay dying in her house in Bow Lane, on one side of James's Street, in Inchicore. It records the young child's first understanding of old age and death.

Commentary

Lines 1–44

This journey is depicted in both a realistic and a mythic way, as in 'Hen Woman'. First, the child has to pass through 'A fringe of jet drops' (line 2) into the darkness of the grandmother's room, just as a legendary hero had to journey down into the darkness of the underworld. The smells of decay and death in the room – of 'disused / organs and sour kidney' (lines 7–8) – make his heart shrink in fear and repulsion. In this atmosphere even familiar things – the grandmother's 'black aprons' (line 10) that he used to find such comfort in – become strange and frightening. There is a sense that the boy feels he is not in control of the situation, that he has been 'carried off / to unfathomable depths' (lines 14–15).

His grandmother, too, is described as both familiar and strange: her mouth is 'still / marked' by 'lines of ill-temper' (lines 23–24), but her hair is spread out on the pillow like that of a young woman. The young boy expresses a mixture of fear and guilt at not wishing to kiss the old woman whom he had once loved. Now she seems like a creature living in a 'pit' (line 44), a witch-like figure whose 'open mouth' (line 36) will lead him into danger. (We are reminded again of the hag figures of myth and legend, a source of danger for the unsuspecting heroes – see Guidelines for 'Hen Woman'.)

Lines 45–80

Forcing himself to show some kind of affection, he buries his head in his grandmother's black aprons, which smell of 'Snuff and musk' (line 49), but he cannot bring himself to kiss her face. Instead, he tries to find some expression of grief within himself, only to succeed in shedding a single 'tear' when he hears his grandmother talking from the bed (perhaps to herself). She is remembering the boy's father's grief when his infant daughter Agnes died. Her sympathetic words remind us that despite the association with darkness and danger that surrounds her, his grandmother had a soft heart.

The speaker recalls his own 'wail of child-animal grief' (line 67) when his little sister died, so different from the bleakness of his feelings now for his dying grandmother. He contrasts his early innocence with his new-found knowledge of the bitterness and hardship of life for someone like his grandmother. Managing to escape from the room ('I broke free', line 76), he soothes his guilt by promising that he would kiss her 'when she was really dead' (line 79).

Lines 81–96

Like all heroic journeys to the underworld, the 'hero' of the poem returns with some reward or insight that he has gained from what happens there. In many legends the hero's encounter with the hag or *cailleach* provides a glimpse of wisdom. So, as in 'Hen Woman', we see how Kinsella blends autobiographical material with mythic imagery, this time creating a moving poem about his grandmother's death and the insight it gave him.

Kinsella's insight is bleak. From his grandmother's words he now realises the yawning gap between the death of an innocent infant and the ugliness and struggle of death in old age, following a long and hard life. This realisation is reinforced by his grandfather's stoical silence by the fireplace as he comes out of the room. But, from a more hopeful perspective, he has also seen his grandmother's emotional side as well as that of his father at the death of 'little Agnes', who seemed to 'vanish' but is yet remembered.

Thinking about the poem

1. A critic has commented that the feeling in 'Tear' is 'a combination of intense revulsion and love'. Would you agree with this view? Give reasons for your answer.

2. Has Kinsella given an honest account of his experience? Support your answer by reference to the poem.

3. How does the poem convey the character of his grandmother? Does she surprise you at any stage?

4. How well does the poet convey the innocence and confusion of a child? Support your answer by reference to the poem.

5. Light, darkness, a journey, witch-like imagery associated with the old woman – what atmosphere do they all create in the poem? How did you respond to this atmosphere?

6. Look carefully at the description of the grandmother in lines 17 to 32. Discuss the view that in this description the grandmother resembles a figure from myth or legend.

7. What lesson did the boy learn from the experience, in your view? Support your answer with examples from the poem.

8. What is conveyed by the contrast between the dying old woman and the death of Kinsella's baby sister, Agnes?

9. From your reading of the poem, how would you describe the poet's vision of life in general?

10. 'Childhood experience is very significant in the poems of Thomas Kinsella.' Discuss this statement in relation to the poems 'Hen Woman' and 'Tear'.

His Father's Hands

I drank firmly
and set the glass down between us firmly.
You were saying.

My father
was saying.   5

His fingers prodded and prodded,
marring his point. Emphas–
emphasemphasis.

I have watched
his father's hands before him   10

cupped, and tightening the black Plug
between the knife and thumb,
carving off little curlicues
to rub them in the dark of his palms,

or cutting into new leather at his bench,   15
levering a groove open with his thumb,
insinuating wet sprigs for the hammer.

He kept the sprigs in mouthfuls
and brought them out in silvery
units between his lips.   20

I took a pinch out of their hole
and knocked them one by one into the wood,
bright points among hundreds gone black,
other children's – cousins and others, grown up.

Or his bow hand scarcely moving,   25
scraping in the dark corner near the fire,
his plump fingers shifting on the strings.

To his deaf, inclined head
he hugged the fiddle's body
whispering with the tune   30

with breaking heart
whene'er I hear
in privacy, across a blocked void,

the wind that shakes the barley.
The wind . . .   35
round her grave . . .

on my breast in blood she died . . .
But blood for blood without remorse
I've ta'en . . .

Beyond that.   40

                              *

Your family, Thomas, met with and helped
many of the Croppies in hiding from the Yeos
or on their way home after the defeat
in south Wexford. They sheltered the Laceys
who were later hanged on the Bridge in Ballinglen   45
between Tinahely and Anacorra.

From hearsay, as far as I can tell
the Men Folk were either Stone Cutters
or masons or probably both.

In the 18   50
and late 1700s even the farmers
had some other trade to make a living.

They lived in Farnese among a Colony
of North of Ireland or Scotch settlers left there

in some of the dispersals or migrations   55
which occurred in this Area of Wicklow and Wexford
and Carlow. And some years before that time
the Family came from somewhere around Tullow.

Beyond that.

*

Littered uplands. Dense grass. Rocks everywhere,   60
wet underneath, retaining memory of the long cold.

First, a prow of land
chosen, and wedged with tracks;
then boulders chosen
and sloped together, stabilized in menace.   65

I do not like this place.
I do not think the people who lived here
were ever happy. It feels evil.
Terrible things happened.
I feel afraid here when I am on my own.   70

*

Dispersals or migrations.
Through what evolutions or accidents
toward that peace and patience
by the fireside, that blocked gentleness . . .

That serene pause, with the slashing knife,   75
in kindly mockery,
as I busy myself with my little nails
at the rude block, his bench.

The blood advancing
– gorging vessel after vessel –   80

and altering in them
one by one.

Behold, that gentleness already
modulated twice, in others:
to earnestness and iteration;   85
to an offhandedness, repressing various impulses.

                            *

Extraordinary . . . The big block – I found it
years afterward in a corner of the yard
in sunlight after rain
and stood it up, wet and black: 90
it turned under my hands, an axis
of light flashing down its length,
and the wood's soft flesh broke open,
countless little nails
squirming and dropping out of it.   95

Glossary		
11	*Plug*: piece of tobacco	
13	*curlicues*: fancy twists	
16	*levering*: movement with a crowbar or other tool	
17	*insinuating*: placing subtly or gradually	
18	*sprigs*: headless or almost headless nails (used here in shoemaking)	
34	*the wind that shakes the barley*: a traditional Irish tune	
42	*Croppies*: Irish rebels of the 1798 rebellion (so-called because they cropped their hair short)	
42	*Yeos*: Yeomen, the British cavalry volunteer force that quelled the Croppy rebellion	
45–6	*Ballinglen between Tinahely and Anacorra*: three townlands in Co. Wicklow	
48	*Men Folk*: male relatives	
53	*Farnese*: a place in Co. Wicklow	
55	*dispersals*: forced departure to new areas	

55	*migrations*: movement from one region or country to another
58	*Tullow*: town in Co. Carlow
60	*uplands*: hilly country
62	*prow*: front part
72	*evolutions*: gradual developments
78	*rude*: crude, rough
80	*gorging*: feeding gluttonously; here, moving relentlessly through blood vessels as in genetic inheritance
84	*modulated*: softened or adjusted
85	*iteration*: repetition
86	*repressing*: keeping hidden or restrained
91	*axis*: straight line about which the parts of a figure are arranged

Guidelines

'His Father's Hands' was published in *Peppercanister One* (1974). Kinsella's interest in his family history developed naturally from his decision, inspired by his study of Carl Jung's psychology, to look inwardly for material for his poems. The information in the poem came to him from a letter from his uncle, Jack Brophy from Tinahely, Co. Wicklow. You can read the complete letter in *A Dublin Documentary* (2006).

Commentary

The poem is divided into five sections, each of which explores a different aspect of family history and relationships.

Lines 1–40

The poem begins with an image of the poet and his father talking and drinking together, possibly arguing, and using their hands in a similar way to make a point: the poet as he sets his glass down 'firmly', the father's finger prodding for emphasis. The imagery of hands creates associations in the poem, as the poet goes on to remember his grandfather's hands as he prepared tobacco for his pipe (significantly, he is remembered as 'tightening' the plug of tobacco) or skilfully mended shoes in his work as a cobbler. Kinsella then introduces the image of the cobbler's block of wood into which he and other cousins (another image of family links) used to knock little headless nails. He recalls, too, his grandfather's hands as they played a traditional tune on the fiddle and hears again how he would whisper the words of the old tune.

For Kinsella, the memory comes back to him 'with breaking heart' (line 31). But he wishes to go beyond his own memories into the earlier history of the family: 'Beyond that' (line 40).

Lines 41–59

In this section Kinsella does go 'beyond' the memory of his more immediate family. A speaker (his uncle, in a letter) recounts the family history to the poet. He tells how the Kinsella family helped many of the rebels of the 1798 rebellion, the Croppies, against the Yeos (Yeomen). Going back further in the eighteenth century, the Kinsellas were stone cutters or masons, or small farmers who lived among migrants from other parts of Ireland or Scotland.

Names of townlands in Wicklow (Ballinglen, Tinahely, Anacorra) convey the sense that these were real people rooted in real places. They were stone cutters and masons – significantly, these are trades that require manual skill. There is a hint of conflict or suffering as the family origins are traced to some of the forced movements of people ('dispersals', line 55) that occurred in the seventeenth century.

Lines 60–70

Here the poet imagines the family 'beyond that', in pre-historic times. **To him it is clear that the family would have had to struggle to establish themselves in their land.** Sacrifice and maybe violence would have been necessary to work the land and provide a living for the people. This realisation causes the poet to respond negatively to the place: 'I do not like this place' (line 66). Although he and his immediate ancestors never experienced that period of family history, in keeping with Jung's theories they share in a racial or unconscious memory of this time. This idea seems to disturb him.

Lines 71–86

Kinsella contemplates the genetic process by which traits are passed down through the generations. He wonders how history and evolution combined to bring about his grandfather's characteristics of patience and gentleness. This changed in the next generation in his son's (Kinsella's father's) seriousness and tendency to repeat himself, and finally produced the poet's 'offhandedness' (line 86), a trait he ruefully attributes to himself.

Lines 87–95

The poem comes full circle as it refers back to the block of wood mentioned in the first and fourth sections. His shoemaker grandfather had worked on it, and Kinsella and his cousins had knocked nails into it. Found many years later, it is now black and falling apart, but the image of the little nails that fall out of it as it breaks **suggests the potential for further life arising from the dead generations. It may also refer to the creative possibilities for the poet** as he continues to explore himself and his family relationships.

Personal experience

As he does in 'Hen Woman' and 'Tear', Kinsella skilfully blends personal material and universal concerns in 'His Father's Hands'. His childhood memories of his grandfather as well as his adult relationship with his father give a focus to the poet's exploration of aspects of his personality and the origins of his creativity. Running through the poem there is a moving awareness of the past, how family history influences later generations, and how family traits are inherited and mutated.

But Kinsella also contemplates questions that have more universal application. Underlying the poem is an awareness of Jung's theory of the collective unconscious (i.e. that people carry within themselves unconscious racial memory, perhaps of trauma or suffering in the past). Kinsella's interest in genetic inheritance mirrors many of the concerns of the twentieth and early twenty-first centuries.

Thinking about the poem

1   How does the poet make the link between himself, his father, his grandfather and his cousins in the poem's first section?
2   Would you agree that the image of 'hands' is particularly effective in conveying family history? Support your answer by reference to the poem.
3   Would you agree that the figure of the grandfather dominates the poem? What impression of him did you get? Support your answer by reference to the poem.
4   How would you describe the poet's father?
5   Explore the image of the cobbler's block as used throughout the poem.
6   How did you respond to the third section of the poem (lines 60–70)?
7   Explore the image of the block of wood and nails in the final part of the poem.
8   'Kinsella's main concern in this poem is to understand himself.' Discuss this statement.
9   Does this poem succeed in conveying how important family history is? Use quotations from the poem to support your answer.
10   How did you respond to this poem?

from Settings: Model School Inchicore

Miss Carney handed us out blank paper and marla,
old plasticine with colours
all rolled together into brown.

You started with a ball of it
and rolled it into a snake curling   5
around your hand, and kept rolling it
in one place until it wore down into two
with a stain on the paper.

We always tittered at each other
when we said the adding-up table in Irish   10
and came to her name.

                                    *

In the second school we had Mr Browne.
He had white teeth in his brown man's face.

He stood in front of the blackboard
and chalked a white dot.   15

'We are going to start
decimals.'

I am going to know
everything.

                                    *

One day he said: 20
'Out into the sun!'
We settled his chair under a tree
and sat ourselves down delighted
in two rows in the greeny gold shade.

A fat bee floated around   25
shining amongst us
and the flickering sun
warmed our folded coats
and he said: 'History . . . !'

                              *

When the Autumn came   30
and the big chestnut leaves
fell all over the playground
we piled them in heaps
between the wall and the tree trunks
and the boys ran races   35
jumping over the heaps
and tumbled into them shouting.

                              *

I sat by myself in the shed
and watched the draught
blowing the papers   40
around the wheels of the bicycles.

Will God judge
our most secret thoughts and actions?
God will judge
our most secret thoughts and actions   45
and every idle word that man shall speak
he shall render an account of it
on the Day of Judgement.

                              *

The taste
of ink off   50
the nib shrank your
mouth.

Glossary

title	*Model School*: the primary school Kinsella attended in *Inchicore*, the Dublin neighbourhood in which he lived as a boy
1	*marla*: a type of modelling material, similar to Plasticine
11	*her name*: the teacher's name is Carney: lessons in the Model School were taught through the medium of Irish and, in the Irish-language addition tables, 4 (*ceathair*) + 9 (*naoi*) sounds rather like 'Carney'
12	*Mr Browne*: Kinsella's teacher, George Browne
42	*Will God judge*: a quotation from the Catechism, which children memorised at school

Guidelines

'Model School, Inchicore' is the first of three poems called 'Settings' that open Kinsella's Peppercanister sequence *Songs of the Psyche* (1985). As the title of the volume suggests, in these poems **Kinsella once again explores the childhood experiences and memories that have made him who he is** (i.e. that have influenced his psyche or mind). A 'setting' implies a background; it also has a musical connotation (as in words 'set' to music).

Kinsella began his education at the Model School, Inchicore, Dublin, near where he lived on Phoenix Street. The Model School had been established in 1811. In accordance with government policy following the foundation of the state in 1922, many of the lessons that Kinsella would have had in the 1930s were taught through the medium of Irish.

Commentary

Lines 1–11

In simple, childlike language and images Kinsella imaginatively re-creates the world of his primary school days. His first teacher, Miss Carney, gives out all the materials needed ('blank paper and marla', line 1) to set him on his way to knowledge. He learns how to make something out of something else (a snake from Plasticine) – a simple experience, but many commentators on the poem have pointed out that a snake is a symbol of knowledge, with mythic and psychological connotations. He is also introduced to the possibilities of language, as illustrated in the wordplay involving the sounds of Miss Carney's name. These are childish experiences, but they look forward to the creative world of the adult poet.

Lines 12–19

His next teacher, Mr Browne, had 'white teeth in a brown man's face' (line 13) – further evidence of the young Kinsella's awareness of wordplay. When Mr Browne begins to teach decimals, the young Kinsella, with a child's innocence, feels he is 'going to know / everything' (lines 18–19). The white dot in the centre of the blackboard seems to the young boy to contain all the seeds of knowledge.

Lines 20–29

Other memories have etched themselves into his consciousness: the happy day they learned about 'History', seated outdoors in the sun. We can almost feel the warmth of the sun and see the 'fat bee' that flew around them. (Might the 'greeny gold shade' of the day suggest the nationalist slant of the lessons?)

Lines 30–37

In autumn there were races and jumps in the playground. The language here re-creates the sheer physical fun and exhilaration the boys felt. Run-on lines without punctuation express the liveliness of their play, as do the verbs of movement: 'piled', 'ran', 'tumbled'.

Lines 38–48

In a moment indicative of Kinsella's later tendency to introspection, he remembers sitting alone in the bicycle shed pondering the lines from the Catechism about God's judgement, which the boys would have memorised in preparation for Confirmation. Here the young Kinsella seems to be waking up to morality and questions of religious importance. We notice the change of language from the simple expression of a child to the biblical-sounding words: 'he shall render an account of it / on the Day of Judgement' (lines 47–48).

Lines 49–52

The final short section contains only one image, but it is a very rich one. **The sensory image of the taste of the ink on the nib of the pen brings the poem back to the child's own experience.** It can also be read in a metaphorical way as the young boy's first encounter with the difficulty of learning, and by extension of writing. It certainly casts an ironic light over his earlier confident assertion 'I am going to know / everything' (lines 18–19).

What the poem reveals

The poem portrays Kinsella as an observant young boy, acutely aware of his surroundings, sensitive to language and keen to learn as much as he can about the world. Knowledge is first of all shown as sensory – the feel of the marla in his hands, the stain on the paper. Then it becomes more abstract, as he encounters mathematics, history and religious knowledge classes. The final image seems to be a metaphorical comment on his experience. But throughout the poem there is a sense of happiness. The boys 'tittered' (line 9), they sat down 'delighted' (line 23) in the sunshine, they 'ran races / jumping over the heaps / and tumbled into them shouting' (lines 35–37).

Thinking about the poem

1   Do you like Kinsella's description of his early schooldays? Which detail particularly appeals to you?

2   Would you agree that Kinsella has succeeded in getting inside the mind of a child in this poem? Refer to the poem in your answer.

3   How would you describe the tone of the poem?

4   How does the poem convey the growing maturity of the child during his primary school days?

5   Explore the sensory images throughout the poem. How do they contribute to the poem's atmosphere?

6   Compare the poem with 'Tear' as a depiction of childhood experience. Which poem do you prefer, and why?

7   Discuss the view that childhood experience has been a rich source of poetic material for Kinsella.

8   Using the poem as a model, write a short description (in poetry or prose) of your own early experiences at school.

from The Familiar: VII

I was downstairs at first light,
looking out through the frost on the window
at the hill opposite and the sheets of frost
scattered down among the rocks.

The cat back in the kitchen.   5
Folded on herself. Torn and watchful.

*

A chilled grapefruit
– thin-skinned, with that little gloss.
I took a mouthful, looking up along the edge of the wood

at the two hooded crows high in the cold   10
talking to each other,
flying up toward the tundra, beyond the waterfall.

*

I sliced the tomatoes in thin discs
in damp sequence into their dish;
scalded the kettle; made the tea,   15

and rang the little brazen bell,
and saved the toast.
Arranged the pieces

in slight disorder around the basket.
Fixed our places, one with the fruit   20
and one with the plate of sharp cheese.

*

And stood in my dressing gown
with arms extended
over the sweetness of the sacrifice.

Her shade showed in the door.   25
Her voice responded:
'You are very good. You always made it nice.'

Glossary

title	*Familiar*: something known or understood; it also has connotations of a ghostly presence
12	*tundra*: vast, level, treeless region with an arctic climate and vegetation; here, the terrain near the Sally Gap, Co. Wicklow
16	*brazen*: brass
25	*shade*: shadow

Guidelines

This is the final part of a seven-part sequence that explores the development of love between the speaker and his wife, Eleanor, from their earliest days in a flat in Baggot Street, to the time of writing (the poem appeared in 1999 in the collection entitled *The Familiar*). In the previous six sections of the poem the speaker portrays Eleanor as lover, poetic muse (source of inspiration) and guide. In this section he paints a more intimate picture of their life together in the domestic setting of their home in Co. Wicklow.

The title clearly conveys the fact that Eleanor is a familiar (intimate) person in his life and that the subject of the poem is the familiar life they lead together. But another meaning of the word 'familiar' is 'a spirit that attends on a person', and this interpretation is also relevant in Kinsella's depiction of their relationship.

Commentary

Lines 1–12
The early lines of the poem set the scene. The poet is up in the early morning and about to prepare breakfast. It is frosty outside. In the kitchen the cat quietly watches

him. As Kinsella works, he observes two crows outside as they fly up towards the treeless terrain of the Sally Gap ('tundra', line 12). They, too, like himself and his wife, are intimate, 'talking to each other' (line 11) as they fly.

Lines 13–21

Preparing breakfast for his wife becomes a sacrificial offering, like a religious ritual. As in many of his poems Kinsella uses sensuous images to convey atmosphere and feeling. He pays careful attention to the food, savouring the look, taste, feel and smell. For example, the 'sliced' (line 13) and 'damp' (line 14) of the tomatoes, the 'sharp cheese' (line 21). Like a priest taking Communion, he takes a mouthful and rings 'a little brazen bell' (line 16) to signal that the meal is ready. As in any ceremony, each action is given its own importance; the food is 'arranged' and 'fixed' (lines 18 to 20).

Lines 22–27

In the final section the priestlike image is even more explicit as he describes how he stretches out his arms 'over the sweetness of the sacrifice' (line 24). The exalted mood of the poem may seem somewhat deflated by the beloved's simple words: 'You always made it nice', but this response also expresses a great deal of love and appreciation. She appears as a 'shade' (line 25), with all the connotations of that word, as shadow, ghost, divine being, to whom reverence is due. **The image adds to a portrait of love as a spiritual experience as well as a physical and emotional one.**

Love poem

Love is a frequent theme in Kinsella's poetry. At the time of writing 'The Familiar' he and his wife were approaching old age; appropriately enough, the poem is set in winter, the end of the calendar year. Their relationship has arrived at the point where simple tasks undertaken for one another, in the ritual of routine (making breakfast, for instance), take on a spiritual dimension as symbols of love.

Religious sacrifice has always had an element of mystery about it. By using it as an analogy of love, Kinsella suggests that mystery also lies at the heart of love – the central theme of the poem 'Echo'.

Thinking about the poem

1. How did you respond to the poem as a love poem?
2. How do the details of the weather, landscape and cat contribute to the atmosphere of the poem?
3. Comment on the significance of the poem's title.
4. What is your interpretation of the image of the two crows that the speaker sees from his window?
5. What impression do you gain of the relationship between the speaker and his beloved?
6. How do the suggestions of priestly offering and sacrifice add to the depiction of the couple's relationship, in your opinion?
7. If you were the recipient of this love poem, would you be flattered? Give reasons for your answer.
8. Compare the poem as a love poem with 'Echo'.
9. You have decided to include this poem in an anthology of your favourite poems by Thomas Kinsella. Say why you would choose it, referring closely to the poem in your answer.

from Glenmacnass: VI Littlebody

Up on the high road, as far as the sheepfold
into the wind, and back. The sides of the black bog channels
dug down in the water. The white cottonheads
on the old cuttings nodding everywhere.
Around one more bend, toward the car shining in the distance.   5

From a stony slope half way, behind a rock prow
with the stones on top for an old mark,
the music of pipes, distant and clear.

*

I was climbing up, making no noise
and getting close, when the music stopped,   10
leaving a pagan shape in the air.

There was a hard inhale,
a base growl,
and it started again, in a guttural dance.

I looked around the edge   15
– and it was Littlebody. Hugging his bag
under his left arm, with his eyes closed.

I slipped. Our eyes met.
He started scuttling up the slope with his gear
and his hump, elbows out and neck back.   20

But I shouted:
              'Stop, Littlebody!
I found you fair and I want my due.'

He stopped and dropped his pipes,
and spread his arms out, waiting for the next move.   25
I heard myself reciting:

'Demon dwarf
with the German jaw,
surrender your purse
with the ghostly gold.'   30

He took out a fat purse,
put it down on a stone
and recited in reply, in a voice too big for his body:

'You found me fair,
and I grant your wishes.   35
But we'll meet again,
when I dance in your ashes.'

He settled himself down once more
and bent over the bag,
              looking off to one side.   40

'I thought I was safe up here.
You have to give the music a while to itself sometimes,
up out of the huckstering

– jumping around in your green top hat
and showing your skills   45
with your eye on your income.'

He ran his fingers up and down the stops,
then gave the bag a last squeeze.
His face went solemn,

his fingertips fondled all the right places,   50
and he started a slow air
                              out across the valley.

                              *

I left him to himself.
And left the purse where it was.
I have all I need for the while I have left   55

without taking unnecessary risks.
And made my own way down to the main road
with my mind on our next meeting.

Glossary		
title	*Glenmacnass*: a waterfall in Co. Wicklow
title	*Littlebody*: leprechaun (from the Irish *lú-chorpán*, 'little body')
1	*sheepfold*: enclosure for penning sheep in
3	*cottonheads*: plants
6	*prow*: projecting front part
14	*guttural*: a throaty sound; here, the deep sound of the uilleann pipes
28	*German jaw*: probably a strong, pointed jaw
43	*huckstering*: selling; here, prostituting your art

Thomas Kinsella

Guidelines

'Littlebody', the sixth part of the poem 'Glenmacnass', is from the collection *Littlebody* (2001). It dramatises an encounter between the speaker and a traditional figure from Irish mythology, a leprechaun (*lú-chorpán* is Irish for littlebody). In the previous sections of the poem the speaker has affirmed his choice of natural beauty over life in the city, and of domestic intimacy over public involvement. Kinsella made this choice when he left his home in Dublin's city centre to live near the Sally Gap in rural Co. Wicklow, also the setting for the poem 'The Familiar'.

Commentary

Lines 1–25

He describes how he climbs far up into the hills reaching an even more remote place, where he is surrounded by black bog and stony slopes. He hears the music of pipes (the traditional music of leprechauns) and comes across the leprechaun, playing his music. Like the landscape that surrounds him, the leprechaun's music is harsh. Its harshness is conveyed by the strong consonance (repetition of consonant sounds) and onomatopoeic effect of the 'g' sounds in 'growl' and 'guttural'.

Littlebody is described in the traditional way, with humped back, carrying his pipes and his bag. An elusive creature, he tries at first to escape from the speaker. But one of the traditions surrounding leprechauns is that they must hand over their purse or crock of gold if they are found, so the speaker duly stops him and demands his reward: 'I found you fair and I want my due' (line 23).

Lines 26–52

Up to this point the tone of the poem has been conversational, as is appropriate for a poem that tells a story. But the dialogue between the speaker and Littlebody is sing-song and ritualistic. The speaker addresses him as 'Demon dwarf / with the German jaw' (lines 27–28), a reference both to his supernatural aspect and the stern, pointed jaw of the traditional leprechaun figure. The 'ghostly gold' (line 30) is the 'magic' crock of gold that leprechauns were said to carry.

Littlebody also replies in a quatrain (four lines). While he is prepared to hand over his purse, ('You found me fair', line 34), he gives the speaker a grim warning: next time they meet it will be when the speaker dies. This is a reminder that leprechauns have an association with death as well as with good luck.

Rather surprisingly, Littlebody now veers away from his traditional role to speak more meaningfully. He tells the speaker that he felt safe in the hills (as indeed the speaker himself does) playing his music for himself rather than having to pander to onlookers or prostitute his art for money's sake. The image of him 'jumping around' in his 'green top hat' (line 44) might remind us of St Patrick's Day traditions. These revelations are followed by a 'slow air' of lament (line 51), perhaps for the times he was forced to do just that.

Lines 53–58

In the final section of the poem the speaker leaves Littlebody alone, realising that he has no need of the leprechaun's gold – in fact it might be a source of sorrow or ill luck for him. He realises that he has 'all I need for the while I have left' (line 55). Ominously, he concludes by saying that his mind is on their 'next meeting' (line 58), which as Littlebody has said, will take place when he dies.

Allegory

An allegory is a story with a second meaning hidden or partially hidden behind its literal one. Clearly Kinsella does not set out to convince us that he has met a leprechaun but decided not to take his purse of gold. There are, however, a number of possible allegorical interpretations we could make of this imagined encounter.

In the first part of the entire poem (not printed here) the speaker referred to how he 'turned away in refusal' from what he termed the 'hissing assemblies', seeking instead the calm and peace of the Wicklow countryside. His meeting with Littlebody dramatises the conflict inherent in this decision. In this context the 'fat purse' (line 31) may represent the material reward or the fame that he (as a poet) may have achieved if he had remained more publicly involved. **But the poem suggests that accepting fame or fortune inevitably leads to prostituting or squandering one's art.** Like Littlebody, then, he is better off seeking to pursue it in solitude, for the sake of the 'music'.

Kinsella the poet is so convinced by Littlebody's words that he leaves him alone. Allegorically speaking, his refusal of the 'ghostly gold' (line 30) represents his determination to avoid Littlebody's mistakes. This may be interpreted as Kinsella's refusal to engage with what has been called the 'business of poetry' (i.e. the public appearances and involvement required of a successful poet). For him, to do so might be one of the 'unnecessary risks' he mentions (line 56) of losing his sense of integrity as a poet.

The final lines remind us that death is a subject Kinsella returns to time and time again. The 'next meeting' (line 58), as in the old superstition, may be the speaker's last.

Thinking about the poem

1 How does the poem convey the remoteness of the place, in the first section?

2 How did you respond to the figure of Littlebody? Do you find him realistic in the context of the poem?

3 How would you describe the atmosphere created in the poem?

4 Bearing in mind the usual depictions of leprechauns, did you find anything surprising about Kinsella's portrayal of Littlebody?

5 What is your interpretation of the lines in the final section: 'I have all I need for the while I have left / without taking unnecessary risks' (lines 55–56)?

6 What is your interpretation of the lines 'You have to give the music a while to itself sometimes, / up out of the huckstering' (lines 42–43)?

7 From your reading of the poem, what have you learned of Kinsella's attitude to writing poetry?

8 Do you consider this poem to be hopeful or pessimistic? Give reasons for your view.

9 Discuss the view that the poem may be a satirical comment on Irish artistic or cultural circles.

10 Is allegory effective as a way of getting a point across? Support your answer by reference to the poem.

from Belief and Unbelief: Echo

He cleared the thorns
from the broken gate,
and held her hand
through the heart of the wood
to the holy well.   5

They revealed their names
and told their tales
as they said that they would
on that distant day
when their love began.   10

And hand in hand
they turned to leave.
when she stopped and whispered
a final secret
down to the water. 15

Guidelines

'Echo' was published in *Peppercanister 27* in 2007. **A love poem, it encapsulates the relationship between a man and woman in beautifully simple images.**

Commentary

A man and woman have returned, many years later, to the place where they first declared their love: a holy well deep in the heart of a wood. Symbolically, this is a place of pilgrimage. Perhaps they wish to express gratitude for the love they have shared. As they had both promised they would, they reveal themselves as intimately as possible: 'They revealed their names / and told their tales' (lines 6–7), in the same way as they had before. In this manner their love comes full circle, as the title 'Echo' might suggest.

But the underlying philosophy of love contained in the poem is not perhaps so straightforward. There are 'thorns' to be cleared (line 1). The 'heart of the wood' (line 4) is not easily found. Might these be metaphors for difficulty and effort? In the closing image we see how the woman has a 'final secret' (line 14) that she has kept. **Perhaps this implies the mystery of love**, the impossibility of ever knowing fully even a beloved partner.

Atmosphere of the poem

The atmosphere created in 'Echo' has the mythic quality of a fairy tale. The man and woman could almost be children wandering through a wood as in many old stories. Thorns feature as symbols in many tales. Holy wells have played a role in legends, Celtic and otherwise. While the title 'Echo' refers to the sound created by talking into the depths of a well, it may also refer to the mythical figure of Echo, who fell in love with the youth Narcissus in the Greek myth.

The tenderness of love is expressed in the couple's simple gestures and words. But there is also sadness in the insight expressed in the last image that is typical of Kinsella's honest appraisal of the love relationship. In an earlier poem (significantly, called 'Echoes') he had said: 'Love I consider a difficult, scrupulous art'.

177

Thinking about the poem

1 Would you agree that the poem is a celebration of love? Refer to the poem in your answer.

2 As well as celebrating love, would you agree that the poem is also realistic about it? Give a reason for your view.

3 Is the title an effective one? Give reasons for your view.

4 Suggest a new title for the poem and explain your choice.

5 Although the poem is short and simply expressed, do you agree that its vision of love is quite complex? Give reasons for your view.

6 Compare 'Echo' with 'The Familiar: VII' as love poems. Which poem do you prefer, and why?

General Questions

1 In his poems, Kinsella has said that he 'attempted to make real, in whatever terms, the passing of time, the frightening exposure of all relationships and feeling to erosion'. With this statement in mind, discuss the poems of Thomas Kinsella.

2 'Love, death and the artistic art are the main concerns of Kinsella in his poems.' Discuss this statement.

3 Kinsella's poems have been praised for their musicality and the power of his visual imagination. Explore these aspects of Kinsella's poems.

4 'Kinsella is always alert and perceptive in his poems to details and their significance.' Discuss this statement.

5 'Kinsella's poems have a strong sense of place but are also universal in their significance.' Would you agree with this view? Support your answer with reference to the poems.

6 'Kinsella's poems see the bleakness of life but also its beauty.' Discuss this statement.

7 'Kinsella gives us great insight in his poems into his childhood and his family relationships.' Choose the poems that you consider give the deepest insight into these family relationships and show how they are effective.

8 'No one else writes like Kinsella.' Explore the aspects of Kinsella's poems that make his voice unique, in your view.

9 'The Impact of Thomas Kinsella's Poetry.' Using this title, write a speech to be given to an audience of your fellow students.

Your speech could include some of the following points:

- Themes make a powerful impact on the reader (e.g. family relationships, childhood memories, love, death).
- Language used is highly effective (e.g. sensuous images, perceptive details, sound effects and patterns).
- Memorable atmosphere evoked in poems.
- Emotional honesty in dealing with difficult subjects.
- Creates vivid sense of time and place.
- Poems are both personal and universal.

10 'Kinsella's poems add greatly to the understanding of the reader.' Do you agree with this assessment? Support your answer by relevant quotation and/or reference to the poems on your course.

Your answer might include some of the following ideas:

- Kinsella's exploration of childhood memories adds to the reader's understanding of this important time in life.
- The stylistic features he uses in evoking his childhood enable the reader to enter fully into his experience.
- He enhances our understanding of difficult issues such as death and suffering by confronting them with honesty.
- By dealing with personal and family relationships he broadens the reader's understanding of these issues.

Sample Essay

'In his poems Kinsella gives us great insight into his childhood experiences and his family relationships.'

Write a response to the poetry of Thomas Kinsella in the light of this statement.

I most certainly agree that reading Thomas Kinsella's poems gives us great insight into his childhood experiences and his family relationships. In 'Dick King', 'Hen Woman', 'Tear' and 'Model School, Inchicore' he evokes for us a world that has long since past, but which has been for him such a rich source of creative inspiration. His emotional honesty in dealing with his family relationships in 'Tear' and 'His Father's Hands', as well as in his experience of love and marriage in 'The Familiar', also made a great impact on me.

[First paragraph indicates the areas that will be covered in the essay and gives initial response]

For Kinsella, childhood experiences provided much material for future poems. In 'Dick King' he pays tribute to a neighbour who lived near the Kinsella family when the poet was a boy. Vivid images such as 'rain on the cobbles / Ripples in the iron trough, and the horses' dipped / Faces under the Fountain in James's Street' evoke a definite time and place: Dublin in the early decades of the twentieth century. He succeeds in giving us a real sense of the man's life and personality. Dick King's life may have been full of hardship – 'season in, season out / He made his wintry bed' – but he was also an 'upright' man who taught the young Kinsella a great deal about the history of their city. Now, as an adult poet, Kinsella acknowledges the kindness of his old friend and expresses his affection for him: he would like to 'wish him well'.

[First poem discussed in response to the question, suitable quotations included]

In 'Tear', however, Kinsella gives us a less positive insight into his childhood experiences. In the poem he recounts how he was 'sent in to see' his dying grandmother. As in 'Dick King', the sense of time and place is created by specific images: the 'fringe of jet drops' that were hanging at the entrance to the old woman's room, the 'smell of disused / organs' and 'the last watery light from the window'. His description of the old woman makes us almost see her, lying 'distracted' in her bed, the covers 'gathered close / up to her mouth'. Her hair was like that of a young woman, 'loosened out' on the pillow, but in the dim light it strangely 'mixed with the shadows / criss-crossing her forehead' so that it was 'like a web of strands'.

The impression we get is of a witch-like figure who is a source of potential danger to the young boy. It was as if his grandmother had ceased to be her familiar self ('my own father's mother') with whom he had a close relationship. She becomes instead someone who might 'turn and tempt me' 'with open mouth'. The image suggests that the boy feels he is being swallowed up in a situation beyond his control. We can identify with his mixed emotions here: he feels compelled to kiss her, but he also feels repelled and frightened at the sight of the dying old woman. With great emotional honesty Kinsella conveys the boy's dilemma. He solved it in his own way, when he 'sank' his face into the 'chill / and smell of her black aprons' at the foot of her bed, and found himself able to produce the single 'tear' of the poem's title.

[Second poem discussed in response to the question, suitable quotations included]

When we read 'Tear' we are conscious that Kinsella is describing a crucial moment in his childhood, and perhaps in everyone's childhood, when they become aware of death for the first time. The boy also learns another lesson from that experience. This could also be labelled a universal truth: that the death of an innocent infant, like that of his sister Agnes, is more affecting than that of an elderly person, whose life may be 'bitter with hard bondage'.

[Discussion of poem combines both aspects of the question and indicates response]

Kinsella's experience of being in primary school is the theme of 'Model School, Inchicore'. This poem is not as emotionally intense as 'Tear', but I was impressed and moved by the manner in which the poet brings us back to his childhood world. The language and imagery is simple and direct. In the earliest class the emphasis is on people and things: the marla they play with, Miss Carney the teacher and the silly pun on her name in Irish. Then we meet Mr Browne, who introduces them to 'decimals'. With a child's innocence Kinsella thinks he is 'going to know / everything'. For most people, childhood is a time when the senses are especially responsive, and Kinsella reflects this when he tells us of the 'flickering sun' that 'warmed our folded coats' and the 'big chestnut leaves' that they played with in autumn. He also succeeds in conveying the young boy's intellectual development as he sits in the shed contemplating what he had been taught in religious knowledge classes. He ends the poem with an image that may be interpreted in a number of ways: 'The taste / of ink off / the nib shrank your / mouth.' Might it suggest the disillusionment that lies in store for many people after their schooldays?

[Third poem discussed in response to the question, suitable quotations included]

Reading these poems it seems to me that Kinsella not only gives us an insight into his childhood experiences but that he goes beyond purely personal memories to give them a universal significance. One of the ways in which he does this is by using images and themes from mythology. In 'Tear', for instance, the boy's situation is described in terms of a journey into the dark, almost like the underworld, where the 'hero' will find something, or learn something. The description of his grandmother, too, has an other-worldly quality. Kinsella's study of the psychology of Carl Jung taught him that the stories in mythology reflect general human experience. Like the young boy in the poem, each of us must learn about death and suffering.

[Personal response given and background information provided]

In 'Hen Woman' there is a similar blend of autobiography and mythology. The young Kinsella sees an old woman grab a hen as it is laying an egg. The egg then smashes down into a 'shore' or sewer opening. This seemingly trivial incident takes on a mythological significance: the old woman emerges from the 'black hole' of her cottage, she is angry and threatening – again, a witch-like figure – and the watching boy not only learns a lesson about the origin of life itself but becomes aware that what he has seen will stay with him for the rest of his life. It will also provide material for poetry: 'I feed upon it still, as you see.' The poem suggests that memory and imagination are inextricably linked, and that childhood experience is crucial in developing artistic awareness.

[Fourth poem discussed in response to the question, suitable quotations included]

Just as I found myself identifying with Kinsella's childhood experiences, I also identified with his exploration of family relationships, especially in 'His Father's Hands', where the image of 'hands' allows him to examine the genetic link between himself, his father and his grandfather. He himself drinks 'firmly', his father's finger 'prodded and prodded', he saw his grandfather 'tightening' the tobacco plug in his pipe and making shoes.

[Links first aspect of discussion with second]

Throughout the poem, as he goes back further into his family's history, he describes how the generations before him worked with their hands – as stone cutters or masons – and earlier still how they seized their territory, 'wedged with tracks'. This leads him to wonder at the mystery of genetic inheritance:

> The blood advancing
> – gorging vessel after vessel –
> and altering in them
> one by one.

The image of the 'countless little nails' that fell from his grandfather's shoemaker's block that ends the poem may be a metaphor for how life continues, generation after generation. Although Kinsella's poem is rooted in his personal family history, I believe we can all respond to this idea, particularly since interest in genealogy and genetics has increased.

[Fifth poem discussed in response to the question, suitable quotations included]

One aspect of Kinsella's work that particularly appeals to me is his emotional honesty, as mentioned previously. This is expressed in his delicate love poems, such as 'The Familiar'. Addressed to his wife, the poem describes a seemingly mundane moment from their lives: preparing breakfast. As he goes through the motions of slicing tomatoes, making tea, fixing their places at the table, the routine becomes a ritual, a ceremony that celebrates their love without any fanfare or emotional drama. The language he uses – the 'little brazen bell', himself standing 'with arms extended' like a priest – creates a religious atmosphere, but the words of his wife that end the poem are plain and almost flat: 'You are very good. You always made it nice.' Placed alongside the religious imagery, these words evoke the simplicity of their life together. His wife is 'familiar' to him in the ordinary meaning of the word, but may also be a 'presence' or inspiration for him and his work. The poem seems to me to celebrate the mysteriousness that surrounds even those most familiar to us in a moving way.

To conclude, I found Thomas Kinsella's imaginative re-creation of childhood utterly convincing and his exploration of relationships emotionally satisfying.

[Final lines emphasise focus of answer and response]

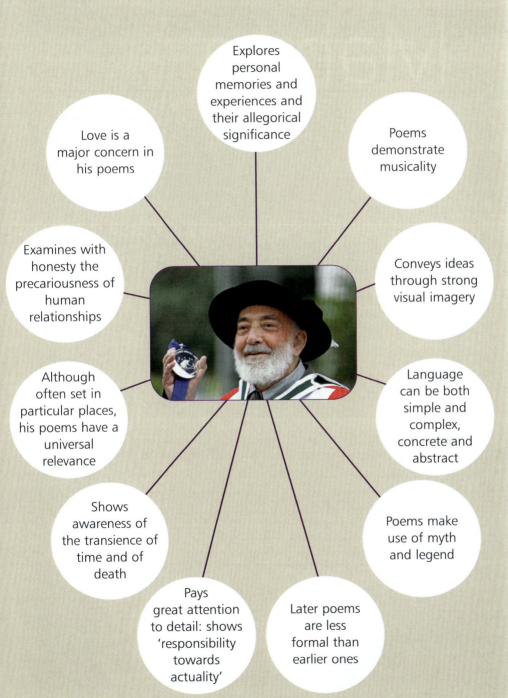

snapshot

Thomas Kinsella

Explores personal memories and experiences and their allegorical significance

Love is a major concern in his poems

Poems demonstrate musicality

Examines with honesty the precariousness of human relationships

Conveys ideas through strong visual imagery

Although often set in particular places, his poems have a universal relevance

Language can be both simple and complex, concrete and abstract

Shows awareness of the transience of time and of death

Poems make use of myth and legend

Pays great attention to detail: shows 'responsibility towards actuality'

Later poems are less formal than earlier ones

Derek Mahon

b. 1941

Biography

Derek Mahon was born on 23 November 1941 in Belfast and brought up in the suburb of Glengormley. His father was an engine-inspector in the Belfast shipyard of Harland and Wolff, where both his grandfathers had also been employed. His mother worked for a time in York Street Flax Spinning Company. He has noted that his parents thus 'embodied the two principal industries in Northern Ireland, shipbuilding and linen'.

Although Mahon's background was working-class Protestant, he played as a child with Catholic children, Glengormley being a mixed neighbourhood. He describes himself in one of his poems as having been a 'strange child with a taste for verse'. He went to secondary school at the Royal Belfast Academical Institution. The poet Michael Longley was a contemporary of his at school and remembers the younger Mahon as already being an accomplished poet at this time.

Like Longley, Mahon went on to study at Trinity College, Dublin. He studied modern languages there, specialising in French. He also began to work seriously at the craft of poetry. Mahon was part of a group of other gifted young poets studying at TCD at the time: Eavan Boland, Brendan Kennelly and Michael Longley. For the first time Mahon felt that there was a poetry-writing community that he could be part of, as well as a thriving literary scene in Dublin. He also studied for a year at the Sorbonne in Paris.

Career

Mahon worked as a teacher in the United States, in Canada and in Ireland, before becoming a journalist and writer in London. He was theatre critic for *The Listener* for a time, poetry editor for *The New Statesman* and features editor of *Vogue*. He was also involved in adapting Irish novels for television, among them Jennifer Johnston's *How Many Miles to Babylon?*, as well as radio adaptations and features. He was writer-in-residence in the University of Ulster (1978/9) and in TCD (1988). He has been a regular contributor of literary journalism and book reviews to *The Irish Times*. For several years in the 1990s Mahon lived in New York and taught at New York University. Having by this time divorced his wife Doreen Douglas, whom he married in 1972, much of his work from New York was addressed to his two children, Rory and Katie, with whom he was no longer living. By 1996 he had returned to live in Dublin. He later moved to Kinsale, Co. Cork.

Poems 1962–78 brings together most of the poems from his first three collections, *Night Crossing* (1968), *Lives* (1972) and *The Snow Party* (1975). *Courtyards in Delft* was published in 1981, *The Hunt by Night* in 1982 and *Antarctica* in 1985. *Selected*

Poems (1991) was the winner of the Irish Times–Aer Lingus Irish Literature Prize for Poetry in 1992. In 1999 he published his *Collected Poems,* with updated versions of many of his poems. His recent collections include *Harbour Lights* (2005), *Life on Earth* (2008) and *An Autumn Wind* (2010).

Mahon edited *The Sphere Book of Modern Irish Poetry* (1972) and, with Peter Fallon, *The Penguin Book of Contemporary Irish Poetry* (1990). He has published several verse translations, including Molière's *School for Wives* and the poems of Philippe Jaccottet from French and a version of Euripides' *The Bacchae* from Greek.

A member of Aosdána and a fellow of the Royal Society of Literature, he has received numerous awards, among them the American Ireland Literary Award and the C. K. Scott-Moncrieff prize for translation.

Social and Cultural Context

Derek Mahon once said in an interview that he considers himself to be a European poet who happens to be Irish, and who just happens to have been born in Belfast. **Each of the three strands of his chosen cultural identity has its place in the development of his work.**

Irish influences

Mahon's work responds in a complex way to the society into which he was born. He is acutely aware of his roots, as the poem 'Grandfather' suggests, revealing a certain admiration for traits that have been associated with the Northern Irish character, such as a degree of rebelliousness and self-reliance. On the other hand, in a poem such as 'Ecclesiastes', he rejects the bigoted attitudes of the churchmen of his native Belfast – a rejection that is tinged with an admission of the attractions of that way of life.

Mahon has never sought to engage with the political problems or the conflict in Northern Ireland. He once said that he felt that as poets in Ulster 'we're supposed to write about the Troubles; a lot of people expect us to act as if it were part of our job – it's not, unless we choose to make it so'. And yet it is true to say that Mahon does not flinch from confronting the issue of violence, even if in a rather oblique way. For instance, in 'Rathlin' he contrasts the violent history of the island with its present peacefulness, but he is also aware of the contemporary conflict in Northern Ireland, the 'bombs that doze in the housing estates'. His attitude to the questions that have caused much grief in Ireland can be seen from his statement that 'whatever we mean by the "Irish situation", the shipyards of Belfast are no less a part of it than a country town in the Gaeltacht'.

The lesson of history is an important theme in his poems. In his long, complex poem 'A Disused Shed in Co. Wexford', he shows an awareness of the many historical conflicts of the past, from the French Revolution to the Jewish Holocaust, while his short poem 'Kinsale' can be read in the light of the historical battle of 1601 that signalled the end of Gaelic Ireland.

Mahon's education at Trinity College, Dublin widened his cultural experience. In the 1960s students at TCD were predominantly Protestant since Catholics were forbidden to attend by the Catholic Church. Mahon, however, met several southern Irish Catholic students at the university, among them the Kerry poet Brendan Kennelly and the Dublin poet Eavan Boland.

Having lived in Dublin while attending college and for some time afterward, Mahon became familiar with life south of the border. An abiding love for the landscape of the west of Ireland is shown in his poems about Inis Oirr, Achill and Donegal. 'Day Trip to Donegal', for instance, is suffused with a love of the sea and a recognition of its power.

International influences

Mahon's assimilation of French literature at university led him to translate classical French texts and modern French poetry. As a student in Paris, he met the Irish writer Samuel Beckett, who had also been educated at Trinity. Like Beckett, Mahon's self-induced exile enabled him to write of his native country as an observer rather than as a participant in the Irish cultural scene.

Many of Mahon's poems reflect an interest in European art. He is conscious of the complex link between poetry and painting that is so important in his work. **His imagery is frequently concerned with the effects of light and shade, as an artist would be.**

Mahon has lived in the United States and some of his poems describe the US landscape and way of life. Although he has returned to Ireland, his poetic vision continues to be truly international. His themes are universal and his frame of reference and allusions contain many diverse cultural echoes.

Mahon has expressed the view that, for him, poetry is primarily an artistic activity rather than an expression of a particular cultural identity: 'for me, poetry is about shape and sound. It's about taking the formless and making it interesting; creating art out of formlessness.'

Derek Mahon

Timeline

1941	Born on 23 November in Belfast
1946–60	Attends Skegoneil Primary School and the Royal Belfast Academical Institution ('Inst')
1960	Begins studies at Trinity College, Dublin (TCD)
1964	Studies at the Sorbonne in Paris
1965	Completes BA degree at TCD
1968	Publishes first collection, *Night Crossing*
1968/9	Travels in North America and France
1970	Moves to London
1972	Marries Doreen Douglas; publishes second collection, *Lives*
1974–7	Works as a journalist and theatre critic in London
1975	Publishes third collection, *The Snow Party*
1977	Son Rory born
1977–79	Writer-in-residence at University of Ulster, Coleraine
1979	Daughter Katie born
1981	Publishes *Courtyards in Delft*
1982	Publishes *The Hunt by Night*
1985	Separates from wife Doreen
1985	Moves to Republic of Ireland
1990–96	Spends time in New York
1996	Returns to Ireland
1999	Publishes *Collected Poems*
2000s	Publishes *Harbour Lights* (2005), *Life on Earth* (2008) and *An Autumn Wind* (2010)

Grandfather

They brought him in on a stretcher from the world,
Wounded but humorous; and he soon recovered.
Boiler-rooms, row upon row of gantries rolled
Away to reveal the landscape of a childhood
Only he can recapture. Even on cold   5
Mornings he is up at six with a block of wood
Or a box of nails, discreetly up to no good
Or banging round the house like a four-year-old –

Never there when you call. But after dark
You hear his great boots thumping in the hall   10
And in he comes, as cute as they come. Each night
His shrewd eyes bolt the door and set the clock
Against the future, then his light goes out.
Nothing escapes him; he escapes us all.

Derek Mahon

Glossary

| 3 | *gantries*: overhead platforms for a travelling crane used in shipbuilding |

Guidelines

'Grandfather' is from the collection *Night Crossing* (1968). Mahon's grandfather was a boiler-maker in Harland and Wolff, the shipbuilders in Belfast where the *Titanic* was built. **In this sonnet the poet paints an interesting portrait of the old man.**

Commentary

Lines 1–9
The poet tells us that his grandfather had been injured at work and then retired. Having recovered, he is no longer concerned with his working life (the 'boiler rooms' and 'gantries') but lives his own rich life, recapturing the freedom of his childhood (lines 3 to 5). He may now be isolated from the real world, and yet there are echoes

of his adult work in the 'box of nails' and the 'banging' noises he makes around the house (lines 6 to 8). He behaves as if he were a young child. Like a 'four year old', too, he is 'never there when you call' (lines 8 and 9). Mahon paints a humorous portrait of a harmless old man.

Lines 9–14

The last six lines of the sonnet offer a slightly different perspective on his grandfather, however. His comings and goings seem to become rather more inexplicable, perhaps a little sinister. He does not say where he has been when he comes home 'after dark', but makes no effort to hide the noise of his 'great boots thumping in the hall' (lines 9 and 10.) Again, he sees no need to apologise for or explain himself.

The colloquial phrase 'as cute as they come' (line 11) suggests that his behaviour is far from aimless. His actions are described now as having a purpose to them. He will 'bolt the door and set the clock' – ordinary everyday actions – but the poem goes on to say that he does them 'against the future' (lines 12 and 13). The word 'shrewd' (line 12) suggests that it is a clever form of self-preservation, an attempt to maintain his independence and dignity in the face of old age and inevitable death. Perhaps in his eccentric behaviour he has found a way of avoiding the problems of real life.

We are left with an impression of an old man who has stubbornly refused to adapt to the conventions of 'normal' elderly behaviour. It is impossible not to feel a certain admiration for the old man.

Tone of the poem

Mahon describes his grandfather with humanity and affection. He clearly identifies with the old man's rebelliousness, but his attitude is not patronising in any way. He seems to recognise his grandfather as an individual, as he accepts that his grandfather's childhood and working life remain a mystery to anyone except himself. He knows his grandfather is not about to explain his behaviour to his family: 'he escapes us all' (line 14). This may be exasperating for everyone else – he is 'never there when you call' (line 9) – but it is part of the old man's strategy for survival. He suggests, too, that his grandfather is perfectly well aware of the world around him: 'Nothing escapes him' (line 14).

Form of the poem

The poem is a sonnet – a poem of fourteen lines, usually divided into eight lines (octet or octave) and six lines (sestet). The octave generally presents a situation and the sestet comments further or develops it. Note that in this sonnet the octave extends into part of line 9. The basic rhyming pattern of a strict sonnet is *abba, abba, cde, cde*, but many poets deviate from this pattern or change it to suit their theme. For instance, 'Grandfather' does not conform exactly to this pattern. In the octave the pattern is *abababba*, in the sestet it is *cdeced*. These breaks with convention seem appropriate for a poem that describes an unusual and eccentric individual.

Sound patterns in the poem

Mahon makes use of sound to reinforce the picture he creates of his grandfather. Alliteration in 'row upon row', 'rolled' leads to 'reveal' and 'recapture' to create a seamless link between the grandfather's work and his childhood. The repetition of the 'u' sound (assonance) in 'wounded but humorous' echoes the sound of someone in pain, while the long 'o' sound in 'row after row' and 'rolled' might suggest wonder at the immensity of the shipyard.

Thinking about the poem

1   How is the grandfather portrayed in lines 1 and 2?

2   Why does the poet refer to his grandfather's working life in lines 3 and 4? Explain your answer.

3   Why also does he refer to his grandfather's childhood in lines 4 and 5?

4   What impression of the grandfather do we get in the last six lines (the sestet) of the sonnet? Is it different from the first eight lines (the octet)? Explain your answer.

5   What does the grandfather's ritual of bolting the door and setting the clock at night suggest about him? How would you explain the phrase 'against the future' (line 13)?

6   Which **one** of these words best describes the grandfather, as he is presented in the poem: secretive, eccentric, innocent, doddering, rebellious or clever. Explain your choice.

7   Do you think that Mahon loved his grandfather? Explain your answer.

8   Would the grandfather have been an easy person to live with? Give a reason for your answer.

9   Explore Mahon's use of sound patterns in the poem and say what effect it creates.

Taking a closer look

1 What do the phrases 'up to no good' (line 7) and 'as cute as they come' (line 11) contribute to the portrait of the old man?

2 Would you describe the tone of the phrase 'Never there when you call' (line 9) as: exasperated, annoyed, amused or accepting? Perhaps you would suggest another word? Explain your choice.

3 What is your interpretation of the last line, 'Nothing escapes him: he escapes us all'?

Imagining

1 Imagine you are the grandfather in the poem. Write a letter to your grandson in which you describe some of your childhood adventures or your working life.

2 Using poetic means, Mahon has given us a vivid picture of his grandfather. From your reading of the poem, write a short descriptive portrait of the man as you imagine him to be.

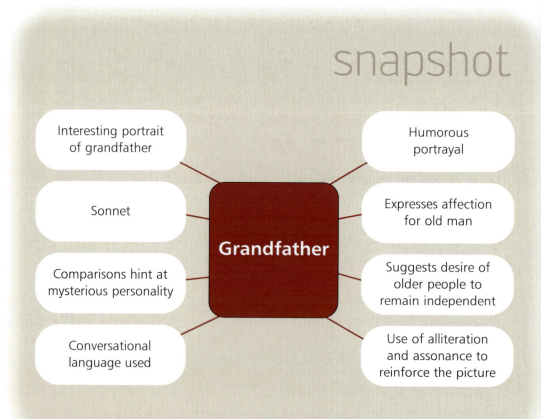

snapshot

Interesting portrait of grandfather

Humorous portrayal

Sonnet

Expresses affection for old man

Grandfather

Comparisons hint at mysterious personality

Suggests desire of older people to remain independent

Conversational language used

Use of alliteration and assonance to reinforce the picture

Day Trip to Donegal

We reached the sea in early afternoon,
Climbed stiffly out; there were things to be done,
Clothes to be picked up, friends to be seen.
As ever, the nearby hills were a deeper green
Than anywhere in the world, and the grave   5
Grey of the sea the grimmer in that enclave.

Down at the pier the boats gave up their catch,
A writhing glimmer of fish; they fetch
Ten times as much in the city as here,
And still the fish come in year after year –   10
Herring and mackerel, flopping about the deck
In attitudes of agony and heartbreak.

We left at eight, drove back the way we came,
The sea receding down each muddy lane.
Around midnight we changed-down into suburbs   15
Sunk in a sleep no gale-force wind disturbs.
The time of year had left its mark
On frosty pavements glistening in the dark.

Give me a ring, goodnight, and so to bed . . .
That night the slow sea washed against my head,   20
Performing its immeasurable erosions –
Spilling into the skull, marbling the stones
That spine the very harbour wall,
Muttering its threat to villages of landfall.

At dawn I was alone far out at sea   25
Without skill or reassurance – nobody
To show me how, no promise of rescue –
Cursing my constant failure to take due
Forethought for this; contriving vain
Overtures to the vindictive wind and rain.   30

Derek Mahon

Glossary

6	*enclave*: a piece of a country that is entirely enclosed within foreign territory
8	*writhing*: twisting
21	*erosions*: eating away, wearing down
30	*overtures*: offers or proposals, especially in negotiations
30	*vindictive*: revengeful

Guidelines

'Day Trip to Donegal' is from the collection *Night Crossing* (1968). **In this poem we can see Mahon's love of the sea and his perception of it as a mysterious, creative force.**

Commentary

Stanza 1

The poem begins as a straightforward narrative with details of preparation for the trip. This is appropriate if we consider that the title is reminiscent of a school composition. At first the language used is conversational: 'things to be done, / Clothes to be picked up' (lines 2–3). The scene is set. The Donegal hills are still a 'deeper green' than anywhere in the world, 'as ever' – the phrase suggests how reassuringly familiar the place is to the poet and his companions (line 4). But words such as 'grave', 'grey' and 'grimmer' hint at a darker vision (lines 5 and 6). You may notice how the alliteration – the repetition of the hard 'g' sounds – in these words indicates this subtle change of mood.

Stanza 2

In the second stanza the poet focuses even more closely on his surroundings. Down at the pier, fish are being landed – a routine commercial event, as the poet recognises in his comment about the price they fetch. But his striking visual image of the fish as a 'writhing glimmer' (line 8) 'flopping about the deck / In attitudes of agony and heartbreak' (lines 11–12) seems to give human qualities and feelings to the fish. **These suggestions of pain and death add to the atmosphere of underlying unease set up in the first stanza.**

Stanza 3

The poet does not describe the actual day he spent at sea. Instead, he seems more interested in the return home, presumably to his native city of Belfast (although it is not named). Donegal seems to recede from his consciousness. The implication is that there is an essential difference in life as experienced in the suburbs and life as it is experienced close to nature in Donegal – the car 'changed-down' in gear as they approached the sleeping suburbs (line 15). Their peacefulness contrasts with the 'gale-force wind' (line 16) they had encountered at sea. **The change is not merely physical but also psychological, as the final two stanzas make clear.**

Stanza 4

All seems well as the companions take their leave of each other: 'Give me a ring, goodnight', and the phrase 'and so to bed . . . ' has echoes of a typical way to end an account of a day's adventures (line 19). **But the last two stanzas plunge us into the terrifying world of the subconscious.** In the speaker's dream the sea has appeared again, but different, as is the case in dreams. The imagery used to describe the experience is vividly sensuous. We can almost hear the sound of the sea and feel its power.

Mahon achieves this effect through the use of carefully chosen sounds and images. Alliteration as in 'slow sea' (line 20) and onomatopoeia as in 'immeasurable erosions' (line 21) and 'muttering' (line 24) reflect the sound and movement of the sea. The image of the water 'marbling the stones / That spine the very harbour wall' (lines 22–23) enables us to visualise its physical power. By deliberately blending the images of the sea with the experience of dreaming – 'spilling into the skull' (line 22) – Mahon conveys the surreal, and sometimes frightening, atmosphere of dreams.

Stanza 5

The dream experience becomes even more nightmarish as the speaker sees himself as lost, cut adrift from everyone and everything. **What is being described here goes beyond physical fear. It is as if being 'far out at sea' (line 25) is a metaphor for alienation, both psychological and spiritual.**

The atmosphere created in the final lines of the poem is utterly intense. The threat posed by the sea, wind and rain (elements of nature) may symbolise the wilderness of the subconscious or the imagination. It is a realm over which we can have no control, but it is central to the work of a poet. Or it may suggest the deepest human fears, of loss and ultimate death, which we must face alone. The fact that Mahon does not name specifically what his fears are adds to the sense of foreboding he conveys.

The imagery here recalls a long tradition in mythology and literature of representing the sea and wind as animate presences that are malevolent and powerful and will not easily be appeased, no more than the human sense of nameless dread can easily be overcome.

In this poem we see how Mahon's imagination works on the ordinary reality of a day trip to a place he knows well, and transforms it so that we are given an insight into the poet's deepest anxieties and fears. The 'trip' (the word has connotations of an out-of-body experience) to somewhere else has brought him back to a sense of himself in the most intense way possible, as a human being who must face his darkest fears alone, with 'no promise of rescue' (line 27).

Structure of the poem

Mahon has organised this poem into five stanzas of six lines made up of rhyming couplets with the pattern *aabbcc* in each. **The very regular form of the poem contrasts with the chaotic feelings he expresses in the final stanza.**

Thinking about the poem

1   What expectations does the title of the poem set up? Are these expectations realised?

2   How would you describe the tone of the first two stanzas? How is it conveyed?

3   Why does the poet describe the fish in such detail? Support your answer by reference to the poem.

4   Was the poet's trip to Donegal as ordinary and uneventful as it seemed? How did it affect him in his later dreams?

5   In what terms does the poet describe the sea? Would you agree that the imagery here is sensuous and intense? Look carefully at words such as 'spilling', 'marbling', 'muttering' (lines 22 to 24).

6   Would you agree that the sense of danger and isolation intensifies in the last stanza? How is this reflected in the language used?

7   How would you account for the sense of fear and disorientation experienced by the speaker?

8   Look carefully at the sound patterns – the full end-rhymes, half-rhymes, alliteration, assonance, consonance – and say what they contribute to the overall impact made by the poem.

9   Discuss 'Day Trip to Donegal' as a nature poem.

10   What does the poem reveal to us about the personality of the speaker?

Ecclesiastes

God, you could grow to love it, God-fearing, God-
chosen purist little puritan that,
for all your wiles and smiles, you are (the
dank churches, the empty streets,
the shipyard silence, the tied-up swings) and   5
shelter your cold heart from the heat
of the world, from woman-inquisition, from the
bright eyes of children. Yes you could
wear black, drink water, nourish a fierce zeal
with locusts and wild honey, and not   10
feel called upon to understand and forgive
but only to speak with a bleak
afflatus, and love the January rains when they
darken the dark doors and sink hard
into the Antrim hills, the bog meadows, the heaped   15
graves of your fathers. Bury that red
bandana, stick and guitar; this is your
country, close one eye and be king.
Your people await you, their heavy washing
flaps for you in the housing estates –   20
a credulous people. God, you could do it, God
help you, stand on a corner stiff
with rhetoric, promising nothing under the sun.

Glossary	
Title	*Ecclesiastes*: one of the books of the Old Testament; an ecclesiast is a preacher or evangelist
2	*purist*: someone who insists on purity in language or art
2	*puritan*: a person of strict moral conduct
3	*wiles*: coaxing, pleasant ways
5	*tied-up swings*: it was formerly the custom in Northern Ireland to close playgrounds on Sundays
7	*woman-inquisition*: questioning by a woman

9	*zeal*: intense, sometimes fanatical, enthusiasm for a cause
10	*locusts and wild honey*: John the Baptist is said to have survived in the desert by eating locusts and wild honey (Matthew, chapter 3)
13	*afflatus*: divine inspiration
17	*bandana*: large handkerchief worn on the head or around the neck
18	*close one eye and be king*: alludes to the words of Erasmus, 'In the kingdom of the blind the one-eyed man is king'
21	*credulous*: gullible
23	*rhetoric*: art of using language to persuade others

Guidelines

'Ecclesiastes', first published in 1968, is contained in the collection *Lives* (1975). **The poem gives us an insight into the Protestant tradition in Ulster into which Mahon was born.** Northern Ireland, particularly in pre-Troubles time (before the late 1960s), had a great number of independent Protestant preachers who would travel around preaching the Bible. 'Ecclesiastes' vividly evokes their way of life and attitudes.

Commentary

Lines 1–8

The first thing we notice about the poem is its tone. You can hear the poet's passion as he addresses himself with a mixture of honesty and contempt. 'God-chosen' is heavily ironic (who knows God's real wishes?), while 'purist' and 'puritan' sound like insults (lines 1 and 2). He acknowledges that for all his outward amiability ('wiles and smiles') he could become a preacher, be attracted to a strict ('puritan') way of life, even as he focuses on its dreariness in images that evoke a gloomy Presbyterian Sunday in his native Belfast – the deserted streets and closed playgrounds. The advantages are that you might avoid the problems of the world or real human relationships with women or children. You may notice how the word 'from' is repeated three times at this point in the poem, as if the speaker is casting out these images from his mind.

Lines 8–16

The tone becomes even fiercer as the poet describes what his life as a preacher would be like. He would live simply – 'wear black, drink water' (line 9) – driven only by religious fervour and 'locusts and wild honey' (line 10). As described in the Bible,

John the Baptist survived for forty days in the desert on a diet of locusts and wild honey.

This brand of religion would not require Mahon to preach forgiveness or understand the complexity of life. Religion, as practised by these preachers, offers no comfort. The word of God ('afflatus' suggests divine inspiration, line 13) is bleak, associated with rain and darkness, harshness and death. This is the tradition within which these preachers work. The poet accepts that it is his tradition, too, as the image of 'the heaped / graves of your fathers' (lines 15–16 suggests.

Lines 16–23
A few evocative images – the 'red / bandana, stick and guitar' (lines 16–17) – conjure up a completely contrasting way of life, that of the romantic 'hippies' of the 1960s and 1970s. Their philosophy revolved around peace and love rather than rigid rules or dogmatic beliefs. The speaker exhorts himself to leave this way of life and take his place among the preachers in his own country.

The phrase 'close one eye and be king' (line 18) recalls the saying of Erasmus: 'In the country of the blind the one-eyed man is king.' It implies religious ignorance allied to power – surely a damning indictment of the whole religious tradition in which the poet grew up. But the fault lies not only with the preachers, but also with the gullible and bigoted people in the 'housing estates' (line 20) who blindly accept their teachings.

With heavy irony the poet suggests that he could easily do this, stand on a street corner 'stiff / with rhetoric' (lines 22–23) or empty words, with nothing of value to say to people. This last line is utterly negative in tone.

Personal experience

Mahon's themes are not often explicitly autobiographical, but 'Ecclesiastes' is one of the few poems in which he comes to terms in some way with his identity as a poet from Northern Ireland.

'Ecclesiastes' expresses Mahon's complex emotional relationship with his native city, Belfast, and with the religious tradition of Protestant Ulster. By constantly repeating the word 'God', the poem forces the reader to look at the vision of God that is put forward in this society. In fact the word takes on different connotations as the poem progresses. In the first line it moves from the opening realisation – 'God, you could grow to love it' – to the irony in the compound adjectives 'God-fearing, God-chosen'. 'God, you could do it' in line 21 is forceful, but the final 'God help you' has overtones of contemptuous pity. However, because much of the irony and the pity are directed at himself, the poem stops short of being a condemnation of a whole way of life.

Form of the poem

You will notice that the poem is not divided into orderly stanzas. It is written in one long verse paragraph, unrhymed, with run-on lines reflecting impassioned speech. Mahon makes use of rhetorical devices such as repetition ('God', 'you could'), alliteration ('darken the dark doors') and Biblical references ('locusts and wild honey') to reinforce his depiction of a preacher's oratory, so that the language and theme of the poem are inextricably linked. The exaggeration in the poem's final line reflects the utterly negative nature of the preacher's message.

Thinking about the poem

1   What exactly are the attractions of the preachers' way of life? Why might they appeal to the poet?

2   Mahon appears to be aware of the inadequacies of the preachers' way of life. How is this inadequacy suggested?

3   Would you agree that the poem satirises a certain kind of religious fanaticism? Look carefully at the religious references and the harsh adjectives used throughout.

4   How would you describe the tone of the poem? Is it consistent throughout?

5   What picture of the Protestant people of Ulster is created for the reader of 'Ecclesiastes'? How did you respond to it?

6   What are Mahon's feelings about his own people, as expressed in the poem?

7   Would you agree that the form of the poem – its language, organisation, rhythm and sound patterns – all contribute greatly to the forcefulness of its effect? Look in particular at the accumulation of images, the imperative mood of the verbs, the run-on lines that carry the poem forward to the implications of the last line.

8   If you were to choose the poem as one of your favourite poems by Mahon, what case would you make for your choice?

9   'Mahon excels at giving a voice to unsympathetic or marginalised characters.' Based on the poems 'Ecclesiastes', 'As It Should Be' and 'After the Titanic', give your opinion of this view.

After the Titanic

They said I got away in a boat
And humbled me at the inquiry. I tell you
　　I sank as far that night as any
Hero. As I sat shivering on the dark water
　　I turned to ice to hear my costly   5
Life go thundering down in a pandemonium of
　　Prams, pianos, sideboards, winches,
Boilers bursting and shredded ragtime. Now I hide
　　In a lonely house behind the sea
Where the tide leaves broken toys and hat-boxes   10
　　Silently at my door. The showers of
April, flowers of May mean nothing to me, nor the
　　Late light of June, when my gardener
Describes to strangers how the old man stays in bed
　　On seaward mornings after nights of   15
Wind, takes his cocaine and will see no-one. Then it is
　　I drown again with all those dim
Lost faces I never understood. My poor soul
　　Screams out in the starlight, heart
Breaks loose and rolls down like a stone.   20
　　Include me in your lamentations.

Derek Mahon

Glossary	
2	*inquiry*: the formal investigation into why the *Titanic* sunk
6	*pandemonium*: chaos, confusion
7	*winches*: machinery used to lift heavy goods
8	*ragtime*: the popular jazz music played by the orchestra as the ship was sinking
15	*seaward mornings*: mornings when the wind blows from the sea
21	*lamentations*: expressions of sorrow and grief

Guidelines

This poem comes from the collection *Lives* (1975). It was originally entitled 'Bruce Ismay's Soliloquy'.

In April 1912 the *SS Titanic* set sail from Southampton, bound for New York. It struck an iceberg off the coast of Newfoundland and sank with the loss of almost 1,500 lives. After the tragedy, an inquiry

was held into the disaster. Among those questioned was Bruce Ismay, the president of White Star Line (the ship's owners) and one of the few male passengers who had managed to escape in the lifeboats. In this dramatic monologue, Mahon gives a voice to Ismay.

The *Titanic* was built at the Harland and Wolff shipyard in Belfast. Perhaps the fact that Mahon's grandfather was a boiler-maker for the ship – the poem contains a reference to boilers bursting – inspired the poet to reconstruct the events and enter imaginatively into the mind of the speaker.

Commentary

Lines 1–8

Bruce Ismay wants to give us his side of the story. From the beginning he distances himself from the verdict of the inquiry: 'They said' (line 1) suggests that he does not agree with the findings. He felt 'humbled . . . at the inquiry' (line 2) and wants to set the record straight, in his own mind. 'I tell you' (line 2) has an honest ring to it, but is there an element of self-delusion in comparing his plight the night that the *Titanic* went down to that of any other 'Hero' (line 4)? He tries to convince his listeners (and perhaps himself also) that he, too, was a victim of the tragedy.

In vivid images **he evokes the atmosphere of chaos as the ship was sinking.** From where he sat 'shivering' in his lifeboat he could hear a 'pandemonium' of sounds as 'prams, pianos' were destroyed, as well as the sounds of 'boilers bursting' and interrupted music: 'shredded ragtime' (lines 4 to 8).

Lines 8–21

Then **he describes his life in the aftermath of the disaster**. Feeling ashamed and guilty, he hides away from the world. Ironically, he has chosen to live by the sea, where the material washed up by the tide seems further to accuse him: 'broken toys and hat-boxes' are left 'silently' at his door (lines 9 to 10). One cannot help but have a sort of sympathy for him as he says that life or the wonders of nature no longer have any meaning for him. Significantly, hearing the sound of wind on the sea disturbs him emotionally, so that he has to numb his senses with cocaine and isolate himself (lines 14 to 16). All the time, too, people are curious about him. He is someone his gardener will gossip about with strangers (lines 13 and 14).

The metaphors and similes in the last few lines convey feelings of utter desolation. It is as if he is forced to relive his experience again and again, to 'drown again' (line 17) with all those who died. His 'poor soul / Screams out in the starlight', his 'heart / Breaks loose and rolls down like a stone' (lines 18 to 19). Although we can detect a note of self-pity here, the speaker seeks to justify why he should be included in any expressions of grief for those who suffered. However, his plea for understanding is diminished somewhat when he admits that he 'never understood' all the 'dim / Lost faces' (lines 17 and 18) – perhaps because most of those who drowned were the poorer passengers in steerage, not part of his own 'costly / Life' (line 5).

Form of the poem

In a dramatic monologue the poet gives a voice to a certain character and tries to make us see things from his or her point of view. Ismay addresses the reader directly and constantly uses the first person, I. His language is mostly conversational and simple, but the imagery at times is highly exaggerated, which adds to our sense of a man tortured by remorse (or wishing to seem as if he is).

A dramatic monologue will also give a glimpse of the views of other people. Ismay tells us that he is socially isolated and an object of curiosity to strangers. He also refers to the 'lost faces' of those who drowned. We must decide whether Ismay's remorse is convincing in the light of such an enormous tragedy for so many people.

Mahon uses alliteration to convey Ismay's experience. In the final lines, for example, the repetition of 's' sounds (sibilance) in 'soul', 'screams' and 'starlight' and the assonance in the long 'o' sounds of 'rolls' and 'stone' echo the sense of grief that pervades the poem.

Thinking about the poem

1   Why, do you think, does the speaker of this poem feel compelled to give his side of the story?

2   What might he mean when he says 'I turned to ice to hear my costly / Life go thundering down' (lines 5–6)? Does what he says later help to explain it further?

3   Does he paint a vivid picture of the disaster, in your view?

4   Do you find it strange that he has chosen to live out his days beside the sea? Why might he have made this decision?

5   From the list of phrases that follow choose **one** that is closest to your own reading of the poem and explain your choice:

>   This man is trying to justify his own cowardly actions.

>   This speaker feels genuinely sorry for what he has done.

>   This speaker has suffered greatly; it would have been better for him to have drowned like the others.

6   What does the speaker of the poem reveal about his personality? Do you find him a sympathetic character?

7   Has the speaker convinced you that he should be included in 'lamentations' (line 21) or grief for the victims? Give a reason for your answer.

8   'Derek Mahon has a great ability to convey the thoughts of others.' Do you agree with this view?

9   Give **two** examples **each** of alliteration and assonance and comment on the effect they create in the poem.

10   Do you like this poem? Give reasons for your opinion.

Taking a closer look

1   Comment on the effectiveness of the simile 'like a stone' in line 20.

2   Choose **two** examples of interesting sounds from the poem and say why you chose them.

Imagining

1   Imagine you are a survivor of the disaster. Write a letter to a friend telling of your memories of that night. Use details from the poem in your letter.

2   Imagine you are a newspaper reporter at Bruce Ismay's inquiry. Write a short report about what you heard and saw.

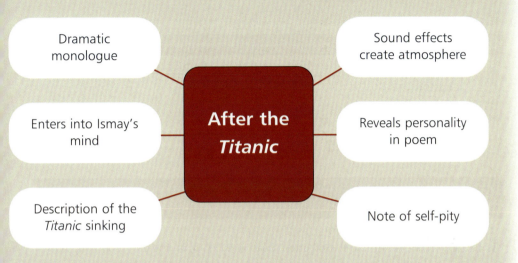

- Dramatic monologue
- Sound effects create atmosphere

After the *Titanic*

- Enters into Ismay's mind
- Reveals personality in poem
- Description of the *Titanic* sinking
- Note of self-pity

Derek Mahon

As It Should Be

We hunted the mad bastard
through bog, moorland, rock, to the star-lit west
And gunned him down in a blind yard
Between ten sleeping lorries
And an electricity generator.   5

Let us hear no idle talk
Of the moon in the Yellow River;
The air blows softer since his departure.

Since his tide-burial during school hours
Our children have known no bad dreams.   10
Their cries echo lightly along the coast.

This is as it should be.
They will thank us for it when they grow up
To a world with method in it.

7 | *Yellow River*: major Chinese river; possibly a reference to a play by Denis Johnston.

Guidelines

'As It Should Be' is from the collection *Lives* (1972). It is **another poem in which Mahon gives a voice to a persona who expresses a distinct and unpopular point of view.**

We enter into the mind of the speaker as he outlines his chilling justification of violence. Although the poem makes no direct reference to any particular conflict, the reference to the 'moon in the Yellow River' suggests a connection with the violence of the Irish Civil War, and, by extension, the conflict in Northern Ireland. Denis Johnston's play *The Moon in the Yellow River* (1931) deals with violence in Civil War times. It includes a particularly brutal episode in which the perpetrator of a plan to destroy a power plant was shot by one of his former comrades, a supporter of the Irish Free State. One of the characters in the play refers to the Chinese poet Lo Pi, who wished to embrace the moon in the Yellow River. This is interpreted as a metaphor for wishing to do the impossible, ideal thing.

Commentary

Stanza 1
From the beginning the speaker assumes an authority to kill that suggests official sanction for his actions. Possibly this is a hint that the speaker is identified with the Irish Free State character in Johnston's play. The enemy is insulted ('mad bastard') and dehumanised as he is 'hunted' like an animal (line 1). The manner of his death is described in chillingly factual terms. There is no sense of fair play: he is 'gunned down in a blind yard' (line 3), trapped between lorries and an electricity generator, from where he could not possibly have escaped.

Stanzas 2 and 3

No pity or remorse is expressed. It is as if the world is a better place without this human being. The speaker firmly rejects any possibility of idealism (the 'moon in the Yellow River', line 7) that may have been associated with his enemy's political views. In fact he sees his violent death, ironically, as easing the fears of violence in the community: the children have had 'no bad dreams' (line 10) since this man's death.

Stanza 4

We hear the voice of fanaticism most clearly in the final stanza. The implications are quite chilling. The hunting down and murdering 'is as it should be' (line 12). There is no room for self-doubt or moral agonising. The world, according to the speaker, will now have 'method in it' – a claim that casts an even more damning, ironic perspective on what he has described. What 'method' is there in the senseless killing of another human being?

Themes of the poem

Although the poem is short, it conveys a great deal about the psychology of the fanatic, whether he has the support of the state or not. An utter inability to consider any course of action other than the one which he sees as right, a total lack of moral questioning and an irrational justification of his actions are all suggested in the poem.

References to nature and the elements – bog, moorland, stars, moon, air, tides, coast – reinforce the idea that the speaker sees his actions as part of the natural course of events, something that hardly needs to be explained.

His conviction that the children 'will thank us for it when they grow up' (line 13) assumes a right to act on behalf of others, even future generations, a belief that has been the basis of fascist regimes. It also betrays a total lack of awareness of how historical attitudes change over time.

As in 'After the Titanic', the poet allows the speaker to reveal the irony of his position, without direct authorial comment. The issues touched on may have their basis in historical events, but the picture of the speaker as it emerges is surely universally applicable to any conflict.

Derek Mahon

Thinking about the poem

1   How does the speaker of 'As It Should Be' justify the violent actions of himself and his companions?

2   Describe the tone of the poem. Look carefully at the use of the plural 'we' and the language and images the poet chooses when describing the events.

3   Which of the lines in the poem do you find the most disturbing? Give reasons for your choice.

4   Does the poem hint at another point of view? How does this affect your interpretation of the poem?

5   'Ecclesiastes' and 'After the Titanic' are two other poems in which Mahon enters the mindset of other characters. Which of the three poems succeed best in doing so, in your view?

6   Discuss the view that the poem is relevant to many contemporary events and conflicts.

A Disused Shed in Co. Wexford

'Let them not forget us, the weak souls among the asphodels.'

Seferis, *Mythistorema*

(for J. G. Farrell)

Even now there are places where a thought might grow –
Peruvian mines, worked out and abandoned
To a slow clock of condensation,
An echo trapped for ever, and a flutter
Of wild-flowers in the lift-shaft,   5
Indian compound where the wind dances
And a door bangs with diminished confidence,
Lime crevices behind rippling rain-barrels,
Dog corners for bone burials;
And in a disused shed in Co. Wexford,   10

Deep in the grounds of a burnt-out hotel,
Among the bathtubs and the washbasins
A thousand mushrooms crowd to a keyhole.

This is the one star in their firmament
Or frames a star within a star. 15
What should they do there but desire?
So many days beyond the rhododendrons
With the world waltzing in its bowl of cloud,
They have learnt patience and silence
Listening to the rooks querulous in the high wood. 20

They have been waiting for us in a foetor
Of vegetable sweat since civil war days,
Since the gravel-crunching, interminable departure
Of the expropriated mycologist,
He never came back, and light since then 25
Is a keyhole rusting gently after rain.
Spiders have spun, flies dusted to mildew
And once a day, perhaps, they have heard something –
A trickle of masonry, a shout from the blue
Or a lorry changing gear at the end of the lane. 30

There have been deaths, the pale flesh flaking
Into the earth that nourished it;
And nightmares, born of these and the grim
Dominion of stale air and rank moisture.
Those nearest the door grow strong – 35
'Elbow room! Elbow room!'
The rest, dim in a twilight of crumbling
Utensils and broken pitchers, groaning
For their deliverance, have been so long
Expectant that there is left only the posture. 40

A half century, without visitors, in the dark –
Poor preparation for the cracking lock
And creak of hinges; magi, moonmen,
Powdery prisoners of the old regime,
Web-throated, stalked like triffids, racked by drought 45
And insomnia, only the ghost of a scream
At the flash-bulb firing-squad we wake them with
Shows there is life yet in their feverish forms.
Grown beyond nature now, soft food for worms,
They lift frail heads in gravity and good faith. 50

They are begging us, you see, in their wordless way,
To do something, to speak on their behalf
Or at least not to close the door again.
Lost people of Treblinka and Pompeii!
'Save us, save us,' they seem to say,   55
'Let the god not abandon us
Who have come so far in darkness and in pain.
We too had our lives to live.
You with your light meter and relaxed itinerary,
Let not our naïve labours have been in vain!'   60

Glossary

Epigraph *asphodels*: lily-like plants, associated with the dead in Greek mythology

Epigraph *Mythistorema*: collection of short poems by the Greek poet George Seferis (1900–71) dealing with the myth of Odysseus in modern form; their themes are often political

Dedication *J. G. Farrell*: novelist (1935–79)

6	*compound*: an enclosure around a house or factory
14	*firmament*: sky
20	*querulous*: complaining
21	*foetor*: a strong, offensive smell
24	*expropriated*: dispossessed
24	*mycologist*: someone who studies fungi
27	*mildew*: a disease on plants
43	*magi*: ancient priests or wise men; here, probably sorcerers
45	*triffids*: monstrous stinging plants invented by the writer John Wyndham in his science-fiction novel *The Day of the Triffids* (1951)
54	*Treblinka*: a Polish concentration camp in which Jews were incarcerated and killed during World War II
54	*Pompeii*: ancient city in Italy, buried when the volcano Vesuvius erupted in 79 ad
59	*light meter*: device for measuring light (in a camera)
59	*itinerary*: plan of a journey

Guidelines

This poem from *The Snow Party* (1985) has been called Mahon's masterpiece. Its impact depends upon our awareness of the symbolic significance the poet gives to the mushrooms in the old shed that he came across in Co. Wexford. **Lonely, abandoned, the mushrooms come to stand for the lost lives of those who have suffered through violence and neglect.** The Irish location of the poem links the suffering of the Irish people throughout history with the suffering of other peoples at other times.

Commentary

Epigraph and dedication

The epigraph 'Let them not forget us, the weak souls among the asphodels' is a plea for remembrance and is echoed throughout the poem.

The poem is dedicated to J. G. Farrell, author of the novel *The Troubles* (1970). The subject matter of the novel may throw some light on the implications of the poem. A historical novel, set in Ireland in the 1920s, it evokes the fate of the Anglo-Irish Ascendancy class by describing the gradual ruin of a hotel, which is burnt down by republicans during the Irish Civil War. This was a time when the Anglo-Irish community felt abandoned politically and emotionally by the British to whom they owed their allegiance.

Mahon has set his poem in a shed in the grounds of a burnt-out hotel, echoing Farrell's novel. Although the poem is not restricted to the theme of the novel, it is interesting that Mahon wrote it as the Protestant people of Ulster (his own people) began to express their sense of abandonment by the British government during the conflict in Northern Ireland in the 1970s.

Stanza 1

From the beginning there is a strong sense of place in the poem, which the language allows us imaginatively to enter. Like the opening shot of a film, the first stanza pans images of emptiness from across several continents – South America, India, Europe – places either once inhabited by people and now abandoned or places hidden from human consciousness. But these places rather eerily may become places where meaning is possible, and so the poem zooms in on the disused shed in Co. Wexford, before focusing more closely on the mushrooms that grow there. This first stanza sets the scene for the rest of the poem, ranging as it does throughout the world, preparing the reader for the historical insights that follow.

Derek Mahon

Stanza 2

The 'thousand mushrooms' (line 13) and their setting are described in a series of precise and rich images. At times we see the world from the mushrooms' point of view. Growing in the outhouse of a derelict hotel, they spend their days straining towards the source of light, which shines in through the keyhole. This source of light is the 'one star in their firmament' (line 14), an image that suggests their pathetic plight and sense of hopelessness.

The mushrooms take on a symbolic function as they are given human qualities and feelings. They are capable of 'desire' (line 16). Pent up in the shed for so long, they have accepted their isolation with 'patience and silence' (line 19). In contrast, the world moves on, 'waltzing in its bowl of cloud' (line 18).

Stanza 3

At times the mushrooms are presented simply as mushrooms: 'foetor / of vegetable sweat' (lines 21–22) suggests the foul smell of vegetable decay. **But their symbolic function is made even more clearly in this stanza as they are linked explicitly with 'civil war days' (line 22).**

Reference to the 'expropriated mycologist' (line 24) who never returned can be explained by an incident in Farrell's *The Troubles*. As in the novel, the decaying world seems to represent the Anglo-Irish who were displaced and ultimately abandoned. Mahon enables us to share in their experience. He names the things they can see and hear: the rusting keyhole, spiders and flies who also have 'dusted to mildew' (line 27), occasional sounds from the outside world: 'gravel-crunching' (line 23) steps, shouts or sounds of vehicles outside.

Stanza 4

The atmosphere becomes even more eerie in the fourth stanza. Powerful, sensuous imagery evokes suffering, death and decay. Visual, aural and tactile images are combined in the mushrooms' 'pale flesh flaking / Into the earth that nourished it' (lines 31–32). We can almost smell and feel the 'stale air and rank moisture' (line 34) in the shed.

Now the mushrooms are perceived as a multitude, symbolic of suffering people within a larger historical framework than those of the abandoned Anglo-Irish of the Irish Civil War. Like imprisoned people everywhere, they seek freedom. 'Elbow room! Elbow room!' (line 36) echoes the German '*lebensraum*' associated with the fate of the Jewish people under Nazi regimes during World War II. (Mahon makes the connection even more explicit in the final stanza, with the reference to the concentration camp at Treblinka.)

As the poem proceeds further, historical associations are established, so that the mushrooms take on their full symbolic weight as forgotten people, casualties of political cruelty or indifference. Like many oppressed people, all they can do is wait for their deliverance.

Stanza 5

In the fifth stanza the focus changes to the moment of discovery on the part of the poet/speaker and his unnamed companions. Hard consonant sounds in 'cracking lock / And creak of hinges' (lines 42–43) have an onomatopoeic effect as the door of the shed is opened. A series of imaginative metaphors follows.

The mushrooms are 'magi' and 'moonmen' (line 43) – mysterious and alien, like imagined inhabitants of the moon who have been without the light of the sun. The shape of the mushrooms also suggests the round moon.

'Powdery prisoners of the old regime' (line 44) has associations with the overthrow of the *ancien régime* during the French Revolution (1789–99). Both the 'p' sound of the alliteration and the word 'powdery' contribute to the richness of the metaphor, recalling both the powdered wigs worn by the French aristocrats and the fragility of the mushrooms.

In the image of the mushrooms as 'Web-throated, stalked like triffids' (line 45), there is a blend of the reality of mushrooms as fungi and the fantastic qualities Mahon sees in them.

As he does throughout the poem, Mahon personifies the mushrooms as he describes them: they suffer thirst and sleeplessness, they are ready to scream in fright when the shed door is opened. Weak and decaying, they 'lift frail heads in gravity and good faith' (line 50). Here the reader is reminded of many scenes of mass suffering that have been captured by the world's media in photographs and on television.

Stanza 6

In the final stanza the silence of the mushrooms is seen as a plea to the world to remember them and the multitudes of the oppressed that they symbolise, among them the Jewish prisoners at Treblinka and the buried inhabitants of Pompeii. The tone of the poem becomes almost biblical as the mushrooms pray that they will not be abandoned again, that their silence and suffering will not be in vain. They seem to acknowledge the power of the poet (notice the pun on the word 'meter', line 59) in speaking on behalf of the powerless.

Derek Mahon

Interpreting the poem

The poem's setting in Co. Wexford and its connections with Farrell's novel have led to its being interpreted as dealing specifically with the twentieth-century Anglo-Irish conflict that culminated in the Northern Ireland Troubles. From this point of view, the plight of the mushrooms can be interpreted as that of the unionists, persisting in their frustrating and stultifying political vacuum. (Bear in mind that the poem was published in 1985, a time when the Unionists were adamantly opposed to any change in the Northern Ireland constitution.)

Some commentators have suggested that this interpretation is too restrictive. Instead, the poem's wide-ranging historical and political references may indicate a wider relevance, as a plea for remembrance on behalf of oppressed people everywhere.

Form of the poem

The poem is organized into six stanzas of ten lines each. Apart from the introductory first stanza, the end of which is marked by a comma, each stanza is self-contained and end-stopped. In effect this means that each stanza works as a paragraph, allowing the poet to make his point or develop his description at some length. You will notice, too, the long line lengths (some have up to twelve syllables), which allow for development and expansion. **The form of the poem is particularly appropriate to its meditative tone and complex historical theme.**

Thinking about the poem

1 Would you agree that the imagery of the first stanza suggests desolation and abandonment? Do you find the effect melancholy or eerie? Explain your answer.

2 What human qualities are ascribed to the mushrooms in the second and third stanzas? How is their plight suggested?

3 How does the language of the poem reflect the passing of time in the second and third stanzas?

4 Is it significant that the mushrooms have been waiting since civil war days, having been abandoned by the mycologist who never came back? What link does this reference create with the places and peoples mentioned in the first stanza?

5 How would you describe the tone and atmosphere of the fourth stanza? Look carefully at the language the poet uses. Do the mushrooms take on an even more poignant weight as metaphors of suffering and loss at this stage in the poem?

6 What echoes of historical suffering are found in the fourth stanza?

7 The moment of entry by the humans, presented in terms of an invasion, provokes a reaction of passive terror in the mushrooms. How does the poet dramatise this?

8 Would you agree that the images in which the mushrooms are presented in the fifth stanza are imaginative, almost surreal? Discuss the contribution made by the sound-effects – alliteration, onomatopoeia – in building the images.

9 In the final stanza the full symbolism of the mushrooms is made apparent. What exactly do they represent? In considering this, take into account not only the explicit historical references of the poem but also the potential contemporary implications for the Protestant people of Northern Ireland.

10 Look carefully at how the six stanzas are formed. Why did the poet choose longer lines and ten-line stanzas for his theme?

11 You have chosen to speak about this poem in a talk entitled 'Introducing Derek Mahon'. Write out the talk you would give.

12 Write a short essay giving your response (positive or negative) to the view that this is 'one of Mahon's finest poems'.

The Chinese Restaurant in Portrush

Before the first visitor comes the spring
Softening the sharp air of the coast
In time for the first 'invasion'.
Today the place is as it might have been,
Gentle and almost hospitable. A girl   5
Strides past the Northern Counties Hotel,
Light-footed, swinging a book-bag,
And the doors that were shut all winter
Against the north wind and the sea mists
Lie open to the street, where one   10
By one the gulls go window-shopping
And an old wolfhound dozes in the sun.

While I sit with my paper and prawn chow mein
Under a framed photograph of Hong Kong
The proprietor of the Chinese restaurant   15

Stands at the door as if the world were young,
Watching the first yacht hoist a sail
– An ideogram on sea-cloud – and the light
Of heaven upon the mountains of Donegal;
And whistles a little tune, dreaming of home.   20

Glossary

Title	*Portrush*: seaside resort in Co. Antrim
13	*chow mein*: Chinese fried noodle dish
18	*ideogram*: in Chinese writing, a written character or symbol that stands not for a word or sound but for the thing itself

Guidelines

'The Chinese Restaurant in Portrush' is collected in the volume *Poems 1962–1978*.

Mahon rarely deals with the Northern Ireland conflict in his poems, but we cannot ignore the implications of the title. Portrush, a seaside town in north Co. Antrim, has been a predominantly Protestant, unionist area of Northern Ireland. This lyrical depiction of the resort as a peaceful, welcoming place must be set against the backdrop of violence and intransigence in Northern Ireland at the time of writing.

Commentary

Stanza 1

The poem celebrates Portrush but also sees its shortcomings. The image of spring with which the poem opens combines pleasant anticipation with an undercurrent of defensiveness: a 'visitor' (line 1) might be seen as part of an 'invasion' (line 3) of the town. The town is 'gentle' but 'almost hospitable' – not totally welcoming yet (line 5). There is a note of regret in line 4: 'the place is as it might have been'. Does the poet seek to recapture the memory of Portrush as it might have been in the past? Or might he be expressing a desire to recapture the town as it might have been had the violence in Northern Ireland not affected it?

Lively visual images – the girl, the gulls, the dog – bring the place to life for the reader. Words such as 'light-footed', 'swinging', 'open', 'window-shopping' and 'sun' set up a contrast to the town as it has been in 'winter', with the 'north wind', 'sea mists' and 'shut' doors. The town seems to be waking up at last.

Stanza 2

When we meet the figures of the poet and the owner of the Chinese restaurant in the second stanza, the scene is one of pleasure and relaxation. The lines that follow have the clarity of a painting. Sitting in the Chinese restaurant under a framed photograph of Hong Kong, the poet relaxes with his paper and his food. He seems then to enter imaginatively into the mind of the proprietor of the restaurant and describes what he sees from that particular perspective as he looks out to sea.

The first yacht on the sea becomes 'An ideogram on sea-cloud' (line 18), like a symbol in Chinese writing. In the background both the poet and the restaurant owner can see the 'mountains of Donegal' (line 19). The image suggests beauty and peace, and the owner of the restaurant responds happily, but there is some poignancy when we recall that he is far away from home.

Themes of the poem

Underlying the poem are themes of identity and belonging. Neither of the main characters in the poem – the poet or the proprietor of the restaurant – 'belong' in Portrush. The poet, a native of Belfast, is one of the town's 'visitors'. He eats his 'foreign' food in a Chinese restaurant, owned by a man who has travelled a long way from his original 'home'. The photograph of Hong Kong on the wall (presumably his former 'home') suggests that it still means a great deal to him, and yet he has chosen to buy a restaurant in Northern Ireland, and therefore he belongs now in Portrush. When he dreams of home, as the last line says, he 'whistles a little tune', but not in a sad or nostalgic way. So the idea of visiting, of movement from one place to another, is central to the poem. Even the background images – the yacht, the Donegal hills – contribute to this idea. **By placing the place names throughout the poem in such close proximity with each other, the poem makes us aware of how one place can be viewed from another.**

Another aspect of the theme of identity that the poem could be said to examine, in an indirect way, is the relationship between the counties of Northern Ireland and of the Republic of Ireland, divided as they are by the border and governed by two different jurisdictions. When we read the poem we are conscious of how close Portrush is to Co. Donegal, and yet the distance between them seems almost as far as that between China and Portrush.

Thinking about the poem

1   What atmosphere is created by the images in the first stanza? Take into account the description of the weather, the girl, the gulls, the dog.

2   What is the poet suggesting in line 4 when he says, 'Today the place is as it might have been'? What feelings may lie behind this?

3   What does the phrase 'as if the world were young' (line 16) suggest to you?

4   Discuss the significance of the notions of place, visitors and home in this poem.

5   Would you agree that the visual images in the second stanza have the clarity and vividness of a painting? What features combine to create this impression?

6   'The poem celebrates the ordinary experiences of life amidst an awareness of their vulnerability to change.' Discuss this view of the poem.

7   Compare 'The Chinese Restaurant in Portrush' with 'Rathlin' and 'Kinsale' as poems that are concerned with place. Which do you prefer, and why?

8   'Mahon is preoccupied with questions of belonging and identity.' Discuss this view in relation to the poem above and **one** of Mahon's other poems.

Rathlin

A long time since the last scream cut short –
Then an unnatural silence; and then
A natural silence, slowly broken
By the shearwater, by the sporadic
Conversation of crickets, the bleak   5
Reminder of a metaphysical wind.
Ages of this, till the report
Of an outboard motor at the pier
Shatters the dream-time, and we land
As if we were the first visitors here.   10

The whole island a sanctuary where amazed
Oneiric species whistle and chatter,
Evacuating rock-face and cliff-top.
Cerulean distance, an oceanic haze –

Nothing but sea-smoke to the ice-cap 15
And the odd somnolent freighter.
Bombs doze in the housing estates
But here they are through with history –
Custodians of a lone light which repeats
One simple statement to the turbulent sea. 20

A long time since the unspeakable violence –
Since Somhairle Buí, powerless on the mainland,
Heard the screams of the Rathlin women
Borne to him, seconds later, upon the wind.
Only the cry of the shearwater 25
And the roar of the outboard motor
Disturb the singular peace. Spray-blind,
We leave here the infancy of the race,
Unsure among the pitching surfaces
Whether the future lies before us or behind. 30

Glossary	
Title	*Rathlin*: an island off the north coast of Co. Antrim
4	*shearwater*: an oceanic bird that skims the water
4	*sporadic*: occasional
12	*Oneiric*: relating to dreams
14	*Cerulean*: dark blue or sea-green
16	*somnolent*: sleepy
16	*freighter*: cargo-carrying boat
22	*Somhairle Buí*: Sorley Boy, chieftain of the MacDonnell clan of Antrim, whose castle was near Ballycastle, the nearest town on the Irish mainland to Rathlin

Guidelines

'Rathlin' is from the collection *Courtyards in Delft* (1981).

Rathlin Island, off the north coast of Co. Antrim, was the scene of a cruel massacre in the year 1575. The Earl of Essex, then Queen Elizabeth's marshal in Ireland, led his troops in a raid on the island. He and his soldiers succeeded in landing without being discovered, taking the inhabitants by surprise. They proceeded to destroy all the island's crops and cattle, before massacring in cold blood all the men, women and children on the island, including the wife and children of Somhairle Buí, chieftain of the MacDonnell clan. Their screams were said to have been heard by Somhairle Buí at his castle on the mainland at Ballycastle, Co. Antrim.

The poem is about a trip the poet takes to the island. His awareness of the island's violent history throws an ironic light on contemporary violence in Northern Ireland.

Commentary

Stanza 1

From the beginning the poet recalls the massacre that took place on Rathlin in a vivid image: the 'last scream cut short' that was followed by 'an unnatural silence' (lines 1 and 2). For a long time the only sounds were the sounds of nature, the cries of the birds and the noise made by crickets. Only the 'metaphysical wind' is a reminder of the past (line 6). The phrase suggests the abstract power of the wind to evoke death and loss. (We might remember that in 'Day Trip to Donegal' Mahon described the wind as 'vindictive'.)

The arrival of the 'visitors' (line 10) and the sound (the 'report', line 7) of the boat's engine seems to disturb the silence of the place, its dreamlike atmosphere. When they land, it is as if they are the 'first visitors', like the first inhabitants of the Garden of Eden.

Stanza 2

Everything on the island is seen as if in a dream. Beautiful visual images convey how peaceful it is. The birds are part of some 'oneiric' or dreamlike species (line 12), the sky is 'cerulean', (intensely blue or sea-green, line 14). All that can be seen is the haze on the ocean and the occasional slow-moving freighter or cargo ship.

But the poem does not retain its dreamlike atmosphere for long. Line 17 – 'Bombs doze in the housing estates' – brings the reader back to reality with a jolt. Threats of violence underlie the lives of ordinary people, just as violence had once destroyed the people of Rathlin. The phrase 'through with history' (line 18) has complex implications that readers may like to tease out for themselves. Does it suggest that Rathlin represents some post-historical place in which history has no relevance, because it all happened so long ago? This would be a comforting thought if it did not follow the ominous reference to the 'bombs' that 'doze' on the mainland, where history is still being made, as it were.

As 'custodians of a lone light' (literally, the lighthouse on the island, line 19), the island and its inhabitants can be seen metaphorically to represent the light of imagination, 'dream-time' (line 9), which offers peace and simplicity. It 'repeats' a 'simple statement' of peace, in contrast to the 'turbulent' sea (lines 19 and 20).

Stanza 3

In the third stanza the mood of the poem changes as we are reminded again of the historical violence that took place on Rathlin, the 'screams' of the women heard by Somhairle Buí. The 'cry of the shearwater' (line 25) and the 'roar of the outboard motor' (line 26) bring to an end the 'singular peace' (line 27) of the island as the poet and his companions leave what he calls the 'infancy of the race' (line 28). The phrase suggests a world of almost primordial innocence.

However, the final lines of the poem leave us with some questions. Does the poet suggest that the violence once known on Rathlin awaits them in the future, or does he suggest that the peacefulness he experienced on the island is what the future holds? Or might the ambiguity here reflect his own uncertainty about this question? Just as the journey has made them 'Spray-blind' (line 27), is the future also confusing?

Themes of the poem

Mahon rarely deals directly in his poems with the violence of what came to be known as the Troubles, but there are many poems, such as 'Rathlin', in which he expresses his unease at the situation. By invoking the violent history of the island he reminds us of the ongoing hostility between the British and the Irish, the source of the contemporary problems in Northern Ireland. We become aware as we read the poem that this historical violence can and may erupt again at any time, and the disturbing implications of this fact.

Images and metaphors

You may notice that Mahon uses the image of speech and its opposite, silence, throughout the poem. 'Silence', 'conversation', even 'report' – although it literally means the backfire noise of the outboard engine it is also possible to see its other meanings as 'rumour' or 'formal account of a case' as relevant to this trip to the island where such atrocities took place. Birds 'whistle and chatter', light from the lighthouse 'repeats / One simple statement'.

As a metaphor for beauty and peace, the image of light occurs frequently in Mahon's poetry. For instance, in 'A Disused Shed in Co. Wexford' light was seen as the mushrooms' saviour. In 'The Chinese Restaurant in Portrush' it suggests hope. The sea and the wind, on the other hand, have represented turmoil in other poems besides 'Rathlin', for instance in 'Day Trip to Donegal'.

Form of the poem

The poem is written in three ten-line stanzas. As in 'A Disused Shed in Co. Wexford', the length of stanzas acts like a paragraph that allows the poet to develop his ideas in a reflective way, as befits a poem dealing with serious and complex issues. There is no regular rhyme pattern, but sounds are repeated throughout, in assonance (e.g. the long 'o' sounds in 'custodians' and 'lone', line 19), consonance (e.g. 'Conversations of crickets', line 5) and sibilance (e.g. 'simple statement', line 20) creating a musical effect.

Thinking about the poem

1 The poem speaks of 'the singular peace' (line 27) on the island of Rathlin. How does the language help to convey this sense of peace?

2 What other perspective on the island is suggested? Do the contrasting images of violence, past as well as present, for instance, contribute to the atmosphere presented throughout the poem?

3 Would you agree that the poem is remarkable for the vividness and sensuousness of its natural imagery? Explain your answer.

4 How would you explain the line 'But here they are through with history' (line 18)? Is this idea echoed elsewhere in the poem?

5 The phrase 'dream-time' occurs in the first stanza. How is the notion of dreams elaborated upon in the poem?

6   What effect has the visit to the island had upon the speaker of the poem? Look carefully at the last two lines.

7   Why has the poet used the image of speech throughout the poem? Support your answer by reference to the poem.

8   Compare the poem with 'Day Trip to Donegal' as a description of nature and an evocation of mood. Which poem do you prefer, and why?

9   Would you agree that Mahon has a remarkable sense of place in his poems? Refer to the poem 'Kinsale' and 'The Chinese Restaurant in Portrush' as well as 'Rathlin' in your answer.

10 Critics have admired Mahon's 'acute eye and precise ear' as a poet. Discuss 'Rathlin' with this in mind.

Antarctica

(for Richard Ryan)

'I am just going outside and may be some time.'
The others nod, pretending not to know.
At the heart of the ridiculous, the sublime.

He leaves them reading and begins to climb,
Goading his ghost into the howling snow;   5
He is just going outside and may be some time.

The tent recedes beneath its crust of rime
And frostbite is replaced by vertigo:
At the heart of the ridiculous, the sublime.

Need we consider it some sort of crime,   10
This numb self-sacrifice of the weakest? No,
He is just going outside and may be some time –

In fact, for ever. Solitary enzyme,
Though the night yield no glimmer there will glow,
At the heart of the ridiculous, the sublime.   15

He takes leave of the earthly pantomime
Quietly, knowing it is time to go.
'I am just going outside and may be some time.'
At the heart of the ridiculous, the sublime.

Glossary

Title	*Antarctica*: the Antarctic is the southern polar region
Dedication	*Richard Ryan*: an Irish diplomat and poet
3	*sublime*: noble, awe-inspiring
5	*goading*: urging on
7	*rime*: frost
8	*frostbite*: damage to body tissue exposed to freezing temperatures
8	*vertigo*: dizziness, tendency to lose balance
13	*enzyme*: a protein that causes a living organism to change but is not changed itself
16	*earthly pantomime*: this world

Guidelines

This poem comes from the collection *Antarctica* (1985).

In 1912 the explorer Captain Robert Scott led an expedition to the South Pole, but he and his men perished in the attempt. An entry in Scott's diary, found after his death, describes how one of the men, Captain L.E.G. Oates, sacrificed himself in order to save food for the others by crawling out into a blizzard, saying only, 'I am just going out and may be some time.' These words have become famous as an example of understatement and of a certain kind of heroism. Mahon dramatises the incident in this villanelle, which matches beautifully the dignity of Oates's last grim resolve.

Commentary

Stanza 1

Oates's words open the poem and form one of the two refrains used throughout. Mahon depicts Oates's companions as nodding wordlessly, pretending that they do not know the true meaning of what he has said. They display the reserve and 'stiff upper lip' that the English were known for at that time.

In exploring the implications of Oates's words, and the reaction of his comrades, Mahon is writing from today's perspective where extreme heroic gestures have become rarer and even slightly suspect. The second refrain, 'At the heart of the ridiculous, the sublime', makes use of our familiarity with the expression 'from the sublime to the ridiculous'. We can see why Mahon might suggest that Oates's words are ridiculous in their failure to register even the smallest amount of emotion and in their glaring understatement. As we know, 'some time' means, in fact, for ever.

On the other hand, Mahon acknowledges the 'sublime' aspect of the event: the nobility and unselfishness with which Oates acted. From this point of view, the lack of emotion expressed by Oates's companions seems more like a brave acceptance of the inevitable.

Stanzas 2 and 3

As Oates climbs to his death, he is depicted in images of suffering and endurance that lend dignity to his famous words. He is seen to be 'Goading his ghost into the howling snow' (line 5), which captures the desperate nature of his situation. He suffers dizziness and frostbite. His experience is far from that suggested by his words 'just going outside', he is dying a lonely death in the cold snow.

Stanza 4

The poem questions present-day attitudes to such acts of 'self-sacrifice' (line 11). Why should they be seen as 'some sort of crime' (line 10)? Such a question would certainly never have been asked in the early twentieth century when the act took place. Generations of British children were brought up to admire Oates without qualification.

Stanzas 5 and 6

Mahon goes on to depict Oates, metaphorically, as a 'Solitary enzyme' or living thing that will glow in the night as a source of inspiration for others (lines 13 and 14). He knew the right thing to do and when to do it, leaving this world – described as an 'earthly pantomime' (line 16) – at a time of his own choosing. The refrain, ending finally with the word 'sublime', now appears as a tribute.

Form of the poem

A villanelle – said to have a singing line – is a form of poem in which there is a sequence of tercets (three lines), with rhyming scheme *aba, aba, aba*. Each tercet ends in a refrain, and there are only two refrains alternating throughout the poem. The set of tercets is rounded off with a quatrain in which the two refrains at last come together, one capping the other. A villanelle is a highly stylised, formal poem that has become associated with meditations on death or grief.

Mahon uses only two rhyme sounds throughout the nineteen lines of his poem: the rhyming 'time' and 'sublime' and the long 'o' sound of 'know', 'snow', 'vertigo' and other words. This could be said to enhance the feeling of emptiness and the sheer monotony of the Antarctic landscape in which the ill-fated expedition took place.

Thinking about the poem

1   Why might the words 'I am just going out and may be some time' be seen as 'ridiculous'?
2   Why are they also 'sublime'?
3   What picture of the members of the expedition do you get from reading this poem?
4   What sort of person was Oates, as suggested in the poem?
5   Choose which of the following phrases, in your opinion, best reveals the poet's attitude:

      He celebrates Oates's heroic act.

      He thinks Oates's act was foolish.

Explain your answer.
6   Does the poem succeed in creating a sense of the awful climate that the explorers experienced? Choose the words and phrases that best create this sense.
7   What is your own response to the issues raised in the poem?
8   Would Oates's action be appreciated nowadays? Give a reason for your view.

Taking a closer look

1   Choose your favourite lines from the poem and give a reason for your choice.
2   Explain what you think Mahon suggests when he asks: 'Need we consider it some sort of crime, / This numb self-sacrifice of the weakest?' (lines 10–11).
3   What attitude to life is expressed in the phrase 'earthly pantomime' (line 16), in your view?

Imagining

1   Imagine you are Captain Oates. In a diary entry for the night before you leave the tent, try to explain what you are about to do and why.

2   Imagine you are one of Oates's companions. You do not want him to sacrifice himself for you and the others. Write what you would say to persuade him not to go.

snapshot

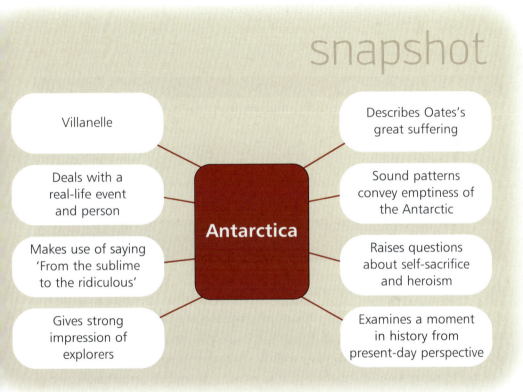

Villanelle

Deals with a real-life event and person

Makes use of saying 'From the sublime to the ridiculous'

Gives strong impression of explorers

Antarctica

Describes Oates's great suffering

Sound patterns convey emptiness of the Antarctic

Raises questions about self-sacrifice and heroism

Examines a moment in history from present-day perspective

Kinsale

The kind of rain we knew is a thing of the past –
deep-delving, dark, deliberate you would say,
browsing on spire and bogland; but today
our sky-blue slates are steaming in the sun,
our yachts tinkling and dancing in the bay   5
like race-horses. We contemplate at last
shining windows, a future forbidden to no-one.

Glossary

Title	*Kinsale*: a fishing village, now a thriving resort in Co. Cork
3	*browsing on*: feeding on

Guidelines

This poem comes from the collection *Antarctica* (1985).

It is difficult to read this poem without remembering the battle that took place in Kinsale in 1601, in which the Irish, led by Red Hugh O'Donnell and Hugh O'Neill, were defeated by the army of Elizabeth I – a decisive victory that altered the course of Irish history. Historians have viewed the defeat as marking the end of the old Gaelic rule of Ireland. Kinsale is now a thriving, fashionable town, well known for sailing activities and tourism. **The contrast between past and present is depicted in the imagery Mahon uses to describe it.**

Commentary

Lines 1–3

There are rich connotations in the phrase the 'kind of rain we knew' (line 1). It was 'deep-delving, dark, deliberate' (line 2) and is perceived as having been 'browsing on spire and bogland' (line 3). The heavy 'd' sounds in the adjectives suggest death and gloom, the burden of remembered history of what happened in Kinsale and its effect on church ('spire') and countryside ('bogland'). As in the poem 'Rathlin', the implication is that Kinsale is 'through with history'. So the rain that we in Ireland once knew is symbolic of a time of suffering and lament in the Irish consciousness, the defeat of the old Gaelic and Catholic order.

Lines 4–6
The images of darkness and sorrow are followed by images of light and movement. The effect is celebratory and carefree. Light, as we have seen in a number of Mahon's poems, signifies hope. The vividly sensuous image of 'our sky-blue slates' 'steaming in the sun' (line 4) captures the new optimistic atmosphere visually and aurally, with sibilance and alliteration giving a musical effect to the words. This musical effect is reinforced by the images of the 'yachts tinkling and dancing' (line 5), while the simile 'like race-horses' (line 6) paints a very attractive picture of the movement of the yachts on the sea. End-rhyme, used throughout, contributes to the sense of harmony that the poem celebrates.

Lines 6–7
The final two lines make the contrast with the past even clearer by looking to the future, a future in which windows will be 'shining' – the image implies happiness and success and, significantly, it will be there for all to enjoy: 'forbidden to no one' (line 7). Is this the new Ireland, free from the shackles of the past, the burden of history? **The attractions of this idea in the Ireland of 1985 (when the poem was published) were obvious, offering a way forward from attitudes that have caused so much grief and strife.**

Might it be significant that the last idea is expressed in a rather sombre way, as the word 'forbidden' suggests? Does this undermine the confident optimism of the poem? It is possible to interpret the images in this poem from an ironic perspective. 'Spire' and 'bogland' contrast greatly with 'race-horses' and 'yachts' and may suggest the desire of the 'new' Irish people to leave aside the old ways of life (religion and the land). From this point of view, the final comment – 'a future forbidden to no-one' (line 7) – is ironic since access to yachts and race-horses requires money.

Thinking about the poem

1   Look carefully at the poet's use of contrast in this short lyric. Might the rain and the sun have a metaphorical significance? Can you say what associations they might carry?
2   Would you agree that the sound patterns of the poem create a musical effect?

3   What is the dominant tone of the poem, in your view? Take into account the images of yachts and race-horses as well as those of spires and bogland.

4   Does the historical significance of Kinsale have any bearing on the theme of the poem, in your view?

5   Mahon has cited the work of the painter Raoul Dufy as an influence on his poetry, and on 'Kinsale' in particular. Dufy has painted watercolours and gouaches depicting harbour scenes, yachts and racecourses. You might like to find some illustrations of Dufy's work and comment on any connections you see between the two artists, painter and poet.

General Questions

1   'Why read the poetry of Derek Mahon?' Write out the text of a talk you would give in response to this title. Support the points you make by reference to the poetry of Derek Mahon on your course.

In your talk, you might include the following reasons:

- His themes are interesting and varied (e.g. explorations of history, individual experiences, personal narrative).
- He is capable of writing from many different perspectives, even unpopular ones.
- His use of language is precise and vivid, his metaphors and images are carefully chosen, his use of sound is musical and evocative.
- He has a keen sense of place to which the reader can respond well.
- He raises important questions, directly or indirectly, about political issues and attitudes.

Remember that you must support your points by detailed discussion of individual poems.

2   'I like (or do not like) the poetry of Derek Mahon'. Respond to this statement, referring to the poetry by Derek Mahon on your course.

Reasons you could give for liking Mahon's poetry include:

- His themes are wide-ranging and relevant to modern life.
- He refuses to be pigeon-holed as a poet from Northern Ireland.
- He enters imaginatively into the minds of others in his poems.
- He uses language in a precise and fresh manner, and often with the eye of a painter.
- Imagery and sound are used to great effect in his work.
- He responds to the beauty of nature and the atmosphere of places.

Reasons you could give for not liking Mahon's poetry include:

- The poet reveals very little about himself in his work.
- He remains too detached from the historical issues and political questions of his time.
- There is a certain lack of emotion in his work.
- When he does engage with political issues, his approach is too indirect.

3   Discuss the importance of history in Mahon's poems.

4   'In his poems Mahon is interested in giving a voice to those who are marginalised, no matter how unpalatable their views are.' To what extent is this true of the poems that are on your course?

5   Write a review of Mahon's poetry for a serious journal.

6   'In his poems Mahon has a keen sense of place'. Discuss.

7   Mahon has been described as a poet of 'great richness, elegance, and technical brilliance'. Do you agree with this opinion of Mahon's poetry? Give reasons for your answer.

8   'Although he rarely deals directly with the Troubles in Northern Ireland, Mahon is acutely aware of the effects of fanaticism and violence on society.' Do you agree with this point of view?

9   'Mahon's poems appeal to both the intellect and the emotions.' Discuss this view.

10   'A wide range of cultural reference makes Mahon's poetry appealing.' Would you agree with this statement?

Sample Essay

Derek Mahon explores people and places in his own distinctive style.

Write your response to this statement, supporting your answer with relevant quotation from or reference to the poems of Derek Mahon.

Derek Mahon's poetry appeals to me for many reasons. I particularly admire his ability to enter into the minds of other people and to communicate their experience. I also admire his gift of describing places so that they come to life for the reader.

[First statements refer directly to the terms of the question and indicate personal response]

The people who inhabit Mahon's poems range from those who are close to him, such as his grandfather in 'Grandfather', and those who are public figures, such as the hapless survivor of the *Titanic* in 'After the Titanic' or the zealous preacher in 'Ecclesiastes'.

[Introduces discussion of people, the first aspect of the question]

Mahon's distinctive style contributes to the effectiveness of these portrait poems. Even though he is describing a close relative in his sonnet 'Grandfather', Mahon shows very little personal emotion, allowing instead the images he uses to convey the personality of the old man. From the beginning of the poem he sets in motion the image of the old man as an outsider, someone who has refused to accommodate the needs and wishes of others. He is 'like a four-year-old' in the way he roams about the house early in the morning 'with a block of wood / Or a box of nails'. As Mahon says, he is 'up to no good' – but the word 'discreetly' hints at the essential privacy of the man, an idea reinforced in the sestet of the sonnet when we hear of his nightly escapades, how he returns home late 'as cute as they come'. This colloquial phrase and the image of him as he 'sets the clock / Against the future' suggest that there is a purpose to his activities. The word 'shrewd' implies that it is a clever form of self-preservation. The impression given is of someone who wishes to maintain his independence in the face of old age and impending death. Although the poem is short and at times wryly humorous, it succeeds in conveying a sense of a complex individual nearing the end of his life.

[First poem referred to, with suitable quotations; discussion includes content and style]

Mahon's poetic method is somewhat similar in 'After the Titanic', to the extent that the poet allows the images to speak for themselves without direct comment. In this poem the speaker is Bruce Ismay, president of the White Star Line, the owners of the *Titanic*. He had survived the disaster and was summoned to speak at the subsequent inquiry. Through the words he gives to Ismay, Mahon evokes the atmosphere of the disaster in vivid images. We can picture the speaker in his boat, 'shivering on the dark water'. A few well-chosen objects – 'prams, pianos, sideboards, winches' – crystallise the contents of the ship as it sinks, with onomatopoeic words and phrases – 'thundering', a 'pandemonium', 'boilers bursting' – conveying the chaos and terror of the event.

[Note how one paragraph links to the next]

Just as Mahon succeeded in capturing the essence of his grandfather's personality, he succeeds here in giving us an insight into the tormented mind of Ismay in the aftermath of the disaster. The metaphors and similes he uses convey a feeling of utter desolation. His 'poor soul / Screams out in the starlight', his heart 'breaks loose and rolls down like a stone'. It is impossible not to feel a certain compassion for the speaker as he now lives his life, isolated and vilified. And yet it is true to say that Mahon's poem has not justified Ismay's actions in any way.

[Second poem referred to, with suitable quotations]

A third poem in which Mahon explores the mind of another person is 'Ecclesiastes'. This poem appeals to me because it conveys not only the mindset of a particular individual, a zealous preacher, but also a whole way of life in a particular place: the Belfast of Mahon's youth. As such it could be said to show Mahon's ability to explore people and places at the one time. As he does in 'After the Titanic' with Bruce Ismay, the poet adopts the voice of another (this time a preacher) in 'Ecclesiastes', but the difference is that in 'Ecclesiastes' he identifies more closely with the speaker. He recognises that the preacher's way of life could have attractions for him. Something in his 'purist little puritan' personality accepts the dreariness of religion as it is practised in his native Belfast: 'the dank churches, the empty streets, / the shipyard silence, the tied-up swings'. He could even 'grow to love it' if it offered a chance to avoid the problems of human relationships and feeling compelled 'to understand and forgive'. These damning words portray the essence of this strict religion preached in Northern Ireland, associated as it is with the 'January rains' and the 'dark doors' of the city. But the poem suggests that this form of religion is destructive. It preaches religious intolerance to a 'credulous' people. It promises them 'nothing under the sun'. 'Ecclesiastes' is one of the few poems in which Mahon comes to terms with his identity as a poet from Northern Ireland, acknowledging honestly the influence it had on his upbringing. The vivid images and impassioned tone of the poem leave us in no doubt about Mahon's complex emotional relationship with the city of his birth.

[Discussion of third poem includes reference to both people and places]

As we have seen, Mahon explores how people think and feel. Through his distinctive and imaginative use of language (what has been called his 'acute eye and precise ear') he also has the ability to make the reader experience a sense of place. We can see this in 'Rathlin', 'The Chinese Restaurant in Portrush' and 'Kinsale'.

[Introduces discussion of place, the second aspect of the question]

In 'Rathlin' he recounts a trip made to the island. It is a peaceful place where the 'natural silence' is 'slowly broken / by the shearwater' – sibilance echoes the sound of the sea – and we can hear the sound of the birds in the onomatopoeic phrase 'whistle and chatter'. Beautiful visual images re-create the atmosphere: the 'oceanic haze' that surrounds it, the 'sea-smoke' that seems to rise to the mountain tops, the 'lone light' of the lighthouse. But Mahon also recalls the violent past of the island, where a cruel massacre took place in the sixteenth century. Similarly, he places its peacefulness in the context of the present-day 'bombs' that 'doze in the housing estates' on the nearby mainland. By doing so he goes beyond surface description to awaken in the reader a sense of the complexity of places and how they have their part to play in the history of a people. The island, he says, is a place that is 'through with history', but it cannot offer reassurance for the future, as the last two lines suggest. It is not clear whether 'the future lies before us or behind'.

[Fourth poem referred to, with suitable quotations]

Mahon explores places not only by imaginative description but also by acknowledging the complex nature of their background and history. We see this at work in both 'The Chinese Restaurant in Portrush' and 'Kinsale'. Both of these locations have connotations within the context of Irish history and politics. Portrush is a seaside resort in Co. Antrim, which has been a predominantly Protestant, unionist area of Northern Ireland. The poem must be set against the backdrop of the Troubles, the Northern Ireland conflict of the late twentieth century. It opens with an image of the spring 'softening the sharp air of the coast / in time for the first 'invasion''. The image suggests the changing season, but the words 'sharp' and 'invasion' have connotations of defensiveness that give the place its own distinct Northern Ireland 'personality'.

The poem goes on to celebrate Portrush. Pleasant images of the carefree girl walking past the hotel, the 'window-shopping' gulls and the old wolfhound as it 'dozes' in the sun bring the place to life for the reader. When we meet the poet he is in a relaxed mood, in a Chinese restaurant, with his 'paper and prawn chow mein', while the proprietor of the restaurant is standing idly at the door, looking out, enjoying the view. The whole scene has the clarity of a painting. But beyond the picture is an awareness of complex connections between places. Mahon provides a number of actual place names – Portrush, the Northern Counties (the name of a hotel here, but nevertheless a geographical region), Hong Kong and Donegal. We cannot ignore the adjective 'Chinese' either. By putting these names in close proximity to each other, Mahon makes us aware of how one place can be viewed from another. It casts an ironic light on the last word of the poem, 'home', which is a subjective idea, varying from one person to another. Without direct comment, as is part of his distinctive style, Mahon leaves the reader to contemplate the complex relationship people have with place.

[Fifth poem referred to, with suitable quotations]

'Kinsale' is a short and in my view very attractive poem. This title has historical connotations as the site of the Battle of Kinsale in 1601, in which the Irish were defeated by the army of Elizabeth 1. This decisive victory altered the course of Irish history. Mahon makes imaginative use of the contrast between the sorrows of the past in his image of the rain, 'deep-delving, dark, deliberate', and the present-day atmosphere of Kinsale with images of light and movement. Visually and aurally the imagery conveys happiness and freedom. Sibilance and alliteration combine in 'our sky-blue slates are steaming in the sun' to create a musical effect, as does the image of 'yachts tinkling and dancing in the bay'. They are 'like race-horses' – an unusual and attractive simile. End-rhyme, used throughout, adds to the sense of harmony. And unlike 'Rathlin', where the poet was unsure about the future, here he sees Kinsale as symbolic of a 'future forbidden to no-one'.

[Sixth poem referred to; note how quotations are incorporated into sentences throughout; as before, discussion includes both content and style]

In conclusion, in exploring people through his poetry Derek Mahon succeeds in conveying a sense of individual experience and personality, while recognising the complexity of the situations in which they find themselves. Similarly, in his exploration of particular places he goes beyond the surface description to convey a sense of their role in the history and emotions of a people. I greatly admire his achievement in doing so.

[Conclusion brings the two aspects of the question together and indicates a final response]

Derek Mahon

snapshot

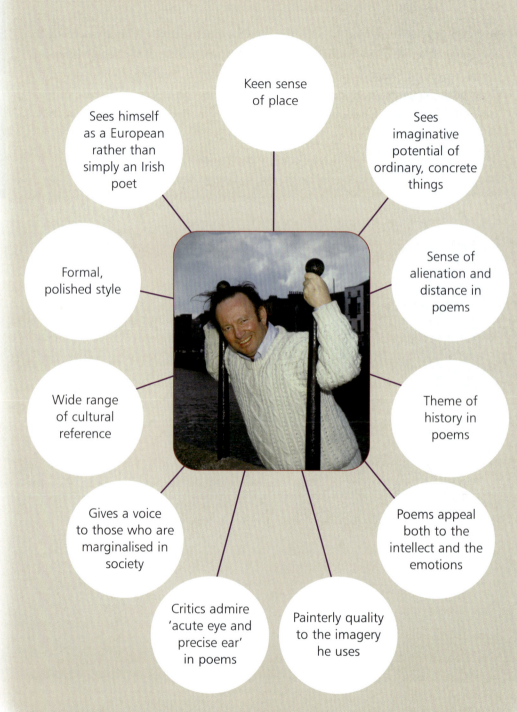

Keen sense of place

Sees himself as a European rather than simply an Irish poet

Sees imaginative potential of ordinary, concrete things

Formal, polished style

Sense of alienation and distance in poems

Wide range of cultural reference

Theme of history in poems

Gives a voice to those who are marginalised in society

Poems appeal both to the intellect and the emotions

Critics admire 'acute eye and precise ear' in poems

Painterly quality to the imagery he uses

Sylvia Plath

1932–63

Biography

Sylvia Plath was born in a seaside suburb of Boston, Massachusetts, in 1932. Both her parents, Otto Plath and Aurelia Schober, were academics and had German ancestry. They believed in the virtues of hard work and were committed to education. Sylvia was a bright, intelligent child and won many school prizes and awards.

When she was eight years old, her father died. On learning of his death, Plath declared, 'I'll never speak to God again.' Anxious to spare Sylvia and her younger brother, Warren, any unnecessary upset, Aurelia did not bring them to the funeral. Her father's death haunted Plath for the remainder of her life.

Otto's death left the family in straitened circumstances. Aurelia took up a full-time teaching job to support her children and Sylvia's grandparents moved in with the family in a house in the prosperous suburb of Wellesley. Plath later wrote that the move to Wellesley marked the end of her idyllic childhood by the sea.

The young writer

All through High School, Plath published poems and stories in local and national newspapers and in her school magazine. In her final year at school *Seventeen*, a national teen magazine, published her short story 'And Summer Will Not Come Again'. It was an important landmark in the young writer's life.

In 1951 Plath won two scholarships, which allowed her to attend Smith College, an exclusive women's college in Massachusetts. Her talent and intelligence were nurtured by the teaching staff there and she continued to have her work published. During her second year at Smith she was awarded a fiction prize by *Mademoiselle*, a fashionable, upmarket magazine for young women.

Personal insecurity

Despite academic, personal and social success, Plath was deeply insecure. The beginning of her third year in college saw her beset by many doubts and uncertainties. A four-week guest editorship at *Mademoiselle* in New York did little to improve matters.

Failure to secure a place on a summer writing course run by Frank O'Connor at Harvard in 1953 caused a crisis, and she was sent for psychiatric treatment. A poorly supervised and administered series of electric shock treatments worsened her condition and she made an attempt to take her own life. She was missing for three days, unconscious in a narrow space under the family home. She recovered her health over a period of six months with the help of a sympathetic psychiatrist.

Smith College offered Plath a scholarship to allow her to finish her degree, and she returned to the college in spring 1954, graduating with distinction. By then she had acquired a growing reputation as a writer.

Cambridge and early career

More success came her way in the form of a prestigious Fulbright scholarship to study at Cambridge University in England. Plath entered Newnham College in October 1955. It was in Cambridge that Sylvia Plath met the poet Ted Hughes. After a whirlwind romance, the couple married on Bloomsday, 16 June 1956. Following a two-month honeymoon in France and Spain, Plath returned to Cambridge to complete her studies. She continued to write, while, at the same time, helping Hughes to organise and send out his work. 'Black Rook in Rainy Weather' was written in this period.

The couple moved to the United States in summer 1957, and Plath taught for a year at Smith College. She found the job taxing and considered herself to be a poor teacher. She was also frustrated that she had so little time to devote to her writing. At the end of the academic year in summer 1958 she resigned her teaching position.

Plath rented an apartment in Boston. It did not go well. She suffered from writer's block and depression. 'The Times Are Tidy' was one of the few poems she completed. She was worried by financial concerns and tried to supplement their income by taking part-time secretarial work.

By summer 1959 things had improved. Hughes continued to write and publish and Plath, too, completed some poems and short stories. The couple then decided to return to England. First, however, they spent two months at a writer's colony in New York state. Relieved of domestic duties, Plath wrote freely and finished a number of the poems that are included in *The Colossus*, the only collection of her work published during her lifetime.

Mother, wife and poet

Frieda Rebecca Hughes, the couple's first child, was born in April 1960 in London. By this time Heinemann had agreed to publish *The Colossus* and Hughes had won the prestigious Somerset Maugham Award. Plath, however, was disappointed by the lack of reaction to *The Colossus* and, while she loved her husband and new daughter, found that the roles of mother and wife took her away from her writing.

1961 was a topsy-turvy year for Plath. It began with the sadness of a miscarriage, followed by an operation to remove an appendix. She likened her recovery from this to a resurrection. A contract with the *New Yorker* magazine boosted her morale and she began work on her novel, *The Bell Jar.*

When Plath became pregnant the couple decided to look for a house in the country, eventually moving, in autumn, to Court Green in Devon, a rambling, crumbling old house with three acres of lawn, garden and orchard. Despite her pregnancy, the care of a young daughter and the practicalities of setting up home in an old house, Plath wrote with great energy in her first months in Devon, though the poems she completed, including 'Finisterre' and 'Mirror', are marked by a sense of threat, fear and menace.

In January 1962 Plath gave birth to her second child, Nicholas. Her experience of birth and her remembrance of her miscarriage in the previous year inform her radio play *Three Women*, which she wrote for the BBC in spring 1962. The poems written later in 1962, most notably 'Elm', are dark meditations on love and self-knowledge.

By summer 1962 Plath's marriage to Hughes had begun to unravel. Hughes became involved with Assia Wevill, the wife of a Canadian poet. He left Court Green. A holiday in Ireland in September failed to save Plath's marriage.

Failing health

Back in Court Green in October and November 1962, Plath, working early each morning, wrote forty of the poems that make up the collection *Ariel*, including 'Poppies in July' and 'The Arrival of the Bee Box'. *Ariel* was published after her death. By any standards, these are remarkable poems.

Writing to a friend, she said, 'I am living like a Spartan, writing through huge fevers and producing free stuff I had locked in me for years.' The strain of writing these intense, personal poems began to affect her health. Her letters to her mother, from this period, are touched with desperation.

In November Plath decided to move back to London. She found a flat in the house where W. B. Yeats had once lived. By December she had closed up Court Green and moved into her new home with her two young children.

In January 1963 some of the worst weather seen in London for decades, allied to the delay in obtaining a phone, and the colds and flu she and the children suffered, cast her down and left her feeling isolated. She was further disheartened by the fact that her new work was, on the whole, rejected by the editors to whom she sent it. The publication of her novel, *The Bell Jar*, under a pseudonym, did little to lift the gloom.

Plath's final poems (including 'Child'), written in late January and early February 1963, reveal that her will to live was almost spent. She sought medical help and was put on a course of anti-depressants. Arrangements were made for her to see a psychiatrist. However, in the early hours of Monday 11 February 1963, overcome by a despairing depression, she took her own life.

Ariel, a collection of her final poems, was published in 1965. Since that time, it has sold over half a million copies. Plath's life, death and poetry have been the subject of much controversy. Understandably, given the tragic circumstances of her death, much of the response to her poetry has sought to relate her work to her life – to find clues in her poetry to explain her suicide or to attribute blame.

The difference between the personality that Plath reveals in her letters home to her mother and the darker personality of her journals has also attracted the attention of critics. Rarely has a poet left such a disputed body of work.

Social and Cultural Context

Plath was born into a male-dominated world. Her father ruled the family. Her mother was the wife and homemaker. Plath attended a college for girls, where she wanted to achieve and be a perfect American girl. Magazines like *The Ladies Home Journal* defined this ideal. A woman should be a wife, a homemaker and a mother, but she was not expected to be a professional or to have her own career. She was to be respectable. There was, in this middle-class culture, a tolerance of male promiscuity but girls were expected to be modest and virginal. Not to marry was to risk being labelled 'unfeminine'.

Plath struggled to escape this ideal of perfection. Her letters to her mother are full of references to her attempts to make a home for herself and Hughes and to win her mother's approval. She was conscious of this tendency in herself, noting in her journal: 'Old need of giving mother accomplishments, getting reward of love.' Her biographer, Anne Stevenson, says of the letters Plath wrote to her mother:

> Letters Home can be seen as one long projection of the 'desired image' (the required image) of herself as Eve – wife, mother, home-maker, protector of the wholesome, the good and the holy, an identity that both her upbringing and her own instinctive physical being had fiercely aspired to.

Search for an identity

Much of Plath's poetry can be seen as a struggle to create a new identity for herself that transcended the cultural limitations imposed upon women. Given society's view of women, Plath found it difficult to find acceptance as a writer outside of women's books and magazines. In her lifetime, her work won serious admiration from only a small number of people. She was more famous for being the wife of the poet Ted Hughes than for being a talented, ambitious and dedicated poet, novelist and short story writer, in her own right.

Plath's desire to fit in at school and be an all-American girl was deepened by her consciousness of her German ancestry. Plath's use of Holocaust imagery and her reference to her father as a Nazi in her poem 'Daddy' indicate a feeling of displacement, a fear that she might, somehow, be tainted by her origins. She also employed Holocaust imagery to speak of the suffering of women.

More than is sometimes acknowledged by critics, Plath was attuned, in a personal way, to the major historical issues of her time. She lived during the period of the Cold War and the ever-present threat of nuclear warfare between the United States and the Soviet Union. She was conscious of the dangers of a nuclear conflict and concerned for the future safety of her children. Plath wrote of these fears in a letter to her mother in December 1961:

> The reason I haven't written for so long is probably quite silly, but I got so awfully depressed two weeks ago by reading two issues of *The Nation* all about the terrifying marriage of big business and the military in America . . . and the repulsive shelter craze for fallout, all very factual, documented and true, that I simply couldn't sleep for nights with all the warlike talk in the papers . . . I began to wonder if there was any point in trying to bring up children in such a mad, self-destructive world. The sad thing is that the power for destruction is real and universal.

The fears expressed here find their way into her poetry in the terrifying imagery of her last poems.

Displacement

For Plath, the opportunity to live and study in England was a partly liberating experience. From England she could view with clarity the consumerism and militarism of US culture. However, she did not always feel at home in England and disliked the shabby inefficiency that she saw in English life. Plath was caught between the two cultures, feeling ambivalent towards both. Her feelings of displacement are important in shaping the poetry she wrote.

Timeline

1932	Born on 27 October in Boston, Massachusetts
1940	Her father dies. Sylvia declares, 'I'll never speak to God again'
1950	*Seventeen* publishes her story 'And Summer Will Not Come Again'
1951	Wins scholarship to the exclusive Smith College for women
1953	Wins guest editorship at *Mademoiselle* magazine; attempts suicide after failing to gain a place on writing course in Harvard
1954	Graduates with distinction from Smith College
1955	Wins Fulbright Scholarship and goes to Cambridge; meets the poet Ted Hughes
1956	Marries Hughes on Bloomsday
1960	Gives birth to Frieda Rebecca Hughes, the couple's first child; publishes first collection, *The Colossus*
1961	Moves to Devon; writes with great energy in first months there; concerned by talk of nuclear warfare
1962	Gives birth to her son, Nicholas; Plath and Hughes separate; writes over 40 poems in October and November; moves to London
1963	Publishes her novel, *The Bell Jar*; takes her own life in February
1965	*Ariel*, a collection of her last poems, is published

Black Rook in Rainy Weather

On the stiff twig up there
Hunches a wet black rook
Arranging and rearranging its feathers in the rain.
I do not expect miracle
Or an accident   5

To set the sight on fire
In my eye, nor seek
Any more in the desultory weather some design,
But let spotted leaves fall as they fall,
Without ceremony, or portent.   10

Although, I admit, I desire,
Occasionally, some backtalk
From the mute sky, I can't honestly complain:
A certain minor light may still
Leap incandescent   15

Out of kitchen table or chair
As if a celestial burning took
Possession of the most obtuse objects now and then –
Thus hallowing an interval
Otherwise inconsequent   20

By bestowing largesse, honour,
One might say love. At any rate, I now walk
Wary (for it could happen
Even in this dull, ruinous landscape); sceptical,
Yet politic; ignorant   25

Of whatever angel may choose to flare
Suddenly at my elbow. I only know that a rook
Ordering its black feathers can so shine
As to seize my senses, haul
My eyelids up, and grant   30

A brief respite from fear
Of total neutrality. With luck,
Trekking stubborn through this season
Of fatigue, I shall
Patch together a content   35

Of sorts. Miracles occur,
If you care to call those spasmodic
Tricks of radiance miracles. The wait's begun again,
The long wait for the angel,
For that rare, random descent.   40

Glossary	
8	*desultory*: changing in a random way
10	*portent*: omen, a sign or indication of a future event
15	*incandescent*: red hot or white hot, shining, luminous
17	*celestial*: heavenly
18	*obtuse*: dull, insensitive
19	*hallowing*: to make holy or sacred
20	*inconsequent*: trivial, insignificant
21	*largesse*: generosity
23	*Wary*: alert, vigilant
25	*politic*: discreet, prudent
31	*respite*: rest, temporary relief
33	*Trekking*: making a long, hard journey
37	*spasmodic*: something that happens in sudden, brief spells

Guidelines

'Black Rook in Rainy Weather' is contained in Plath's first collection, *The Colossus* (1960). It was originally published in the English journal *Granta*, while she studied at Cambridge.

The poem alerts us to many features of Plath's style:

- **The confident handling of rhyme and stanza form.**
- **The exploration of emotions and states of mind.**
- **The use of weather, colours and natural objects as symbols.**
- **The dreamlike or surreal world of the poem.**

This poem explores the nature of poetic inspiration, and the necessity of such inspiration to ward off the speaker's fear of total neutrality. There is no simple relationship between the 'I' of the poem (the persona or speaker) and the writer. In fact, many of her poems can be read as Plath trying out different identities.

Commentary

Describing the world

The poem begins with a clear description of the rook, sitting 'Arranging and rearranging feathers in the rain' (line 3). The sight is ordinary. The speaker of the poem tells us that she does not expect a 'miracle / Or an accident / To set the sight on fire' (lines 4–6). The words 'miracle' and 'fire' set up a contrast between the damp weather (the reality) and the fire of vision (the poet's imagination). The speaker is not expecting anything to happen. Her muse, her inner vision, seems to have deserted her. So she describes what she sees, content to let the world be as it is.

The word 'portent' (line 10) suggests the tradition of seeing the weather as a warning of things to come. The colour black is also associated with the ancient art of divination or prediction. In pre-Christian times a poet was considered to be a seer, a person possessed with the supernatural power of vision. This idea informs the poem's exploration of inspiration.

Inspiration

In stanza 3 the poet confesses that although she would like the sky to speak to her, she is not complaining. The reason for this is that the speaker believes that even the most ordinary object, such as a 'kitchen table or chair' (line 16), may appear transformed as if it was possessed by some heavenly fire. This visionary experience is described, in lines 19 to 22, in terms of heavenly generosity and love.

Although not stated directly, the poem suggests that poetic inspiration is like a gift from heaven. It is not within the control of the poet. It is not a matter of will

or determination. **Inspiration, when it happens, has the quality of accident, favour and giftedness about it.** Nor is it that the poet is inspired, but rather that the world is transformed in the poet's presence. The adjectives 'incandescent' (line 15) and 'burning' (line 17) suggest the force and power of the experience of inspiration.

The speaker tells us that she is waiting for the angel, the symbol of heavenly visitation and inspiration, 'to flare / Suddenly at my elbow' (lines 26–27). The description of the landscape as 'dull, ruinous' (line 24) suggests how much the poet wants the angel to appear, while the adjective 'sceptical' in the same line implies that she is trying not to hope too much.

Fear and hope

Yet, the rook gives her reason to hope, for in catching a sight of him, she feels a lifting of her spirit and 'A brief respite from fear / Of total neutrality' (lines 31–32). These two lines are key to understanding the emotional centre of the poem. **Without vision, without the inspiration to write, the poet fears 'total neutrality'.** The words suggest a state of non-being, a blank. (This kind of fear is expressed in a number of other poems, including 'Poppies in July'.)

In lines 32 and 36 the speaker's voice falters, overcome by fatigue but hoping, 'With luck', to 'Patch together a content / Of sorts'. **The final stanza is balanced between faith and scepticism, between 'miracles' and 'tricks' (line 38). However, the poet's belief, or desire to believe, or need to believe, is expressed in the beautiful ending.** The image of the angel's 'rare, random descent' (line 40) calls to mind Pentecost, when, according to the biblical account, tongues of fire appeared over the apostles and they were filled with the Holy Spirit.

It is clear from this poem that for the speaker/poet, the threat to her well-being is posed by a fear of 'neutrality' (line 32). She is afraid that without moments of vision and the reassurance of her creativity, life and identity will be intolerable.

Style and form of the poem

The poem is written in unrhymed five-line stanzas, a form that Plath also uses in 'The Times Are Tidy' and 'The Arrival of the Bee Box'. The form allows for flexibility in rhythm and pacing. Reading the poem aloud allows you to hear the intricate sound patterns that Plath creates and the way in which she marries sound to the emotional tone of the poem. Consider, for example, the long, vowel sounds and the alliteration in line 33, which capture the effort and drudgery in going on: 'Trekking stubborn through this season'.

Thinking about the poem

1   What attitude to the rook and the weather does the speaker of the poem express in the first two stanzas? What do these stanzas suggest to you about the speaker?

2   How do you understand the idea of celestial burning, as presented in the poem? In your experience can ordinary objects be seized in the way described in lines 14 to 22 of the poem?

3   Consider the character of the speaker of the poem, as suggested by the adjectives ('wary', 'sceptical', 'politic') in lines 23 to 25. Having read the poem, what additional adjectives would you use to describe the speaker?

4   What is the fear referred to at the outset of stanza 7? Consider the possible meanings of the word 'neutrality' (line 32). How might the rook allay this fear? What is the relationship between the rook and the celestial burning referred to in the fourth stanza?

5   What is it that the speaker hopes to achieve, 'With luck' (lines 32–35)? What is your reaction to this hope?

6   What belief is expressed in the final stanza? How is the belief qualified?

7   'The wait's begun again' (line 38). Comment on the word 'again'.

8   'Trekking stubborn through this season / Of fatigue' (lines 33–34). Write a note on these lines and the way in which sound and sense combine.

9   The beauty of the last two lines of the poem has been remarked on by critics. What, in your view, makes them beautiful?

10 Examine the stanza form employed by the poet and comment on it.

11 Comment on the images of heat and light in the poem, and their relevance to the theme of the poem.

12 Consider the title of the poem and its relevance to the theme of the poem.

13 What does the poem say to you about imagination and the vision of the poet?

14 'The speaker of the poem is poised between hope and despair.' Comment on this view of the poem, supporting your answer by reference to the poem.

15 'Behind the controlled language of the poem there is a glimpse of a fearful and nightmarish personal world.' Is this a fair assessment? Support your answer by reference to the poem.

The Times Are Tidy

Unlucky the hero born
In this province of the stuck record
Where the most watchful cooks go jobless
And the mayor's rôtisserie turns
Round of its own accord.   5

There's no career in the venture
Of riding against the lizard,
Himself withered these latter-days
To leaf-size from lack of action:
History's beaten the hazard.   10

The last crone got burnt up
More than eight decades back
With the love-hot herb, the talking cat,
But the children are better for it,
The cow milk's cream an inch thick.   15

Sylvia Plath

Glossary	
2	*province*: here, a historical period; the word also carries the derogatory suggestion of a place that is culturally backward
2	*stuck record*: something that is going nowhere, as when a needle on a record player gets stuck on the vinyl surface of a record
3	*watchful cooks*: from the Middle Ages onwards the poisoning of food was common in attempts on the lives of the powerful; thus, cooks had to be vigilant, wary and politic
4	*rôtisserie*: traditionally, a pointed rod with a turning handle on which meat is skewered and roasted; today, an electric cooking apparatus, with a rotating spit
7	*lizard*: used here as a synonym for dragon
10	*hazard*: danger, risk; here, personal adventure
11	*crone*: withered old woman, witch

Guidelines

'The Times Are Tidy' was published in the 1960 collection, *The Colossus.* The poem was written during the summer of 1958, after Plath had resigned from her job as a teacher at Smith College.

This is one of the few Plath poems in which the 'I' persona does not appear. **The poem is a straightforward social comment on the blandness of contemporary culture compared with the fairy-tale world of the past.** (As a way of keeping up her German, the language of her ancestors, Plath read *Grimm's Fairy Tales.*)

Commentary

Stanza 1

The tone of the poem is ironic. It begins with a statement: 'Unlucky the hero born / In the province of the stuck record'. The suggestion is that the present is an unheroic age, with little opportunity for adventure or valour.

Stanza 2

The second stanza introduces the figure of the knight riding to battle the dragon ('lizard', line 7). There is no career, we are told, in such heroism. The word 'career' (line 6) suggests the difference between the heroic age of the past (not specified in time or place) and the career-minded world of the late 1950s. The stanza concludes with the statement: 'History's beaten the hazard' (line 10). Adventure is dead. It is impossible to read Plath's assessment of the bland safety of public life without thinking of the hazards that she feared in her private world.

Stanza 3

There is an ironic edge to the regret that announces: 'The last crone got burnt up / More than eight decades back' (lines 11–12). Magic and mystery, it seems, have died with her. The 'but' that introduces the two last lines is unconvincing; the speaker does not really believe that 'the children are better for it' (line 14) or that the thick cream is compensation.

Interestingly, around the time Plath wrote 'The Times Are Tidy', she and Ted Hughes were experimenting with a Ouija board. Plath found these sessions both intriguing and entertaining. She also shared Hughes' interest in tarot cards and horoscopes. **The consumer culture, rapidly developing in urban America, was too sanitised and removed from the superstitious beliefs that attracted her.** Perhaps the poem hints at the difference between Hughes' home county of Yorkshire in northern England, where superstitions still survived, and the urban culture of the United States, where they had disappeared.

Form of the poem

The poem shows Plath's attention to the craft of poetry. In each stanza there are interesting patterns of sound. Look, for example, how the vowel sounds 'o' and 'u' are woven into stanza 1. The 'k' sound in the first word of the poem is repeated at intervals and concludes the poem. The stanzas and rhymes are carefully worked. You might like to consider if all the rhymes are successful. Consider the lizard / hazard rhyme of stanza 2. Are the words well chosen?

Thinking about the poem

1. How is the disappearance of the world of fairy-tale adventure suggested in the first stanza?

2. Comment on the phrase 'the stuck record' (line 2) and the attitude it conveys.

3. Give examples of the people of whom it might be said they rode 'against the lizard' (line 7).

4. What is the meaning of the statement 'History's beaten the hazard' (line 10).

5. How do you interpret the references to 'the love-hot herb' and 'the talking cat' (line 13)?

6. In your opinion, does the speaker believe that the gains referred to in the last two lines compensate for the losses mentioned in the rest of the poem? Support your answer by reference to the poem.

7. Describe the tone and mood of the poem and the attitude it expresses towards the contemporary world. Refer to the title of the poem, in your answer.

8. Is this a well-crafted poem? Explain your answer.

9. The poem is dismissed by some critics as a mere 'exercise'. What is your assessment of the poem?

Morning Song

Love set you going like a fat gold watch.
The midwife slapped your footsoles, and your bald cry
Took its place among the elements.

Our voices echo, magnifying your arrival. New statue.
In a drafty museum, your nakedness   5
Shadows our safety. We stand round blankly as walls.

I'm no more your mother
Than the cloud that distils a mirror to reflect its own slow
Effacement at the wind's hand.

All night your moth-breath   10
Flickers among the flat pink roses. I wake to listen:
A far sea moves in my ear.

One cry, and I stumble from bed, cow-heavy and floral
In my Victorian nightgown.
Your mouth opens clean as a cat's. The window square   15

Whitens and swallows its dull stars. And now you try
Your handful of notes;
The clear vowels rise like balloons.

Glossary	
3	*elements*: earth, air, water and fire
9	*Effacement*: obliteration, erasure
11	*flat pink roses*: presumably the patterned wallpaper
13	*cow-heavy*: the poet's amused reference to her breasts heavy with milk

Guidelines

Plath wrote 'Morning Song', a poem on the birth of her daughter, in spring 1961, ten months after Frieda's birth, and shortly after a miscarriage. It was first published in *The Observer* newspaper in May 1961 and was later included in her posthumous collection *Ariel*, published in 1965. In November 1962 Plath arranged the poems for her collection, placing 'Morning Song' first so that the manuscript would begin with the word 'love' and end with the word 'spring' from the poem, 'Wintering'. (The published collection does not follow her wishes.)

'Morning Song' is clearly a celebration of birth, but there is also a suggestion of loss and separation in the imagery of the poem. The poem begins with the word 'love' and ends with the music of the child's cry rising 'like balloons'. In between it charts the mother's journey from her initial disorientation to her joyful acceptance of her baby.

Commentary

Estrangement

'Morning Song' opens with a bold statement and a striking image: 'Love set you going like a fat gold watch.' There is little sense of the miraculous or the mysterious in the slap that sets the child crying. The child's cry is described as 'bald' (line 2). It seems to express a basic instinct and, therefore, takes 'its place among the elements' (line 3). **The voice of the narrator, the mother, seems puzzled by what is happening, even as she speaks to her child. The sense of estrangement is captured in the imagery of the second stanza, where things seem out of proportion.** For example, 'Our voices echo, magnifying your arrival' (line 4).

The baby is like an exhibit in a museum, around whom the adults stand, unable to make sense of what it is they are looking at. The museum imagery is striking. The description of the baby as a 'New statue' (line 4) may indicate that the baby resembles a perfect work of art. The baby's fragility, her 'nakedness' in the 'drafty museum' (line 5), causes the parents to feel anxious about their ability to protect and safeguard the child they have brought into the world. This doubt is suggested in the phrase 'Shadows our safety' (line 6); *a* line that will support many interpretations. The word 'blankly' (line 6) is particularly significant as it implies that the experience of birth has somehow robbed the parents of their identity.

The sense of estrangement leads to a declaration in stanza 3, which rehearses an often-expressed fear in Plath's work: the fear of effacement, of annihilation. She fears that the birth of her child will rob her of her identity, just as the rain creates a mirror (in the form of a puddle or pool of water) in which the cloud is reflected and can see its own dispersal by the wind. This is a complex image of the relationship between mother and daughter.

Mother's protective response

There is a change in tone in the fourth stanza. The sound of the child's breath, symbolising its fragile, though insistent, hold on life, evokes the mother's protective response. After the estrangement of the opening stanzas, where the mother's response was frozen into an attitude of a blank wall in a museum setting, a more recognisable, domestic world appears. In contrast to the immobility of the second stanza, the child's cry stirs the mother into activity. Having regained her composure and her sense of self, she can laugh at herself: 'cow-heavy and floral / In my Victorian nightgown' (lines 13–14).

The speaker is now involved with her child, filled with wonder as her 'mouth opens clean as a cat's' (line 15). The image resonates with amused delight. The quality of happiness continues in the imagery of the growing light. **The poem ends on a note of elation as the child's 'clear vowels rise like balloons'** (line 18).

Form of the poem

The poem is written is unrhymed three-line stanzas. The first line has ten syllables, which is the standard line length in English poetry. What is interesting in the poem is how Plath breaks the line to achieve certain effects. Look, for example, how the short line 10 creates a space that is filled by 'flickers' on line 11, so that that we almost hear the child's breath in the sound and rhythm of the stanza.

Thinking about the poem

1   Comment on the importance of the words 'love' and 'elements' in the first stanza of the poem.
2   In what way is the child a 'New statue' (line 4)?
3   Explain, as clearly as you can, the museum imagery in stanza 2. What does it suggest about the relationship between the adults and the new-born child?
4   Tease out the meaning of the statement, 'your nakedness / Shadows our safety' (lines 5–6).
5   What is the tone of the declaration, 'I'm no more your mother' (line 7)?

6 What kind of relationship between mother and child is described in the cloud, mirror and wind imagery of the third stanza? Is it a distinctive view or does it express a general truth?

7 What does the moth imagery in stanza 4 suggest about the child?

8 What picture of the new mother is created in stanzas 4 and 5?

9 What is your favourite image in the poem? Explain your choice.

10 'Although tender in tone, the poem is clear-sighted and unsentimental.' Discuss this view of the poem.

11 'Even though the poem celebrates motherhood, the mother appears as an isolated and estranged figure.' Do you agree with this assessment of the poem? Support your answer by reference to the poem.

12 How do you imagine Frieda Hughes reacting to this poem about her birth?

Finisterre

This was the land's end: the last fingers, knuckled and rheumatic,
Cramped on nothing. Black
Admonitory cliffs, and the sea exploding
With no bottom, or anything on the other side of it,
Whitened by the faces of the drowned.   5
Now it is only gloomy, a dump of rocks –
Leftover soldiers from old, messy wars.
The sea cannons into their ear, but they don't budge.
Other rocks hide their grudges under the water.

The cliffs are edged with trefoils, stars and bells   10
Such as fingers might embroider, close to death,
Almost too small for the mists to bother with.
The mists are part of the ancient paraphernalia –
Souls, rolled in the doom-noise of the sea.
They bruise the rocks out of existence, then resurrect them.   15
They go up without hope, like sighs.
I walk among them, and they stuff my mouth with cotton.
When they free me, I am beaded with tears.

Our Lady of the Shipwrecked is striding toward the horizon,
Her marble skirts blown back in two pink wings.   20
A marble sailor kneels at her foot distractedly, and at his foot
A peasant woman in black
Is praying to the monument of the sailor praying.
Our Lady of the Shipwrecked is three times life size,
Her lips sweet with divinity.   25
She does not hear what the sailor or the peasant is saying –
She is in love with the beautiful formlessness of the sea.

Gull-coloured laces flap in the sea drafts
Beside the postcard stalls.
The peasants anchor them with conches. One is told: 30
'These are the pretty trinkets the sea hides,
Little shells made up into necklaces and toy ladies.
They do not come from the Bay of the Dead down there,
But from another place, tropical and blue,
We have never been to.   35
These are our crêpes. Eat them before they blow cold.'

Glossary	
Title	*Finisterre*: English name for Finistère, the westernmost part of Brittany, France
1	*land's end*: the literal meaning of 'Finisterre'; from earliest times it was believed that the horizon marked the end of the created world
1	*fingers*: here, rocks jutting into the sea; the imagery suggests the desperate clinging of a drowning person
3	*Admonitory*: warning
7	*Leftover soldiers*: maimed veterans of the Algerian war
10	*trefoils, stars and bells*: wildflowers, identified by shape rather than name
13	*paraphernalia*: bits and pieces, miscellaneous items; here Plath is referring to the belief that the mists are the souls of the dead and associating this superstition with Finisterre
19	*Our Lady of the Shipwrecked*: statue commemorating lives lost at sea

Guidelines

'Finisterre' was among a group of poems that Plath wrote in autumn 1961, shortly after moving to Devon with her husband, Ted Hughes, and their daughter, Frieda. **Although this was one of the happiest periods of her personal life, the poems she wrote are dark.**

In June 1960 Plath and Hughes motored through Brittany, swimming along the rocky coastline of Finisterre. They also stopped at Berck-Plage, a seaside resort with a sanatorium for soldiers wounded in the Algerian war. Plath saw maimed soldiers limp among the holiday makers. The experience made a profound impression and called to mind her father's death, following the amputation of his leg. **The poems she wrote about Brittany – 'Finisterre' and 'Berck-Plage' – share a sense of death and menace, contrasting images of permanence and stability with those of formlessness and annihilation.** In this regard, it is worth bearing in mind that 'Finisterre' was written during a period when there was a serious risk of nuclear conflict between the Soviet Union and the United States. Plath wrote of her fears in a letter to her mother in December 1961.

The ocean played an important part in Plath's childhood and is a constant in the imagery of her poems. In a letter to her mother, written in 1958, she said, 'I am going back to the ocean as my poetic heritage.' She also wrote in her journal a note on the title of another of her poems, 'Full Fathom Five', which gives an insight into the importance of the sea for her:

> 'Full Fathom Five' . . . has the background of *The Tempest*, the association of the sea, which is a central metaphor for my childhood, my poems and the artist's subconscious, of the father image . . . and the pearls and coral highly wrought to art; pearls sea-changed from the ubiquitous grit of sorrow and routine.

As a twelve-year-old, Plath saw Shakespeare's *The Tempest*, a play that begins with a shipwreck, and she later associated Ariel's song, 'Full fathom five, thy father lies; / Of his bones are coral made', in that play with her own dead father.

Commentary

Different interpretations

At one level, 'Finisterre' is a description of a seaside resort. It depicts the rocky shoreline and the cliffs that surround the bay known as the Bay of the Dead. It describes the mists that rise from the sea, and the statue of Our Lady of the Shipwrecked, a memorial to the sailors who died at sea. The poem concludes with a description of the stalls and the trinkets sold by the local peasants. At another level,

'Finisterre' is a symbolic poem, in which the meeting of ocean and land is presented in terms of the recurrent drama of death and rebirth, of entrapment and freedom, and of form and formlessness. As with other Plath poems, the symbolic language sends the reader off in many directions. Thus, 'Finisterre' can support different interpretations.

Form and formlessness

The vocabulary of the opening stanza suggests a pattern of force – 'knuckled', 'cramped', 'exploding' and 'cannons' – and of annihilation – 'end', 'last', 'nothing', 'Black' and 'bottom'. It is as if the Bay of the Dead is a site of battle between the sea and the land.

In the second stanza Plath sees, in the relationship between the sea mist and the rocks, an archetype or symbol of death and resurrection. In describing the rocks and the sea mist, the poem juxtaposes the fixed and the fluid. The fixed forms of the rocks seem threatened by the formlessness of the sea and the mist, but they survive.

The imagery of fixed forms and formlessness appears in the third stanza where the statue of Our Lady of the Shipwrecked is said to be 'in love with the beautiful formlessness of the sea' (line 27).

Final stanza

There is a shift of tone in the fourth stanza. We are back in the world of the living, on firm land. The peasants sell 'pretty trinkets' (line 31) to the tourists. The locals do not want their souvenirs to be associated with the Bay of the Dead. They tell her that the trinkets come from 'another place, tropical and blue' (line 34).

This place is like the world of Plath's childhood or the world of her poetry. She takes elements from the sea of her unconscious and makes them into poems. The poem ends with the peasants offering her some sustenance. They urge her to eat before the food goes cold. Although eating is associated with nurture, the final word of the poem, 'cold', returns to the idea of death that haunts the poem.

Thinking about the poem

1. The first five lines give a vivid account of the beliefs/fears once held about the sea. Describe these. Is there a relationship between these fears/beliefs and the private fears of speaker of the poem?

2. How is Finisterre regarded now, according to lines 6 to 9? Comment on the rock imagery in these lines.

3. Examine the description of the flowers and the mist in stanza 2. How are both associated with death?

4. Comment on Plath's use of the verb 'bruise' in line 15. Is it effective?

5. 'I walk among them, and they stuff my mouth with cotton. / When they free me, I am beaded with tears' (lines 17–18). What do you make of these lines and the drama they describe? (Are the mists/souls presented as hostile? Do they prevent her from speaking? Is the speaker in the poem more in sympathy with the ancient or the modern view of the place . . . ?)

6. How is Our Lady of the Shipwrecked presented in the third stanza? Is it a surprising representation?

7. Comment on the phrase, 'the beautiful formlessness of the sea' (line 27).

8. In lines 31 to 35 the peasants speak of 'the pretty trinkets that the sea hides', which come from a place far away. How do you interpret these lines?

9. Does the poem end on a hopeful note? Give reasons for your answer.

10. In your view, is the speaker of the poem attracted to the sea? Plath regarded the sea as an image of the artist's subconscious. What does the description of the sea in the poem suggest about Plath's subconscious and its concerns?

11. The poem arose from a holiday visit to a seaside resort. What does her treatment of this visit in the poem suggest to you about the personality and imagination of the poet? Support the points you make by quotation from the poem.

12. Choose one stanza from the poem and write a response to the sounds and imagery of the stanza.

Sylvia Plath

Mirror

I am silver and exact. I have no preconceptions.
Whatever I see I swallow immediately
Just as it is, unmisted by love or dislike.
I am not cruel, only truthful –
The eye of a little god, four-cornered.   5
Most of the time I meditate on the opposite wall.
It is pink, with speckles. I have looked at it so long
I think it is a part of my heart. But it flickers.
Faces and darkness separate us over and over.

Now I am a lake. A woman bends over me,   10
Searching my reaches for what she really is.
Then she turns to those liars, the candles or the moon.
I see her back, and reflect it faithfully.
She rewards me with tears and an agitation of hands.
I am important to her. She comes and goes.   15
Each morning it is her face that replaces the darkness.
In me she has drowned a young girl, and in me an old woman
Rises toward her day after day, like a terrible fish.

Glossary	
1	*preconceptions*: opinions or ideas formed in advance but not based on real knowledge or experience
14	*agitation of hands*: hand wringing; a similar symbol of distress is used in 'Child' to convey the speaker's anguish

Guidelines

'Mirror' was one of a group of poems written in Autumn 1961, days before Plath's twenty-ninth birthday and shortly after she and Ted Hughes moved to Court Green in Devon. Plath was pregnant with her second child at the time. This was one of the last poems she wrote before the birth of her baby, Nicholas.

As in 'Elm', Plath employs the technique of personification to achieve a sinister effect. She was well read in folk and fairy tales and may have taken the idea of a talking mirror from this tradition. Mirrors occur in many of Plath's poems. Perhaps, they suggest the dangers of judging ourselves too harshly, or of seeking perfection. Or they may suggest the lonely drama of living and dying, as it was, in the end, for Plath herself.

Commentary

Opening statement

The poem begins with a precise statement: 'I am silver and exact.' 'Silver' connotes something valuable but it also suggests something inanimate and, therefore, heartless. The adjective 'exact' is ambiguous. It suggests accuracy and correctness. However, there is a more sinister meaning to the verbal form of the word. 'To exact' is to extort or demand payment. **So the opening statement can be read in quite different ways. The surface meaning: I am valuable and accurate. Or the implied meaning: I am heartless and demand payment. The opening statement succeeds in expressing both meanings simultaneously, moving back and forth between the ordinary and the symbolic.**

If we identify the mirror with the perceiving self, then the opening statement suggests a harsh and unforgiving way of viewing the self. It suggests a lack of self-love. Is the voice of the mirror to be interpreted as the voice of the woman whose image the mirror reflects? Is the voice of the poem an aspect of Plath's own voice? Or should we keep a distance between the poet and the speaker of the poem? There are no correct answers to these questions. Different readers read the poem in different ways. Moreover, Plath's poetry succeeds in communicating on a number of levels, in any individual poem, without losing its sense of focus.

Final image

In the final image of the poem (the 'old woman' rising 'like a terrible fish', lines 17 and 18), **Plath suggests many fears and insecurities: the fear of time and old age; the fear of annihilation; the fear of entrapment and alienation; and the fear of losing control.** The image may also perhaps suggest a daughter's fear of her mother, which is the reading that the critic David Holbrook gives to these lines.

World of the poem

The world of the poem is a bleak and unloving one. The perceiving and recording intelligence is cold and inhuman. It gives nothing creative, warm or assuring to the woman. The image of the lake in the second stanza is striking. Like the bottom in 'Elm', the sea in 'Finisterre' and the bee box in 'The Arrival of the Bee Box', the lake represents the dark and fearful inner life. The woman is alone and has no one else to turn to, except the moon and the candles.

Form of the poem

Plath uses the nine-line stanza, which she also used in 'Finisterre'. The line length is irregular but the lines are mostly long. On the page, the two stanzas of the poem appear to mirror each other. The cold tone of the poem is reflected in the carefully phrased statements and the harsh 'k' sounds of the first stanza.

Many of the lines form complete sentences. This contributes to the impression of exactitude that the mirror claims for itself. A sense that is also reflected in the many short words with final voiced consonants ('exact', 'just', 'god', 'pink', 'part' and so on), which create an impression of cold precision. For some readers, the controlled accuracy of the language of the poem emphasises the agitation and disturbed feelings that lie behind the carefully chosen words and phrases.

The run-on line (line 17) that continues with 'rises' in the last line of the poem works brilliantly to mirror the shock of the 'old woman' rising like a 'terrible fish'.

Thinking about the poem

1. What qualities does the mirror attribute to itself in the first four lines of the poem? What is your reaction to the claims the mirror makes for itself? What is your reaction to the tone of these lines?
2. In what sense might a mirror be said to 'swallow' what it sees (line 2)?
3. 'I am not cruel, only truthful' (line 4). Consider this statement. Is the voice of the poem cruel? Is it a masculine or a feminine voice? Are mirrors always truthful? What governs what a person may or may not see in a mirror?
4. Why does the mirror refer to the moon and candles as 'liars' (line 12)?
5. What is the woman's attitude to the mirror and the mirror's attitude to the woman? What is your attitude to the woman?

6   Comment on the images of the final lines of the poem and the impact they have on you. Where else is there a sense of dread or panic in the poem?

7   What does the poem say to you about fear and insecurity and the prospect of growing old?

8   'The exact and precise nature of the mirror is reflected in the language and structure of the poem.' In the light of this statement, comment on the language and form of the poem.

9   'The world reflected by the mirror is one in which the female persona suffers and is alone.' Do you agree with this reading of the poem? Support the points you make by quotation from the poem.

10 'The voice of the mirror is the harsh inner voice that every woman carries within herself.' Give your response to this statement, supporting the points you make by quotation from the poem.

Pheasant

You said you would kill it this morning.
Do not kill it. It startles me still,
The jut of that odd, dark head, pacing

Through the uncut grass on the elm's hill.
It is something to own a pheasant,   5
Or just to be visited at all.

I am not mystical: it isn't
As if I thought it had a spirit.
It is simply in its element.

That gives it a kingliness, a right.   10
The print of its big foot last winter,
The tail-track, on the snow in our court –

The wonder of it, in that pallor,
Through crosshatch of sparrow and starling.
Is it its rareness, then? It is rare.   15

But a dozen would be worth having,
A hundred, on that hill – green and red,
Crossing and recrossing: a fine thing!

It is such a good shape, so vivid.
It's a little cornucopia.   20
It unclaps, brown as a leaf, and loud,

Settles in the elm, and is easy.
It was sunning in the narcissi.
I trespass stupidly. Let be, let be.

Glossary

3	*jut of that odd, dark head*: jerky, forward movement of the head; the way the head of the pheasant leaned forward
12	*our court*: courtyard; Court Green is the name of the house in Devon where the poem is set; also suggests a royal court and picks up on the mention of the kingliness of the bird
13	*pallor*: paleness
14	*crosshatch*: shading by a series of intersecting lines; here, the prints left by the pheasant overlap those left by other birds to create a crosshatch pattern
20	*cornucopia*: treasure; literally means horn of plenty, a Roman symbol of abundance
23	*narcissi*: daffodil-like plants, with white or yellow flowers; there were thousands of bulbs planted around Court Green

Guidelines

Plath wrote 'Pheasant' in April 1962, in a period of enormous creativity in which she wrote a number of fine poems within days of each other. The poem had its origins in Plath's glimpse of a pheasant standing on a hill at the back of her house.

Some critics read the poem in terms of the relationship between the speaker and the person she addresses. The 'you' of the poem is often identified with Ted Hughes, Plath's husband, who came from a Yorkshire family that was well used to hunting and fishing.

Commentary

Dramatic opening

The poem opens in a dramatic fashion. The speaker reports the intention of 'you' to kill the pheasant, which she has seen on the hill behind their house. The opening line has the quality of an accusation: 'You said you would kill it this morning.' The repetition of the pronoun 'you' and the use of the verb 'kill' are striking. **'You' is associated with death, is a killer or a potential killer.**

The plea

The speaker pleads for the pheasant's life. The plea in line 2 is direct and simple, 'Do not kill it.' This is not an order as the speaker feels obliged to supply reasons for this request. She says that the pheasant has the capacity to startle her, as it paces through the grass on the hill. She is fascinated by the movement and shape of its head. And because the pheasant is on their land, she feels a pride of ownership. She feels it is an honour to be visited by this kingly bird. The adjective 'dark' (line 3) suggests that the pheasant is unknowable and therefore remains a mystery to her.

The speaker continues her plea for the bird in the third stanza, arguing that the pheasant 'is simply in its element' (line 9). To the speaker's mind, this naturalness gives the bird a kingly quality, a right to exist, without fear or favour. **The implicit argument is that it is the 'you' and the 'I' who are the outsiders, the interlopers.** In stanza 6 the speaker indulges in a flight of fancy, wondering what it would be like to have a hundred (dozen) pheasants 'green and red' (line 17) on the elm's hill. **The green and red hues of the pheasant are symbols of life and passion.**

Anguished voice

In stanza 7 the focus returns to the pheasant. This one alone is a source of delight. It is a 'cornucopia' (line 21), with its fine shape and vivid colouring. She watches as it unclaps its wings and makes itself comfortable in the tree. **There is almost envy in the statement that the pheasant 'Settles in the elm, and is easy' (line 22). This ease is not shared by the speaker.**

The tone of the poem takes on an edge as the speaker describes herself as trespassing stupidly on the pheasant, sunning itself in the narcissi. And then the emotion, which has been controlled throughout 'Pheasant', breaks out in the urgent plea that concludes the poem: 'Let be. Let be.' **The repeated phrase captures the**

anguish of the speaker, while the echoing rhyme of the final two lines captures the intensity of the plea. This is a trace of the anguished voice that we hear in 'Elm, 'Child', ' Mirror' and 'Poppies in July'.

Critical interpretation

For some critics, the plea is not for the pheasant but for the poet herself. Plath wrote 'Pheasant' in April 1962 during a tense period in her relationship with Ted Hughes. Some critics read the poem as being about Plath's marriage. She is the narrator and Hughes is the 'you' whom she addresses. The pheasant represents the marriage itself, under threat from the male. It is he who is intent on destroying it. Plath pleads for it. She pleads for its beauty and wonder, and for the life and passion that animate it. The fact that it is the female who makes the plea suggests that the relationship of power is an unequal one, with the male possessing the authority to take or spare life, as he wills. (In 'The Arrival of the Bee Box', the narrator says she will be a sweet god and spare the lives of the bees.) For the critic Linda Wagner-Martin, 'Pheasant' rests on the fear that the male will not listen to the female's plea for the life that deserves to exist. The male is a silent, powerful presence in the poem. The female is the pleading supplicant.

Form of the poem

'Pheasant' is a beautifully achieved poem. It has a conversational quality. Yet, apart from the final line, Plath uses a nine-syllable line, and there are subtle rhymes and half-rhymes throughout the poem. The rhyme scheme is a version of terza rima, a form in which the last word in the middle line of each stanza provides the rhyme for the next stanza. What is so impressive about 'Pheasant' is the way Plath follows a strict form while never losing the conversational feel of the poem.

Thinking about the poem

1   What is the dramatic situation suggested by the opening and closing of the poem?

2   What reasons does the 'I' give to support her plea, in stanzas 1 and 2?

3   From the evidence of stanzas 3 to 5, is the speaker sure of her reasons for wanting the pheasant spared? Quote from the poem in support of your answer.

4   In stanzas 7 and 8, what is the speaker's attitude to the pheasant and where is it most evident?

5   'At the end of the poem, it is the speaker who feels like an outsider.' Do you agree with this reading of the poem? Give reasons for your answer.

6   'The difference between 'Pheasant' and 'Black Rook in Rainy Weather' is that in the former there is no movement from the outside to the inside. It is the bird, rather than the poetic persona who is the centre of the poem.' *Or* 'In 'Pheasant' the poetic persona pleads for herself in pleading for the bird.' Which of these two readings of the poem is closest to your own. Support the points you make by quotation from the poem.

7   In writing about 'Pheasant', Ted Hughes speaks of Plath achieving a 'cool, light, very beautiful moment of mastery'. Write a note on the kind of mastery achieved by Plath in 'Pheasant'. You might like to consider some or all of the following in your answer: the choice of verbs and their effect; the descriptions of the pheasant; the dramatic language; line length and syllable count; the stanza form. In considering these, be alert to the sounds of the poem and their effect.

8   If, as some critics suggest, the poem describes the relationship between the poet and her husband, what kind of relationship is portrayed? (In the above Commentary it is assumed that the speaker of the poem is a woman. Is this a fair assumption? Does the poem support it?)

9   If you were encouraging someone to read 'Pheasant' for the first time, how would you describe the poem and your reaction to it?

Elm

for Ruth Fainlight

I know the bottom, she says. I know it with my great tap root;
It is what you fear.
I do not fear it: I have been there.

Is it the sea you hear in me,
Its dissatisfactions?   5
Or the voice of nothing, that was your madness?

Love is a shadow.
How you lie and cry after it
Listen: these are its hooves: it has gone off, like a horse.

267

All night I shall gallop thus, impetuously,   10
Till your head is a stone, your pillow a little turf,
Echoing, echoing.

Or shall I bring you the sound of poisons?
This is rain now, this big hush.
And this is the fruit of it: tin-white, like arsenic.   15

I have suffered the atrocity of sunsets.
Scorched to the root
My red filaments burn and stand, a hand of wires.

Now I break up in pieces that fly about like clubs.
A wind of such violence   20
Will tolerate no bystanding: I must shriek.

The moon, also, is merciless: she would drag me
Cruelly, being barren.
Her radiance scathes me. Or perhaps I have caught her.

I let her go. I let her go   25
Diminished and flat, as after radical surgery.
How your bad dreams possess and endow me.

I am inhabited by a cry.
Nightly it flaps out
Looking, with its hooks, for something to love.   30

I am terrified by this dark thing
That sleeps in me;
All day I feel its soft, feathery turnings, its malignity.

Clouds pass and disperse.
Are those the faces of love, those pale irretrievables?   35
Is it for such I agitate my heart?

I am incapable of more knowledge.
What is this, this face
So murderous in its strangle of branches? –

Its snaky acids hiss.   40
It petrifies the will. These are the isolate, slow faults
That kill, that kill, that kill.

Glossary		
Dedication		*Ruth Fainlight*: writer and friend of Plath
1		*the bottom*: the furthest point that can be reached; here, the deepest point in the subterranean world
1		*tap root*: the main root that goes deep into the soil
6		*voice of nothing*: silence, the absence of inspiration
19		*clubs*: stout-ended sticks used as weapons

Guidelines

'Elm' is a poem that went through numerous drafts before Plath completed it in April 1962. It follows on from the last line of 'Pheasant', in which the bird settles in the elm tree at the back of their house 'and is easy'. Plath took up the word 'easy' at the end of 'Pheasant' and began to explore the elm as something that is not easy.

Commentary

Title

The title refers to a wych elm that grew on a prehistoric mound at the back of Court Green, the house in Devon that Plath shared with Ted Hughes before the break-up of their marriage. In silhouette, the branches of the wych elm make strange, tangled shapes. Plath described the branches of the tree as an 'intricate nervous system'. She plays upon the visual appearance of the elm and its great age in giving it human characteristics. As Anne Stevenson, one of Plath's biographers, observes, the wych elm becomes 'witch' elm in the poem, a frightening, sinister presence.

Stanza 1

In the opening stanza the elm declares her knowledge. It is a dark and deep knowledge, one that has explored 'the bottom' (line 1), the thing that 'you' (the narrator) fears – implying the journey into the deepest part of the self or to the worst periods of one's life. The phrase also suggests the bed of a lake or river where the mud and sludge gather. The imagery here is reminiscent of that in 'Mirror'. The elm shows no sympathy and offers no comfort to the narrator. **The elm resembles an inner voice that is harsh and mocking.**

Stanza 2

In the second stanza the elm asks if the narrator hears the 'dissatisfactions' (line 5) of the sea, as the wind sounds in its branches. The sea is an important and complex symbol in Plath's poetry. It often represents formlessness and annihilation, as in 'Finisterre', or her childhood before the death of her father. After he died, Plath thought of him as drowned and described the creation of pearls as coming from the 'grit of sorrow and routine'. Thus, for Plath, the sea represents creativity and the subconscious of the artist.

The questions posed by the elm seem intended to taunt the narrator. The elm suggests that perhaps the sound is the 'voice of nothing' – the sound of silence, which it equates with the narrator's 'madness' (line 6). Silence – the absence of inspiration – was the cause of severe depression in Plath, who constantly feared that her poetic gift had deserted her.

Stanzas 3 and 4

Stanza 3 continues in a mocking vein. The elm compares its sounds to the pounding of horses' hooves. These hooves, it says, are the sound of love running away from the narrator. **The elm mocks the abandoned narrator's need and desire for it. Love's absence is a 'shadow' (line 7) that hangs over her life.** There is also an interesting ambiguity in the verb 'lie'. As with 'Pheasant', written during the same month, it is worth bearing in mind that Plath's marriage was in crisis at the time she wrote 'Elm'.

Stanza 5

The elm offers the narrator an alternative to the sound of the horse's hooves: 'the sound of poisons' (line 13). The movement from unattainable love to poison is similar to the movement in 'Poppies in July', where poison and annihilation are opposed to a life of intensity. Like the sound of madness, the sound of poisons is silent. Plath worried about the threat of nuclear warfare and the poisoning of the environment. Her fear is reflected in the imagery of this stanza, with its suggestions of acid rain and nuclear dust. The 'big hush' (line 14) may be the deathly silence induced by chemicals (arsenic is a component in many weed and insect killers) in the atmosphere and in the soil or it may be the hush following a nuclear explosion.

Stanzas 6 and 7

The nuclear imagery is continued into stanzas 6 and 7, where the sunset and the violent wind seem to characterise the flash and blast of a nuclear bomb. **The references to suffering – 'scorched', 'wires', 'violence', 'shriek' – speak as much to the suffering endured by Plath's body in the electric shock treatment she received for depression, as they do to the violence endured by the body of the elm.**

The difference established between the elm and the narrator in the first stanza becomes less apparent. In speaking of itself, the elm speaks for the narrator, and the narrator, increasingly, seems identifiable with Plath herself. This, in turn, leads to an intensifying of the emotional strain in the poem.

Stanzas 8 and 9

The elm/narrator continues to describe her suffering. Now it is the 'merciless' moon who is responsible. There are sixty-one references to the moon in Plath's poetry and none of them is benevolent. The moon is sterile and mocking. It is associated with women but it cannot create life (it is 'barren', line 23). 'Barren' is an adjective Plath uses often to indicate a strong dislike or horror of someone. A barren woman is, Plath suggests in another poem, like an empty museum. '*Diminished and flat, as after radical surgery*' is a startling and disturbing image that suggests a woman after a mastectomy.

Line 27 is a key line in interpreting the poem: **the elm suggests that the narrator's nightmares have taken them over and made them what they are: 'How your bad dreams possess and endow me.' From this point on, the elm and the narrator speak with one voice.** In 'The Moon and the Yew Tree', Plath says that the trees of the mind are black. The elm is black and expresses some of the dark, incomprehensible fears that occupy the narrator's mind.

Stanzas 10 and 11

The litany of the narrator's fears begins in stanza 10 and continues in stanza 11. A **bird-like predatory cry, 'this dark thing' (line 31), seems to represent the unconscious of the narrator.** It is fearful, threatening and malignant. It is as if she is a stranger to herself, terrified by forces that she cannot control and a destructive need for love. The imagery reminds us of the incomprehensible sounds in the box in 'The Arrival of the Bee Box'.

Stanzas 12 to 14

Stanza 12 returns to the need for love and the feeling that love, like the passing clouds, is unattainable. There is something pitiful in the question that concludes this stanza: 'Is it for such I agitate my heart?' (line 36).

But this question is not pursued, as the narrator admits she is incapable of more knowledge. However, even as she confesses to her inability to bear more knowledge, more knowledge must be borne. The elm's face forces itself into her consciousness bringing the knowledge of what that face represents. It is a Medusa-like face. Medusa symbolises duality, a double nature that is beautiful and horrifying, seductive and destructive. Is the narrator seeing her own nature in this face?

The 'snaky acids' of the branches 'hiss' (line 40) and the face freezes the will. Anyone who looked on Medusa (whose hair was a tangle of snakes) was turned to stone. The imagery also recalls the serpent in the Garden of Eden and suggests a correspondence between the elm and the Tree of Knowledge. The 'acids' of line 40 are the poisons that kill over time. The repetition of 'kill' in line 42 suggests both a violent frenzy and a hysterical fear of that violence.

The end of the poem, with its nightmarish imagery, a product of the narrator's imagination, suggests that it is the individual poisons ('the isolate, slow faults', line 41) that build up over time within the body (and the mind) that kill. **The repetition in the last line creates a feeling of inevitability, as if the narrator feels doomed, unable to escape the faults that kill.** It is interesting to note that the verb 'kill' also appears in the first line of 'Pheasant'.

Voice of the poem

In the poem, as in many others, Plath personifies a natural object (the elm) and gives it a voice. The voice is at once the 'voice' of a tree, as reported by the narrator, and the voice of the narrator herself.

The voice of the elm is knowledgeable, distressed and, at times, cruel and taunting. The elm addresses a 'you', the poetic persona of the poet, on the subject of fear, love, suffering and despair. Many critics read the second half of the poem as spoken by this 'you' and read the voice as anguished and fearful. The second part of the poem speaks of the need for love, its absence and a destructive inner force. However, to describe the poem in this way is, arguably, misleading. In each utterance of the tree, we can catch a trace of the woman's voice and, in effect, the voices blur and merge, as if the voice of the elm is the inner voice of the woman.

As with many of Plath's poems, the poetic persona seems very harsh in her view of herself. The end of the poem suggests the recognition of some inner faults that will lead to her death. The absence of love intensifies the activity of the dark owl-like thing, whose malignity she fears. As in 'Child', 'Mirror' and 'Poppies in July' the poetic persona is anguished and speaks in a voice that is, by the end of the poem, anguished and fearful.

Atmosphere of the poem

The technique of personification creates a surreal, even nightmarish effect. The world of 'Elm' is not unlike the world of a Brothers Grimm fairy tale, or the world of the subconscious: it is dark and frightening. The vocabulary of the poem captures this nightmarish world: 'terrified', 'dark' 'malignity', 'murderous', 'acid', 'kill'. It is also worth bearing in mind that, **in the heightened atmosphere of the Cold War, there was much discussion about the prospect of nuclear warfare,** so much so that Plath wrote to her mother a couple of months before she completed 'Elm' about the 'mad, self-destructive world' in which they lived. This atmosphere may also have contributed to the imagery of the poem, especially in stanza 5 where it suggests the aftermath of a nuclear bomb.

Form of the poem

Compared with the careful structure of 'Pheasant', 'Elm' is written in a looser manner, with lines of varying lengths. The lack of formal certainty mirrors the swarming content of the poem. Interestingly, the critic Hugh Kenner believes that Plath's abandonment of formal structures in her later poetry encouraged her to explore states of mind and emotions that were unsafe and which, ultimately, contributed to her suicide.

Thinking about the poem

1   What impression of the elm is created by its statements in the first stanza?
2   Examine the questions posed by the elm in stanza 2. What do they suggest about the elm and the person it addresses?
3   What image of love is created in stanzas 3 and 4? Is the elm comforting or cruel in these stanzas? Explain your answer.
4   Stanzas 5 to 9 describe the elements of rain, sun, wind and moon and their relationship to the elm. What aspect of each is emphasised? How does each affect the elm? What, in your view, is the most striking image in these stanzas?
5   What is the elm's attitude to the moon? Where is this attitude most apparent?
6   What do stanzas 5 to 9 suggest about the nature of the elm's existence? Select the words or phrases that strike you most forcefully.

7   What relationship is suggested between the elm and the 'you' of the poem in the statement: 'How your bad dreams possess and endow me' (line 27)? The line can be read as either the elm addressing the woman or the woman addressing the elm. What is the effect of each reading? How do you read it?

8   The last five stanzas are rich, complex and difficult. How does the narrator view herself? What images strike you as particularly disturbing or vivid? What is your reaction to the use of the word 'faults' (line 41)? What is the tone of the extraordinary last line of the poem?

9   'In 'Elm' the boundary between outside and inside is blurred. It is as if the "you", the poetic persona, takes the elm into herself.' In the light of this statement, describe the poetic personae of 'Elm' and the nature of the world, physical and psychological, that they inhabit. Refer to the imagery and vocabulary of the poem in your answer.

10   There is no single reading of 'Elm' that will do justice to its rich complexity. Here are three of the many readings proposed for the poem. Give your opinion of each.

   (a)   *The poem's narrator confesses that she is searching desperately for someone to love. Because of this hysteria, she realises that some deadly force within her has been triggered into action by the loss of love. The disintegration of love, the poem says, is a sure death warrant for the speaker.* (Paul Alexander)

   (b)   *'Elm' describes the effects of nuclear and chemical damage upon a tree and a woman. 'I have suffered the atrocity of sunsets', the speaker explains, and further, 'My red filaments burn and stand, a hand of wires.' . . . 'Elm' is one of the many poems in which Plath explores the consequences of isolation, and argues against the impulse to hold oneself as separate from the rest of the world.* (Tracy Brain)

   (c)   *In the poem, originally titled, 'The Elm Speaks', wych elm becomes witch elm, a frightening mother-double of the poet, who offers death as the only possible love substitute. Between the taproot of the tree and the murderous face of the moon, the poet, 'incapable of more knowledge' is forced into a terrible acknowledgement of 'faults' – suddenly a new word in Sylvia's poetic lexicon. The poem suggests them as somehow built into her nature, bent like a crooked tree by traumatic childhood events: 'These are the isolate slow faults / That kill, that kill, that kill.'* (Anne Stevenson)

11   'The poem vividly conveys suffering, self-doubt and despair.' Give your response to this assessment of 'Elm', supporting the points you make by quotation from the poem.

12   'Elm' is a poem with many striking visual images. Perhaps you might like to offer your own creative response to, or interpretation of, the poem, in visual form.

Poppies in July

Little poppies, little hell flames,
Do you do no harm?

You flicker. I cannot touch you.
I put my hands among the flames. Nothing burns.

And it exhausts me to watch you   5
Flickering like that, wrinkly and clear red, like the skin of a mouth.

A mouth just bloodied.
Little bloody skirts!

There are fumes that I cannot touch.
Where are your opiates, your nauseous capsules?   10

If I could bleed, or sleep! –
If my mouth could marry a hurt like that!

Or your liquors seep to me, in this glass capsule,
Dulling and stilling.

But colourless. Colourless.   15

Sylvia Plath

Glossary	
10	*opiates*: opium comes from the unripe seed of the poppy
10	*nauseous capsules*: tablets that cause sickness or discomfort
13	*liquors*: a solution of a drug or chemical in water
13	*glass capsule*: a bell jar, of the kind used in scientific experiments or to hold a specimen

Guidelines

Plath wrote 'Poppies in July' in July 1962, at Court Green in Devon, during the break-up of her marriage. The poetic persona addresses the flowers in a voice that is overwrought and anguished. Anne Stevenson, Plath's biographer, sets the poems that Plath wrote in the final months of her life in a biographical context. She says that these poems report on 'the weather of her inner universe' and the two poles that governed it: rage and stasis. 'At the depressed pole there was a turning in on herself, a longing for non-being as in 'Poppies in July'.'

Commentary

Title

Red poppies are a common sight in the English countryside in summer. The poppy is also a flower of remembrance for the war dead. In Keats' poem 'To Autumn', the poppy is associated with sleep and ease. As Plath develops the symbolism of the poppy, it takes on a dark and destructive resonance, indicative of a troubled state of mind.

Couplets 1–4

From the first line we realise that the speaker of the poem is troubled. The opening line greeting the poppies – 'Little poppies, little hell flames' – seems to be spoken by two different people. 'Little poppies' suggests a sentimental relationship to the flowers. However, this impression is immediately destroyed by the negative energy of 'little hell flowers' and the association that the speaker makes between the red poppies and the flames of hell. After only one line, we suspect that the poem is not really about the poppies. It is about someone in an excited and disturbed psychological state.

This disturbance is carried into the second line, where the speaker asks: 'Do, you do no harm?' **The word 'harm' is striking and from here on the speaker explores and contemplates the different kinds of harm that she associates with the flowers.** The poppies are associated with danger and death.

The second couplet (lines 3 and 4) continues the imagery of 'flames' begun in line 1. The movement of the red petals is like the flickering of flames. The speaker says she puts her hands among the flames (the petals of the flowers) but 'Nothing burns' (line 4). It is as if the speaker is cut off from feeling and sensation, an idea taken up later in the fifth couplet and linked to the imagery of being contained in the glass jar.

The speaker cannot touch the poppies but she can watch them, though she finds their movement exhausting (line 5). In a striking visual image, she compares the poppies to a mouth and immediately develops the comparison to bloodied mouths and bloodied skirts. The bloodied mouth may suggest violence. Plath often associated red with love, and love with violent emotion that incorporated danger, excitement and vitality. Famously, in her first meeting with Ted Hughes, she bit him on the cheek and he left with blood running down his face.

In poetry, blood is a complex symbol, suggesting hurt, violence, danger, excitement and vitality. The reference to 'little bloody skirts' (line 8) may suggest the stain of menstrual blood and the association of female sexuality with a wound. The tone of 'little bloody skirts' suggests disgust or irritation. It could also be an indirect and derogatory reference to Assia Wevill, the woman with whom Hughes was having an affair. Indeed, Ronald Hayman, one of Plath's biographers, suggests that 'Poppies in July' is directed at Assia Wevill.

Couplets 5–7
In the fifth couplet **the speaker changes tack and focuses on the by-products of poppies: the colourless fumes, their opiates.** She seems frustrated that she cannot inhale the fumes that bring drowsiness and ease, or find the opium tablets that make you feel sick or unwell.

In the sixth couplet we realise how distressed the speaker is. She expresses the wish that she could either bleed or sleep, suffer or escape. In other words, **the speaker seems trapped, unable to live life to the full or escape from it.** Either suffering or sleeping, it seems, would bring relief to her. The couplet concludes with the startling and passionate exclamation, 'If my mouth could marry a hurt like that' (line 12). It is a strange, wild and fascinating statement of longing and captures the desperation of the speaker to live life in a different way from the way she is living it now. It encompasses all the related imagery at work in the poem: life, death, violence, sexuality, addiction, sickness.

The seventh couplet (lines 13 and 14) expresses an alternative wish, namely that the fumes of the poppy will seep into the glass jar where she is trapped, dulling and stilling her senses. This is a death wish, which involves no blood or violence just a colourless fume that will drain the colour out of life. The image of the 'glass capsule' (the bell jar) is a recurrent one in Plath's work. References to bell jars and liquor suggest hospital and museum specimens kept in chemical solutions. Plath witnessed such specimens when she posed as a medical student and observed an anatomical dissection. The experience proved traumatic. In this case, the imagery suggests that the speaker sees herself as trapped in a glass jar, like an exhibit in a museum.

The poem concludes with a chilling wish for annihilation in place of her present inability to feel or experience life.

Interpreting the poem

The poem is complex and invites a variety of interpretations and you may not fully agree with the one offered here. It is clear that the speaker is distressed and acting out a psychological drama in her words. She is deeply unhappy and feels trapped. She wants something to change in her life or she wants her life to end. There are two impulses at work in the poem, one associated with the vibrant colour red and the other with the absence of colour. One symbolises a life of physical, even violent, intensity and the other the total annihilation of consciousness.

Style and form of the poem

The poem is dramatic. It progresses in short dramatic statements, governed by careful punctuation, which are organised into unrhymed, irregular couplets. The use of exclamation marks and question marks adds to the dramatic impact and the poem moves through a range of tones in its short fifteen lines, including fascination, frustration, disgust and repulsion, intense desire and longing. Plath is brilliant at weaving intricate patterns of sound that mirror the sense of the lines. You can almost hear the crackle of the flames in the opening six lines. This is achieved by the onomatopoeic effect of the 'c' and 'k' sounds used. A completely different effect is achieved in the final three lines of the poem where the soft 's' sounds and the long 'u' and 'ou' vowels create a sense of ease and quiet.

Thinking about the poem

1. Based on the first two lines of the poem, what is the state of mind of the speaker?

2. Why, in your view, does the speaker want to experience the sensation of burning by putting her 'hands among the flames' (line 4)?

3. In the fourth couplet, the speaker compares the poppies to 'a mouth just bloodied' and 'little bloody skirts'. What is the impact of these comparisons?

4. In the fifth couplet, the speaker says she cannot touch the fumes of the poppies. Why, in your view, can she not touch them?

5. The speaker asks about opiates and tablets in line 10. What do her questions tell us about what she is thinking?

6. 'If I could bleed or sleep!' (line 12). If the speaker is neither bleeding nor sleeping, what kind of existence is she experiencing? Explain your answer.

7   What does the reference to 'this glass capsule' (line 13) say to you about how the speaker views her life?

8   What is the wish expressed by the speaker at the end of the poem? How does the wish make you feel?

9   Which **two** of the following statements best describe your view of the poem?

> It is a poem about feeling trapped.
>
> It is a poem about wanting to escape.
>
> It is a poem abut feeling numb.
>
> It is about wanting to live life to the full.
>
> It is a poem about annihilation.

Explain your choice using reference to the text.

10 Which of the following statements is closest to your own feelings for the speaker of the poem?

> I admire the speaker.
>
> I feel sorry for the speaker.
>
> I am fascinated by the speaker.

Explain your choice.

Taking a closer look

1   Comment on the phrase 'little hell flames' (line 1) – considering each of the three words – and its impact upon you.

2   The phrase 'I cannot touch' is used twice in the poem (lines 3 and 9). How does it add to your understanding of the predicament of the speaker?

3   'If my mouth could marry a hurt like that!' (line 12). In your opinion, what longing is expressed in this line?

4   'The poem 'Poppies in July' has little to do with poppies and a great deal to do with the mind that perceives them.' Give your response to this statement, supporting the points you make by quotation from the poem.

Imagining

1   Imagine that you are asked to make a short film to accompany a reading of the poem. Explain how you would use music, sound effects, colour, images, etc. to capture the atmosphere of the poem.

2   Imagine you are the poet. Write **two** diary entries that give your reaction to the poem a long time after you first wrote it.

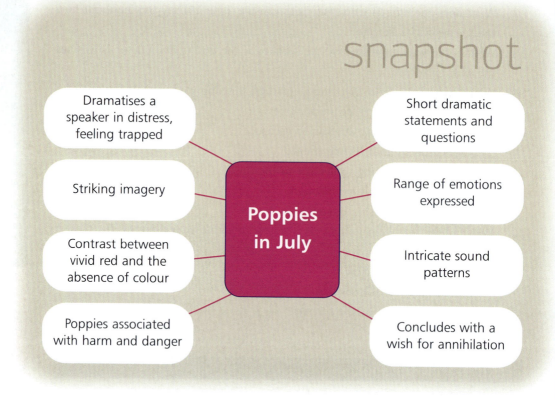

snapshot

Dramatises a speaker in distress, feeling trapped

Striking imagery

Contrast between vivid red and the absence of colour

Poppies associated with harm and danger

Poppies in July

Short dramatic statements and questions

Range of emotions expressed

Intricate sound patterns

Concludes with a wish for annihilation

The Arrival of the Bee Box

I ordered this, this clean wood box
Square as a chair and almost too heavy to lift.
I would say it was the coffin of a midget
Or a square baby
Were there not such a din in it.   5

The box is locked, it is dangerous.
I have to live with it overnight
And I can't keep away from it.
There are no windows, so I can't see what is in there.
There is only a little grid, no exit.   10

I put my eye to the grid.
It is dark, dark,

With the swarmy feeling of African hands
Minute and shrunk for export,
Black on black, angrily clambering.   15

How can I let them out?
It is the noise that appals me most of all,
The unintelligible syllables.
It is like a Roman mob,
Small, taken one by one, but my god, together!   20

I lay my ear to furious Latin.
I am not a Caesar.
I have simply ordered a box of maniacs.
They can be sent back.
They can die, I need feed them nothing, I am the owner.   25

I wonder how hungry they are.
I wonder if they would forget me
If I just undid the locks and stood back and turned into a tree.
There is the laburnum, its blond colonnades,
And the petticoats of the cherry.   30

They might ignore me immediately
In my moon suit and funeral veil.
I am no source of honey
So why should they turn on me?
Tomorrow I will be sweet God, I will set them free.   35

The box is only temporary.

Glossary		
13	*swarmy*: moving in large numbers	
22	*Caesar*: Roman emperor	
29	*colonnades*: row of columns, in this case ringlets	
32	*moon suit*: spacesuit, protective clothing worn by astronauts	

Guidelines

In 1962 Plath and Hughes decided to take up beekeeping. (Plath's father had been an expert on bees.) In October, following their separation, Plath wrote a sequence of bee poems that explore the nature of the self and self-identity; personal fears; complex relations and attitudes towards freedom and control. Of the five poems in the sequence, 'The Arrival of the Bee Box' is the one that can stand on its own.

The poem may be taken at face value: it describes the arrival of the bee box and the speaker's response to it. **The box both frightens and fascinates the speaker of the poem. However, the bee box is often read as a symbol for the inner life of the speaker or a symbol for poetry itself, a formal shape which contains a swarm of ideas and feelings.**

Commentary

Stanza 1

The poem opens on a note of wonderment as the speaker seems surprised by the bee box and by the fact that she is responsible for its presence, 'I ordered this'. The verb 'ordered' introduces a major theme of the poem: the question of power and control.

Lines 3 and 4 introduce the first of the surreal images that run through the poem. The speaker says she would compare the box to 'the coffin of a midget / Or a square baby' except for the noise coming from it. The box, like the bell jar imagery that is evident in much of Plath's work, symbolises entrapment and confinement and, as the poem progresses, the noise coming from it is the sound of the bees agitating for release.

Stanza 2

The second stanza is the most straightforward in the poem. It opens with two direct statements: 'The box is locked. It is dangerous.' The speaker says she has to live with the box overnight and cannot keep away from it. Lines 9 and 10 describe the box in terms that bring to mind a windowless prison cell. **This stanza reveals the speaker's fascination with the contents of the box.** In Greek mythology, Pandora, out of curiosity, opened a container and released harm and sickness into the world. All the contents of the box escaped except hope. The box in this poem resembles Pandora's in the mixture of fear and hope that it excites in the speaker.

Stanza 3

Plath was influenced by the surrealist painter Giorgio de Chirico, and his use of symbols taken from the subconscious to create ominous, disturbing images. She was also interested in African sculpture and folktales. Both interests – surrealism and Africa – come together in the imagery of the third stanza.

The speaker tells us that she can see only darkness when she puts her eyes to the grid. It is not an empty darkness but one which the speaker associates with 'African hands' (line 13), a reference to the Black slave-workers exported from Africa on slave ships to work as manual labourers on plantations. In a surreal, disturbing image, the speaker sees these 'hands' as 'minute and shrunk' (line 14).

Like the African slaves, the bees are workers and they must clamber over each other to move around in their cramped conditions. The use of the word 'angrily' (line 15) suggests the danger and aggression that the speaker senses within – the threat posed by the contained but angry bees. Some commentators have suggested that the series of images linking the bees to African slaves could only have been made by a White writer.

Stanza 4

The opening line of the fourth stanza, 'How can I let them out?', is ambiguous. Given the anger of the bees the question may mean 'How can I let them out *safely*?' On the other hand, it could mean 'How can I *possibly* let them out *now that I know what they are like*?' **It is as if the speaker doubts her capacity to cope with the bees, and their dangerous potential.** She tries to identify the source of her dismay and attributes it to the noise and its incomprehensibility: she fears what she does not

understand. The potential for destruction that she senses in the bee box is captured in the comparison to the mob which, in Roman times, demanded public killings for their amusement (line 19).

Stanza 5

Listening to the 'furious Latin' (line 21), the speaker feels unable to control the mob, as Caesar did, by the power of his words. Their language is, after all, 'unintelligible' (line 18) to her. But then **the speaker grows more confident. She defines the situation and the solution to the problem with a new clarity** in lines 23–24: 'I have simply

ordered a box of maniacs. / They can be sent back.' The situation is not out of control. In the final line of the stanza, another possibility occurs to her. The bees might be left in their box, without food. Then it will become a coffin. Ownership gives her the power of life and death. She is like a slave owner.

Stanza 6

The sixth stanza brings a change of tone. The possibility of allowing the bees to die is no longer entertained. Instead, she thinks of how they might be released without causing harm to herself. **The speaker is calmer, although still curious.** She wonders if the bees will forget her. It is an intriguing question. Does she mean 'forget' in the sense of not wanting to exact revenge upon her for bringing them there in the first place?

She thinks of the idea of escaping by becoming a tree. In Greek mythology, the God Apollo, mad with love and desire, pursued the nymph Daphne, who called on her father, Peneus, for help and was turned into a laurel tree.

The speaker seems to suggest that the laburnum and cherry trees may well be the result of a similar transformation. The drooping flower-covered branches of the laburnum are likened to blond ringlets and the blossom of the flowering cherry tree to the ruffled petticoats that were popular in the 1950s and 1960s (lines 29 to 30).

Stanza 7

The seventh stanza presents another possibility: the bees might ignore her in her beekeeper's suit, which she describes as a spacesuit topped with the type of veil traditionally worn by women mourners at a funeral, another comparison which shows that the speaker's mind swarms with ideas and associations.

Line 33 is a simple statement – 'I am no source of honey' – and it prompts the question, 'So why should they turn on me?' **This reveals the speaker's fear that the bees might hurt her.** The question is really an attempt by the speaker to persuade herself that the bees will not harm her. And taking comfort, she speaks with calm authority in line 35: 'Tomorrow I will be sweet God. I will set them free.' **She anticipates the pleasure of exercising her power in a generous way, though the action itself is postponed.**

Final line

There is a note of optimistic triumph in the final line of the poem, 'The box is only temporary.'

Interpreting the poem

The poem can be read as the story of an inexperienced beekeeper who orders a box of bees and is then afraid to release them. However, because Plath employs symbols and works by association, and because she was interested in the unconscious, her poems tend to be interpreted in a variety of ways. Here are examples of how some readers have interpreted this poem:

- The White female beekeeper wants to free the Black bees but she is appalled by them and frightened of what they might do to her.
- The poem depicts a psychological drama between the inner turmoil of the speaker, who is a version of Plath, and the outer, formal control that the speaker exerts on her feelings.
- It is about the kind of poetry that Plath wrote and the dangers involved in writing it. The bees represent her mind and all the repressed feelings, memories and ideas it contains. This is the dangerous subject-matter that both fascinates and appals her. The box represents the poem, the structure that contains and controls the dangerous swarming content of her mind.
- The beekeeper opening the box is like a person releasing repressed feelings or a poet exploring dark themes: all are likely to get hurt.

Style and form of the poem

The poem is written in five-line unrhymed stanzas. The language is direct and powerful. From the opening 'this', the speaker utters her words in short, sharp bursts. The dramatic impact is heightened by the repetition of key words such as 'dark', 'black' and 'I' ('I' appears five times in the fifth stanza alone).

The run-on lines and conversational words create the impression of someone telling a personal story. Look, for example, at the way the sound echoes in the first stanza in the words 'square', 'chair', 'were' and 'there'. The 'r' sound is repeated throughout the poem and occurs in the final word: 'temporary'. As always in Plath's poetry, there is an intricate pattern of sound woven through the text.

Because of the narrative structure and the use of the present tense, we get a sense of the flow of time and live the experience with the speaker.

Interestingly, the last line of the poem falls outside the five-line stanza structure. The speaker announces her intention to free the bees in a line that seems to escape the formal structure of the poem.

Thinking about the poem

1   How does the speaker describe the bee box in the first stanza? Do you find the imagery of the first stanza strange, disturbing or amusing? Explain your answer.
2   Based on the evidence of stanza 2, what is the speaker's attitude to the bee box?
3   Explain as clearly as you can the reference to 'African hands' (line 13) and the comparison the speaker makes between them and the bees.

4   What, according to the speaker in stanza 4, appals her most of all about the bees?

5   In stanza 5, the speaker grows more confident. Speaking as the 'owner' what actions are open to her?

6   In stanza 6, the speaker considers ways in which the bees might be released without causing harm to herself. What options does she consider?

7   What announcement does the speaker make in stanza 7? What is the tone of this announcement?

8   What, in your view, does the final line add to the poem? Does the poem end on a note of optimism?

9   Which **one** of the following statements best describes your view of the poem?

    It is a poem about bees.

    It is a poem about psychological fears.

    It is a poem about writing poetry.

    Explain your choice using reference to the text.

10   What impression of the poet do you form from reading the poem? What words or phrases help to create this impression of Plath?

Taking a closer look

1   'The box is locked, it is dangerous' (line 6). Comment on Plath's use of the word 'dangerous' and what you think it adds to the poem.

2   'With the swarmy feeling of African hands' (line 13). Describe the impact of this line on you.

3   'I will be sweet God' (line 35). Write a note on this statement and what it means in the context of the poem.

4   'In the poem, there is both a desire to trust the bees and a fear of trusting them, but in the end, the fear is overcome.' Do you agree with this reading of the poem? Explain your answer.

Imagining

1   You are the speaker of the poem. Write a diary entry describing your experience of having the bee box in your possession overnight. The entries should catch some of the conflicting feelings evident in the poem: fear, fascination, repulsion, intended kindness, etc.

2   Choose a song or a film that, in your opinion, has a similar atmosphere to that created in the 'The Arrival of the Bee Box'. Explain your choice.

3   Suggest an alternative title for the poem. Explain your suggestion.

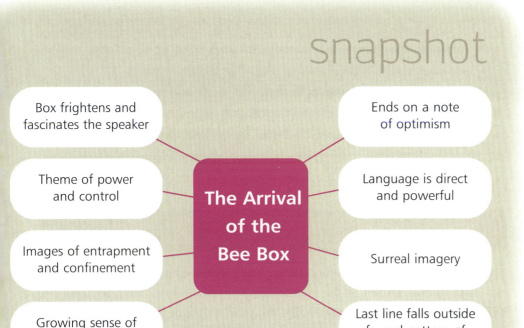

snapshot

The Arrival of the Bee Box

Box frightens and fascinates the speaker

Theme of power and control

Images of entrapment and confinement

Growing sense of calm in the poem

Ends on a note of optimism

Language is direct and powerful

Surreal imagery

Last line falls outside formal pattern of the poem

Child

Your clear eye is the one absolutely beautiful thing.
I want to fill it with colour and ducks.
The zoo of the new

Whose names you meditate –
April snowdrop, Indian pipe,   5
Little

Stalk without wrinkle,
Pool in which images
Should be grand and classical

Not this troublous   10
Wringing of hands, this dark
Ceiling without a star.

Glossary

4	*meditate*:	reflect upon; this is picking up the imagery of reflection
5	*snowdrop*:	small, white-flowering plant that blooms in spring
5	*Indian pipe*:	small, woodland flower
10	*troublous*:	agitated, unsettled, disturbed; taking up the idea of classical and grand in the preceding line, Plath uses an old-fashioned, literary word

Guidelines

'Child' appeared in Plath's collection *Winter Trees*, published in 1971, eight years after her death. It was written at the end of January 1963, shortly after her son's first birthday and less than two weeks before she took her life at the age of thirty. It is a beautifully phrased and composed poem in which a mother expresses her frustrated wishes for her child.

Commentary

Stanza 1

'Child' opens dramatically with the mother addressing her child in what is the longest line in the poem. **She tells the child that its eye is the one thing in her life that is beautiful**: 'Your clear eye is the one absolutely beautiful thing.' The line tells us as much about the mother and the world she inhabits as it does about the child.

The mother then expresses her wishes for her child. She wants to create a world of excitement and colour to fill the child's eye: 'I want to fill it with colour and ducks. / The zoo of the new'. These lines work brilliantly. The random progression from 'colour' to 'ducks' captures the unpredictability and pleasure of the world she wants to show her child. The phrase 'the zoo of the new' expresses not only the potential of the world to delight, but also the humour and inventiveness of the mother who wants to bring this world to her child.

Stanza 2

The mother begins to describe the joyful world she wants to offer to her child: 'April snowdrop, Indian pipe' (line 5). The verb 'meditate' (to reflect upon, line 4) suggests that the child has not yet seen these beautiful flowers. The placing of the word 'Little' on its own in line 6 emphasises the smallness of the child. **For the mother, the child is her April snowdrop, the symbol of spring and new beginnings.**

Stanza 3

The child is also 'Little / Stalk without wrinkle' (lines 6–7) – delicate, young and unblemished like the flowers. Line 8 picks up on the imagery of reflection, which began with 'clear eye' in the opening line and continued in line 4 with 'meditate'. **Now the child's eye is a 'pool'. The mother thinks that 'grand and classical' images should fill it.** The image of a pool creates a different set of associations from the image of an eye: the world reflected in a pool is an unstable one that can quickly lose its shape and dissolve into formlessness.

Stanza 4

The final stanza gives us the image that fills the child's eye. It is a classic image of despair: the 'wringing of hands' (line 11). It symbolises the mother's anguish. Her anguish is intensified by her inability to give her child what she feels the child deserves. **The speaker is reduced to expressing her own anguish.** Her failure to fill the child's world with joy adds to her gloom: her world is now a 'dark / Ceiling without a star' (lines 11–12).

Interpreting the poem

It is difficult not to read this poem in the biographical context in which it was written – two weeks before Plath took her life. The poem presents a speaker who has lost confidence in her ability to create joy, a mother unable to escape her own anguish and despair, but anxious to spare her child the sight of it. She does not want the child's clear eye to witness the pain she endures, yet she lacks the strength and self-belief – not the humour, imagination or inventiveness – to make things otherwise.

Style and form of the poem

The poem is written in unrhymed, three-line stanzas. 'Child' is a testimony to Plath's skill and judgement as a poet. Every word is carefully chosen. The words 'Little' (line 6) and 'dark' (line 11), for example, are perfectly placed. The despair that underlies the poem is managed and controlled.

Thinking about the poem

1 'The first line of the poem shows the mother's love for her child.' Do you agree? Explain your answer.

2 On the evidence of lines 2 and 3, what kind of world does the mother want to create for her child?

3 What is the effect of the flower names mentioned in the second stanza? Explain your answer.

4 What are the conditions in which the images in a pool might appear 'grand and classical' (line 9)? Do these conditions exist in the child's life?

5 What does stanza 4 tell us about the mother? What feeling does the mother have for her child? What feeling do you have for the mother?

6 This poem presents us with a picture of a woman who is deeply troubled.' Do you agree with this assessment of the poem? Explain your answer.

7 Which of the following statements is closest to your own view of the poem?

> It is a poem about love.
>
> It is a poem about despair.
>
> It is a poem about innocence.

Explain your choice.

Taking a closer look

1 'Your clear eye' (line 1). Comment on Plath's use of the adjective 'clear' at the beginning of the poem.

2 Comment on the use of the word 'zoo' (line 3) and the mood and ideas it generates.

3 Consider the phrase 'grand and classical' in line 9. Write a note on both words and the kind of images you associate with each.

4 Comment on the placing of the words 'Little' in line 6 and 'dark' in line 11.

Imagining

1 If you could write a letter to Sylvia Plath, after reading 'Child', what would you say to her?

2 What music would you select to accompany a reading of this poem? Explain your choice.

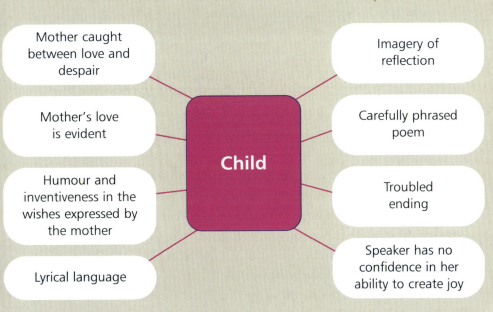

Mother caught between love and despair

Mother's love is evident

Humour and inventiveness in the wishes expressed by the mother

Lyrical language

Child

Imagery of reflection

Carefully phrased poem

Troubled ending

Speaker has no confidence in her ability to create joy

General Questions

1   Give your personal response to the poetry of Sylvia Plath, describing the impact of the poems upon you. Support your answer by relevant quotation from the poems you have studied.

Here are some possible areas that you might focus on in your answer:

- Her themes, for example love and despair.
- The anguished voice of some of her poems.
- The startling imagery and symbolism employed in the poems.
- Her skill as a poet.
- The relationship between her life and her poetry.

2   What in your view are the emotions and the emotional experiences explored in Plath's poetry and how are these conveyed in the language and imagery of the

poems? Support the points you make by quotation from the poems you have studied.

3   'The poetic techniques employed by Plath succeed in making the world of her poetry a strange and terrifying one.' In the light of this statement, discuss the world of Plath's poetry. Support your answer by quotation from the poems you have studied.

4   'Plath's poems make most sense when they are read as biographical.' Do you agree with this view of Plath's poetry? Explain your answer, supporting the points you make by quotation from the poetry by Plath on your course.

5   'Death and annihilation are the themes that dominate Plath's poetry.' Is this an accurate assessment? Support your point of view by quotation from the poems you have studied.

6   'Plath's poetry presents a vivid portrait of an individual whose life is tormented and anguished.' Do you agree with this reading of Plath's work? Support the points you make by quotation from the poems by Plath on your course.

7   Write an essay in which you outline your reasons for liking or not liking the poetry of Sylvia Plath. You must refer to the poems of Plath on your course.
Possible reasons for liking the poetry include:
- The uniqueness of the poetic voice.
- The striking imagery and symbolism.
- The vitality and energy of the writing.
- The exploration of emotions and extreme states of mind.
- The exploration of women's experiences.
- The impact of the poetry upon the reader.
- The variety of themes.
- Plath's skill as a poet.

Possible reasons for not liking the poetry include:
- The themes of isolation and estrangement.
- The cruelty of the world of many of the poems.
- The absence of happiness in many of the poems.
- The obscurity of the imagery.
- The troubled nature of the poetic persona.
- The complexity of the relationship explored in the poetry.
- The feeling of despair in many of the poems.
- The effect of the poems upon the reader.

8   'The movement of Plath's poetry is from the outside world to the inner world, from landscape to mindscape.' Discuss this statement in relation to **two** of the poems by Plath on your course.

9   Select your favourite poems by Plath and explain what it is you admire about them. Support the points you make by quotation from the chosen poems.

10 'In Plath's poetry, of course, this slightly old-fashioned point of view of the sanctity of domesticity is wedded to a tormented modern consciousness.' (Margaret Dickie)

> 'For all her harrowing and courageous record of suffering, Sylvia Plath died in the end because she could not sustain confidence in her true potentialities which could free her.' (David Holbrook)

Write an essay on Plath's poetry in support of **one** of the views above. Support the points you make by quotation from the poems you have studied.

Sample Essay

What in your view are the emotions and the emotional experiences explored in the poetry of Sylvia Plath and how are these conveyed in the language and imagery of the poems? Support the points you make by quotation from the poems you have studied.

Sylvia Plath's poetry is a poetry of emotional extremes and while there are moments of joy and optimism in her poems, the prevailing mood is dark and filled with fear, suffering and despair. The mood of her poetry is conveyed in dramatic monologues in which the speakers use memorable, haunting and sometimes terrifying imagery to convey their feelings.

[Opening paragraph sets up answer]

'Black Rook in Rainy Weather' was published during the time Plath spent in Cambridge as a student and probably captures the contrast between the sunny weather of Plath's Boston and the wet and dark atmosphere of autumn in England. The 'black' and 'rainy' adjectives of the title tell us all we need to know about the kind of experience that inspired the poem. However, the poem uses the dark colours of the bird and the gloomy atmosphere as symbols to represent the emotional mood of the speaker, the poetic persona of the poem. The landscape is described as 'dull, ruinous'. The autumn weather is now a 'season of fatigue' where the speaker is 'trekking stubborn'. The double consonant sounds and the long vowels capture the effort required by the speaker just to keep going. The speaker hopes for a break in the weather, for 'spasmodic tricks of radiance' that might give her 'A brief respite from fear / Of total neutrality'. Almost out of nowhere a poem that began by describing a bird in the rain gathers together all its imagery and poetic energy to announce its theme: the speaker's fear of a complete loss of identity. This theme runs through Plath's poetry and is expressed in striking imagery.

[Important theme introduced; first poem discussed]

Consider, for example, the museum imagery of 'Morning Song', where the newborn is described as a museum exhibit and the parents 'stand round blankly as walls'. The word 'blankly' is particularly striking. And it is immediately followed by the speaker of the poem announcing that she feels no more the mother of a child than a cloud is mother to a pool of water that shows the cloud 'its own slow / Effacement at the wind's hand'. As a reader, you want to shout 'Stop'. How can a poem that begins with the birth of a child move so quickly to the loss and disappearance of the mother? And while the poem ends on an optimistic note, it is the imagery of effacement and the word 'blankly' that stay in the mind.

[Reader response introduced; second poem discussed]

'Finisterre' is one of the few Plath poems that does not have a poetic persona or narrator and this results in the poem being less emotionally engaging than some of the others. However, what is clear is that the poem circles the theme of identity and fixed forms versus formlessness. The poem describes the statue of Our Lady of the Shipwrecked and says that 'She is in love with the beautiful formlessness of the sea'. It is a line that requires a bit of teasing out. What it seems to convey is an attraction to the loss of identity that was feared in the poems I have already discussed. The attraction is revealed in the long vowels and the soft sibilant sounds of the line, which reflect the seductive power of the formless sea. It is a dangerous form of seduction. This ambiguity towards annihilation becomes more pronounced in the poems that Plath wrote towards the end of her life.

[Third poem widens the discussion]

Of course, it is always dangerous to generalise about a poet's work, for as soon as we do, a poem appears that questions the validity of what we have claimed. Take, 'Pheasant', for example. The poem is brilliantly dramatic, with a woman pleading to a man to spare a pheasant he has threatened to kill. The basis of her plea is the definite shape and identity of the bird. Its solidity attracts her: 'it is such a good shape, so vivid'. And the poem itself is a good shape, written in carefully constructed three-line stanzas. The speaker sees the bird as belonging where it is. It is she who feels like a trespasser and pleads for the pheasant to be left alone: 'I trespass stupidly. Let be, let be'. Interestingly, the simplicity of the language indicates the heart-felt nature of the plea.

[Fourth poem introduced to show awareness of other aspects of the poet's work]

The repetition of 'Let be' at the end of the poem, suggests that the speaker is emotional and overwrought. The emotion is held in check by the tight structure of the poem. Certainly the speaker who addresses the poppies in 'Poppies in July' is anguished and emotional. The imagery is terrifying. The speaker sees the poppies as 'hell flames' and is disappointed that 'nothing burns' when she places her hands among them. The sinister, surreal imagery of the poem, conveys the distress of the speaker, who addresses the flowers as 'A mouth just bloodied' and 'Little bloody skirts'. Unable to feel pain or inflict harm upon herself, the speaker expresses a chilling wish for annihilation, where the fumes of the poppies would seep into her in her 'glass capsule' and dull and still her senses until life was drained of all its colour. The reference to a glass capsule suggests that the speaker feels trapped, and is so dissatisfied with life that death seems to be an attractive alternative to her current situation.

[Argument in new paragraph follows on from discussion in previous one; fifth poem discussed]

Of course at this stage the reader is asking, 'Why?' Why are the speakers in Plath's poems so fearful and afraid? Three poems offer two different answers. In 'Child', one of the last poems she completed before taking her own life, it is because the mother has lost confidence in herself and in her ability to create the kind of joyful world she would like for her child. She wants to fill her child's eye with 'The zoo of the new'. It is such a brilliant phrase – simple, zany, unforgettable. It shows a mother who is inventive and fun. But this is not enough for the speaker. She is anxious and in despair and does not want her child's 'clear eye' to witness her pain and distress. The speaker does not believe herself capable of being the mother she would like to be. It is such a sad poem.

[Sixth poem discussed; notice how short quotations are used throughout the answer]

In 'Elm', the speaker's terror is related to 'this dark thing / That sleeps in me.' This is the darkest imagery in all her poems, full of terror and self-hatred. The dark thing inside her is malignant and the poem concludes with an image of poisonous acids killing the self. The repetition of the verb 'kill' at the end of the poem suggests a frenzy of uncontrollable violence. This is a poem on the furthest edge of emotion and self-analysis.

[New paragraph continues the thread of argument running through the essay]

The idea of the uncontrollable violence and darkness that the speaker senses within herself is also evident in 'The Arrival of the Bee Box', where the bees represent a fascinating dark force that she senses within but which she does not understand. They speak in 'unintelligible syllables' and 'furious Latin'. The bees 'appal' her but she tells us that she 'can't keep away' from them. The box contains them but the speaker wants to see them free, even though she understands they could harm her, turn on her, just as the slow faults referred to in 'Elm' have the capacity to kill. However, 'The Arrival of the Bee Box' concludes with the speaker determined to release the bees. The last triumphant statement declares: 'The box is only temporary.' As a reader you fear for the safety of the speaker who would release such dark and dangerous things upon herself.

[Begins to draw entry to conclusion]

Reading the poetry of Sylvia Plath is to encounter a succession of speakers who live on the edge, who seem on the point of being overwhelmed by doubt and fear and a lack of belief. The wonder of the poetry is that out of such dark material Sylvia Plath makes such beautifully crafted poems. The tragedy for the poet was that, in her own life, she was not able to contain her personal fears within such tightly controlled structures.

[Strong conclusion]

Wrote all the poems within a period of seven years; died aged thirty

Voice of the poems is sometimes anguished

Writes about her life but no simple relationship between her life and her poetry

Poems have a dreamlike or surreal quality

Writes about the importance of love and motherhood

Imagery influenced by the threat of nuclear warfare

Writes about nature, the weather and children

Images of entrapment and release

Explores extreme emotions and extreme states of mind

Poems are poised between celebration and despair

Poems carefully composed and beautifully phrased

Adrienne Rich

b. 1929

STORM WARNINGS
AUNT JENNIFER'S TIGERS*
THE UNCLE SPEAKS IN THE DRAWING ROOM*
LIVING IN SIN
THE ROOFWALKER
OUR WHOLE LIFE
TRYING TO TALK WITH A MAN
DIVING INTO THE WRECK
FROM A SURVIVOR
POWER

Biography

Adrienne Rich's most recent books of poetry are *Tonight No Poetry Will Serve* (2011) and *Telephone Ringing in the Labyrinth* (2007). She edited Muriel Rukeyser's *Selected Poems* for the Library of America. *A Human Eye: Essays on Art in Society*, appeared in April 2009. She was the 2006 recipient of the National Book Foundation's Medal for Distinguished Contribution to American Letters. She lives in California.

Social and Cultural Context

As one of the leading American poets of the twentieth century, Adrienne Rich has engaged with many of the controversial ideas of her time. Almost from the beginning she saw poetry not solely as a means of expression for its own sake, but also as a way in which to bring about change. She has blended poetry with politics throughout her career.

As a young woman she struggled with the conflict between the traditional roles of marriage and bringing up children, and artistic ambition. The poems in her first collection were famously praised by W. H. Auden as being 'neatly and modestly dressed; speak quietly but do not mumble; respect their elders but are not cowed by them'. This is an ironic comment in the light of her subsequent career when she became committed to what the critic Albert Gelpi calls 'the poetics of change'.

Feminism

In 1950s America, as elsewhere in the western world, women poets were not encouraged to share in the same aspirations as their male counterparts. When poets such as Sylvia Plath and Adrienne Rich began to describe their experiences as women and mothers, there was as yet no wider cultural recognition that these experiences could be legitimate themes for poetry. Rich later recognised that her own work had been influenced primarily by male writers. Attitudes began to change when the women's liberation movement gathered force in the 1960s. Feminists began to enquire into the rights of women and their position in society. They analysed what they called 'the patriarchal society' in which males are the dominant power and found it wanting. Adrienne Rich was in the forefront of the movement, as her poems testify. In exploring sexual politics, Rich developed influential theories of the relationship between language, power and sexuality. These issues continue to be explored to this day.

Although it was to the women's movement that Rich gave her greatest attention, she and her husband Alfred Conrad were politically involved in the Civil Rights movement also sweeping the USA in the 1960s. Issues concerning education, especially that of black Americans and other ethnic minorities, were highly controversial. Rich's involvement with disadvantaged students led her to further examination of the relation of language to power and the class struggle.

Throughout the 1960s, too, an anti-war movement constantly protested against American involvement in Vietnam. Rich, by this time a radical feminist fully committed to social justice, was immersed in this.

Poetic journey

In her poems Rich records her journey with searing honesty from compliant daughter, to wife and mother, to feminist and political activist. She has not tried to diminish the emotional upheavals that accompanied her disintegrating marriage, her ex-husband's suicide, or her realisation of her lesbian sexuality. Stylistically, her poems seem to echo the tumultuous times in which she reached the peak of her career, from the formalism and control of her earlier work to the looser, more experimental style of her later poems.

Now in her eighties, Adrienne Rich continues to write, give lectures and interviews, and play an active role in political debates. Asked in 1994 if she thought writing political poetry (what the interviewer referred to as 'poetry of witness') was a good use of her time, she answered:

> I wouldn't say it isn't a good use of my time because it's really at the very core of who I am. I have to do this. This is really how I know and how I probe the world ... I happen to think [poetry] makes a huge difference.

At the poet's request, we have not included guidelines or questions with the poetry of Adrienne Rich.

Timeline

1929	Born in Baltimore, Maryland
1951	Educated at Radcliffe College, Harvard. Publishes first poems, *A Change of World*
1953	Marries Alfred Conrad
1955–9	Birth of sons David, Paul and Jacob
1966	Moves with family to New York
1968	Begins teaching at City College, New York
1970	Suicide of Alfred Conrad
1971	Increasingly identifies with women's movement
1974	Wins the National Book Award
1976	Begins life with Michelle Cliff
1984	Moves to California
1986–93	Professor of English, Stanford University
1991	Member of the American Academy of Arts and Sciences

Storm Warnings

The glass has been falling all the afternoon,
And knowing better than the instrument
What winds are walking overhead, what zone
Of gray unrest is moving across the land,
I leave the book upon a pillowed chair   5
And walk from window to closed window, watching
Boughs strain against the sky

And think again, as often when the air
Moves inward toward a silent core of waiting,
How with a single purpose time has traveled   10
By secret currents of the undiscerned
Into this polar realm. Weather abroad
And weather in the heart alike come on
Regardless of prediction.

Between foreseeing and averting change   15
Lies all the mastery of elements
Which clocks and weatherglasses cannot alter.
Time in the hand is not control of time,
Nor shattered fragments of an instrument
A proof against the wind; the wind will rise,   20
We can only close the shutters.

I draw the curtains as the sky goes black
And set a match to candles sheathed in glass
Against the keyhole draught, the insistent whine
Of weather through the unsealed aperture.   25
This is our sole defense against the season;
These are the things that we have learned to do
Who live in troubled regions.

Glossary	
1	*the glass*: the barometer
11	*undiscerned*: not seen or noticed
23	*sheathed*: enclosed in
25	*aperture*: opening

Aunt Jennifer's Tigers

Aunt Jennifer's tigers prance across a screen,
Bright topaz denizens of a world of green.
They do not fear the men beneath the tree;
They pace in sleek chivalric certainty.

Aunt Jennifer's fingers fluttering through her wool   5
Find even the ivory needle hard to pull.
The massive weight of Uncle's wedding band
Sits heavily upon Aunt Jennifer's hand.

When Aunt is dead, her terrified hands will lie
Still ringed with ordeals she was mastered by.   10
The tigers in the panel that she made
Will go on prancing, proud and unafraid.

Glossary	
1	*prance*: to bound from the hind legs, to move proudly
2	*topaz*: a precious stone of yellow/tangerine colour
2	*denizens*: inhabitants
4	*chivalric*: knightly, courtly
10	*ordeals*: severe trials

The Uncle Speaks in the Drawing Room

I have seen the mob of late
Standing sullen in the square,
Gazing with a sullen stare
At window, balcony, and gate.
Some have talked in bitter tones   5
Some have held and fingered stones.

These are follies that subside.
Let us consider, none the less,
Certain frailties of glass
Which, it cannot be denied,   10
Lead in times like these to fear
For crystal vase and chandelier.

Not that missiles will be cast;
None as yet dare lift an arm.
But the scene recalls a storm   15
When our grandsire stood aghast
To see his antique ruby bowl
Shivered in a thunder-roll.

Let us only bear in mind
How these treasures handed down   20
From a calmer age passed on
Are in the keeping of our kind.
We stand between the dead glass-blowers
And murmurings of missile-throwers.

Glossary	
title	*drawing room*: sitting room
7	*follies*: foolish things
16	*grandsire*: grandfather
16	*aghast*: horrified

Living in Sin

She had thought the studio would keep itself;
no dust upon the furniture of love.
Half heresy, to wish the taps less vocal,
the panes relieved of grime. A plate of pears,
a piano with a Persian shawl, a cat   5
stalking the picturesque amusing mouse
had risen at his urging.
Not that at five each separate stair would writhe
under the milkman's tramp; that morning light
so coldly would delineate the scraps   10
of last night's cheese and three sepulchral bottles;
that on the kitchen shelf among the saucers
a pair of beetle-eyes would fix her own –
envoy from some village in the moldings …
Meanwhile, he, with a yawn,   15
sounded a dozen notes upon the keyboard,
declared it out of tune, shrugged at the mirror,
rubbed at his beard, went for cigarettes;
while she, jeered by the minor demons,
pulled back the sheets and made the bed and found   20
a towel to dust the table-top,
and let the coffee-pot boil over on the stove.
By evening she was back in love again,
though not so wholly but throughout the night
she woke sometimes to feel the daylight coming   25
like a relentless milkman up the stairs.

Adrienne Rich

Glossary	
title	*Living in Sin*: living together without being married
1	*studio*: one-room apartment used also as artist's workroom
3	*heresy*: opinion opposed to the usual belief
6	*picturesque*: beautiful as in a picture
8	*writhe*: to twist violently; here, to creak

10	*delineate*: draw
11	*sepulchral*: gloomy, like a tomb
14	*envoy*: messenger
14	*moldings*: mouldings, strips of wood used for decorative purposes
26	*relentless*: non-stop

The Roofwalker

for Denise Levertov

Over the half-finished houses
night comes. The builders
stand on the roof. It is
quiet after the hammers,
the pulleys hang slack.   5
Giants, the roofwalkers,
on a listing deck, the wave
of darkness about to break
on their heads. The sky
is a torn sail where figures   10
pass magnified, shadows
on a burning deck.

I feel like them up there:
exposed, larger than life,
and due to break my neck.   15

Was it worth while to lay –
with infinite exertion –
a roof I can't live under?
– All those blueprints,
closings of gaps,   20

measurements, calculations?
A life I didn't choose
chose me: even
my tools are the wrong ones
for what I have to do.   25
I'm naked, ignorant,
a naked man fleeing
across the roofs
who could with a shade of difference
be sitting in the lamplight   30
against the cream wallpaper
reading – not with indifference –
about a naked man
fleeing across the roofs.

Glossary

dedication *for Denise Levertov*: Levertov was a poet (1923–97) born in England but who moved to America. Rich may be responding, in part, to Levertov's poem 'From the Roof', in which a woman bringing in the washing on her Manhattan rooftop becomes the transformer and the transformed, watching and taking part in the sensuous, teeming life beneath her

5	*pulleys*: device for lifting heavy weights
7	*listing*: leaning to one side
19	*blueprints*: a guide or model of how things should be done

Our Whole Life

Our whole life a translation
the permissible fibs

and now a knot of lies
eating at itself to get undone

Words bitten thru words   5
meanings burnt-off like paint
under the blowtorch

All those dead letters
rendered into the oppressor's language

Trying to tell the doctor where it hurts   10
like the Algerian
who walked from his village, burning

his whole body a cloud of pain
and there are no words for this

except himself   15

Glossary

2	*permissible*: allowable
5	*thru*: American version of 'through'
8	*dead letters*: undelivered letters
9	*oppressor*: one who governs tyrannically

Trying to Talk with a Man

Out in this desert we are testing bombs,

that's why we came here.

Sometimes I feel an underground river
forcing its way between deformed cliffs
an acute angle of understanding   5
moving itself like a locus of the sun
into this condemned scenery.

What we've had to give up to get here –
whole LP collections, films we starred in,
playing in the neighbourhoods, bakery windows   10
full of dry, chocolate-filled Jewish cookies,
the language of love-letters, of suicide notes,
afternoons on the riverbank
pretending to be children

Coming out to this desert   15
we meant to change the face of
driving among dull green succulents
walking at noon in the ghost town
surrounded by a silence

that sounds like the silence of the place   20
except that it came with us
and is familiar
and everything we were saying until now
was an effort to blot it out –
coming out here we are up against it   25

Out here I feel more helpless
with you than without you
You mention the danger
and list the equipment

we talk of people caring for each other 30

in emergencies – laceration, thirst –

but you look at me like an emergency

Your dry heat feels like power

your eyes are stars of a different magnitude

they reflect lights that spell out: EXIT 35

when you get up and pace the floor

talking of the danger

as if it were not ourselves

as if we were testing anything else.

Glossary

4	*deformed*: misshapen
5	*acute angle*: sharp, pointed
6	*locus*: place. Also a term in geometry, meaning a location defined by a group of elements
17	*succulents*: juicy, fleshy plants such as cacti
31	*laceration*: torn flesh
34	*magnitude*: measure of star's brightness

Diving into the Wreck

First having read the book of myths,
and loaded the camera,
and checked the edge of the knife-blade,
I put on
the body-armor of black rubber   5
the absurd flippers
the grave and awkward mask.
I am having to do this
not like Cousteau with his
assiduous team   10
aboard the sun-flooded schooner
but here alone.

There is a ladder.
The ladder is always there
hanging innocently   15
close to the side of the schooner.
We know what it is for,
we who have used it.
Otherwise
it's a piece of maritime floss   20
some sundry equipment.

I go down.
Rung after rung and still
the oxygen immerses me
the blue light   25
the clear atoms
of our human air.
I go down.
My flippers cripple me,
I crawl like an insect down the ladder   30
and there is no one
to tell me when the ocean
will begin.

First the air is blue and then
it is bluer and then green and then 35
black I am blacking out and yet
my mask is powerful
it pumps my blood with power
the sea is another story
the sea is not a question of power
I have to learn alone 40
to turn my body without force
in the deep element.

And now: it is easy to forget
what I came for
among so many who have always 45
lived here
swaying their crenellated fans
between the reefs
and besides
you breathe differently down here. 50

I came to explore the wreck.
The words are purposes.
The words are maps.
I came to see the damage that was done
and the treasures that prevail. 55
I stroke the beam of my lamp
slowly along the flank
of something more permanent
than fish or weed.

the thing I came for: 60
the wreck and not the story of the wreck
the thing itself and not the myth
the drowned face always staring
toward the sun
the evidence of damage 65

worn by salt and sway into this threadbare beauty
the ribs of the disaster
curving their assertion
among the tentative haunters.

This is the place.   70
And I am here, the mermaid whose dark hair
streams black, the merman in his armored body
We circle silently
about the wreck
we dive into the hold.   75
I am she: I am he

whose drowned face sleeps with open eyes
whose breasts still bear the stress
whose silver, copper, vermeil cargo lies
obscurely inside barrels   80
half-wedged and left to rot
we are the half-destroyed instruments
that once held to a course
the water-eaten log
the fouled compass.   85

We are, I am, you are
by cowardice or courage
the one who find our way
back to this scene
carrying a knife, a camera   90
a book of myths
in which
our names do not appear.

Glossary	
1	*myths*: folklore, legends
9	*Cousteau*: Jacques Cousteau (1910–2001) French underwater explorer and film-maker
10	*assiduous*: diligent, hard-working
11	*schooner*: a swift sailing vessel
20	*maritime floss*: thread used at sea
21	*sundry*: various
42	*element*: the water (one of the four elements – earth, air and fire are the others)
47	*crenellated*: notched with round or scalloped projections
48	*reefs*: a chain of rocks at or near the surface of water
55	*prevail*: triumph
69	*tentative*: done provisionally
79	*vermeil*: gilded metal
84	*log*: daily record of ship's progress

From a Survivor

The pact that we made was the ordinary pact
of men & women in those days

I don't know who we thought we were
that our personalities
could resist the failures of the race   5

Lucky or unlucky, we didn't know
the race had failures of that order
and that we were going to share them

Like everybody else, we thought of ourselves as special

Your body is as vivid to me   10
as it ever was: even more

since my feeling for it is clearer:
I know what it could and could not do

it is no longer
the body of a god   15
or anything with power over my life

Next year it would have been 20 years
and you are wastefully dead
who might have made the leap
we talked, too late, of making   20

which I live now
not as a leap
but a succession of brief, amazing movements

each one making possible the next

Glossary	
1	*the pact*: agreement i.e. of marriage
17	*you*: the poet's estranged husband, Alfred Conrad

Power

Living in the earth-deposits   of our history

Today a backhoe divulged   out of a crumbling flank of earth
one bottle   amber   perfect   a hundred-year-old
cure for fever   or melancholy   a tonic
for living on this earth   in the winters of this climate   5

Today I was reading about Marie Curie:
she must have known she suffered   from radiation sickness
her body bombarded for years   by the element
she had purified
It seems she denied to the end   10
the source of the cataracts on her eyes
the cracked and suppurating skin   of her finger-ends
till she could no longer hold   a test-tube or a pencil

She died   a famous woman   denying
her wounds   15
denying
her wounds   came   from the same source as her power

Glossary		
2	*backhoe*: mechanical digger	
2	*flank*: side	
4	*melancholy*: sadness, depression	
6	*Marie Curie*: Polish-born chemist and physicist (1864–1934). Having come to France and married Pierre Curie, she did pioneering research on radioactivity. The Curies discovered radium. Marie Curie was the first person to be awarded the Nobel Prize twice. She died of leukaemia caused by exposure to high levels of radiation	
8	*bombarded*: attacked	
11	*cataracts*: a condition in which the lens of the eye becomes opaque, causing partial blindness	
12	*suppurating*: oozing pus	

General Questions

1   Write an essay on the poetry of Adrienne Rich with the title: 'Adrienne Rich: woman of our time'.

2   'Adrienne Rich: a poet of conflict.' Write an essay on this aspect of Adrienne Rich's poetry.

3   Adrienne Rich has been called 'witness, visionary, prophet'. Would you agree that these words apply to her as a poet?

4   'Adrienne Rich's poems are more interesting for what she says rather than how she says it.' Would you agree with this view of Adrienne Rich's work?

5   'Adrienne Rich has documented her development as a woman and as a poet with great honesty.' Would you agree with this view?

6   'Adrienne Rich's early poems are more appealing than her later ones.' To what extent would you agree with this view?

7   'Rich's poems tell us a great deal about the society in which she lives.' Discuss this view of her poetry.

8   'Adrienne Rich's poems portray men in an unfair light.' Do you agree with this view?

9   'The appeal of Adrienne Rich's poetry.' Using the above title, write an essay outlining what you consider to be the appeal of Rich's poetry. Support your points by reference to the poetry of Adrienne Rich on your course.

    In your answer, you could consider some of the following points:
    - her choice of themes is interesting and contemporary e.g. relations between men and women, the nature of power, political issues
    - she confronts the issues she deals with honestly and fearlessly
    - her use of language is always fresh and exciting
    - she reveals her own personality and concerns in many of her poems, etc.

10 Write about the feelings that Adrienne Rich's poetry creates in you and the aspects of her poetry (content and/or style) that help to create those feelings. Support your points by reference to the poetry by Adrienne Rich on your course. You might include some of these points in your answer:
    - you respond well to the issues she deals with – they are relevant to people's lives, including your own
    - you share in the anger she expresses, whether directly or indirectly, at oppression of women and the politically powerless
    - you sympathise with the personal problems she has faced, as expressed in her work, e.g. her husband's death
    - you appreciate the way in which the form of her poetry changed in response to changes in her own life, e.g. from her early to her later work, etc.

NB Of course, it may be that the feelings her work creates in you are negative! In this case, you could make some of the following points:

- you consider the issues she deals with irrelevant to the present day
- you find her attitudes to certain issues (e.g. the relations of men and women) inflexible and exaggerated
- you feel she depicts men unfairly
- you find her use of language too detached
- you react negatively to her desire to change the world.

Sample Essay

Write an introduction to the poetry of Adrienne Rich for new readers.

I am delighted to have been asked to write an introduction to the poetry of Adrienne Rich for new readers. In her poetry Adrienne Rich has dealt with some of the most important ideas of the twentieth century: the changing role of women in society and the effect it has had on the relationships between men and women. She has never been afraid to confront these issues, no matter how painful it may have been for her as a woman and as a poet. For these reasons, new readers will find her work stimulating and challenging, as I certainly did when I first encountered her work.

[The introduction covers the poet's ideas and use of language, e.g. imagery.
It also refers to the tone and atmosphere of her poems]

From her earliest years as a poet Rich was aware that she was writing and living in a tradition that had been established by males – what is called a 'patriarchal' society. One of her earliest poems, 'Aunt Jennifer's Tigers', dramatises the position of women in the society of her youth, as she saw it. 'Aunt Jennifer' is a creative artist in her own right. The 'tigers' she embroiders are described in images of fearlessness and pride: they 'prance across a screen'. They are 'proud and unafraid'. There is a suggestion that like all good works of art they will have a life of their own, regardless of their creator: they will 'go on prancing'. In contrast, the images associated with Aunt Jennifer as a woman show her as timid and uncertain: her fingers 'fluttering' through her wool, her 'terrified hands'. Perhaps the image that dramatises Aunt Jennifer's plight most is that she is living under the 'massive weight of Uncle's wedding band'. It is as if she cannot bring herself to realise the contradiction between her ambitions as an artist and as a woman in her traditional role as wife, subservient to her husband. In my opinion these issues have a relevance to all readers, of whatever gender, who are trying to come to terms with gender roles in their lives.

[Note how short quotations are used as a part of sentences]

A similar contradiction appears in another poem, 'Living in Sin'. Here the speaker describes the different experiences men and women have in their domestic lives. For the male figure in the poem – clearly an artist – living with a woman has not changed his way of life at all. He is still free to produce his pictures – 'a plate of pears / a piano with a Persian shawl'. There is no obstacle to his creative urge. But the woman, like Aunt Jennifer, is weighed down by her role as housewife. Her struggle to keep the house clean is shown in images that could be amusing – the 'pair of beetle-eyes' that seem to challenge her from the kitchen shelf, an 'envoy' or messenger from a whole 'village' of them in the paintwork – if they weren't also a reminder of the sheer drudgery and monotony of housework. The tone of the poem is so heartfelt that we must assume Rich is basing this on personal experience. It is far from the romantic notions she had of what 'living in sin' might mean. However, Rich does not blame men entirely for this situation, as it is the woman alone who is 'jeered by the minor demons', urging her to behave like a housewife. But she does hint that relations between the sexes will not remain as simple as they once seemed to be: the woman is 'not so wholly' in love as she was before.

Both of the poems I have mentioned express dissatisfaction with the role of women in society, but at this stage Rich still writes in the third person, as if the problems had little to do with her. But in 'The Roofwalker' she writes from a personal point of view. The central image of workers repairing a roof becomes a metaphor for her own life as a woman and as a poet, at a particular moment in time. The roof workers take risks. Like them, Rich is 'due to break my neck'. She can no longer live as she used to, following the 'blueprints' or 'calculations' that she 'didn't choose'. We know from Rich's life that her father dictated how she was to be educated, and how she wrote poems initially in the style of the male poets that had preceded her. We also know that she became involved in the women's movement in the 1960s. Now we have a sense in this poem that she is preparing for change, aware that this will leave her vulnerable: 'naked, ignorant'. Once again, I suggest that for many of us, men and women, change is a frightening experience, and Rich has given us a vivid metaphor for any feelings of panic that we may have in confronting these issues.

[Third poem discussed; use of biographical details]

Another metaphor that Rich uses to express her predicament as a woman on the brink of change is that of 'diving into the wreck', in the poem of the same name. Many poems use the metaphor of a journey as a starting-point for a discovery or new insight. The image of the sea, too, has often featured as a source of knowledge. As the speaker descends deeper and deeper into the 'wreck' at the bottom of the sea, it may be that she is exploring the depths of her subconscious, trying to find the truth about the myths that men and women have told about themselves. There is a sense of adventure and mystery in the poem. What she finds in the wreck may not be

Adrienne Rich

completely destroyed: perhaps there are 'treasures' as well as 'damage'. Here, she may be 'mermaid' and 'merman' – all distinctions between the sexes have disappeared. Is the poet suggesting that the fixed gender roles accepted in society have led to the metaphorical 'wreck' in the first place? Readers new to Rich's poetry will find that although this is not a poem that can be easily explained, it works its magic through the mysterious atmosphere it creates. I certainly found it quite challenging, initially, but I hope that new readers will be entranced by the mysterious atmosphere it creates, as I came to be.

[Discussion of fourth poem linked to previous paragraph]
[Personal response]

New readers should respond positively too to Rich's expressions of vulnerability. Her themes are relevant to the experience of many women in the 1960s, and later, as the women's movement progressed, but she still writes movingly and in a personal way. One of her simplest and most affecting poems is 'From a survivor', written after the death by suicide of her husband, Alfred Conrad. It must have been a difficult poem to write. She remembers with sadness how they married, full of hope for the future, making what was the 'ordinary pact / of men and women in those days'. These words, although simple, say a great deal about how relationships between men and women were to change during the lifetime of their marriage. They were happy and in love: 'like everybody else, we thought of ourselves as special' – and unaware that they were about to 'share' in the 'failures of the race' by experiencing marriage breakdown. Now that he is dead, she can look back and see how, once, as her husband he had 'power over my life'. But she seems also to regret that he 'might have made the leap / we talked, too late of making' – perhaps he too could have faced change in their lives, and lived to experience life as she does, as a 'succession of brief, amazing moments'.

[Fifth poem discussed]

In this poem, we see Adrienne Rich confronting the emotional fallout from the feminist movement. Even readers who may not be convinced by her feminist views cannot fail to respond to her honesty in facing painful truths about her experiences and the effectiveness of the language she uses.

In conclusion, I would like to think that new readers will respond as positively as I have done to the challenges and rewards of Adrienne Rich's poetry, and appreciate the poetic journey she reveals to us.

[Note how the opening paragraph indicates the direction of the essay while the final paragraph gives it a sense of closure]

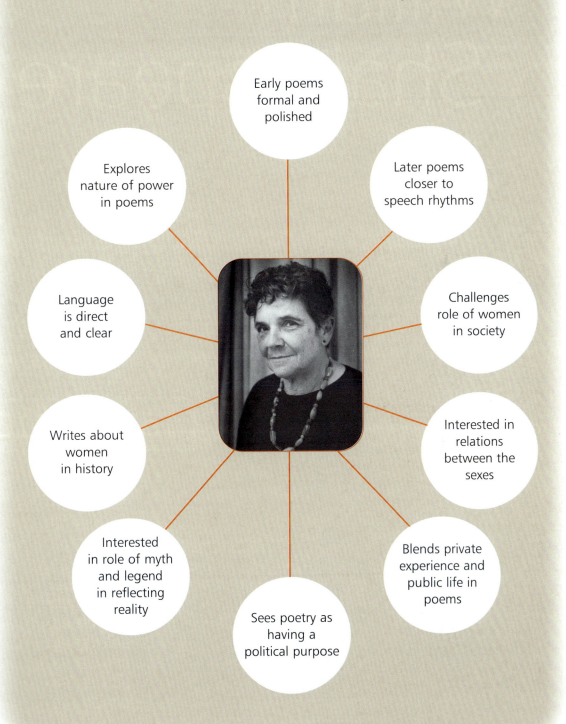

Early poems formal and polished

Explores nature of power in poems

Later poems closer to speech rhythms

Language is direct and clear

Challenges role of women in society

Writes about women in history

Interested in relations between the sexes

Interested in role of myth and legend in reflecting reality

Blends private experience and public life in poems

Sees poetry as having a political purpose

William Shakespeare

1564–1616

Biography

Eighteenth-century editor George Steevens claimed, 'all that we know of Shakespeare is that he was born at Stratford-on-Avon, married and had children there; went to London, where he commenced [as an] actor, and wrote plays and poems; returned to Stratford, made his will, and died'.

What passes for Shakespeare's biography is, in fact, a tissue of documentary records, mainly of trivial facts; traditions, legends and anecdotes, often of doubtful value; references to Shakespeare in the works of his contemporaries; and, most unsatisfactory of all, assumptions based on passages in the plays and sonnets. In the absence of a substantial volume of undisputed facts, biographers are often forced to fall back on terms such as 'perhaps', 'it is probable', 'it is likely', 'it is almost certain', and so on.

What do we know

It is known that Shakespeare's father, John, came into Stratford from a neighbouring farm in the 1550s, practised a variety of trades, achieved prosperity, owned property and became a leading citizen of the town, which at that time had a population of about one thousand.

Shakespeare was christened at the parish church at Stratford on 26 April 1564. It can be taken for granted that he attended the local grammar school, only half a mile from his home, until he was aged sixteen. In Shakespeare's day, grammar school education was focused almost exclusively on the study of the Latin language and its literature. Students also learned rhetoric, which is the art of public speaking.

In 1582 Shakespeare married Anne Hathaway. She was aged twenty-six; he was eighteen. They had three children. Their only son, Hamnet, died in 1596, aged eleven. No record of Anne Hathaway exists between the baptism of her children and the drafting of her husband's will in 1616, the year of his death.

By the 1590s Shakespeare was an actor and a rising dramatist, based in London. By 1595 he was a sharer in an acting company. Two years later he was able to buy New Place, the second largest property in Stratford. Between 1590 and 1603 he spent most of his time in London, writing plays, arranging for their performance and sometimes acting in them. Of the twenty-six plays he wrote during this period, *Hamlet* (1601) is the most celebrated. Between 1603 and his death thirteen years later in 1616, Shakespeare wrote his four other tragic masterpieces: *Othello, King Lear, Macbeth* and *Anthony and Cleopatra*. His great plays were all performed at the Globe theatre in London, in which he was a shareholder.

Shakespeare combined supreme creative ability with practical instincts and an impressive business sense. Records from the last decade of his life show him acquiring considerable property in and around his place of birth and in London, and shrewdly protecting his legal interests. In addition to houses, he purchased over one hundred acres of farmland and an interest in tithes, which guaranteed a substantial income. When debts owing to him remained unpaid, he was quick to sue the defaulters, even in petty cases.

Publications

Shakespeare appears to have taken far less interest in the fate of his writings than in his property and investment income. He did not oversee the publication of the editions of his plays published during his lifetime. These are carelessly printed and contain many errors. Much of his most celebrated work was still in manuscript form when he died, and remained so until two of his friends and colleagues, John Heminges and Henry Condell, published his complete plays in 1623 in an edition now known as the First Folio. This substantial volume contains all the plays now attributed to Shakespeare, except *Pericles*.

The sonnets were probably written and revised over the course of two decades. They were first published in 1609. It is unclear whether Shakespeare had any involvement in this publication.

Social and Cultural Context

Shakespeare wrote his sonnets in an era when sonnet sequences were highly fashionable.

Conventional themes

It is important to bear in mind that Shakespeare's favourite themes in his sonnets are the same as those of a large number of his contemporaries in the sonnet form. Many sonnets from the period deal with time, decay, death, love, friendship, jealousy or poetic immortality. This is because Shakespeare and his contemporaries were drawing heavily for both themes and formulations on the work of two great classical poets, Ovid and Horace. The nature of Shakespeare's debt to these poets is well documented by J. B. Leishman in his book *Themes and Variations in Shakespeare's Sonnets*.

Meaning of 'love'

The kind of friendship, or love, between the male speaker of the sonnets and the young man whose outstanding qualities he is celebrating does not necessarily carry homosexual implications. In Sonnet 20 the speaker calls the young man 'the master mistress of my passion', but in the same sonnet appears to make a distinction between his platonic love for his friend and the very different kind of love the latter will experience with an adoring woman: 'Mine be thy love, and thy love's use their treasure'.

The idea that the friendship of a man for a man was more profound and noble than his love for a woman was a favourite theme in classical and Renaissance literature, the conventions of which had a considerable influence on Shakespeare's poetic practice. It is in this context that we should consider the relationship between the speaker and his friend in these sonnets.

Are the sonnets autobiographical?

Any sensible approach to Shakespeare's sonnets must be based on our answer to a fundamental question: are the sonnets poems in which Shakespeare unlocked his heart, or are they simply conventional literary exercises, having no reference, or very little at least, to real persons or events?

If we insist on looking for Shakespeare's personal history in the sonnets, we are faced with the problem that the best efforts of scholars for centuries have failed to establish with certainty – or even probability – the identity of the central figures (the young man, the dark lady, the rival poet). Given the considerable number of possible contenders for these roles, an approach to the sonnets as autobiography is at best only tentative, and at worst absurd. There is simply not enough unimpeachable evidence.

In the light of this, it is tempting to dismiss altogether the idea that Shakespeare had himself or any actual contemporaries in mind when he wrote the sonnets. This would mean reading the sonnets as conventional literary exercises in which Shakespeare uses a speaker to express a variety of moods, emotions and views on a variety of themes.

There are several good reasons for believing that Shakespeare was not bringing his personal experiences to light in the sonnets. If he did harbour a hopeless passion for a fair young man and was at the time betrayed, is it likely that he would have exposed these painful circumstances in sonnets circulated among his friends before they were published?

In several of the sonnets, the speaker makes the claim, usual among writers in the form, that these very poems will immortalise the young man and defy the ravages of time. If the speaker represents Shakespeare, and is not merely rehearsing a

William Shakespeare

conventional formula, how do we account for the fact that Shakespeare appears not to have taken the trouble to have the sonnets published and so to ensure the immortality so often promised to their unnamed subject?

There is the further consideration that all of Shakespeare's contemporaries who wrote sonnets dealt with themes, experiences and attitudes to loved ones that are very similar to these found in Shakespeare's sonnets. It would be odd if so many representative English poets all underwent the same ordeal at the hands of those they admired!

It is safest to assume that Shakespeare's sonnets are not autobiographical, but rather follow a rigid set of conventions and explorations on the themes of being deeply and hopelessly in love and of poetic immortality for both speaker and beloved.

Shakespeare's Sonnets: Recurring Themes

A few great, simple, conventional themes dominate the entire sonnet sequence. These are:

- The ravages of time and its destruction of youth and beauty (Sonnets 12, 60, 65, 73).
- The joys, sorrows and compensations of love (Sonnets 18, 23, 29, 30).
- The power of great art – in this case great poetry – to defy time (Sonnets 18, 60, 65).
- The definition of true love (Sonnet 116).
- The miseries of life (Sonnets 66, 94).

The eleven prescribed sonnets on this course all consist of various forms of address by a speaker to a young, handsome man whose friendship he treasures and who gives his life its meaning. These eleven sonnets may be divided into two groups.

First group of sonnets

Sonnets 12, 18, 60 and 65 belong to the first group. In each of these poems, youth and beauty – specifically that of the young man – are considered in relation to the merciless destruction wrought by time. Also in each of them, the speaker seeks some means of defying the ravages of time.

In Sonnet 12, having provided a catalogue of time's destructive dealings with human beings, the speaker suggests that the only defence against time's scythe is for the young man to marry and leave heirs who will perpetuate his beauty after time has taken him away, by repeating his face and features.

In Sonnets 18, 60 and 65, the speaker proposes to preserve the young man's beauty from oblivion by invoking the classical convention that poetry will confer immortality on its subject, as well as on the poet. In Sonnet 18, the speaker promises an eternal, unfading summer to the young man: as long as time lasts he will last, because as long as the earth holds people able to read, they will be conscious of the young man and his glory:

> So long as men can breathe, or eyes can see,
> So long lives this, and this gives life to thee.

Sonnet 60 invokes a darker, grimmer picture of time as it fights to destroy the beauty of men as soon as they reach the perfection of maturity. Again, as in Sonnet 18, the speaker's best hope of preserving the young man's memory from the wreckage is to immortalise him in verse that will long outlive him:

> And yet to times in hope my verse shall stand,
> Praising thy worth, despite his cruel hand.

In Sonnet 65, three kinds of time and their common effects are considered. We have geological time, which destroys the materials of which the earth is made, as well as the boundless sea; archaeological time, which wastes the strongest creations of man such as the impregnable walls of castles and gates of steel; and human time, which shows no mercy to man, time's best jewel, but tries to hide him for eternity in its treasure chest. Against this overwhelming power exerted by time, the speaker can only oppose black lines of verse, which, for all their fragility, will ensure the immortality of one splendid young man and save him from oblivion. To the question of who can prevent time's destruction of human beauty, the speaker has only one answer:

> O none, unless this miracle have might:
> That in black ink my love may still shine bright.

It is worth remembering that the young man being promised immortality in this sonnet (and in Sonnets 18 and 65) is not necessarily a real individual. It is likely that he is a conventional idealised character of the type addressed in many sonnets by Shakespeare's contemporaries. In one of Michael Drayton's sonnets, for example, the speaker (who is not necessarily the poet) promises a similar kind of immortality to the unnamed person he admires:

> So shalt thou fly above the vulgar throng,
> Still to survive in my immortal song.

William Shakespeare

Second group of sonnets

Sonnets 23, 29, 30, 66, 73, 94 and 116 celebrate the speaker's love for the young man and dwell on the significance of this love as a compensation for the sorrows and troubles of life.

Within this second group, there are variations of emphasis. Sonnets 29 and 30 may be considered together, since they belong to a group in which the speaker declares that his friend is a compensation for his shortcomings in talent and fortune, as well as for all the failures and disappointments he has encountered. In Sonnet 29, he contemplates his present wants and troubles in a depressed state of mind. In Sonnet 30, he torments himself with a depressing survey of his past griefs and losses. In both, the mere thought of his friend is enough to restore him to supreme happiness: in Sonnet 29 to convert him from the outlook of a wretched outcast to that of a royal personage, and in Sonnet 30 to compensate him not only for disappointment and unfulfilled ambition, but also for the death of other dear friends.

The remaining five sonnets deal with love and its expression. Sonnet 23 suggests a depth of feeling so intense that the speaker lacks the eloquence to express it adequately. He is therefore obliged to ask the young man to read his love for him in his poems.

Sonnet 66 records the speaker's love for his friend in a very different mode. Having chronicled the evils of human existence and expressed a longing for death as a relief from these, he is restrained by only one consideration: that if he dies he will be deserting his friend, thus suggesting that the relationship is not one-sided – that the young man may in some sense reciprocate his love.

Sonnet 73 reads like a pathetic appeal for love. The speaker depicts himself as declining into old age and hopes that the young man's love for him will grow stronger as he realises how little time their love has left to run.

Sonnet 94 is a disillusioned account of a disappointed friendship ending in the sad reflection that even seemingly virtuous people can become their own opposites.

Sonnet 116, the finest of all the sonnets, transcends the individual circumstances of the others and considers love as an absolute value. The speaker defines perfect love (the marriage of true minds) as being constant and unchangeable like the Northern Star, and triumphantly defying time. He goes on to argue that his own love has these qualities. In some of Shakespeare's other sonnets, we find attempts to discover permanence in the midst of transience and waste of beauty. For example, Sonnet 12 advocates the perpetuation of beauty through offspring ('breed') and Sonnets 18, 60 and 65 promise the immortality of the beloved through poetry. Sonnet 116 celebrates the power of love to transcend time.

Shakespeare's Sonnets: Language

Like every poet, **Shakespeare makes continuous use of figurative language**. Figurative language is distinct from literal language and involves the description of one thing in terms of another. Metaphor is the basic figure of speech in Shakespeare's sonnets.

Simile and metaphor

There is a close association between metaphor and simile. In metaphor, the comparison is usually implied; whereas in simile, it is openly proclaimed. Along with simile, metaphor is the writer's chief mode of achieving concreteness and vitality, which are characteristics of Shakespeare's best sonnets.

When Shakespeare writes, in Sonnet 60, 'Like as the waves make towards the pebbled shore / So do our minutes hasten to their end', he is using a simile. When he writes, in Sonnet 30, 'When to the sessions of sweet silent thought / I summon up remembrance of things past', he is using a metaphor. It is clear from these two examples that metaphor is capable of a greater range of suggestiveness than simile, and that its implications are wider and richer. The simile, by its very nature, is limited to a comparatively small area of suggestion.

By means of successful metaphor, Shakespeare achieves strength and clarity of impression. A vivid metaphor can impress its meaning more memorably and more indelibly than almost any passage of abstract discourse, however well written. For example the following (from Sonnet 65):

> O how shall summer's honey breath hold out
> Against the wrackful siege of batt'ring days

Personification

Shakespeare also makes telling use of personification throughout the sonnets, particularly in his treatment of time and chance as enemies of beauty. Personification, which in Shakespeare's sonnets becomes part of a dense web of metaphor, involves the attribution of human qualities to such abstractions as time and beauty.

A good example of Shakespeare's handling of personification with memorable effect is found in Sonnet 60:

> Time doth transfix the flourish set on youth,
> And delves the parallels in beauty's brow

Another, equally impressive, example is this from Sonnet 65:

> O fearful meditation! Where, alack,
> Shall time's best jewel from time's chest lie hid?

Timeline

1564	Born in Stratford-upon-Avon in the English Midlands to John Shakespeare and Mary Arden
1570s	Probably attends grammar school, where Latin and rhetoric (the art of public speaking) are important subjects
1582	Marries Anne Hathaway when she was 26 and he was 18
1583	Birth of his first daughter, Susanna
1585	Birth of his twin son and daughter, Hamnet and Judith
1593	Publishes a long narrative poem: *Venus and Adonis*
1594	Publishes a second narrative poem: *The Rape of Lucrece*
1594	An established actor and successful playwright, he joins the Lord Chamberlain's Men and becomes a sharer in the company's profits
1596	Death of his son, Hamnet
1603	Death of Elizabeth I and coronation of James I
1603	James I confers his patronage on Shakespeare and his fellow players, who become the King's Men
1609	First publication of his sonnets, many of which had been circulating privately for over a decade
1616	Dies on 23 April; his monument survives in Holy Trinity Church, Stratford-upon-Avon
1623	First publication of his collected plays

Sonnet 12

When I do count the clock that tells the time,
And see the brave day sunk in hideous night;
When I behold the violet past prime,
And sable curls all silvered o'er with white:
When lofty trees I see barren of leaves,   5
Which erst from heat did canopy the herd,
And summer's green all girded up in sheaves
Borne on the bier with white and bristly beard:
Then of thy beauty do I question make,
That thou among the wastes of time must go,   10
Since sweets and beauties do themselves forsake,
And die as fast as they see others grow,
And nothing 'gainst time's scythe can make defence
Save breed to brave him, when he takes thee hence.

Glossary

1	*count the clock*: mark the passage of the hours, count the clock's chimes
2	*brave*: beautiful, radiant
3	*past prime*: faded, beyond its best
4	*sable*: dark brown
5	*barren*: bare
6	*erst*: once, formerly
6	*canopy the herd*: shade the animals (from the heat of the sun)
7	*green*: fresh crops
7	*girded*: bound securely
7	*sheaves*: bundles
8	*bier*: carriage or wooden frame used for carrying the dead to their graves
9	*question make*: enquire, think about
11	*forsake*: abandon (themselves by changing their state and no longer being sweet and beautiful)
13	*scythe*: a tool for cutting grass; here, time is personified as the reaper
14	*breed*: children
14	*brave*: defy

Guidelines

In this sonnet we have a succession of varied images, each illustrating the changes brought about by time. These are concrete images, drawn from the familiar experiences of the natural world. What is interesting about Shakespeare's handling of these images is the way in which they succeed each other as they reflect shifting emotions.

Commentary

Lines 1–8

The powerful spirit of time works out its progress in an irresistible way through the clock, the day, the violet, the greying hair of ageing human beings, trees dropping their leaves and, most memorably, the harvesting of 'summer's green' (line 7) crops. The telescoping of images in these lines creates a powerful imaginative effect.

In lines 7 and 8 the harvest of sheaves being carried home is transformed into a body in a funeral procession: the vehicle on which the sheaves are carried becomes the bier conveying a corpse to its grave. The 'white and bristly beard' belongs equally to the sheaves and to the aged corpse, and 'girded up' refers simultaneously to the bound sheaves and the girdle about the waist of the dead man. In a grimly ironical touch, the grain that keeps us alive is transmuted into the dead body we will become in time. These lines feature the functional use of alliteration to stress time's power over all things, human as well as natural ('summer's', 'sheaves', 'green', 'girded', 'Borne', 'bier', 'bristly beard').

Lines 9–14

This consideration of time's effects causes the speaker to begin thinking about his friend's beauty and how his friend must eventually join those things destroyed by time. All beautiful things must die and be replaced by other beautiful things.

The identification of man's fate with that of nature and natural beauty is central to this sonnet, and is reinforced in the final two lines. Nothing can resist the hand of time. Time is here personified as the reaper, indiscriminately at work with his scythe, cutting off both human lives and ripe grain. The association between the two is powerfully reinforced by the disturbing ceremonial depicted in lines 7 and 8. The only defence against the destructive power of time is to leave offspring behind after death to defy him.

William Shakespeare

Thinking about the poem

1   Sonnet 12 has many images of change. Make a list of these. How do they illustrate the main theme of the poem?

2   Lines 7 and 8 have been much admired by critics. Why, do you think, is this so? What do the lines suggest to you?

3   Why is time such a menacing figure?

4   Is there anything that can defy the effects of time?

5   To what kind of person is the poem addressed?

6   Why does Shakespeare contrast 'brave day' with 'hideous night' in line 2?

7   In the first eight lines Shakespeare makes much use of colour. How do the various colours mentioned (violet, sable, silver, white, green) relate to the main theme of the poem?

8   Distinguish between the human images and the images of nature in the sonnet. How are they related?

9   In the third quatrain (lines 9 to 12), there is a change of emphasis. Say what this is.

10   Show how the third quatrain follows logically from the first two.

11   The sonnet features a clear opposition between time and death on the one hand, and beauty on the other. How is this opposition resolved?

12   Is this poem pessimistic or optimistic, or both? Explain your answer by close reference to the sonnet.

13   The sonnet is arranged in the form of an argument (i.e. it is designed to persuade). Comment on this idea.

14   Why is there so much emphasis on beauty in this sonnet? Support your answer by reference to the poem.

Sonnet 18

Shall I compare thee to a summer's day?
Thou art more lovely and more temperate:
Rough winds do shake the darling buds of May,
And summer's lease hath all too short a date:
Sometime too hot the eye of heaven shines,   5
And often is his gold complexion dimmed;
And every fair from fair sometimes declines,
By chance, or nature's changing course, untrimmed;
But thy eternal summer shall not fade,
Nor lose possession of that fair thou ow'st,   10
Nor shall death brag thou wander'st in his shade,
When in eternal lines to time thou grow'st:
So long as men can breathe, or eyes can see,
So long lives this, and this gives life to thee.

Glossary		
2	*lovely*: kind or gentle
2	*temperate*: not extreme; here, even-tempered
3	*May*: in Shakespeare's time, May ran from our mid-May to our mid-June
4	*lease*: a temporary grant of property that expires on an agreed date; here, a metaphorical way of saying that summer passes all too quickly
4	*date:* duration
5	*eye of heaven*: the sun
6	*dimmed*: obscured by clouds
7	*fair*: every beautiful thing, beauty
8	*untrimmed*: deprived or stripped of its beauty (trimmings)
10	*ow'st*: own, possess
12	*lines*: verse, poetry; also descendants
12	*grow'st*: become part of
14	*this*: this sonnet, which will keep the friend's name alive for as long as people are alive to read it

Guidelines

This sonnet again illustrates Shakespeare's tendency to think metaphorically. The speaker's initial impulse is to make his friend's beauty the subject of a simile, only to realise that to compare him to a summer's day would not do justice to his beauty. Day here may well refer not to a single day in summer, but to the season as a whole.

Commentary

Like many of the sonnets, including Sonnet 12, this one is relatively simple in style. The emotions of the speaker are not expressed in far-fetched comparisons. The diction is plain and often monosyllabic. The metaphors are based on the homely, everyday experiences of common life.

Lines 1–8

In the octave of the sonnet (the first eight lines), **the metaphors derive from two sources: the brevity and volatility of summer** and the more mundane business of leaseholding. The octave also dwells on some of the imperfections of summer; it is neither as beautiful nor as temperate as the speaker's friend; its winds can be rough and injurious; it is too short; its sunshine can be too warm or sometimes obscured by cloud, and during its course the beautiful things of nature can be divested of their beauty ('untrimmed', line 8).

The various imperfections of summer throw the friend's perfections into relief. Unlike summer, he cannot lose his natural beauty, or be the captive of death or decay. Instead, he will enjoy the eternity of loveliness that this and the other sonnets will ensure for him by celebrating for ever his youthful beauty.

The metaphoric character of the sonnet is best expressed in lines 4 to 6. The implications of the metaphors become clearer when we translate the concrete images they invoke into abstract language. The right enjoyed by the personified summer (its 'lease') to remain a tenant of the earth runs only for a short period. This is a vastly more arresting way of saying that summer passes all too quickly. The metaphors of the next two lines are commonplace; the sun is first pictured as the bright eye of heaven and then as a person whose golden features are often obscured.

Lines 9–14

The key line in the poem as a whole is 'But thy eternal summer shall not fade' (line 9). The key word in the line is 'eternal'. The suggestion is that while the splendour of summer fades quickly, the friend's splendour will live on. It will last as long as time itself does. Death will not take possession of it (line 11). The rhyming couplet of lines

13 and 14 explain why this is true: he will enjoy immortality because the poet's verse will keep his memory alive for coming generations. **Each time a person reads this poem, his friend is given a new lease of life.**

Thinking about the poem

1   How would you describe the tone of line 11?
2   What is the speaker's main concern in this poem?
3   Is there an element of boastfulness in lines 13 and 14?
4   What view does the speaker take of the significance of great poetry?
5   Do you find this a sincere, honest poem? Explain your answer.
6   What theme does this sonnet share with Sonnet 12?

Taking a closer look

1   The first eight lines of the sonnet feature a number of images of change. What is the purpose of these images in the scheme of the poem as a whole?
2   The last six lines feature images of permanence and durability. What function do these images perform?
3   How do the early images of change make the later images of permanence so striking?
4   In what respects might the person to whom this sonnet is addressed find it flattering?
5   What is the significance of the contrast between images of light and images of darkness?
6   The speaker tells the person he addresses that his 'eternal summer shall not fade' (line 9). How can this be?

Imagining

1   If you were to make a film that interprets this sonnet, what images would you include and what kind of music would you select as a musical score?
2   Write a short letter to William Shakespeare telling him about your thoughts and feelings on the poem. Refer to the text of the poem in your letter.

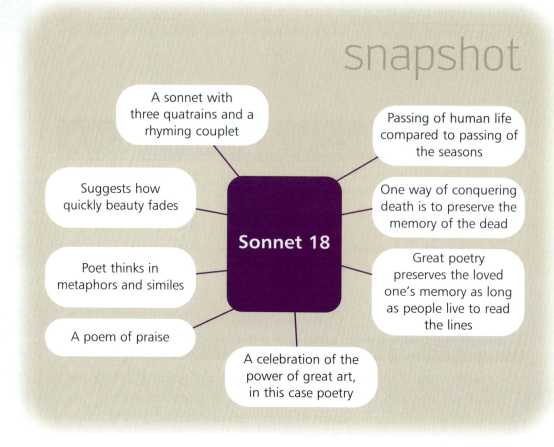

snapshot

A sonnet with three quatrains and a rhyming couplet

Passing of human life compared to passing of the seasons

Suggests how quickly beauty fades

Sonnet 18

One way of conquering death is to preserve the memory of the dead

Poet thinks in metaphors and similes

Great poetry preserves the loved one's memory as long as people live to read the lines

A poem of praise

A celebration of the power of great art, in this case poetry

Sonnet 23

As an unperfect actor on the stage,
Who with his fear is put besides his part;
Or some fierce thing, replete with too much rage,
Whose strength's abundance weakens his own heart;
So I, for fear of trust, forget to say   5
The perfect ceremony of love's right,
And in mine own love's strength seem to decay,
O'ercharged with burden of mine own love's might:
O let my books be then the eloquence
And dumb presagers of my speaking breast,   10

Who plead for love, and look for recompense,
More than that tongue that more hath more expressed:
O learn to read what silent love hath writ!
To hear with eyes belongs to love's fine wit.

Glossary

1	*unperfect actor*: an actor who does not know his part properly
2	*fear*: nerves
2	*besides*: out of, not at ease with (and therefore is unable to fulfil his role in the play)
3	*replete with*: full of
5	*for fear of trust*: unable to trust myself
6	*right*: entitlement, due
8	*O'ercharged*: overpowered
8	*might*: power, strength
9	*books*: writings, poetry
9	*eloquence*: impressive manner of speaking or writing
10	*dumb presagers*: silent indicators
10	*breast*: heart
11	*recompense*: reward, recognition (returned love)
12	*that tongue*: the words of another
14	*fine wit*: superior intelligence and perception

Guidelines

The speaker of this sonnet, tongue-tied in the presence of his friend, is unable to express his feelings face to face and must therefore put them in verse.

Commentary

Lines 1–8

The difficulty experienced by the speaker in trying to convey his powerful feelings is presented in two similes, which form the substance of the octave. The poem opens with a theatrical simile: the speaker compares himself to an ill-prepared actor, not properly versed in his part, whose nervousness makes his performance poor.

In lines 3 and 4 the simile for his condition changes: he is now like a wild beast (a 'fierce thing') helpless with excessive rage; this violent rage undermines its own strength and prevents him from taking action. The third line involves an ambiguity, since rage also means lust, giving the line a second meaning: like one made impotent by excessive lust. This meaning looks forward to lines 7 and 8.

In lines 5 and 6 the speaker picks up the stage simile of the first two lines. Not knowing how his words would be received were he able to say them, he is too nervous to express or act out his love in proper form. The 'perfect ceremony of love's right' (line 6) suggests a formal, ritual declaration. The insecure lover is like the badly prepared actor of lines 1 and 2.

Lines 7 and 8 develop the simile of lines 3 and 4, just as lines 5 and 6 correspond to lines 1 and 2. The force and strength of the speaker's love are so overpowering that they paralyse his will: the power of his love takes away his power to express it, leaving him tongue-tied.

Lines 9–14

The sestet is concerned with how the speaker will give expression to his overwhelming love for his friend. As he finds it impossible to do it in person, he must let his poems (the 'books' of line 9) be the silent interpreters or representatives of his feelings.

In lines 11 and 12 we find a characteristic example of Shakespeare's fondness for wordplay. The speaker's poems, composed in honour of his friend, will plead for the love and recognition he seeks: 'More than that tongue that more hath more expressed'. The main meaning of this line appears to be: I hope my poems may enjoy greater recognition from you (the first 'more' meaning greater) than the words of some rival, who has more fully and eloquently (the second 'more') praised more (the third 'more') of your outstanding qualities than I have. Within this general pattern of meaning there is the possibility of ambiguity. The second 'more', for example, may mean more strong expressions of love as well as more of your outstanding qualities, while the third 'more' may mean either with greater flattery or at greater length.

In the rhyming couplet the speaker asks his friend to read his poems so that he may understand the depth of his feelings for him. It is a sign of intelligence and perception on the friend's part to be able to hear the poet's speaking voice in the words of his poems.

Thinking about the poem

1 Explain the use of the actor image in the sonnet.

2 In what respect is an insecure lover like an actor?

3 The sonnet is based on a paradox, which is a way of conveying a truth by means of an apparent contradiction. Identify the central paradox (see especially lines 4 and 7), and show how it is used to make an essential point.

4 An 'unperfect actor' (line 1) may be defined as one who is not word perfect. How does the speaker eventually overcome this problem?

5 What feelings does the speaker betray? Do these feelings change as the poem proceeds?

6 In many sonnets the last six lines mark a change of tone or a change of focus. Show how this occurs in this sonnet.

7 In line 9 the speaker refers to his 'books'. What role does he hope these will play?

8 Some editors print 'looks' instead of 'books' in line 9. What difference would this make to the sonnet as a whole? Can you think of any objections to 'looks'?

9 Show how lines 5 and 6 comment on lines 1 and 2, and how lines 7 and 8 comment on lines 3 and 4.

10 The speaker has a problem. What is this problem? How does he propose to solve it?

Sonnet 29

When in disgrace with fortune and men's eyes
I all alone beweep my outcast state,
And trouble deaf heav'n with my bootless cries,
And look upon myself, and curse my fate,
Wishing me like to one more rich in hope,   5
Featured like him, like him with friends possessed,
Desiring this man's art, and that man's scope,
With what I most enjoy contented least;
Yet in these thoughts myself almost despising,
Haply I think on thee, and then my state,   10
Like to the lark at break of day arising,
From sullen earth sings hymns at heaven's gate;
For thy sweet love remembered such wealth brings
That then I scorn to change my state with kings.

Glossary

1	*in disgrace*: out of favour
1	*fortune*: most often imagined as a woman who might smile on a person one moment and frown on him or her the next
2	*state*: condition
2	*beweep*: lament, cry for
3	*bootless*: useless, hopeless (because heaven ignores them)
6	*Featured like*: with the same features as, look the same as
7	*art*: skill, learning
7	*scope*: range of abilities or opportunities; or possibly freedom
10	*Haply*: perhaps
12	*sullen*: gloomy, dull
14	*change*: exchange, swap

Guidelines

The primary concern of the speaker in the octave is with his present wants and troubles. The sestet shows him triumphing over these as he thinks of his friend, in whom he finds consolation for all his ills.

Critics who favour the biographical approach to Shakespeare's sonnets, and see in them a set of references to the poet's life, tend to find this sonnet particularly revealing. It has, for example, been suggested that the reference to 'my outcast state' (line 2) reflects Shakespeare's sense of social inferiority at being an actor, and that lines 7 and 8 refer to his own poems. The power of Sonnet 29 does not, however, derive from whatever it may vaguely suggest about Shakespeare's attitude to his acting or his poetry. The sonnet is impressive because he is able to give the complaints, and the consolation, a universal significance independent of an individual case.

Commentary

Structurally, the sonnet is based on a thematic and linguistic contrast between the octave and the sestet.

Lines 1–8

The octave is devoted to a generalised account of the speaker's complaints against a personified fortune. He is held in low esteem: his cries for help are futile ('bootless', line 3) as they fall on deaf ears.

He sees one contemporary who appears to have an outstanding future in store ('rich in hope', line 5), another who is handsome, another who is surrounded by friends. He wishes himself like all of these. He sees another whose learning ('art', line 7) he envies, and yet another whose range of opportunity ('scope', line 7) he would like to enjoy. He is, paradoxically, least happy in the pursuit of his favourite activity.

Lines 9–14

In the sestet the speaker turns his back on the melancholy mood of the octave as the thought of his friend dispels his feelings of self-disgust. **The reversal of mood from octave to sestet is reflected in diction and rhythm.** The linguistic transition from the gloomy reflections of the octave to the joyful mood of the sestet is best illustrated by contrasting the mournful tones of 'I all alone beweep my outcast state' (line 2) with the soaring rhythms of 'Like to the lark at break of day arising' (line 11).

The beginning of the sestet raises questions of tone. Line 9 may be read as the speaker's faintly ironical and humorous comment on the self-pity expressed in the octave, which makes him almost despise himself.

The 'state' of line 10 refers back to the 'outcast state' of line 2. In fact, the word is used three times in the sonnet: first in a depressing context in its association with outcast, here in joyful harmony with the melodious lark and later in comparison with the enviable wealth of kings.

The sonnet features some subtle linguistic effects. In line 12, 'sullen' means dull and heavy, contrasting with the bird rising in the lighter air, but it also suggests gloomy and sombre as a contrast to the breaking light of dawn. The polar opposites – 'sullen earth' and 'heaven's gate' – of this line perfectly reflect the contrast between the two states of mind expressed in the sonnet as a whole.

William Shakespeare

343

Thinking about the poem

1   How would you describe the speaker's mood in the first four lines?

2   Explain how lines 5 to 8 help to clarify what the speaker expresses in lines 1 to 4.

3   In lines 9 to 12 there is a noticeable change of tone and attitude. Comment on this. How is this change to be accounted for?

4   Is there any evidence in the sonnet that the speaker's miseries arise from self-pity?

5   How exactly does the speaker find a cure for his miseries?

6   The poem begins in a mood of depression and ends in one of almost pure joy and triumph. Trace the stages through which misery is replaced by happiness.

7   Why does the speaker make so much of his miseries in the early part of the poem?

8   Rhythm and movement in a poem often play an essential part in conveying meaning. With this in mind, contrast lines 1 to 4 with lines 9 to 14.

9   Explain the contrast between 'state' in line 2 and 'state' in line 14.

10 Lines 3 and 12 have contrasting images of heaven. What is the significance of the contrast?

Sonnet 30

When to the sessions of sweet silent thought
I summon up remembrance of things past,
I sigh the lack of many a thing I sought,
And with old woes new wail my dear time's waste;
Then can I drown an eye (unused to flow)   5
For precious friends hid in death's dateless night,
And weep afresh love's long since cancelled woe,
And moan th'expense of many a vanished sight.
Then can I grieve at grievances foregone,
And heavily from woe to woe tell o'er   10
The sad account of fore-bemoaned moan,
Which I new pay, as if not paid before;
But if the while I think on thee, dear friend,
All losses are restored, and sorrows end.

Glossary

1	*sessions*: a court of enquiry into the condition of a person's estate
3	*sigh*: feel sorrow for, regret
6	*dateless*: endless, without limit
8	*th'expense*: the loss
8	*sight*: may mean sigh, which would mean that the speaker is lamenting the sighs of grief that wasted him long ago (there was an old belief that sighing involved loss of blood and damaged the health)
9	*foregone*: over and done with
10	*heavily*: laboriously, sorrowfully
10	*tell o'er*: count over, enumerate each
11	*fore-bemoaned moan*: a sorrow already mourned for
12	*new pay*: pay for again

Guidelines

The role of the speaker's friend in this sonnet is the same as that attributed to him in Sonnet 29: the speaker's losses and griefs (this time belonging to his past life) are redeemed when he thinks of his friend.

Commentary

Lines 1–8

The sonnet is densely metaphorical. The two opening lines introduce an incomparable metaphor. If he were not using metaphorical language, Shakespeare might have written: when I sit alone and contemplate the past. The metaphor he opens with is a legal one, and extends through the entire sonnet, although some of the terms with legal connotations may also be interpreted as book-keeping metaphors. Among the words in the sonnet with legal connotations are 'sessions', 'summon', 'dateless', 'cancelled', 'tell o'er', 'account', 'losses' and 'restored'.

We have to imagine a court ('the sessions') presided over by 'thought' (line 1), the purpose of which is to enquire into the conditions of the speaker's life, particularly his past losses. Sessions were judicial proceedings to discover the losses and assets of a person's estate. In this sonnet the court being held is in the speaker's mind and the estate being examined is the speaker's life. The session takes place in silence – because it consists of thought, not of spoken words – and it is sweet because the speaker is in a bitter-sweet mood. The witness summoned to testify on the speaker's past distresses is his memory ('remembrance of things past', line 2).

Together with sorrows and disappointments, the speaker feels another grief: the destruction ('waste') of the most precious ('dear') part of his life (line 4). At such times he weeps, although he is not used to weeping (line 5), for friends who are dead (death is depicted as a night without end in which precious friends are hidden). He also weeps for forgotten sorrows caused by love and for other losses.

The main current of the poem is one of tender emotion, however there is a counter-current of irony running through it, directed by the speaker towards himself. The speaker is aware of the faintly disturbing, even tasteless, implications of his recurring self-pity. This is clear, for example, in line 8, where he consciously exposes himself to subtle self-mockery. When he says that he can 'moan th'expense of many a vanished sight', he means that his present moan, like the sighs ('sight' means sigh) that have already escaped from him, involves a fresh loss of vital energy (in accordance with contemporary medical opinion that sighing led to a loss of blood). As one critic puts it, the speaker is thus saying something like: 'I waste my time and energy regretting the time and energy wasted in regrets'.

Most readers of Sonnet 30 find the first eight lines greatly superior to the those in the sestet. These lines are a sensitive, touching lament for past losses, tinged with self-pity (as suggested in the catalogue of mournful responses to past experience: 'I sigh', 'I drown an eye', 'weep afresh', 'moan').

Lines 9–14

A book-keeping or accounting metaphor is suggested in lines 9 to 12, with the speaker having to count or check ('tell o'er', line 10) a ledger in which are recorded past grievances and woes that he has already paid for in grief but must continue to pay for in further grief. He counts each of these with a sad heart, and as he does, he again grieves over them.

The self-criticism implied at line 8 gives a clue to the proper interpretation of lines 9 to 12. This is not the speaker, or Shakespeare, unconsciously lapsing into windy, embarrassing rhetoric. Instead, it represents a piece of self-mockery and self-awareness on the part of the speaker, who is conscious that his emotion is excessive even as he is expressing it. However we read the last six lines of the sonnet, they represent a falling off from the splendour of the opening. This is true of a number of the other sonnets, very few of which, as M. M. Reese points out, 'live up to the excitement promised in their opening lines'.

The sonnet culminates in a graceful tribute to the speaker's friend in the final rhyming couplet: thoughts of the friend restore all the speaker's losses and end his sorrows.

Thinking about the poem

1　The theme of this sonnet is a variation of that of Sonnet 29. In what way do these two sonnets resemble each other?

2　In Sonnets 29 and 30 the friend's love is a sufficient compensation for the speaker's griefs. However, the extent of the compensation is not the same in the two sonnets. Comment on this idea.

3　In Sonnet 30 the sounds of the words are particularly significant in expressing meaning. Comment, for example, on the sound pattern in lines 1 and 2 and in lines 7 to 11.

4　Show how the speaker's increasing misery is reflected in his choice of words.

5　How would you describe the mood of the first twelve lines?

6　It is sometimes remarked that this sonnet is uneven in quality. Do you find a difference in quality between, for example, lines 1, 2 and 6 on the one hand, and lines 10 and 11 on the other? Explain your response.

7　The speaker is clearly indulging in self-pity. Is this overdone? Give reasons for your opinion.

8　What tactical purpose does the speaker's pessimism serve? In answering this, consider the last two lines of the sonnet.

9　The positive claim made in lines 13 and 14 reverses all that has gone before. Do you find this reversal convincing?

10　Comment on the significance of the reference to 'precious friends' in line 6 and 'dear friend' in line 13.

11　Comment on the use of repetition in this sonnet. Do you find it effective, or tiresome? Explain your answer.

William Shakespeare

Sonnet 60

Like as the waves make towards the pebbled shore,
So do our minutes hasten to their end,
Each changing place with that which goes before,
In sequent toil all forwards do contend.
Nativity, once in the main of light,   5
Crawls to maturity, wherewith being crowned
Crooked eclipses 'gainst his glory fight,
And time, that gave, doth now his gift confound.
Time doth transfix the flourish set on youth,
And delves the parallels in beauty's brow;   10
Feeds on the rarities of nature's truth,
And nothing stands but for his scythe to mow.
And yet to times in hope my verse shall stand,
Praising thy worth, despite his cruel hand.

Glossary

4	*sequent toil*: each wave pushes the one before it as it moves forward, just as each minute displaces the one that went before
5	*Nativity*: birth, here representing a newborn infant
5	*main*: broad expanse (also of land, sea or sky)
6	*wherewith*: with maturity
7	*Crooked eclipses*: a term from astrology that means evil, hostile influences on the lives of people. Many people in Shakespeare's day believed that human life was influenced by the position of the heavenly bodies at one's birth. Eclipses of the sun and moon were seen as signs of coming disasters
8	*doth*: does
8	*confound*: destroy, reverse
9	*transfix*: destroy, damage
9	*flourish set on youth*: physical beauty or bloom of the young
10	*delves the parallels*: digs furrows or trenches (i.e. creates wrinkles)
10	*brow:* forehead
11	*rarities*: the best specimens or features
11	*truth*: perfection, particularly perfect beauty
12	*scythe*: a tool for cutting grass; here, time is personified as the reaper

Guidelines

Here Shakespeare is dealing with a commonplace idea that is the main theme of many of his sonnets: time will inevitably destroy youth and beauty, but the speaker's verse will survive the cruel hand of time and thus ensure the perpetuation of his friend's beauty.

Commentary

Lines 1–8

This sonnet is particularly rich in metaphor. In the first four lines the slow, inexorable passing of time is the subject of an impressive simile: the passing minutes, like the waves, press forward one after another in steady succession. From line 5 onwards, we move from simile to metaphor.

Lines 5 to 8 involve complex uses of language. The abstract noun 'Nativity' (line 5) stands for the newborn infant who, once he has entered the sphere of independent existence, moves slowly to maturity. When he has been crowned with the glory of maturity, however, malignant astrological influences plot his downfall. At this stage, time, which has given the gift of youth and beauty, paradoxically destroys what it has given ('doth now his gift confound', line 8).

Both 'Nativity' and 'main of light' (line 5) have associations with astrology. Shakespeare is thinking of the moment of birth in relation to the position of the planets and the Elizabethan notion of the universe as a hollow sphere filled with light. 'Main' also means a broad expanse of water. Thus, 'main of light' means ocean of light, and the lines carry the suggestion of life as a sea-voyage doomed to disaster. It is also possible that lines 5 to 7 convey an image of life's journey in terms of the sun's journey through the heavens, with the sun at its height ('maturity') in line 6, and subject to disastrous eclipse in line 7. However we interpret the metaphors in these four lines, the general sense remains the same: the glories of early life are doomed to extinction.

Lines 9–14

The metaphor in line 9, 'Time doth transfix the flourish set on youth', is difficult to interpret in detail, although the general sense of the line is that time destroys or impairs physical beauty (i.e. the beauty associated with youth). The image may be derived from warfare and suggests time with its dart or spear cutting through the crest or helmet of youth. 'Flourish' can also mean a blossom, and so the line may suggest time causing the bloom of youth to fade.

Line 10 has a marvellously concrete image of the ageing process. The 'parallels' are the furrows of an ageing face, and time digs ('delves') these furrows on the face of beauty as a labourer digs trenches.

In line 11 time destroys and consumes the choicest feature ('rarities') that nature has brought to perfection ('truth'). Line 12 features the conventional image of time as the reaper: in the end time is ready to claim (through death) its human victim, just as the reaper gathers in the harvest.

The rhyming couplet at the end of the sonnet offers the traditional measure of hope and consolation – a defence against the cruel processes of time. In spite of the destruction wrought by time on youth and beauty, the speaker's verse will celebrate the glory of his friend in better times yet unborn, existing only in the imagination ('hope').

Thinking about the poem

1   In the first four lines the speaker makes a general comment on the passage of time. In the next four he is more specific. Explain.

2   Explain the contrasts between 'hasten' (line 2) and 'Crawls' (line 6).

3   The final two lines of the sonnet make it clear that it is addressed to someone whose beauty is endangered by time. What is the significance of the first twelve lines for the person being addressed?

4   Does the sonnet as a whole offer a pessimistic account of human life? Explain your answer.

5   In line 12, the speaker says of time that 'nothing stands but for his scythe to mow'. In the following two lines, however, he claims that his own verse will defy time. How can this seeming contradiction be explained?

6   Here, as in his other sonnets, Shakespeare makes effective use of rhythm and movement to enact his meanings. The first two lines of the poem illustrate this, in the majestic sweep of the open vowels of the first line, which contrast with the hurried movement of the short ones in the second line. Can you give other examples?

Taking a closer look

1   How does Shakespeare create the impression that time is not merely an abstract force, but also a personality?

2   Does Shakespeare seem to believe in a world ruled by forces friendly to humans? Explain with reference to this poem.

3   This sonnet features a rapid movement from one metaphor to another. Explain.

4   How would you describe the tone of the final two lines?

5   Consider the idea that the power of this sonnet lies less in its ideas, which are commonplace, than in the remarkable images the poet uses to convey those ideas.

6   Choose two images from the sonnet that seem to be more impressive than the rest. Explain your choice.

Imagining

1   You have been asked to suggest two suitable titles for this sonnet. Explain your suggestions.

2   Imagine that you are the person to whom this poem is addressed. Describe your reaction.

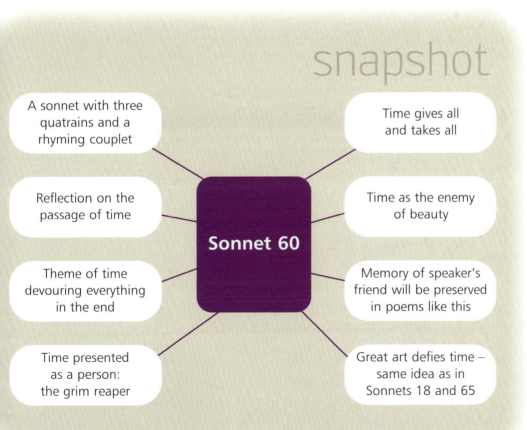

snapshot

A sonnet with three quatrains and a rhyming couplet

Reflection on the passage of time

Theme of time devouring everything in the end

Time presented as a person: the grim reaper

Sonnet 60

Time gives all and takes all

Time as the enemy of beauty

Memory of speaker's friend will be preserved in poems like this

Great art defies time – same idea as in Sonnets 18 and 65

Sonnet 65

Since brass, nor stone, nor earth, nor boundless sea,
But sad mortality o'er-sways their power,
How with this rage shall beauty hold a plea,
Whose action is no stronger than a flower?
O how shall summer's honey breath hold out   5
Against the wrackful siege of batt'ring days,
When rocks impregnable are not so stout,
Nor gates of steel so strong, but time decays?
O fearful meditation! Where, alack,
Shall time's best jewel from time's chest lie hid?   10
Or what strong hand can hold his swift foot back?
Or who his spoil o'er beauty can forbid?
O none, unless this miracle have might:
That in black ink my love may still shine bright.

Glossary	
2	*sad mortality*: death and awful destruction
2	*o'er-sways*: overcomes
3	*with this rage*: against the violence and anger of death
3	*hold a plea*: mount a defence
4	*action*: power to preserve itself (also legal process)
6	*wrackful*: destructive, devastating
7	*impregnable*: invincible, cannot be broken
7	*stout*: strong, robust
9	*fearful meditation*: terrifying thought
9	*alack*: alas (exclamation of alarm)
11	*his*: time's (personified as a fast runner)
12	*his spoil*: time's destruction (of beauty)
12	*forbid*: prevent

Guidelines

Thematically, this sonnet is similar to Sonnet 60. The speaker is conscious that in the face of universal, rampant decay, fragile beauty, particularly that of his friend, can endure only by being immortalised in poetry.

Commentary

Lines 1–8

The speaker notes that not even the strongest things in nature can avoid decay. We may imagine that a durable metal like brass will last for ever, but it will not. The same is true of stones, earth and sea. 'Sad mortality' (calamitous destruction, line 2) overwhelms these strong things. This being the case, the speaker asks in lines 3 and 4, what defence can beauty offer against time's destructive fury, given that the power of beauty to preserve itself is no stronger than that of a flower? If strong things cannot survive, what hope is there for fragile beauty?

On the face of it, the metaphor in lines 3 and 4 appears to be a legal one. 'Plea' and 'action' suggest a lawsuit, in which beauty is delicately pleading before the raging, hostile court of time, but its case ('action') seems hopelessly weak. 'Action', however, has a double function. As well as being an element in the legal metaphor of lines 3 and 4, it also becomes part of the siege metaphor of lines 5 to 8. In these lines, the summer flowers with their 'honey breath' (line 5) represent beauty, here besieged by the destructive ('wrackful', line 6) army of time, one of whose members is winter. The defence seems hopeless, since even rock and steel cannot hold out against time.

Lines 9–14

Alarmed by the situation he has set out in lines 1 to 8, the speaker asks if beauty ('time's best jewel', line 10) can be hidden so that it may escape being encased in 'time's chest' (i.e. avoid passing into oblivion, line 10). Since beauty is a personification of the speaker's beloved friend, the image also suggests a desperate demand: how shall the loved one escape the grave? The primary image of line 10 is of beauty as a jewel, lent by time for humans to enjoy for a while. The human beneficiaries are anxious to hide the gift from time, who will take it back and keep it under lock and key in the final prison of beauty ('time's chest' or the coffin).

In lines 8 to 12 the rhythm and movement convey a sense of futile desperation at the impossibility of arresting the destructive progress of time. In line 11 time is personified as a runner whose swift, measured stride cannot be restrained, and in line 12 it is a destroyer whose plunder of beauty cannot be prevented.

The final couplet offers a qualified hope. The defeat of beauty by time can be prevented only if the speaker/poet can perform the miracle of perpetuating the memory of the beloved in immortal verse.

Thinking about the poem

1   What purpose is served by the references in line 1 to 'brass', 'stone', 'earth' and 'sea'?

2   What is 'this rage' referred to in line 3?

3   The contest between beauty and time is an unequal one. How does the speaker suggest this?

4   Which detail most effectively suggests the power of time?

5   Early in the poem the speaker examines the effect of time on nature. At what point does he begin to consider time in relation to human beings?

6   How would you describe the speaker's attitude to nature in lines 3 to 6?

7   Describe the varying images of time emerging from the poem. It may be helpful to imagine time assuming different personalities.

8   What is the tone of lines 9 to 12?

9   In the last two lines of the sonnet, does the speaker appear absolutely confident that he can preserve his friend's beauty for future ages? Give reasons for your answer.

10   Sonnet 60 also deals with the devastation of beauty by time. Do Sonnets 60 and 65 differ significantly in their approach to the subject?

11   Show how the speaker presents his ideas through images rather than through statements.

12   Show how the sounds in the poem help to suggest the contrast between the strength of time and the weakness of beauty.

Sonnet 66

Tired with all these for restful death I cry:
As to behold desert a beggar born,
And needy nothing trimmed in jollity,
And purest faith unhappily forsworn,
And gilded honour shamefully misplaced,   5
And maiden virtue rudely strumpeted,
And right perfection wrongfully disgraced,
And strength by limping sway disabled,
And art made tongue-tied by authority,
And folly, doctor-like, controlling skill,   10
And simple truth miscalled simplicity,
And captive good attending captain ill:
Tired with all these, from these would I be gone,
Save that to die I leave my love alone.

William Shakespeare

Glossary		
1	*Tired with all these*: tired of the evils listed in lines 2 to 12
2	*desert*: worth, merit; here, personified as people of merit
3	*nothing*: people of no value
3	*trimmed in jollity*: dressed in fine clothes
4	*forsworn*: betrayed
6	*strumpeted*: falsely accused of promiscuity
7	*right*: true, genuine
8	*limping sway*: weak, indecisive rule of those in power
9	*art*: skills of learning and science; here, writers
12	*captain*: one who dominates, an overlord
13	*be gone*: like to escape (i.e. through death)

Guidelines

Structurally, Sonnet 66 differs from all the others. It departs from the common pattern by avoiding the usual division into octave and sestet, and the separation of the first twelve lines into quatrains. It provides a summary of conventional complaints, featuring the evils from which death would deliver the speaker. There is no need to imagine that Shakespeare is here making a catalogue of the earthly wrongs that trouble him, or indeed any other individual: similar catalogues, though consisting of different complaints, are found in the work of other contemporary writers of sonnets.

Commentary

The main value of Sonnet 66 is the economical, epigrammatic phrasing, which ensures that each line has a wealth of meaning. The best parallel to Sonnet 66 is Hamlet's 'To be or not to be' soliloquy, where the speaker is convinced that only the fear of what might come after death could restrain a wise man from escaping life's 'sea of troubles' once and for all. The speaker in Sonnet 66 is restrained by consideration for his friend, whom his death would leave solitary and perhaps uncared for.

The first two lines can be misunderstood: 'these' in line 1 does not refer to anything mentioned in previous sonnets. Rather, it refers to the evils about to be enumerated. 'As' in line 2 means for example. The dominant figure of speech in the sonnet is personification: a series of abstract nouns stand for the people who embody the qualities these nouns represent.

The speaker lists the wrongs that he is weary of:
- Seeing people of merit, people who are truly deserving (personified in 'desert', line 2) but are born into poverty.
- Worthless individuals of no merit and lacking significant gifts or qualities (personified in 'needy nothing', line 3, a strong term of condemnation), who are decked out in gaudy finery ('jollity'). Lines 2 and 3 offer a contrast between two opposing kinds of people, neither category getting what it deserves.
- Values and principles (personified in 'faith', line 4) that should command loyalty and respect, but are disastrously betrayed. 'Faith' here may also mean 'love'.
- Rank and titles (personified in 'honour', line 5) wrongly and shamefully conferred on people who do not deserve them.
- The reputations of virtuous women (personified in 'maiden virtue', line 6) being ruined by those who falsely brand them as unchaste or a prostitute.
- People who are true and honest (personified in 'right perfection', line 7) but have been given a bad reputation. Line 7 expands the point made in line 6.

- The efforts of a vigorous people or citizenry (personified in 'strength', line 8) being undermined and frustrated by weak and indecisive rulers.
- Censoring writers (personified in 'art', line 9) to prevent them from expressing ideas, or dealing with subjects, which those in authority find offensive.
- Ignorant people (personified in 'folly', line 10) posing as experts ('doctor-like'), who control and direct the activities of those who really have the skills and knowledge.
- Mistakenly treating people who are honest and straightforward (who represent 'simple truth', line 11) as if they were simple-minded ('simplicity').
- Goodness dominated by evil – good people who are helpless (personified in 'captive good', line 12) at the hands of evil people who use them to advance their own interests.

The speaker contemplates death in order to escape these evils, however, the problem is that if he dies, he would be deserting his beloved friend, leaving him alone and thus unprotected from the corrupt world he has just described.

Thinking about the poem

1 Throughout the sonnet, the speaker makes use of personification (e.g. 'nothing' stands for somebody having nothing). What advantage does the poem gain from this?

2 The sonnet is a roll-call of the evils of human life. Given that the speaker is a writer, how many of these evils could have been experienced by him personally? How many could not? Explain your answer.

3 Does the poem as a whole give the impression that it is dealing with strictly personal experiences? Explain your answer.

4 The speaker longs for death as a way of escape from mortal evils. Do the evils he lists justify his longing?

5 Read Sonnet 30, which also lists some of the miseries that are part of human life. There are, however, differences in approach between the two sonnets. Comment on these.

6 The role of the friend in this sonnet differs from his role in Sonnet 30. In what way?

7 In the end the speaker does not want to die. Do you find the reason he gives convincing?

8 Do the final two lines of the sonnet make a satisfactory ending? Explain your answer.

9 Consider this sonnet as a comment on the theme of appearance versus reality.

10 Sonnet 66 is one of the most pessimistic of all the sonnets. What makes it so?

Sonnet 73

That time of year thou mayst in me behold,
When yellow leaves, or none, or few do hang
Upon those boughs which shake against the cold,
Bare ruined choirs where late the sweet birds sang;
In me thou seest the twilight of such day   5
As after sunset fadeth in the west,
Which by and by black night doth take away,
Death's second self that seals up all in rest;
In me thou seest the glowing of such fire
That on the ashes of his youth doth lie,   10
As the deathbed, whereon it must expire,
Consumed with that which it was nourished by;
This thou perceiv'st, which makes thy love more strong,
To love that well, which thou must leave ere long.

Glossary

1	*thou*: the young male friend to whom the sonnet is addressed
3	*shake against*: tremble or shiver in anticipation of
8	*Death's second self*: 'black night' (line 7) is a traditional image of death; night is a period of rest (sleep) for all things, just as human life ends in rest when the coffin is closed or sealed
8	*seals up*: closes; may also allude to the stitching up or 'sealing' of the eyes of a hawk
9	*fire*: vigour
14	*leave*: do without
14	*ere*: before

Guidelines

Sonnet 73 explores how the young friend to whom the sonnet is addressed may perceive the older speaker.

Commentary

The structure of this sonnet is clearly outlined by the varied repetitions that occur in lines 5, 9 and 13 ('In me thou seest the twilight', 'In me thou seest the glowing', 'This thou perceiv'st') and by the development of a new metaphor in each quatrain. If we examine the metaphoric words, we shall be able to trace the progression from a season to a day to a fire, which is the unifying metaphor of the poem, since fire is the element that regulates the seasons and days through the sun.

First quatrain

The first quatrain is an extremely complex one. The speaker pictures himself in the late autumn or early winter of his life. The human lifespan is pictured in terms of a year, and human decay in terms of seasonal decay. The speaker's advancing age is conveyed through the image of a desolate forest, whose leaves have all but disappeared. The bare trees call to mind the ruined arches of churches or monasteries, now half-open to the sky. The 'sweet birds' (line 4) are those who recently sang in the summer trees. They are also those, whether choirboys, monks or nuns, who sang in the choir-stalls of monasteries before these were dissolved in the reign of Henry VIII and allowed to fall into ruin.

Line 4 has attracted considerable critical comment. In his classic study of ambiguity in poetry, William Empson traces some of the possible meanings involved in this line, which he finds effective in several ways at once. This is because ruined monastery choirs are places in which to sing:

> . . . because they involve sitting in a row, because they are made of wood, are carved into knots and so forth, because they used to be surrounded by a sheltering building crystallised out of the likeness of a forest, and coloured with stained glass and painting like flowers and leaves, because they are now abandoned by all but the grey walls coloured like the skies of winter.

The fate of the trees, the birds and the churches reminds us of the physical decay of the speaker.

Second quatrain

The span of human life is seen in terms of a day in lines 5 to 8. The metaphor introduced here, with night as 'Death's second self' (line 8), is a conventional, commonplace one. If life is a day, the speaker has reached twilight. Just as night will soon take twilight away, so death, of which night is a classic image, will deprive the speaker of life. The metaphor in line 8 may well have a double reference: Shakespeare may have in mind the sealing up or closing of a coffin or the stitching up of the eyes of a hawk, a method used by the falconer to blindfold it.

Third quatrain

Lines 9 to 12 introduce a new image of the final extinction of life as a fire dying on its own ashes. The vital flame of youth has died down, and what remain are glowing embers lying on the ashes of a more vital, glorious past. The glow will fade away completely when bodily vitality has been exhausted. Line 12 involves a characteristic Shakespearean paradox: the fire is wasting away (is 'consumed') on the dead ashes, which are the remains of the fuel that had to be consumed to nourish it. In other words, time fostered and nourished youthful life, only to consume it in old age. The third quatrain presents a fine balance between two contrasting ideas: the finality of death ('ashes', 'deathbed', 'consumed') and the speaker's sense of lingering, flickering life ('glowing', 'nourished').

Rhyming couplet

The ageing of the speaker and his closeness to death, as described in the first twelve lines, mean that the speaker's young friend should love him all the more because he will not have him for very much longer.

Thinking about the poem

1   In the first eight lines there is an intimate connection between the processes of nature and human growth and decay. Show how this works.
2   In his sonnets Shakespeare conveys his meanings through images rather than through abstract statements. This sonnet is particularly rich in pictorial effects. Describe each successive picture as it appears to you.
3   Each group of four lines has its own picture, separate from the rest. How are the pictures related?
4   The images in the first four lines are fused together. In this context 'choirs' (line 4) is a most significant word. Consider all the possible meanings these lines are capable of.
5   What is the relationship between love and death in this sonnet?

6 The sonnet reflects on the approach of old age and death. Describe the speaker's mood as he contemplates these.

7 In what sense is this sonnet a persuasive poem?

8 Read Sonnet 66 in conjunction with this one. Discuss points of resemblance and difference between the two.

9 How do the rhythm and movement of the sonnet reflect the meaning of the poem and the outlook of the speaker?

10 What light does the poem throw on the relationship between the speaker and the friend he is addressing?

11 This sonnet has been described as a mournful meditation on life. Is this description justified?

Sonnet 94

They that have power to hurt and will do none,
That do not do the thing they most do show,
Who, moving others, are themselves as stone,
Unmoved, cold, and to temptation slow,
They rightly do inherit heaven's graces,   5
And husband nature's riches from expense;
They are the lords and owners of their faces,
Others but stewards of their excellence.
The summer's flower is to the summer sweet,
Though to itself it only live and die,   10
But if that flower with base infection meet,
The basest weed outbraves his dignity:
    For sweetest things turn sourest by their deeds;
    Lilies that fester, smell far worse than weeds.

Glossary		
1	*They... do none*: people who are capable of doing harm to others but will not do.
2	*That do not...show*: that do not do what they look most capable of doing.
3	*Who moving... stone*: who affect others deeply, but remain unaffected, like a stone.

4	*To temptation slow*: Not easily tempted.
5	*Rightly*: Truly
5	*Inherit heaven's graces*: they inherit all sorts of graces from heaven.
6	*And husband... expense*: they do not squander the gifts of nature they have been given.
6	*Expense*: wasteful spending.
7	*They are the lords... faces*: they are in complete control of the appearance they present to the world.
8	*Others... excellence*: others, having no control, are not true owners of their beauty, but merely squander it.
9	*The summer's... sweet*: The flower that blooms in the summer gives out its sweetness into the summer.
10	*Though... live and die*: Even though it blooms alone and dies alone bearing no fruit.
11–14	*But if that flower... weeds*: If the flower is attacked by disease and corruption, then the coarsest weed makes a finer display than it does. When the force of something good turns to evil activity it becomes most evil; corrupting the best is always the worst kind of corruption.

Guidelines

The sonnet leaves itself open to two contrary interpretations. On the one hand that it presents a flattering portrait of a truly virtuous type of man, even though the final lines suggest that even the most virtuous people are liable to be corrupted; and on the other hand that the portrait is far from favourable, in fact that it is deeply critical.

There is also the possibility that the sonnet is about a certain type of seemingly virtuous person, who is not as virtuous as he seems. The poem may not be about a type of individual, but a particular one, a friend of the speaker who has shown himself a false friend and that the sonnet is a bitter account of his friend's abandonment or their former friendship.

There is no agreement among critics that the sonnet is ironical in tone (what is being said about the friend is not what is meant). This assumes, of course, that the sonnet deals with one individual, thus we might say that the speaker means what he says in lines 1-8. However, the irony may lie in the fact that he knows and expects the reader to realise that the friend is not that kind of person at all, but only seems to be. This may explain the final lines.

Lines 9-12

In lines 1-8 we see what the speaker thought the friend ought to be like, but the last four lines suggest that he is instead a festering lily, one of the seemingly best people who have become the worse. Overall, it seems more reasonable to think of the sonnet as a disillusioned account of a disappointed friendship, expressed in terms of bitter irony, and ending in the sad reflection that even seemingly virtuous people can become their own opposites. The obvious bitterness of the final two lines suggests that the emotion is deeply felt, and that the sonnet is not simply a reflection on people in general, but about the personal experience the speaker has had of an individual.

Thinking about the poem

1   The sonnet has some impressive images. Choose your favourite one and explain why you have done so.

2   What do you think this sonnet is about? Explain your answer.

3   Is this poem (a), sad, (b) angry, (c) flattering, (d) critical? Comment on your choice.

4   What does this poem tell us about human nature?

5   In the final four lines of the sonnet there is a change of tone. Describe this change. How would you account for it?

6   What kind of person is being described in this sonnet? Do you think we are expected to admire him or to have doubts about him? Would you like this kind of person as a friend?

7   Are there any hints in the poem that the speaker is not entirely impressed by the character he is depicting?

8   Where do we find the suggestion in the poem that a person's actions are more important as a test of character than his/her outward appearance?

Sonnet 116

Let me not to the marriage of true minds
Admit impediments; love is not love
Which alters when it alteration finds,
Or bends with the remover to remove.
O no, it is an ever-fixed mark,   5
That looks on tempests and is never shaken;
It is the star to every wand'ring bark,
Whose worth's unknown, although his height be taken.
Love's not time's fool, though rosy lips and cheeks
Within his bending sickle's compass come;   10
Love alters not with his brief hours and weeks,
But bears it out even to the edge of doom.
If this be error, and upon me proved,
I never writ, nor no man ever loved.

Glossary

1	*Let me not*: May I never
1	*marriage of true minds*: friendship between people with like minds (i.e. the speaker and his friend)
2	*impediments*: obstacles, hindrances
4	*bends*: is inclined
5	*ever-fixed mark*: permanent sea-mark or beacon
8	*wand'ring bark*: lost ship
8	*height*: altitude
9	*time's fool*: something to be mocked by time, something that passes away
10	*his bending sickle*: time's curved blade
10	*compass*: limits, range
11	*his*: time's
12	*bears it out*: survives defiantly, endures
12	*edge of doom*: the last day, the Day of Judgement
13	*error*: false, deception

Guidelines

Sonnet 116 has long been considered one of the finest of Shakespeare's sonnets, particularly for its language. Tucker Brooke remarks that in it Shakespeare has employed:

> One hundred and ten of the simplest words in the language and the two simplest rhyme-schemes to produce a poem which has about it no strangeness whatever except the strangeness of perfection.

Commentary

The poem's opening statement echoes the marriage service in the Anglican Book of Common Prayer: 'If any of you know cause, or just impediment, why these two persons should not be joined in Holy Matrimony, ye are to declare it.' The 'impediment' mentioned in the marriage service is any hindering circumstance that might render the marriage invalid. Shakespeare is applying the word not to the marriage of a man and a woman, but to the marriage of minds (i.e. a faithful, loving friendship between two people of compatible dispositions). The statement means: may I never accept that there are obstacles to the love of two faithful people.

The rest of the poem, if we leave out the rhyming couplet at the end, is a series of statements about love, which are really attempts to define it. The loving relationship of the first two lines is defined negatively (lines 2 to 4 and lines 9 to 11) and positively (lines 5 to 8 and line 12).

Love is not
Love is not genuine love if it alters due to a change of circumstances, infidelity or the effects of time on beauty. Nor is true love inconstant. This idea is expressed in line 4, where 'bends with the remover to remove' means that one party is inclined to withdraw when the other party does the same thing (i.e. withdraws his or her love).

In lines 9 to 11 the speaker states that love is not the plaything of time: the destruction of beauty (the only quality on which inconstant love might depend) comes within the scope and power of time, but faithful love is not affected by the passing of hours and weeks.

Love is
On the positive side, faithful love is presented in terms of metaphors of permanence and stability. It is seen as a sea-mark or beacon (line 5) about to endure the ferocity of storms. It is like the Northern Star by which a navigator is able to keep a ship on course, whose altitude ('height') is known, but whose influence ('worth') can

never be calculated (line 8). In line 12 the speaker claims that love staunchly endures to the end in the face of the most extreme hazards: 'the edge of doom' suggests a deep abyss.

Rhyming couplet

In the rhyming couplet that closes the sonnet the speaker affirms his own loving constancy. He is saying that his definition of true love is correct, and also that true love exists, as his own case shows. The couplet means: If what I have said about true love is false, and if this can be proved against me by citing my own case as evidence, then I have never written anything, and no man's love has ever been real.

Thinking about the poem

1   How does the speaker suggest that what he thinks of as true love is a spiritual, rather than a physical, thing?
2   What relationship is suggested here between love and time?
3   In Shakespeare's other sonnets on the themes of love and time, much of the emphasis is on change, decay and impermanence. How is this sonnet different?
4   How would you describe the words used in the poem? What does the choice of words tell us about the speaker's attitude?
5   Compare this sonnet with Sonnet 60 from the point of view of language. Which poem is simpler in its expression? Which do you find the more satisfying?
6   List the images of true love in this poem, and comment on their common purpose.
7   What is the tone of this poem?
8   Why is love not 'time's fool' (line 9)?
9   Comment on the way in which one idea is balanced against another. What effects are achieved by this balance?
10 Rhythm and movement are significant in this poem. In what way?

Fear No More the Heat o' the Sun

Guiderius
Fear no more the heat o' the sun,
   Nor the furious winter's rages,
Thou thy worldly task has done,
   Home art gone and ta'en thy wages,
Golden lads and girls all must,   5
As chimney-sweepers, come to dust.

Arviragus
Fear no more the frown o' the great,
   Thou are past the tyrant's stroke,
Care no more to clothe and eat,
   To thee the reed is as the oak: 10
The sceptre, learning, physic, must
All follow this and come to dust.

Gui.   Fear no more the lighting-flash.
Arv.   Nor th'all-dreaded thunder-stone.
Gui.   Fear not slander, censure rash.   15
Arv.   Thou hast finish'd joy and moan.
Both All lovers young, all lovers must
       Consign to thee and come to dust.

Gui.   No exorciser harm thee!
Arv.   Nor no witchcraft charm thee!   20
Gui.   Ghost unlaid forbear thee!
Arv.   Nothing ill come near thee!
Both Quiet consummation have,
       And renowned be thy grave!

Glossary

2	*rages*: storms
4	*ta'en*: taken
8	*tyrant's stroke*: power of a wicked, unjust, dictatorial ruler to inflict the severest punishment, even death
11	*sceptre*: king's staff of office; here standing for the king himself
11	*learning*: knowledge; here referring to the scholar
11	*physic*: medicine; here referring to the doctor
14	*thunder-stone*: a meteorite, a mass of solid matter whose fall from the sky is accompanied by a sound like thunder
15	*slander*: a false, malicious statement intended to injure someone's reputation
15	*censure rash*: blame or condemnation without sufficient evidence
16	*moan*: complaint, lament
18	*Consign to thee*: agree to enlist or sign up (in the ranks of death)
19	*exorciser*: a person capable of conjuring up spirits
21	*Ghost unlaid forbear thee*: may you be left alone by spirits not yet banished or laid to rest
22	*ill*: evil
23	*consummation*: death
24	*renowned*: famous, honoured

Guidelines

This song is taken from *Cymbeline*, one of Shakespeare's later plays. Cymbeline is the King of Britain. His two sons, Guiderius and Arviragus, are stolen from him and brought up in Wales by one of his nobles whom he has wronged. His daughter, Imogen, remains at his court, falls in love with Posthumus, the son of one of his warriors, and marries him. When Imogen's mother dies, Cymbeline marries a wicked widow with a brutal, foolish son named Cloten. The new queen decides that Cloten should marry Imogen. When it is discovered that Imogen has married Posthumus, the latter is banished. A wicked character named Iachimo convinces Posthumus that Imogen has been unfaithful to him in his absence. Mad with rage, Posthumus instructs his servant Pisanio to take Imogen to Wales and kill her. Moved by Imogen's goodness and innocence, Pisanio spares her, giving her a medicinal drug to comfort her. This drug turns out to be a powerful sleeping potion. Imogen puts on boy's clothes, and finds the cave where her unknown brothers, Guiderius and Arviragus, live. She introduces herself to them as Fidele. They show great kindness to their new acquaintance. When Imogen takes the drug given to her by Pisanio, she falls into a death-like sleep. Guiderius and Arviragus, thinking her dead, cover her with flowers and sing this lament.

The comments of Guiderius and Arviragus on the supposedly dead Fidele provide a moving context for the lament. Guiderius hopes that Fidele may not, after all, be dead. He says (in Act 4, Scene 2, lines 215–18):

> Why, he but sleeps:
> If he be gone he'll make his grave a bed:
> With female fairies will his tomb be haunted,
> And worms will not come to thee.

The events of the play unfold to make the beautiful lament of Imogen's brothers premature. *Cymbeline* is a romance, not a tragedy. The good characters are finally rewarded and the evil Cloten is decapitated. Imogen forgives her deceived and repentant husband, Posthumus. Cymbeline has his sons restored to him and all ends in happiness and peace.

Commentary

The impulse behind this lament (or dirge) is to draw whatever consolation is possible from death, so that those who are left behind may not succumb to absolute despair.

The varieties of consolation to be drawn from the event are expressed in the first four lines of each of the first three stanzas. This catalogue of mortal ills will no longer have meaning to the dead, thus inspiring the thought that death is to be welcomed rather than feared.

The dirge balances against this idea of welcome death another commonplace: that death is inevitable. This is expressed in the final two lines of the first three stanzas, and is driven home with sad directness by the rhyming of 'must' and 'dust' at the end of each.

Stanza 1

The dead person is beyond the reach of the misery of extreme weather and of hard work, and is thus to be envied.

Death comes to all human beings, whatever their rank or social status. The essential contrast here is between privileged boys and girls endowed with both beauty and wealth – 'golden' (line 5) suggests the glow of youth and beauty as well as the possession of wealth and privilege – and those, such as chimney-sweeps, who are neither beautiful nor rich. There is a disturbing pun on 'dust' in line 6. Chimney-sweeps necessarily 'came to dust' by virtue of their trade, but the real purpose of the line is to remind us that the most beautiful and prosperous youths and maidens have no better defence against becoming dust in the grave than have the poor dusty chimney-sweeps.

Stanza 2

The dead person is beyond the displeasure of great people, the danger to life posed by tyrants, and the struggle to provide for bodily needs, and is thus to be envied. Much of the power and interest of this song derives from the way in which the dominant ideas are brought to life in terms of concrete illustrations. For example, instead of generalising about the threats posed to everyday mortals by those in power, Shakespeare suggests their menace is 'the frown o' the great' and 'the tyrant's stroke' (lines 7 and 8).

Death comes to all human beings, whatever their role in life. People and their offices are identified by reference to significant items associated with them: kings, scholars and doctors become 'sceptre, learning, physic' (line 11).

Stanza 3

The dead person is beyond the reach of misfortune caused by sudden disasters, slander or criticism, and is thus to be envied. Death comes to all lovers.

Stanza 4

The final six lines are a series of charms and spells, invoking protection for the departed spirit from evil influences.

Thinking about the poem

1   Two ways of looking at death are considered in this song. Describe them.
2   Examine how the images in this song help to convey contrasting attitudes to death.
3   Discuss the relationship in the poem between general statements and the way they are brought home to the imagination.
4   Consider this song as an illustration of Shakespeare's fondness for wordplay.
5   Some of Shakespeare's sonnets deal with themes similar to those in this song. Develop this idea.
6   Do you find this song consoling or depressing?
7   Would the ideas presented here be likely to help somebody mourning a loved one? Do you find any single idea in the song more convincing than any other?

General Questions

1. Time in its many guises dominates many of Shakespeare's sonnets. Explore this idea.
2. Examine the treatment of love in the sonnets.
3. Shakespeare's poetry is remarkable for its metaphorical richness. Consider how imagery is used to express and develop central themes.
4. Many of the sonnets involve conflict and contrast between opposing ideas and themes. Discuss.
5. Discuss the sonnets as poems of hope and defiance.
6. Examine the attitudes to life and living reflected in Shakespeare's poetry.
7. Jan Kott has written that 'the first theme of the sonnets is the attempt to preserve beauty and love from the destructive action of time'. Discuss.
8. Consider the theme of change as a major feature of the sonnets.
9. J. B. Leishman refers to 'the frequently recurring topic of compensation' as a positive feature of Shakespeare's poetry. Examine Shakespeare's treatment of this topic.
10. In the sonnets, Shakespeare affirms the existence of something unchangeable in a world of change, and of something eternal in transient mortality. Discuss the ways in which he does this.

Sample Essay

Write an introduction to the sonnets of Shakespeare on your course, with particular emphasis on (a) the major themes in the sonnets and (b) their language and imagery.

The first significant theme that comes to mind is best described as the theme of devouring time, a common topic in the literature of all ages. This theme is powerfully expressed in Sonnet 60 ('Like as the waves'), in which everything leads to the conclusion that after time has devoured youthful beauty, leaving nothing but the wreckage of humanity, death comes and takes away this wreckage: 'And nothing stands but for his scythe to mow'. Time is personified in a paradoxical way, being the giver of natural beauty and the eventual agent of its destruction: 'And time, that gave, doth now his gift confound'. Like a farmer wielding a spade in a field, time digs furrows in beautiful foreheads ('delves the parallels in beauty's brow').

[First theme identified. Theme illustrated by reference to one sonnet and by quotation and comment]

Sonnet 73 ('That time of year') also deals with the theme of devouring time. In this case, the progress of the seasons through time, and of the hours through the course of a day, are paralleled by the gradual disintegration of the human being. In the course of time, the glow of youth fades. Time gave this glow, and prepares to swallow it up in death. Thus, human life is 'Consumed with that which it was nourished by'.

[Second sonnet identified in support of the first point and reinforced by quotation]

In Sonnet 12 ('When I do count') the process of decay through time is again given forceful treatment. Decay is here shown to pervade all the processes of nature as well as the course of human life. This decay is presided over by time. Dark hair is replaced by grey; beautiful day is sunk in hideous night; trees lose their leaves, while beautiful things wither as they see others grow. The only way to defeat time is to leave offspring behind, but this does not entirely console those who die. Apart from offspring, 'nothing 'gainst time's scythe can make defence'.

[A third sonnet has been identified to make and support the first point]

Sonnet 65 ('Since brass, nor stone'), in which time is personified as the great destroyer, is another example of this theme. The destructive power of time is even more dramatically and forcefully expressed here than it was in Sonnet 60. Even the strangest and apparently most durable things on earth must finally surrender to time's power to destroy them: brass, stone, earth and the 'boundless sea'. When these mighty forces cannot resist the ravages of time, what chance does fragile beauty have against the assaults of this violent and angry agent of decay. There is a pathetic note in the expression of this idea:

> How with this rage shall beauty hold a plea,
> Whose action is no stronger than a flower?

Then the speaker moves to consider the fate of human beings, the most precious of all things created by time ('time's best jewel'). What force can prevent time from destroying people and their beauty, just as it destroys other earthly things? Here, the answer is the same as that given in Sonnet 60: the miracle of great art will preserve at least the memory of people whom poets love and admire after their death, and so in a sense keep them alive.

[A fourth sonnet has been discussed to enlarge the range of reference]

Time is associated in the sonnet with other themes, the most prominent of these being love, death and beauty. Time is the agent of death as well as of birth, it is both the creator and the destroyer of beauty. In the sonnets, two forces are presented as being able to outlive the ravages of time: great art (in Shakespeare's case great poetry) and true love.

[New themes identified]

The most memorable account of the power of true love to overcome all that time can do is found in Sonnet 116 ('Let me not'). Genuine love, which in this sonnet means true friendship ('the marriage of true minds') is a permanent thing. It never diminishes or alters even when the attitude of friends may change ('Or bends with the remover to remove'). It resists the changes brought about by time and circumstances. All around it things may change, but it remains constant, like a sea-mark or beacon that defies storms and tempests, or like the Northern Star, a permanent fixture in the sky on which sailors may always rely as a guide to their ships.

The ability of love to defy the destructive power of time is asserted in two powerful lines:

> Love's not time's fool, though rosy lips and cheeks
> Within his bending sickle's compass come

The key words here are 'time's fool'. A fool is somebody to be mocked or despised. In other sonnets time mocks the things it destroys: earth, brass, stone, oceans, beauty and mortal life. These two lines put love in a different category from all the rest. Unlike all other things, love resists the changes time brings and even defies time's ultimate weapon, death:

> Love alters not with his [time's] brief hours and weeks,
> But bears it out, even to the edge of doom.

Thus, love is seen as the ultimate survivor. It alone resists the passage of time. It alone survives until the Day of Judgement ('doom'). At that stage, time and death will be no more, and love will last through eternity.

[Further discussion of themes illustrated by detailed reference to one sonnet]

The themes of the sonnets are commonplace enough. Poets had been dealing with the same themes for thousands of years before Shakespeare wrote his sonnets. The real triumph represented by Shakespeare's handling of the themes of time, death, decay, beauty and love lies in his use of language and imagery. The sonnets show that Shakespeare is the great master of figurative language: metaphor, simile, personification, for example; and the master of suggestive sound in his handling of such devices as alliteration and assonance. To test this, all we have to do is to write a paraphrase of any of the sonnets using non-figurative language, omitting all similes and metaphors, as well as personification, alliteration and assonance. The result will be a set of bald statements lacking any merit as poetry. The real merit of the sonnets lies in the poetic form in which Shakespeare conveys the themes he has chosen.

[Response to second part of question introduced; paragraph links the
two parts of the answer]

In Sonnet 12, for example, Shakespeare is saying that time wastes all natural things. This is something all of us know. Shakespeare, however, impresses this idea on our imagination in a series of striking images:

> And summer's green all girded up in sheaves
> Borne on the bier with white and bristly beard

In these few words there is a wealth of meaning and suggestion. 'Summer's green' describes the fresh green crops of summer. These are bound up ('girded up') into sheaves of barley after they have ripened. The next line is a triumph of imagination. The ripened sheaves are carried away on a cart, described here as a bier, which is a carriage or wooden frame used in Shakespeare's day to convey corpses to their graves. We are thus invited to imagine two scenes related to the themes of ripening and decay. We picture a vehicle carrying bound sheaves of barley. We also picture the corpse of a white-bearded man, ready for burial, with a girdle tied around his waist. Decay through time in humankind and nature, a universal theme, is thus impressed on the imagination in two lines and in simple language.

[First point illustrated by reference, quotation and brief analysis of an appropriate sonnet]

The imagery of the sonnets is all the more impressive because it is largely visual, as if the poet were creating a picture in words. A fine example is found in the opening lines of Sonnet 73

> That time of year thou mayst in me behold,
> When yellow leaves, or none, or few do hang
> Upon those boughs which shake against the cold,
> Bare ruined choirs where late the sweet birds sang;

The main point of this description is that the leafless trees of the forest remind us of the physical decay of the speaker. The words themselves conjure up a beautiful picture of a forest in late autumn or early winter. The phrase 'Bare ruined choirs' suggests another picture and a further layer of meaning. The bare trees are the arching ruins of English monasteries, open to the heavens. The 'sweet birds', as well as being the summer birds who sang when the trees were in leaf, are also choirboys, monks or nuns, who sang in the monasteries before they were closed by order of King Henry VIII and allowed to fall into ruin in the sixteenth century.

[Another sonnet introduced to make a second point]

Sonnet 60 has other memorable images of time's progress and the devastation it causes. Its unhindered progress is conveyed in lines that also suggest the swift passage of a human life:

> Like as the waves make towards the pebbled shore,
> So do our minutes hasten to their end,

In the same sonnet another visual image shows us what time does to human beauty. Again, time is personified as a tiller of the soil. The farming landscape is pictured as a human face. The farmer ploughing the field is an image of time digging furrows ('delves the parallels') in a hitherto smooth human face.

In most of the sonnets the sounds of the words are a central part of the meaning being conveyed. Sonnet 30 ('When to the sessions') is a good example of this. In the opening lines, the speaker announces his intention to summon memories of his past life before the court of his mind. His mood is solemn and reflective:

> When to the sessions of sweet silent thought
> I summon up remembrance of things past,
> I sigh the lack of many a thing I sought

The soft hissing sounds running through these lines (sessions, sweet, silent, summon, remembrance, past, sigh, sought), along with the slow rhythms, mirror the contemplative mood. The lament for dead friends provides an immediate contrast:

> Then can I drown an eye (unused to flow)
> For precious friends hid in death's dateless night

In the second of these lines the strong emphasis created by alliteration ('friends hid in death's dateless night') reflects the finality of death. In the same way, the mournful vowel sounds express the speaker's self-torture in the following lines:

> And heavily from woe to woe tell o'er
> The sad account of fore-bemoaned moan

[A third sonnet introduced in further support of the second part of the question]

This brief introduction to just some of Shakespeare's sonnets highlight some of the major themes: the devouring effect of time on life and beauty, and the ability of great poetry and true love to triumph over time. It has also illustrated how Shakespeare's handling of these themes in his masterful use of language and imagery gives the sonnets their power.

[Brief concluding paragraph]

William Shakespeare

snapshot

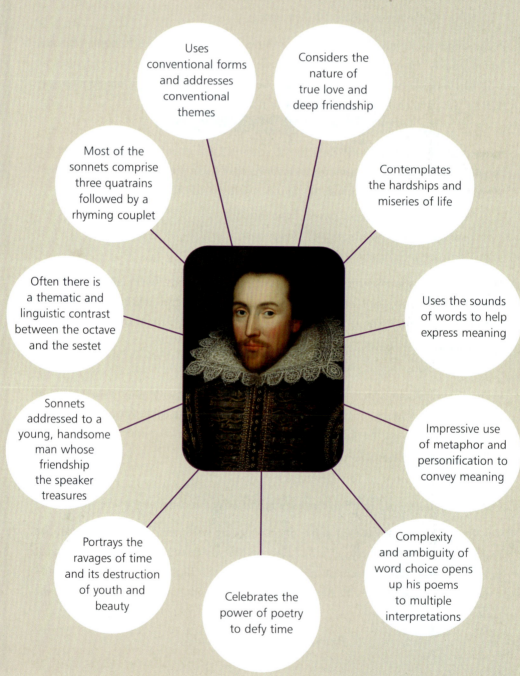

Uses conventional forms and addresses conventional themes

Considers the nature of true love and deep friendship

Most of the sonnets comprise three quatrains followed by a rhyming couplet

Contemplates the hardships and miseries of life

Often there is a thematic and linguistic contrast between the octave and the sestet

Uses the sounds of words to help express meaning

Sonnets addressed to a young, handsome man whose friendship the speaker treasures

Impressive use of metaphor and personification to convey meaning

Portrays the ravages of time and its destruction of youth and beauty

Complexity and ambiguity of word choice opens up his poems to multiple interpretations

Celebrates the power of poetry to defy time

William Wordsworth

1770–1850

TO MY SISTER
SHE DWELT AMONG THE UNTRODDEN WAYS*
A SLUMBER DID MY SPIRIT SEAL
COMPOSED UPON WESTMINSTER BRIDGE
IT IS A BEAUTEOUS EVENING, CALM AND FREE*
THE SOLITARY REAPER
from *THE PRELUDE*: SKATING*
from *THE PRELUDE*: THE STOLEN BOAT
LINES COMPOSED A FEW MILES ABOVE TINTERN ABBEY

Biography

William Wordsworth, the greatest of the English Romantic poets, was born in Cumberland in northern England in 1770. He was raised in the Lake District, a place remarkable for the beauty of its landscape, which had a profound and permanent effect on his life and poetry.

He had to endure the loss of his mother when he was eight years old and of his father when he was thirteen. His sister, Dorothy, became the main support of his life, but his most passionate relationship was with the natural world with which he communed in a particularly intense way.

As a youth, he enjoyed the freedom to roam his native countryside, to absorb its influences and spend time with country people. Such experiences are reflected everywhere in his poems. His dealings with nature, and its benevolent influence on his entire being, are memorably celebrated in 'Tintern Abbey', perhaps his greatest work.

From 1787 to 1791 Wordsworth studied at St John's College, Cambridge. His university career was not particularly distinguished. In 1790, the year following the fall of the Bastille, he went on a walking tour of the Alps and France. He was deeply affected by the optimism generated by the French Revolution.

He lived in France from November 1791 to December 1792, where he fell in love with Annette Vallon, who bore him a child but whom he did not marry. His initial enthusiasm for the French Revolution was tempered by the murderous horrors it generated, and by the outbreak of war between France and England. Wordsworth abandoned Annette and their daughter and returned to England. He visited them some years later in more settled times (see his sonnet 'It Is a Beauteous Evening').

Influential poet

After his departure from France, Wordsworth was troubled by emotional conflicts and intellectual doubts. Two people helped him to recover his balance. One was his sister, Dorothy, with whom he settled in Dorset in southern England. The intensity of his devotion to her is revealed in such poems as 'Tintern Abbey' and 'To my Sister'. Another healing agent was the poet Samuel Coleridge, whom he met in 1795. Coleridge became his best friend and literary collaborator. They jointly published *Lyrical Ballads* in 1798. This was one of the most influential books of poetry ever published in Britain. It contained Wordsworth's 'Tintern Abbey' and Coleridge's 'Rime of the Ancient Mariner'. It is fair to describe the volume as heralding the emergence of modern poetry, with its emphasis on the self as the central subject.

In his 'Preface' to the second edition of *Lyrical Ballads*, published in 1800, **Wordsworth challenged earlier poetic practice and announced a radical new approach to poetic composition.** He outlined his view that the conventional, elaborate, artificial poetic style of the previous age was no longer adequate, and that poets should employ colloquial language, the kind used by people in their everyday lives. However, as his own poetry demonstrates, this aim was not easy to put into practice.

Wordsworth wanted to reform the content, as well as the language, of poetry. His principal objective, he declared, was 'to choose incidents and situations from common life, and to relate or describe them, throughout, as far as possible, in a selection of language really used by men'. Among Wordsworth's most important achievements was his success in making commonplace incidents and simple people profoundly interesting and moving.

Having received a legacy from a friend in 1790 Wordsworth had been able to devote himself to writing. In 1799 he and Dorothy returned to the Lake District to live at Dove Cottage, Grasmere. In 1802 he married Mary Hutchinson. As his fame grew, he attracted official recognition. In 1813 he was appointed Stamp Distributor for Westmoreland, a position not entailing significant work but providing a secure income while he wrote. The final mark of public approval came in 1843, when he was appointed Poet Laureate.

Poetic output

Wordsworth's poetic output is massive, but uneven. There are enough great poems and passages of great poetry to give him an assured place as one of the supreme English poets. He had, however, written all his important work by the time he was forty years old.

His most ambitious achievement is the long autobiographical poem *The Prelude*, which he began in 1798 and revised at intervals throughout his life. The greatness of this poem lies in its incomparable rendering of episodes from his childhood in passages of sustained imaginative intensity (see 'The Stolen Boat' and 'Skating').

Many commentators suggest a connection between Wordsworth's abandonment of his revolutionary principles and his poetic decline. By the second decade of the nineteenth century he had become a champion of the established political and social order, and a strong upholder of the Church of England. His poetry lost much of its imaginative power and often became dull, tame and conventional by his own best standards. He became increasingly addicted to rhetoric and moralising comment.

William Wordsworth

Taken as a whole, Wordsworth's poetry is the record of a massive exploration of a developing self-consciousness and its intimate relationship with the natural world. His single great subject is his spiritual, emotional and intellectual history, the landscape of his mind being continually reflected, as it is so memorably in 'Tintern Abbey', in the beauty of the natural world. His profound understanding of the communion between the inner self and outward nature, and of the intimate bonds between human beings and the natural world, makes him appear a thoroughly modern poet.

Social and Cultural Context

In many respects Wordsworth was a revolutionary who brought a fundamentally new approach to the writing of English poetry, both in its style and in its subject matter. As such, he is considered one of the key poets of the Romantic Movement that transformed cultural attitudes in the early nineteenth century.

Poetic style

Many of his great predecessors of the classical age, particularly John Dryden, Alexander Pope, Thomas Gray and Oliver Goldsmith, favoured the formal, elaborate poetic diction associated with that age, which tended to draw clear distinctions between the language of prose and the language of poetry. One of Wordsworth's main aims was to simplify poetic language and make it more natural. He argued that there should not be any essential difference between the language of prose and that of poetry, which should be the language of normal speech.

In many of his poems, Wordsworth puts this theory into practice. 'To My Sister', 'She Dwelt Among the Untrodden Ways', 'A Slumber Did My Spirit Seal' and 'The Solitary Reaper' are written in simple, comprehensible language. On the other hand, it is often pointed out that in such poems as 'Tintern Abbey', Wordsworth employs a more learned diction and a more complex syntax (word order) than one is likely to find in the language of everyday life. In parts of the poem, the diction is quite remote from that of ordinary speech ('tranquil restoration', 'this corporeal frame', 'abundant recompense' and 'deeply interfused', for example).

Poetic subject matter

Wordsworth's 'Preface' to *Lyrical Ballads* defended his choice of simple incidents and humble people as subjects for his poetry. He used language and incidents from what he called 'low and rustic life' because in such life people are simpler, more direct, more natural and less affected in expressing their passions than people living in more sophisticated settings. **He departed from tradition in arguing that poetry does not have to deal with specifically 'poetic' subjects or with grand, dignified themes.** Instead, he believed poetry should explore subjects of permanent interest to ordinary human beings.

The subjects most congenial to Wordsworth were 'storm and sunshine, the revolution of the seasons, cold and heat, loss of friends and kindred, injuries and resentment, gratitude and hope, fear and sorrow'. Such preferences are described in 'The Solitary Reaper', where he wonders what the reaper's themes are:

> Perhaps the plaintive numbers flow
> For old, unhappy, far-off things,
> And battles long ago:
> Or is it some more humble lay,
> Familiar matter of to-day?
> Some natural sorrow, loss or pain,
> That has been, and may be again?

Wordsworth's treatment of external nature, landscape, flora and fauna, is perhaps his most distinctive contribution to English poetry. He is one of the great poets of landscape and one of the most descriptive poets. However, his interest in nature is not confined to recording impressions of the countryside and its inhabitants.

He constantly evokes the outward appearances of natural objects, but he is much more interested in another kind of landscape – that of his own mind. **In some of his finest poems, the real theme is the subtle relationship between nature in all its forms and meanings and the mind and heart of the poet who contemplates it.** This relationship is seen by Wordsworth as uniformly beneficial to those who devote themselves to the service and contemplation of nature. 'All which we behold', he tells his sister in 'Tintern Abbey', is 'full of blessings'. In another remarkable passage in the same poem, Wordsworth expresses his sense of the inseparable unity of God, man and nature. His reference to 'motion and a spirit . . . that rolls through all things' implies a belief in a divine being pervading the world and sustaining it.

Wordsworth could not accept the eighteenth-century idea of a 'mechanical' universe from which God had withdrawn after creating it. He thought instead in terms of a living universe (called nature), which was being continuously created and renewed by a creator who was intimately involved in all its parts and activities. (Compare the poems of Gerard Manley Hopkins for their expression of a similar view of the link between God and nature.)

Timeline

1770	Born in Cumberland, in the English Lake District, an area remarkable for the beautiful landscape
1787–91	Undistinguished academic career at St John's College, Cambridge
1790	Walking tour in France: deeply affected by the French Revolution; a legacy of £900 enables Wordsworth to live frugally on the interest and to concentrate on writing
1791–2	In France, where he falls in love with Annette Vallon, who has his child, Caroline
1798	Publishes *Lyrical Ballads* in collaboration with Coleridge; a radical new work, the cornerstone of English Romanticism
1798	Begins work on *The Prelude*, his great autobiographical poem
1802	Marries Mary Hutchinson
1813	Appointed Stamp Distributor for Westmoreland
1813	Settles at Rydal Mount, Grasmere, where he lives for the rest of his life
1815–50	No longer a political radical, he becomes conservative and orthodox
1843	Appointed Poet Laureate, a token of his acceptance as part of the establishment
1850	Dies; posthumous publication of *The Prelude*, which had taken fifty years to evolve

To My Sister

It is the first mild day of March:
Each minute sweeter than before,
The redbreast sings from the tall larch
That stands beside our door.

There is a blessing in the air,   5
Which seems a sense of joy to yield
To the bare trees, and mountains bare,
And grass in the green field.

My sister! ('tis a wish of mine)
Now that our morning meal is done,   10
Make haste, your morning task resign;
Come forth and feel the sun.

Edward will come with you; – and, pray,
Put on with speed your woodland dress;
And bring no book: for this one day   15
We'll give to idleness.

No joyless forms shall regulate
Our living calendar:
We from today, my Friend, will date
The opening of the year.   20

Love, now a universal birth,
From heart to heart is stealing,
From earth to man, from man to earth:
– It is the hour of feeling.

One moment now may give us more   25
Than years of toiling reason:
Our minds shall drink at every pore
The spirit of the season.

William Wordsworth

Some silent laws our hearts will make,
Which they shall long obey: 30
We for the year to come may take
Our temper from to-day.

And from the blessed power that rolls
About, below, above,
We'll frame the measure of our souls: 35
They shall be tuned to love.

Then come, my Sister! Come, I pray,
With speed put on your woodland dress;
And bring no book: for this one day
We'll give to idleness.   40

Glossary

13 | *Edward*: the boy messenger who carried the poem to Wordsworth's sister, Dorothy; he was really Basil Montagu, the son of Wordsworth's friend of the same name

Guidelines

This poem is a verse-letter, addressed by Wordsworth to his sister, Dorothy, in March 1798, and first published in *Lyrical Ballads* in the same year. The original title of the poem was 'Lines written at a distance from my house and sent, by my little boy, to the person to whom they are addressed'. **The poem expresses one of Wordsworth's favourite ideas: the close communion of people and nature.**

Commentary

The good life

'To My Sister' is one of a number of poems in which Wordsworth considers the relative merits of a life devoted to study and a life spent in communion with nature. In all these poems his preference is clear: wild nature has infinitely more to offer human beings than a lifetime of reading. This explains the request that is at the heart of the poem (lines 14–16):

> Put on with speed your woodland dress;
> And bring no book: for this one day
> We'll give to idleness.

In an associated poem, 'The Tables Turned', Wordsworth had been even more extreme in his dismissal of a bookish life as a source of wisdom and knowledge than he is in 'To My Sister', commenting scornfully on the way in which 'our meddling intellect' can misshape 'the beauteous forms of things'. 'The Tables Turned' has a celebrated stanza that expresses the central idea of 'To My Sister':

> One impulse from a vernal wood
> May teach you more of man,
> Of moral evil and of good,
> Than all the sages can.

The power of nature

When the poet tells his sister that 'one moment' in the presence of nature at its best can give them 'more / Than years of toiling reason' (lines 25 and 26), he is not advocating idle outdoor rambling. Instead, he is asking her to subscribe to a new ethic that will allow the blessings of joy, tranquillity and love to flow into her heart if only she will give herself up to the observation and contemplation of nature. **The soul will find itself enriched through seeing, hearing and touching natural objects.**

Many of Wordsworth's poems take a similarly benevolent view of the influence of nature in all its aspects on human beings. In 'To My Sister' it is 'the blessed power that rolls / About, below, above' (lines 33–34). In 'Tintern Abbey' nature is 'a motion and a spirit . . . that rolls through all things' (lines 100–102). The love and benevolence experienced by people who put themselves into harmony with nature is not a process working in only one direction. In 'To My Sister' love is a universal force moving gently and silently from one person to another, but also moving 'from earth to man, from man to earth' (line 23).

William Wordsworth

Thinking about the poem

1. What does this poem tell us about the relationship between the speaker and his sister?

2. Does the speaker make a good case for a positive response to the invitation he offers in stanza 3?

3. In stanza 4, the speaker suggests that he and his sister should devote their entire day to idleness. What value does he attach to idleness in this context? What will a day of idleness achieve?

4. The speaker thinks it a good idea to date 'The opening of the year' (line 20) to this mild March day. Mention some details in the poem which inspire this idea.

5. The poem contrasts two ways of living. Describe these. Stanzas 4 to 7 will help you here.

6. Stanza 8 refers to 'some silent laws' that the hearts of brother and sister will make and obey. What kind of laws might these be?

7. What is 'the blessed power' mentioned in stanza 9?

8. What might the speaker mean when he talks about drinking 'The spirit of the season' (line 28)? Give reasons for your answer.

9. A number of key words sum up the speaker's attitude to his subject. Choose four of these, and give reasons for your choice.

10. How does Wordsworth convey his sense of the intimate relationship between humankind and nature?

11. What idea of human happiness is conveyed in the poem?

12. Explain the references to love in the poem. The sixth stanza gives an important clue.

13. Why does Wordsworth dismiss 'years of toiling reason' (line 26)?

14. Wordsworth suggests a connection between the present and the future. What is this connection? A careful reading of stanzas 8 and 9 will help you with this answer.

15. Compose a reply, either in verse or prose, to the invitation offered in the poem.

The 'Lucy Poems'

'She Dwelt Among the Untrodden Ways' and 'A Slumber Did My Spirit Seal' are part of a group of five poems, traditionally referred to as the 'Lucy poems'. The identity of the woman to whom the poems refer has not been established. Some critics argue that since most of Wordsworth's poems in the collection to which the 'Lucy poems' belong are based on fact, and since Wordsworth's mind was essentially factual, it would be rash to claim that Lucy is entirely fictitious. Others have suggested that she represents a woman whom Wordsworth loved in his youth and who died young. One scholar has speculated that Lucy was Margaret Hutchinson, younger sister of the woman whom Wordsworth eventually married. Margaret died at the age of twenty-four.

The matter is complicated by the fact that in some of his poems Wordsworth associates the name Lucy with his beloved sister and close friend, Dorothy. If, however, Lucy is Dorothy, or if Dorothy is the inspiration for the 'Lucy poems', why does Wordsworth represent Lucy as having died? Coleridge, who believed that Lucy was Dorothy, offered an explanation. 'Most probably,' Coleridge wrote to a friend, 'in some gloomier moment he had fancied the moment when his sister might die.'

She Dwelt Among the Untrodden Ways

She dwelt among the untrodden ways
Beside the springs of Dove.
A Maid whom there were none to praise
And very few to love;

A violet by a mossy stone   5
Half hidden from the eye!
– Fair, as a star when only one
Is shining in the sky.

She lived unknown, and few could know
When Lucy ceased to be;   10
But she is in her grave, and, oh,
The difference to me!

Glossary	
2	*Dove*: three English rivers bear this name, it is uncertain which of them Wordsworth had in mind; 'springs of Dove' may suggest that Lucy is associated with sources of peace, given the usual symbolic significance of the dove

Guidelines

This is one of the 'Lucy poems'. Wordsworth composed it at Goslar in Germany in 1799. He and his sister, Dorothy, spent a long, severe winter there, in cramped and poor lodgings. The weather made trips into the surrounding countryside impossible. It may be that the pessimism of the poem is partly due to the poet's unhappy, confining experience of winter.

Commentary

Stanza 1

The poem's simple language conceals difficulties when we come to decide on meaning. For example, the reader may wonder at the 'untrodden ways' of the first line. 'Ways' suggest roads or paths that are well worn, but in the context of the poem we are invited to think of them as places where people do not walk: they are 'untrodden'.

It is only when we refuse to take 'untrodden ways' literally, and regard the term as a metaphor, that a satisfactory meaning emerges. Understood metaphorically, 'untrodden' suggests an innocent, simple existence, unspoiled by the world, and 'ways' refers to a way of life. The two words taken together thus imply that Lucy lived in a remote place in harmony with nature. The rest of this stanza suggests that it is a lonely, isolated existence.

Stanza 2

The second stanza appears to offer another contradiction. The two images describing Lucy – the half-hidden violet and the single, clearly visible star – seem at odds with each other. How can Lucy be partly hidden from sight and at the same time be the only object to be seen in the sky? This contradiction is resolved if we think of Lucy as having once inhabited the ordinary world, where  her simplicity was almost hidden from view, and where, as the final stanza tells us, she 'lived unknown' except to nature. Now that she inhabits another world, she can be imagined as a single, beautiful star, adorning the heavens.

Stanza 3

The poem does not end on this consoling note. Lucy was beautiful and innocent, and close to nature, but these things could not preserve her from death. **The bleak, simple**

ending of the poem expresses the terrible finality of death, as if all that there was to Lucy has ended in the grave. There is no suggestion that she has, in death, been united with nature or with God.

Thinking about the poem

1 What are 'the untrodden ways' (line 1)?
2 Why were there 'none to praise' (line 3) Lucy?
3 Describe the mood of stanza 1. Does this mood change in the other two stanzas?
4 Do you find the imagery in the second stanza appropriate to Lucy?
5 Describe your own feelings as you read the poem.
6 Can you suggest a link between the fourth line of stanza 1 and the final two lines of stanza 3?
7 Comment on the language of the poem. In what ways does it suit the theme?

Taking a closer look

1 Both 'untrodden' and 'ways' (line 1) have more than one meaning. Consider what this ambiguous use of language may tell us about Lucy.
2 In the second stanza, the two images (the violet and the star) appear to contradict each other, if both apply to Lucy. Comment on this.
3 Identify all the ambiguities in the poem, and discuss their significance.
4 How does Wordsworth suggest an identity between Lucy and her natural environment?
5 Compose a story based on the content of this poem.

Imagining

1 Imagine that Lucy has left a diary. Write **two** entries for such a diary, explaining her way of life.
2 Imagine you are living in Lucy's neighbourhood. Write your impressions of her and her way of living.
3 Imagine that you are asked to make a short film dealing with the life and death of Lucy, featuring scenes from the place in which she passed her life and an interview with the speaker of this poem. Briefly describe the content of your film.

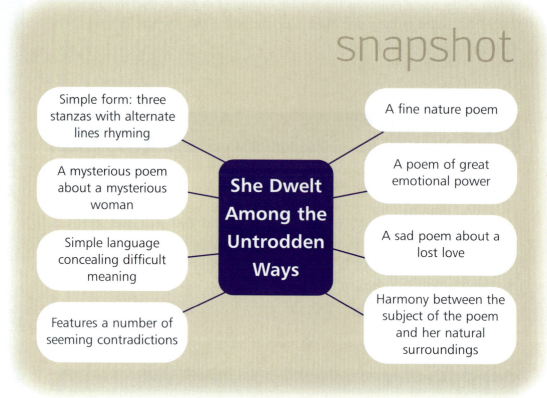

snapshot

Simple form: three stanzas with alternate lines rhyming

A fine nature poem

A mysterious poem about a mysterious woman

She Dwelt Among the Untrodden Ways

A poem of great emotional power

Simple language concealing difficult meaning

A sad poem about a lost love

Features a number of seeming contradictions

Harmony between the subject of the poem and her natural surroundings

A Slumber Did My Spirit Seal

A slumber did my spirit seal;
I had no human fears:
She seemed a thing that could not feel
The touch of earthly years.

No motion has she now, no force;   5
She neither hears nor sees;
Rolled round in earth's diurnal course,
With rocks, and stones, and trees.

Glossary		
5	*motion, force*: both terms are used in Newtonian physics
7	*diurnal*: daily

Guidelines

This poem is based on the contrast between the first stanza, with its seeming assurance that Lucy will never die, and the second, which records the cold reality of her death.

Commentary

Stanza 1
The first two lines describe a condition to which Wordsworth refers elsewhere in his work. The 'slumber' (line 1) that insulates his senses from troublesome, irritating realities is a creative sleep of the senses, inducing a state in which the soul and imagination are most fully alive. This is the condition described in 'Tintern Abbey', in which 'we are laid asleep / In body, and become a living soul' (lines 45–46). The optimism induced by this happy state gives way to the ultimate dismemberment of Lucy described in the second stanza.

Stanza 2
The poem expresses a more pessimistic view of life and death than 'She Dwelt Among the Untrodden Ways'. Here, Lucy is not imagined as having been a violet or a star. Her present status is presented in terms of negatives: she has no movement of her own, no force, no hearing, no sight, no existence. But while she has no motion of her own, she is, paradoxically, not motionless. She is made to share in the movement of the world and all it contains: she rolls in unison with rocks, stones and trees as the earth makes its daily ('diurnal') course around the sun.

Death as a happy state
Wordsworth's poem introduces us to a novel and a complex notion. He imagines Lucy rolled round in the earth's daily course through the heavens with rocks and stones and trees. The poem, however, makes us feel that rocks and stones and trees are alive and that the rotation of the earth is a living movement. It is worth remarking that both Wordsworth and his sister, Dorothy, thought of death as of lying awake in the grave. Wordsworth demonstrated this idea by lying in a trench, eyes shut, listening to the waterfalls and the birds, and thought how pleasant it would be to lie thus in the grave, to hear the peaceful sounds of the earth.

Alternative readings

There is room for legitimate argument over the mood and tone of the second stanza. If it makes us feel that Lucy is as dead as stones or trees, being propelled mechanically by the movement of the earth, it can only be regarded as pessimistic. Another reading is possible. Wordsworth may be suggesting that the movement of the earth is a positive, living thing, and that everything in creation is part of a great unified scheme that embraces God, humankind and nature.

When he wrote this poem Wordsworth seems to have believed in pantheism. This was the doctrine that the souls of human beings are temporarily separated fragments from the totality of creation, with which, in the end, they will be reunited. This idea is more fully explored in 'Tintern Abbey', where in lines 100–102 Wordsworth expresses his consciousness of:

> A motion and a spirit, that impels
> All thinking things, all objects of all thought
> And rolls through all things

Wordsworth rejoices in the belief that 'the mind of man' (line 99) is an intimate part of a reality that includes the ocean, 'the living air / And the blue sky' (lines 98–99). If he could find this a cause for joy, there is no reason to suggest that he could have regarded Lucy's intimate connection with 'earth's diurnal course' (line 7) and such natural objects as rocks, stones and trees as a cause for pessimism.

A poem by A. E. Housman, 'The Night Is Freezing Fast', is interesting for its expression of an idea quite similar to that in 'A Slumber Did My Spirit Seal'. In Housman's poem, a dead man who hated the cold:

> Has woven a winter robe,
> And made of earth and sea
> His overcoat for ever,
> And wears the turning globe.

Thinking about the poem

1   Two statements are at the heart of the poem: (a) the speaker thought that his subject (baby, girl or woman) could not die; (b) she is dead. How would you interpret the relationship between these two statements?

2   Consider the second stanza as a comment on the first. What kind of comment is it?

3   What kind of slumber sealed the speaker's spirit? Was it merely a sleep of illusion or self-deception?

4   How could the person described in the first stanza have seemed immortal?

5   Are we to understand from the second stanza that death has deprived his subject of her soul, and that she is now merely lifeless matter? Give reasons for your answer.

6   Is this a happy or a sad poem? Does it offer hope or consolation? Give reasons for your answer.

7   Wordsworth tended to identify human beings with the natural world. How does he do this here?

8   How can the subject of the poem be said to have 'No motion' and 'no force' (line 5) when she is 'Rolled round in earth's diurnal course' (line 7)?

Composed upon Westminster Bridge, September 3, 1802

Earth has not anything to show more fair:
Dull would he be of soul who could pass by
A sight so touching in its majesty;
This City now doth, like a garment, wear
The beauty of the morning; silent, bare.   5
Ships, towers, domes, theatres and temples lie
Open unto the fields, and to the sky;
All bright and glittering in the smokeless air.
Never did sun more beautifully steep
In his first splendour valley, rock or hill;   10
Ne'er saw I, never felt, a calm so deep!
The river glideth at his own sweet will:
Dear God! the very houses seem asleep;
And all that mighty heart is lying still!

Glossary

5	*bare*: not covered in smoke or vapour

Guidelines

The idea for this sonnet occurred to Wordsworth as he and his sister, Dorothy, were travelling through London by coach on the way to Dover, where they embarked for France. Dorothy recorded the circumstances in her journal:

> We mounted the Dover coach at Charing Cross. It was a beautiful morning. The city, St Paul's, with the river and a multitude of the boats made a most beautiful sight, as we crossed Westminster Bridge. The houses were not overhung by their cloud of smoke, and they were spread out endlessly, yet the sun shone so brightly, with such a pure light, that there was something like the purity of one of nature's young grand spectacles.

Commentary

Delayed response

The title of the sonnet does not give an accurate impression of its composition. Many of Wordsworth's poems were not written as immediate responses to particular experiences, and this was one of them. The coach journey that inspired the sonnet was made around five o'clock on the morning of 31 July. He did not write about it until over a month later, by which time the impressive scene had sunk deep into his consciousness. This delay in composing was an example of a principle in which he strongly believed, what he called 'emotion recollected in tranquillity'.

The sonnet was not, to use another famous phrase of Wordsworth's, the 'spontaneous overflow of powerful emotions'. Like 'The Solitary Reaper', it seems to have owed something to Wordsworth's reading. One of his contemporaries John Thelwall had published a book in 1793 containing a passage describing the view of London from Highgate Hill. Some of the language in Thelwall's work anticipates lines 6 and 7 of the sonnet. Thelwall wrote:

> No sooner did I behold the vast metropolis expanding beneath my feet, see turrets, spires and cupolas thronging round the still more magnificent dome, than wonder and delight rushed immediately to my heart. Nature perhaps was knocking at my bosom.

Wordsworth associated big cities with noise and smoke. He loved the wild countryside. In the early nineteenth century, however, London still retained a partially rural atmosphere. Most of the city occupied the northern bank of the River Thames and was, as Wordsworth records, 'Open unto the fields, and to the sky' (line 7) on the southern side of the river.

Landscape as a living thing

Wordsworth was criticised for what appeared to be a contradiction in lines 4 and 5: 'This City now doth, like a garment, wear / The beauty of the morning; silent, bare'. Those who found fault with the lines wondered how the city could be wearing beauty like a garment and still be bare. Wordsworth knew better than his critics. He pointed out to a friend that the contradiction was in the words only. London was bare, in the sense that it was not covered in smoke or vapour. It was clothed since it was attired in the beams of the morning sun, as lines 6 to 10 make clear. The ships and buildings glitter 'in the smokeless air' (line 8), while the sun steeps the city, clothing it in light, more beautifully than it steeps any splendid rural landscape.

The sentiments in the final three lines of the poem are characteristic of **Wordsworth's view of landscape, whether urban or rural, as a living thing in sympathy with humanity and with human characteristics.** The river glides 'at his own sweet will', the 'houses seem asleep' and the 'mighty heart' of the city is 'lying still' (lines 12 to 14).

Thinking about the poem

1   This poem suggests that a great city can be as beautiful as any countryside. How is this suggestion conveyed?

2   Which details of the poem convey the beauty of the city? Is there more to this beauty than the 'Ships, towers, domes, theatres and temples' (line 6)?

3   What is the significance of the fact that the city is sleeping, and that it is still early morning?

4   Do you get the impression that the speaker might not enjoy his experience of London if he were there later in the day?

5   In line 12 we are told that 'the river glideth at its own sweet will'. Why is this detail important?

6   How does the speaker suggest that the city is a living thing? What qualities does it seem to have in common with a person?

7   Does the poem suggest that the speaker prefers the city to the countryside?

8   Taking the first line of the poem as a starting point, show how the thirteen lines that follow develop the idea conveyed in it.

9   On the evidence of the poem, how can the speaker say that he has never experienced 'a calm so deep' (line 11)?

10 Select **three** images in the poem that you find impressive, and give reasons for your choice.

It Is a Beauteous Evening, Calm and Free

It is a beauteous evening, calm and free,
The holy time is quiet as a Nun
Breathless with adoration; the broad sun
Is sinking down in its tranquillity;
The gentleness of heaven broods o'er the Sea;   5
Listen! the mighty Being is awake,
And doth with his eternal motion make
A sound like thunder — everlastingly.
Dear Child! dear Girl! That walkest with me here,
If thou appear untouched by solemn thought,   10
Thy nature is not therefore less divine:
Thou liest in Abraham's bosom all the year,
And worship'st at the Temple's inner shrine,
God being with thee when we know it not.

Glossary		
1	*beauteous*: beautiful
5	*broods o'er*: sits over (like a bird protecting its eggs)
6	*the mighty Being*: the sea, also meaning nature and God
7	*doth*: does
9	*Dear Child*: Caroline, Wordsworth's daughter
12	*Abraham's bosom*: heaven; taken from Christ's parable of the rich man and the poor man, when the latter dies he is 'carried by angels into Abraham's bosom' (Luke, chapter 16, verse 22)
13	*Temple's inner shrine*: the most sacred part of the Temple of Jerusalem, entered by the high priest only once a year

Guidelines

This sonnet may be read as a sequel to that on Westminster Bridge. The coach journey that took Wordsworth and his sister through London was a stage in a trip to Calais in France, where the Wordsworths met Annette Vallon, with whom William had had a love affair during a previous visit to France. Annette was the mother of their child, Caroline, who was born in December 1792. Caroline, who is the subject of this sonnet – the 'Dear Child, dear Girl' (line 9) to whom it is addressed – was in her tenth year when Wordsworth wrote it. At the time of the visit to Calais, Wordsworth had arranged to marry Mary Hutchinson. In spite of this, he and Dorothy spent four weeks in Calais in unattractive lodgings, with little to do but walk on the sands with Annette and Caroline. Dorothy wrote in her journal that the four walked by the seashore almost every evening.

The sonnet shows that Wordsworth was by no means indifferent to Caroline, whose upbringing he had left to Annette. There is a suggestion that he hoped to find in her some reflection of his own mystical ecstasies when brought into communion with nature. It is evident that he was disappointed in not finding this, realising that she appeared 'untouched by solemn thought' (line 10).

Commentary

This sonnet divides itself naturally into two parts. **The first eight lines describe the beauty of the setting, while the final six offer a reflection on the significance of the splendid scene for Caroline, to whom the entire poem is addressed.** The beauties of nature evoked in the first part appeal profoundly to Wordsworth. They provide evidence of the 'eternal motion' (line 7) of 'the mighty Being' (line 6), who controls and orders all things.

The real significance of the final six lines lies in the revelation that the 'Dear Child' is not moved by nature in the same way as Wordsworth is. In spite of this, however, she is still blessed, still in close communion with the God of nature.

Wordsworth's altered religious views

The language of this sonnet is significant. It suggests that by August 1802, when he composed it, Wordsworth had become an orthodox Christian. In 'Tintern Abbey', which appeared in 1798, there are some indications that he found it difficult to think of God as a being separate from nature. Towards the end of that poem, he tells Dorothy that the natural world is the supreme object of his devotion ('I, so long / A worshipper of nature, hither came / Unwearied in that service', lines 151–153). In the same poem, it is nature, not God, which makes human beings morally good and which leads 'from joy to joy' (line 125).

In this sonnet the language is much closer to that of conventional religion. Wordsworth pictures a nun quietly adoring God, describes 'the gentleness of heaven' brooding over the sea (line 5), invokes biblical references to heaven such as 'Abraham's bosom' (line 12) and the inner shrine of the Jewish temple as the ultimate place of worship (line 13), and refers to the Christian God in the final line. The final six lines can be interpreted only as a Christian blessing on Caroline. The opening simile comparing the evening to a praying nun conveys a sense of the sacred mystery the poet feels in contemplating nature.

Thinking about the poem

1   Who is 'the mighty Being' of line 6? Has this 'Being' more than one identity?
2   What is the connection between line 6 and lines 10 to 14?
3   Why does Wordsworth say that his daughter worships 'at the Temple's inner shrine' (line 13)? What kind of experience is he describing?
4   What kind of relationship between human beings and nature does the poem suggest? Where does the Christian God fit into this relationship?
5   Identify the words and expressions in this poem that give it a strongly religious colouring.
6   How would you describe the mood of the poem?
7   Does the speaker's daughter share his experience of the scene?

Taking a closer look

1   Choose **one** image from the poem that appeals to you, and explain why you have chosen it.
2   Why might the 'mighty Being' make 'a sound like thunder' (lines 6 to 8)?
3   This poem conveys a sense of the joy of nature. Which details contribute to this sense?
4   Write a short piece on what the beauty of nature can do for human beings.
5   What does this poem tell you about the kind of person the speaker is?

Imagining

1   Imagine that Caroline wrote in her diary about the evening with her father on Calais beach. Write the account that she might have written.

2   You have been asked to make a short film based on this poem. Describe how you would try to create atmosphere, how you would use sound effects, and your choice of background music.

3   Suppose that, before writing the sonnet, Wordsworth made some notes outlining his ideas on what it might contain. Write your version of these notes.

4   The title of this sonnet is simply borrowed from its first line. It was not chosen by Wordsworth. Suggest a suitable title he might have chosen to convey the mood and atmosphere of the episode.

snapshot

It Is a Beauteous Evening, Calm and Free

Two-part structure: eight lines of description and six lines addressed to his daughter

Biblical and other images associated with the Christian faith

God and nature closely connected

The spirit of nature moves through all things

A personal poem, mainly about the poet's daughter

Reflects on his daughter's present failure to share the speaker's solemn thought

Daughter still enjoys God's continuous protection

Poem informed by deep religious feeling

William Wordsworth

The Solitary Reaper

Behold her, single in the field,
Yon solitary Highland lass!
Reaping and singing by herself;
Stop here, or gently pass!
Alone she cuts and binds the grain,   5
And sings a melancholy strain;
O listen! for the vale profound
Is overflowing with the sound.

No nightingale did ever chaunt
More welcome notes to weary bands   10
Of travellers in some shady haunt,
Among Arabian sands;
A voice so thrilling ne'er was heard
In springtime from the cuckoo bird,
Breaking the silence of the seas   15
Among the farthest Hebrides.

Will no one tell me what she sings?
Perhaps the plaintive numbers flow
For old, unhappy, far-off things,
And battles long ago;   20
Or is it some more humble lay,
Familiar matter of today?
Some natural sorrow, loss or pain,
That has been, and may be again?

Whate'er the theme, the maiden sang   25
As if her song could have no ending;
I saw her singing at her work,
And o'er the sickle bending;
I listened, motionless and still;
And, as I mounted up the hill,   30
The music in my heart I bore,
Long after it was heard no more.

Glossary		
6	*melancholy strain*: sad tune	
7	*vale profound*: deep valley	
9	*chaunt*: sing (from the French *chanter*)	
11	*shady haunt*: oasis	
18	*plaintive numbers*: sad verses	
21	*lay*: song	

Guidelines

In September 1803 Wordsworth visited the Scottish Highlands with his sister, Dorothy, who kept a diary in which the inspiration for the poem is described. It is clear from the diary that 'The Solitary Reaper' is based both on Wordsworth's direct observation of the scene he describes, and on his reading. During their tour, the Wordsworths encountered small companies of reapers at harvest time. Dorothy remarked that it was not uncommon 'in the more lonely parts of the Highlands to see a single person so employed', as is the case in the poem. The language of 'The Solitary Reaper' bears a remarkable resemblance to that in a passage from a book that Wordsworth had read. This book, written by his friend Thomas Wilkinson, was entitled *Tours to the British Mountains*. Wilkinson records the following:

> Passed near Loch Lomond a female who was reaping alone. She sung in Erse (Scots Gaelic), as she bended over her sickle, the sweetest human voice I ever heard. Her strains were tenderly melancholy, and felt delicious, long after they were heard no more.

Before finalising the poem, Wordsworth made a number of changes to the lines. For example, line 10 was originally 'So sweetly to reposing bands'; line 13 was 'No sweeter voice was ever heard'; and line 29 was altered from 'I listened till I had my fill'.

Commentary

'The Solitary Reaper' combines description with reflection. The descriptive element in the poem is found in the first and fourth stanzas, which provide the framework for the inspired reflections of stanzas 2 and 3. There is a clear structure: the speaker begins with straightforward description, then reflects on what he has described, then speculates on the meaning of the girl's song, and finally recalls what the episode has meant to him after time has elapsed.

The descriptive stanzas draw particular attention to two aspects of the reaper's singing: its melancholy beauty and the difficulty of its language, which the speaker of the poem cannot comprehend. The 'melancholy strain' (line 6) of the singing gives rise to a flight of imaginative fancy on the poet's part. The sound that overflows the Highland valley is as refreshing as the song of the nightingale in an Arabian oasis or that of the cuckoo in the remote Hebrides.

The speaker's failure to understand the singer's language inspires the finest stanza of the poem. Here, as he speculates on the nature of her theme, the only evidence he has is that it is a sad one, given the melancholy tone of her singing. At this point, the speaker moves from the delighted contemplation of the voice of a humble singer to a profound reflection on universal human suffering, expressed in simple, unadorned language (see lines 18 to 24).

The poem is remarkable for the way in which its rhythm and movement help to enact its meaning and reflect the contours of the speaker's feeling. For example, the movement of the verse perfectly matches the rising emotion in lines 5 to 8.

Thinking about the poem

1 Why is the speaker so impressed by the song?
2 Is it significant that he does not know the meaning of the song?
3 How does he compensate for his ignorance of its meaning?
4 The song has a significance for the speaker beyond its immediate context. What is this?
5 There is an air of mystery about the speaker's experience. How does he convey this?
6 The poem has a clear structure. Show, by referring to details from the poem, how each of the four stanzas develops a different emphasis.
7 Was this poem written as an immediate response to the speaker's experience? Look to the poem for evidence.
8 The poem combines joy with sadness. How are these sentiments conveyed?
9 How would you describe the tone of the poem?
10 Would the poem have been better if the speaker fully understood the girl's language and summarised for us what she was singing about?
11 Write an appreciation of the poem, stressing the things in it that appeal to you.

The Prelude

'Skating' and 'The Stolen Boat' are extracts from *The Prelude*, Wordsworth's immense autobiographical poem in fourteen books. He began to compose it in 1799 and completed it in 1805. It was not published until 1850, after the author's death.

The most impressive passages in *The Prelude* occur in the first two books, which deal with the poet's childhood and schooldays. His moving account of his youth given in these two books offers vital evidence of the development of his mind. The impressions of his early years formed the deepest layer of Wordsworth's fascination with nature.

The first book of *The Prelude*, to which both 'Skating' and 'The Stolen Boat' belong, illustrates Wordsworth's consciousness of the intimate link between external nature and the human mind, an idea developed with eloquence and subtlety in 'Tintern Abbey'. In *The Prelude*, nature is a living being with a soul and motivation of its own, linked with the human soul and its purposes. **Such episodes as 'Skating' and 'The Stolen Boat' are descriptions of incidents in Wordsworth's childhood. These incidents convinced him that nature was a moral and spiritual presence, influencing his mind in the way a good teacher can, although also in mysterious ways.**

In 'The Stolen Boat' we have a moving account of the moral influence of nature, which has the power to trouble his mind and awaken his conscience after he has committed a trivial offence. The effect of the experience is profound, haunting his mind by day and troubling his dreams, driving pleasant images of nature from his consciousness. The 'huge and mighty forms' that violate his peace of mind have an important function in the scheme of Wordsworth's beliefs. The passage underlines his conviction that there is a close relationship between breaches of the moral law (theft, for example) and the harmony of nature. Disruption in one sphere involves disharmony in the other: a person's activity cannot be isolated from the natural world of which he or she is a part.

In a key passage of *The Prelude* Wordsworth refers to certain events in people's lives that he calls 'spots of time', which have a decisive influence on the minds of those who experience them. These events, which may simply be feelings, sights or impressions, such as individual episodes of skating or boating, can leave indelible marks on the mind and can have healing or morally enhancing effects. By means of such experiences, Wordsworth believed that 'our minds are nourished / And invisibly impaired'. When he looked back on some particularly vivid 'spots of time' in his life, he was able to restore his spirits. See 'Tintern Abbey', lines 22 to 31.

William Wordsworth

from The Prelude: Skating

And in the frosty season, when the sun
Was set, and visible for many a mile
The cottage windows blazed through twilight gloom,
I heeded not their summons: happy time
It was indeed for all of us – for me   5
It was a time of rapture! Clear and loud
The village clock tolled six – I wheeled about,
Proud and exulting like an untired horse
That cares not for his home. All shod with steel,
We hissed along the polished ice in games   10
Confederate, imitative of the chase
And woodland pleasures – the resounding horn,
The pack loud chiming, and the hunted hare.
So through the darkness and the cold we flew,
And not a voice was idle; with the din   15
Smitten, the precipices rang aloud;
The leafless trees and every icy crag
Tinkled like iron; while far distant hills
Into the tumult sent an alien sound
Of melancholy not unnoticed, while the stars   20
Eastward were sparkling clear; and in the west
The orange sky of evening died away.
Not seldom from the uproar I retired
Into a silent bay, or sportively
Glanced sideway, leaving the tumultuous throng,   25
To cut across the reflex of a star
That fled, and, flying still before me, gleamed
Upon the glassy plain; and oftentimes,
When we had given our bodies to the wind,
And all the shadowy banks on either side   30
Came sweeping through the darkness, spinning still
The rapid line of motion, then at once
Have I, reclining back upon my heels,
Stopped short; yet still the solitary cliffs
Wheeled by me – even as if the earth had rolled   35

With visible motion her diurnal round!
Behind me did they stretch in solemn train,
Feebler and feebler; and I stood and watched
Till all was tranquil as a dreamless sleep.

Glossary	
6	*rapture*: extreme delight
8	*exulting*: rejoicing
9	*shod with steel*: wearing skates
10–11	*games confederate*: games in which all joined in
11	*imitative of*: in imitation of
16	*smitten*: struck forcibly
16	*precipices*: vertical or nearly vertical cliffs
17	*crag*: a rough, steep rock or point
19	*tumult*: noisy crowd
19	*alien*: strange, not belonging to the place
20	*melancholy*: sadness, gloominess
23	*tumultuous throng*: noisy, disorderly crowd of other skaters
24	*sportively*: joyously
26	*reflex*: reflection in the ice
28	*glassy plain*: frozen stretch of water
31–32	*spinning still / The rapid line of motion*: the rapidly moving line of fellow skaters, still spinning
6	*diurnal round*: daily movement of the earth
37	*in solemn train*: the cliffs (of line 34) stretched out as though in a formal procession

Guidelines

In this passage Wordsworth describes his experience as a child skating on a frozen lake on a winter's evening. This episode suggests how deeply impressionable a child he was: decades after the event described here, he could recall its details with dramatic intensity.

Commentary

What is most immediately impressive about the passage is its immense vitality. The strong, surging rhythms contribute significantly to this. For example, 'I wheeled about, / Proud and exulting like an untired horse' (lines 7–8), 'So through the darkness and the cold we flew' (line 14), 'leaving the tumultuous throng' (line 25).

The passage is filled with sound, movement and colour. Wordsworth is particularly successful in his description of the ice-bound landscape with its metallic hardness. For example, 'All shod with steel, / We hissed along the polished ice' (lines 9–10), 'every icy crag / Tinkled like iron' (lines 17–18).

The skating episode is also remarkable for its variety. The noisy crowd of young skaters, not an idle voice among them, is brought to life using the terms of a woodland hunt: 'the resounding horn, / The pack loud chiming, and the hunted hare' (lines 12–13). In contrast to this lively din, we have the restrained response of the far distant hills, which 'Into the tumult sent an alien sound / Of melancholy not unnoticed' (lines 19–20).

There is also a splendid contrast between 'So through the darkness and the cold we flew' (line 14) and 'in the west / The orange sky of evening died away' (lines 21–22).

Lines 23–39

The poet distances himself from the noisy scene. But, even after he has stopped skating and reclined back upon his heels, he continues to feel the effects of the vigorous exercise he has been engaged in: 'yet still the solitary cliffs / Wheeled by me' (lines 34–35). This is a normal sensation in the circumstances. Wordsworth, however, gives it a further significance. He feels as though he is experiencing the earth revolving on its axis: 'as if the earth had rolled / With visible motion her diurnal round' (lines 35–36). Here **Wordsworth is recording a kind of mystical experience: his sense of being at one with nature and the earth.** As his

consciousness of this communion deepens, impressions of the external world recede, and all becomes peaceful: 'tranquil as a dreamless sleep' (line 39). This experience resembles what is described in the second stanza of 'A Slumber Did My Spirit Seal':

No motion has she now; no force;
She neither hears nor sees;
Rolled round in earth's diurnal course
With rocks and stones and trees.

Thinking about the poem

1   This extract gives us a picture of a winter landscape. Comment on the ways in which the poet builds up the details of this picture.

2   The poet connects himself enthusiastically with his surroundings. Give examples.

3   The extract reveals Wordsworth's descriptive power at its best. Choose some instances from the poem, commenting on the reasons for your choice.

4   How does Wordsworth convey his enjoyment of the exercise?

5   There is a transition in the extract from 'we' to 'I'. Can you suggest any significance in this? Pay particular attention to line 23 and the lines that follow.

6   Give your response to the extract, saying how it makes you feel, whether you can identify with the poet's experience, and whether it recalls a similar experience that you have had.

7   Why, in your opinion, is Wordsworth so enthusiastic about this episode ('It was a time of rapture!', line 5)? What does his response tell you about him?

Taking a closer look

1   Skating is the official subject of the poem, but is there another one?

2   Wordsworth conveys the idea that he and his fellow skaters form part of the landscape. How does he do this?

3   Wordsworth offers suggestions of a communion between himself and nature. Consider some of these suggestions.

4   Discuss the role of imagery, rhythm and movement in conveying the meaning and atmosphere of the poem. Pick out some lines that particularly suggest the rapid motion of the skaters.

5   How does the poem suggest that nature has a benevolent influence on humankind?

6   Mention some instances from the poem in which the sounds of the words echo their meaning.

William Wordsworth

Imagining

1 You want to make a short film based on this passage. Describe the kind of atmosphere you would create, and say what kind of music, sound effects and images you would use.

2 Choose another title for this passage. The title you choose should describe your own response as you read the passage.

3 Suppose Wordsworth had written a diary entry about his experience of skating. Write out what you think he might have written.

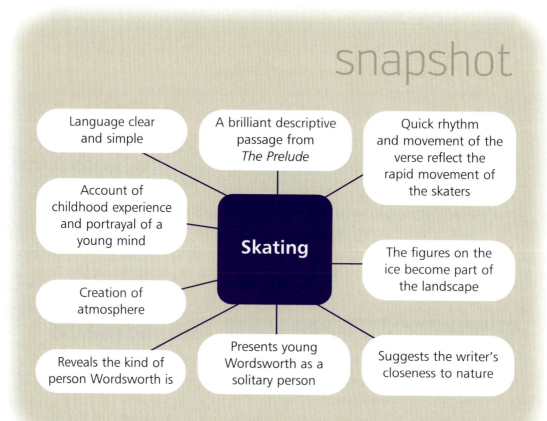

snapshot

Language clear and simple

A brilliant descriptive passage from *The Prelude*

Quick rhythm and movement of the verse reflect the rapid movement of the skaters

Account of childhood experience and portrayal of a young mind

Skating

The figures on the ice become part of the landscape

Creation of atmosphere

Reveals the kind of person Wordsworth is

Presents young Wordsworth as a solitary person

Suggests the writer's closeness to nature

from *The Prelude*: The Stolen Boat

One summer evening (led by her) I found
A little boat tied to a willow tree
Within a rocky cave, its usual home.
Straight I unloosed her chain, and stepping in,
Pushed from the shore. It was an act of stealth   5
And troubled pleasure; nor without the voice
Of mountain echoes did my boat move on;
Leaving behind her still, on either side,
Small circles glittering idly in the moon,
Until they melted all into one track   10
Of sparkling light. But now, like one who rows,
Proud of his skill, to reach a chosen point
With an unswerving line, I fixed my view
Upon the summit of a craggy ridge,
The horizon's utmost boundary; for above   15
Was nothing but the stars and the grey sky.
She was an elfin pinnace; lustily
I dipped my oars into the silent lake,
And, as I rose upon the stroke, my boat
Went heaving through the water like a swan,   20
When, from behind that craggy steep till then
The horizon's bound, a huge peak, black and huge,
As if with voluntary power instinct,
Upreared its head. I struck and struck again,
And growing still in stature the grim shape   25
Towered up between me and the stars, and still,
For so it seemed, with purpose of its own
With measured motion like a living thing,
Strode after me. With trembling oars I turned,
And through the silent water stole my way   30
Back to the covert of the willow tree;
There in her mooring place I left my bark,
And through the meadows homeward went, in grave
And serious mood; but after I had seen
That spectacle, for many days my brain   35

Worked with a dim and undetermined sense
Of unknown modes of being; o'er my thoughts
There hung a darkness, call it solitude
Or blank desertion. No familiar shapes
Remained, no pleasant images of trees,   40
Of sea or sky, no colours of green fields;
But huge and mighty forms that do not live
Like living men, moved slowly through the mind
By day, and were a trouble to my dreams.

Glossary

1	*her*: nature
13	*unswerving*: straight
17	*elfin pinnace*: a little boat that might have belonged in a fairy tale
23	*instinct*: possessed
36	*undetermined*: vague

Guidelines

Elsewhere in *The Prelude* Wordsworth mentions the two impulses that dominated his early years: beauty and fear: 'Fair seed-time had my soul, and I grew up / Fostered alike by beauty and by fear'. In the skating episode, the controlling influence is beauty: the young Wordsworth enjoys an evening of delightful movement and reflection in a splendid setting. In 'The Stolen Boat', on the other hand, he describes an evening dominated by fear.

The central theme of this episode is well described in a central passage in 'Tintern Abbey' (lines 109–111), in which Wordsworth recognises in nature:

> The anchor of my purest thoughts, the nurse,
> The guide, the guardian of my heart, and soul
> Of all my moral being.

'The Stolen Boat' shows this principle in action, as nature enforces a moral lesson on the young man.

Commentary

The phrase in parentheses in line 1 – '(led by her)' – suggests that nature has prompted him to break the moral law by taking someone's boat without permission in order to teach him the consequences of such acts. Even as he takes the boat, his conscience is not entirely clear: he recognises the theft as 'an act of stealth / And troubled pleasure' (lines 5–6). He nevertheless enjoys his trip on the lake, in much the same way as he enjoys the more innocent sport of skating. He is 'Proud of his skill' (line 12) as an oarsman, his ability to make his boat go 'heaving through the water like a swan' (line 20).

At the height of his enjoyment, however, **nature intervenes to trouble his imagination and arouse his moral sense** (lines 21–24):

> . . . from behind that craggy steep till then
> The horizon's bound, a huge peak, black and huge,
> As if with voluntary power instinct,
> Upreared its head . . .

The intimate bond between external nature and the human mind is again emphasised as the 'grim shape' (line 25) of the mountain peak continues to grow until it towers between the frightened boy and the stars. By this point it has, in his ignited imagination, become 'a living thing' (line 28), with a mind and purpose of its own, pursuing him to where he returns the boat.

Thinking about the poem

1. What is the significance of 'led by her' in the first line?
2. The speaker has mixed feelings as he takes the boat. How are these conveyed?
3. What impression is conveyed by the images of the landscape? How do these add to the meaning?

William Wordsworth

4   Why is the speaker 'in grave / And serious mood' (lines 33–34) as he makes his way home?

5   What, in your opinion, are the 'unknown modes of being' (line 37)?

6   Compare the speaker's reflections on the episode (lines 31 to 44) with those in 'Tintern Abbey' (lines 107 to 111), as reflections of his view of nature.

7   This passage gives a moving account of childhood guilt. How was the 'act of stealth' (line 5) punished? Was the punishment likely to have a lasting effect?

8   How does the young wrongdoer respond to his experience? How would you respond to a similar one?

9   As the speaker begins his journey, he hears 'the voice / Of mountain echoes' (lines 6–7). What does this voice seem to be telling him? Is this voice part of a pattern of similar experiences recorded in the extract?

10   Does the speaker enjoy his journey in the boat?

11   Describe the change of mood that overcomes the speaker from line 22 on.

12   What causes him to steal his way back to the mooring place?

13   What makes him think of the huge, black peak as 'a living thing' (line 28)?

14   Is the speaker's fear of the threatening peak simply caused by his guilty feeling at having stolen the boat, or is there a deeper cause?

15   Is there a hint that the speaker has been led into breaking the moral law by a great external force in order that he may learn a lesson? Is this what is implied in line 1?

Lines Composed a Few Miles Above Tintern Abbey

Five years have passed; five summers, with the length
Of five long winters! and again I hear
These waters, rolling from their mountain-springs
With a soft inland murmur. Once again
Do I behold these steep and lofty cliffs,   5
That on a wild secluded scene impress
Thoughts of more deep seclusion; and connect
The landscape with the quiet of the sky.
The day is come when I again repose
Here, under this dark sycamore, and view   10

These plots of cottage-ground, these orchard tufts,
Which at this season, with their unripe fruits,
Are clad in one green hue, and lose themselves
'Mid groves and copses. Once again I see
These hedgerows, hardly hedgerows, little lines   15
Of sportive wood run wild; these pastoral farms,
Green to the very door; and wreaths of smoke
Sent up, in silence, from among the trees!
With some uncertain notice, as might seem
Of vagrant dwellers in the houseless woods,   20
Or of some Hermit's cave, where by his fire
The Hermit sits alone.
These beauteous forms,
Through a long absence, have not been to me
As is a landscape to a blind man's eye;
But oft, in lonely rooms, and 'mid the din   25
Of towns and cities, I have owed to them,
In hours of weariness, sensations sweet,
Felt in the blood, and felt along the heart;
And passing even into my purer mind,
With tranquil restoration – feelings too   30
Of unremembered pleasure; such, perhaps,
As have no slight or trivial influence
On that best portion of a good man's life,
His little, nameless, unremembered, acts
Of kindness and of love. Nor less, I trust,   35
To them I may have owed another gift,
Of aspect more sublime; that blessed mood,
In which the burthen of the mystery,
In which the heavy and the weary weight
Of all this unintelligible world,   40
Is lightened – that serene and blessed mood,
In which the affections gently lead us on –
Until, the breath of this corporeal frame
And even the motion of our human blood
Almost suspended, we are laid asleep   45
In body, and become a living soul;

William Wordsworth

While with an eye made quiet by the power
Of harmony, and the deep power of joy,
We see into the life of things.
                                        If this
Be but a vain belief, yet, oh! how oft –   50
In darkness and amid the many shapes
Of joyless daylight; when the fretful stir
Unprofitable, and the fever of the world,
Have hung upon the beatings of my heart –
How oft, in spirit, have I turned to thee,   55
O sylvan Wye! thou wanderer through the woods,
How often has my spirit turned to thee!

    And now, with gleams of half-extinguished thought,
With many recognitions dim and faint,
And somewhat of a sad perplexity,   60
The picture of the mind revives again;
While here I stand, not only with the sense
Of present pleasure, but with pleasing thoughts
That in this moment there is life and food
For future years. And so I dare to hope,   65
Though changed, no doubt, from what I was when first
I came among these hills; when like a roe
I bounded o'er the mountains, by the sides
Of the deep rivers, and the lonely streams,
Wherever nature led – more like a man   70
Flying from something that he dreads than one
Who sought the thing he loved. For nature then
(The coarser pleasures of my boyish days,
And their glad animal movements all gone by)
To me was all in all. – I cannot paint   75
What then I was. The sounding cataract
Haunted me like a passion: the tall rock,
The mountain, and the deep and gloomy wood,
Their colours and their forms, were then to me
An appetite, a feeling and a love,   80
That had no need to a remoter charm,

By thought supplied, nor any interest
Unborrowed from the eye. – That time is past,
And all its aching joys are now no more,
And all its dizzy raptures. Not for this 85
Faint I, nor mourn nor murmur; other gifts
Have followed; for such loss, I would believe,
Abundant recompense. For I have learned
To look on nature, not as in the hour
Of thoughtless youth; but hearing oftentimes 90
The still, sad music of humanity,
Nor harsh nor grating, though of ample power
To chasten and subdue. And I have felt
A presence that disturbs me with the joy
Of elevated thoughts; a sense sublime 95
Of something far more deeply interfused,
Whose dwelling is the light of setting suns,
And the round ocean and the living air,
And the blue sky, and in the mind of man:
A motion and a spirit, that impels 100
All thinking things, all objects of all thought,
And rolls through all things. Therefore am I still
A lover of the meadows and the woods,
And mountains; and of all that we behold
From this green earth; of all the mighty world 105
Of eye, and ear – both what they half create,
And what perceive; well pleased to recognise
In nature and the language of the sense
The anchor of my purest thoughts, the nurse,
The guide, the guardian of my heart, and soul 110
Of all my moral being.
                              Nor perchance,
If I were not thus taught, should I the more
Suffer my genial spirits to decay:
For thou art with me here upon the banks
Of this fair river; thou my dearest Friend, 115
My dear, dear Friend; and in thy voice I catch
The language of my former heart, and read

My former pleasures in the shooting lights
Of thy wild eyes. Oh! yet a little while
May I behold in thee what I was once,   120
My dear, dear Sister! and this prayer I make,
Knowing that Nature never did betray
The heart that loved her; 'tis her privilege,
Through all the years of this our life, to lead
From joy to joy: for she can so inform   125
The mind that is within us, so impress
With quietness and beauty, and so feed
With lofty thoughts, that neither evil tongues,
Rash judgments, nor the sneers of selfish men,
Nor greetings where no kindness is, nor all   130
The dreary intercourse of daily life,
Shall e'er prevail against us, or disturb
Our cheerful faith, that all which we behold
Is full of blessings. Therefore let the moon
Shine on thee in thy solitary walk;   135
And let the misty mountain winds be free
To blow against thee: and, in after years,
When these wild ecstasies shall be matured
Into a sober pleasure; when thy mind
Shall be a mansion for all lovely forms,   140
Thy memory be as a dwelling place
For all sweet sounds and harmonies; oh! then,
If solitude, or fear, or pain, or grief
Should be thy portion, with what healing thoughts
Of tender joy wilt thou remember me,   145
And these my exhortations! Nor, perchance –
If I should be where I no more can hear
Thy voice, nor catch from thy wild eyes these gleams
Of past existence – wilt thou then forget
That on the banks of this delightful stream   150
We stood together; and that I, so long
A worshipper of Nature, hither came
Unwearied in that service; rather say
With warmer love – oh! with far deeper zeal

Of holier love. Nor wilt thou then forget   155
That after many wanderings, many years
Of absence, these steep woods and lofty cliffs,
And this green pastoral landscape, were to me
More dear, both for themselves and for thy sake!

Glossary	
Title	*Tintern Abbey*: ruined medieval abbey in Monmouthshire, east Wales
56	*Wye*: River Wye, which at this point in its course forms the border between England and Wales
115	*dearest Friend*: Wordsworth's sister, Dorothy, who was his companion, mentor and confidante for the greater part of his life; the entire section (lines 111 to 159) is addressed to her

Guidelines

The full title of the poem is 'Lines Composed a Few Miles Above Tintern Abbey, on Revisiting the Banks of the Wye During a Tour. July 13, 1798'. It is a dramatic lyric, since the speaker is presented in a particular situation, expresses his feelings and addresses himself to another person. Wordsworth declared:

> No poem was composed under circumstances more pleasant for me to remember than this. I began it upon leaving Tintern, after crossing the Wye and concluded it just as I was entering Bristol in the evening, after a ramble of four or five days, with my sister. Not a line of it was altered, and not any part of it written down till I reached Bristol.

Tintern Abbey, a great ecclesiastical ruin even in Wordsworth's day, was founded by Cistercian monks in 1131. It was dissolved in 1537 in the course of Henry VIII's campaign against religious foundations. During the Romantic era of the late eighteenth and early nineteenth centuries it was fashionable to look with nostalgia at such great memorials of the medieval past; they became favourite subjects for writers and graphic artists. However, the inclusion of Tintern Abbey in the title of this poem is misleading. The poem is about the Wye Valley, and does not mention the abbey.

In many of his poems, Wordsworth made use of the work of other writers (see the Guidelines for 'The Solitary Reaper'). In 'Tintern Abbey' he alludes to Gilpin's *Tour of the Wye*, a popular work of his day, in the opening passage of his poem. 'Many of the furnaces on the banks of the river,' Gilpin wrote, 'consume charcoal, which is manufactured on the spot; and the smoke, which is frequently seen issuing from the sides of the hills, and spreading its thin veil over a part of them, beautifully breaks their lines, and unites them with the sky'. Compare this with lines 9 to 18 of the poem.

Commentary

Lines 1–22

The significant feature of this passage is its emphasis on the physical sameness of the scene since the speaker last saw it five years previously. This sameness is continuously underlined –'again I hear' (line 2), 'Once again' (lines 4 and 14), 'I again repose' (line 9). The scene, then, remains the same. The only change over the five years is in the speaker's response to what he sees. **He spends the rest of the poem trying to understand why his perception of nature has changed.**

Lines 22–49

Wordsworth remembers what the landscape has meant to him in the five years that have passed since he made his last visit. The passage embodies his theory of memory, of 'emotion recollected in tranquillity'. **The memory, as he explains in *The Prelude*, selects certain 'spots of time', happy moments of past experience, which can nourish and repair our minds whenever we are depressed.**

The blessings he has owed to the vivid recollection of the Wye Valley as seen five years before are of four kinds.

- Physical: 'Felt in the blood, and felt along the heart' (line 28) – the restorative effect of recalling nature's beauty on his physical being.
- Mental: 'passing even into my purer mind' (line 29) – the refreshing impact of thoughts of the loveliness of the natural environment on his mind.
- Moral: his feelings of 'unremembered pleasure' (line 31) inspire him to do good and to perform 'acts / Of kindness and of love' (lines 34–35).
- Mystical: the most sublime gift he owed to the 'beauteous forms' imprinted on his mind is the deepest of all his experiences – a mystical vision 'into the life of things' (line 49) and the unity of all creation in an infinitely joyful being. The 'serene and blessed mood' evoked in lines 37 to 50 is the one experienced by mystics in a state of ecstatic trance as they lose their sense of individual identity and enter a tranquil communion with a great invisible presence.

This passage expresses one of Wordsworth's most powerfully held convictions: that nature is able to shape and influence the human mind rather as a teacher might do, though in vaguer, more mysterious ways. The same idea is taken up in lines 109 to 111.

Lines 49–57

See also lines 20 to 49, 62 to 65 and 123 to 59. All of these passages relate to the same theme: the power of natural beauty to impress itself on the mind and refresh the human spirit in times of sadness and despair.

Lines 58–111

This passage opens with a flooding back into the poet's mind of experiences now half-extinguished. The 'sad perplexity' of line 60 is a sense of loss in the contrast he recognises between the memory of things past and the scene before him.

He proceeds to record the successive stages in the development of his attitude to nature:

- His boyhood response was essentially physical: his movements were 'glad animal' ones (line 74).
- In his youth, five years ago (lines 66–85), his delight was visual and auditory and emotion was dissociated from thought. This time has now passed and he is disturbed by the possibility of estrangement from nature and from his former ability to love nature without anxiety.
- His present mature response involves his discovery that nature offers not merely sensation and emotion, but a complete system of ideas to live by. This he sees as 'Abundant recompense' (line 88) for the 'aching joys' (line 84) he has lost. This mature response has been called, for want of a better term, 'undoctrinal pantheism'. Pantheism places the emphasis on God's presence or immanence in nature. For the pantheist, God is not separate from creation, but permeates it – 'rolls through all things', as Wordsworth puts it in line 102.

His perception of nature now combines an intellectual and moral response with the purely emotional response of his last visit. Lines 88 to 111 convey this changed outlook. The new elements in his perception are a deep awareness of the 'still, sad music of humanity' (line 91) and a morally elevating 'presence' (line 94) in nature. The 'still, sad music of humanity' is a key phrase in the poem. Wordsworth has learned that his love for external nature is not necessarily incompatible with a loving concern for human nature – for the joys and sorrows of human beings.

In lines 106 and 107 Wordsworth expresses the idea that, between them, the human mind and the mind of nature form a complete creative force (hence the eye and the ear only 'half create').

William Wordsworth

Lines 111–159

The 'dearest Friend' of line 115 is Wordsworth's sister, Dorothy. The role of Dorothy in the poem is interesting. She is the unspeaking listener to whom the entire poem is addressed. She is also a convenient point of reference for some of the main concerns of the poem, helping Wordsworth to identify more precisely some of his earlier attitudes ('in thy voice I catch / The language of my former heart', lines 116–117). Dorothy still takes the same primitive, unsophisticated delight in natural things that he once felt (see lines 75 to 83): a delight that has nothing to do with thought, being compounded of pure joy and affection. In looking at her he can now relive his past, and pray that she, like him, will achieve a deeper, more mature response with her 'wild ecstasies' (line 138) eventually giving way to 'a sober pleasure' (line 139). Nature will also exert a moral influence and sustaining power over her in times of solitude, fear, pain and grief.

The language of lines 121 to 155 is explicitly religious, full of echoes of traditional Christian piety. The 'prayer' (line 121) is, however, addressed not to the Christian God but to Nature. The phrase 'A worshipper of Nature' (line 152) was one that Wordsworth later regretted. In a letter written over sixteen years after 'Tintern Abbey', he claimed that this was 'a passionate expression used incautiously', and that he had not intended to make nature a god.

In the final four lines Wordsworth turns his eyes back to the landscape, giving the poem a circular movement.

Wordsworth's spiritual autobiography

This is one of the great English nature poems. It celebrates the beauties of the English landscape, and the first paragraph is a fine piece of pastoral description. However, **the poem is as much about Wordsworth as it is about nature**. The emphasis is on what the scenes Wordsworth now beholds, and first saw five years ago, mean to him – emotionally, intellectually, spiritually and morally. What we have, then, is mainly spiritual autobiography, which for Wordsworth is a record of his developing relationship with nature and the changing character of that relationship. The main concern of the poem is with the changes that have taken place in his feelings and outlook since he first saw the woods and the cliffs of the Wye Valley, five years before.

Three phases

Three main phases in his spiritual development can be identified in the poem. The first gets only a passing mention. Wordsworth describes his childhood response to nature in terms of muscular enjoyment, 'glad animal movements' (line 74). This aspect is developed in 'Skating'.

The second phase is traced by Wordsworth to his first visit to the Wye Valley five years earlier. Then his attitude to nature was one of purely visual delight. He threw himself into this delight out of violent need. His enjoyment was sensuous and devoid of the deeper pleasure that thought might supply. It was a time of 'aching joys' (line 84) and 'dizzy raptures' (line 85), ultimately unsatisfying because they were purely emotional responses.

The third phase is Wordsworth's present, mature attitude to nature. He may no longer feel 'dizzy raptures', but this loss has been more than counterbalanced by what he has gained. Two of these gains ('other gifts', line 86) he sees as being particularly important: he has achieved a new understanding of the tragic plight of humanity (its 'still, sad music', line 91); and he frequently senses the presence within and all around him of a universal, infinite spirit – the divine force that moves all things. He has learned to unite nature and humanity in his affections and has come to feel that all life is united in one joyful, benevolent being. His horizons have greatly expanded in the space of five years. To the emotional response of his last visit, he can now add an intellectual and a moral response.

A system of ideas

By the time of his second visit the poet has learned to find in nature not merely sensation and emotion, but a system of ideas, a doctrine by which to live and a system of moral values (i.e. a religious system). It is not surprising, then, that he can describe himself towards the end of the poem as a 'worshipper of Nature' (line 152), much as a religious person might feel conscious of a steady commitment and dedication. In keeping with this attitude, the language of the poem, particularly as it moves towards its conclusion, has profoundly religious, indeed Christian, associations, which is not to say that 'Tintern Abbey' is a Christian poem. The address to Dorothy has the form and expression of a prayer. There is a distinctively Christian vocabulary: 'Rash judgments' (line 129), 'Shall e'er prevail against us' (line 132), 'cheerful faith' (line 133), 'full of blessings' (line 134), 'deeper zeal / Of holier love' (lines 154–155).

William Wordsworth

Thinking about the poem

1 In 'Tintern Abbey', Wordsworth values nature for its own sake. Where is the evidence in the poem for this? Why might Wordsworth call himself 'A worshipper of nature' (line 152)?

2 Write on the importance of memory in 'Tintern Abbey'.

3 Wordsworth is often described as an extremely subjective poet, creating a world that is a reflection of his own mind. Does 'Tintern Abbey' confirm this impression? Is Wordsworth merely exploiting nature to make it conform to his ideas?

4 Wordsworth is less concerned with outward appearances in 'Tintern Abbey' than with the value and meaning of these. Comment on this idea.

5 Nature takes on many different meanings and significances in the poem (as comforter, source of visual delight, mystical presence, and so on). Identify as many examples of these as you can.

6 Consider the idea that nature is a personality in 'Tintern Abbey', and that Wordsworth relates to it as he might to another person. If nature is a personality, what are its principal qualities?

7 Discuss 'Tintern Abbey' as a happy, optimistic account of experience.

8 Examine 'Tintern Abbey' under the heading 'Loss and Gain'.

9 Might Wordsworth fairly be described as a prophet of modern environmentalism? Give reasons for your answer.

10 Discuss Wordsworth's examination in 'Tintern Abbey' of the idea of nature as an active agent, working on the human mind like a benevolent teacher of morality. Do we find the same principle at work in any of his other poems? What can nature teach us, according to this poem?

11 The poem describes Wordsworth's changing views on nature, and its meaning for him. Discuss the way in which his views change with time. How does he account for the changes?

General Questions

1 Discuss the proposition that Wordsworth's poetry is largely the history of his own mind, and that it is profoundly self-centred.

2 Wordsworth is constantly preoccupied with the influence of nature on human beings, particularly on himself. Discuss the meaning and significance of nature in his poems.

3   There is a strong moral emphasis throughout Wordsworth's poetry. Where do his moral ideas originate?

4   Wordsworth's primary intention was to relate poetry as closely as possible to common life, to appeal to the normal interests of human beings. Examine his poems from this point of view.

5   Much of Wordsworth's best poetry is based on the recollection of moments of insight and awareness. Explore this idea.

6   Wordsworth is one of the great descriptive poets in the language. Consider this aspect of his poetry.

7   In several poems, Wordsworth stresses the power of beautiful present experiences to make us happy in the future. See 'Tintern Abbey' (lines 61–65) and the final stanza of 'The Solitary Reaper'. Write an essay based on Wordsworth's belief that the 'beauteous forms' of nature can provide us with 'life and food' for future years.

8   Wordsworth is often described as a decidedly 'modern' poet. Consider some features of his poetry that you think might justify this description.

9   Do the poems suggest that Wordsworth had a generally optimistic outlook?

10 Write an essay in which you give your reasons for liking and/or not liking Wordsworth's poetry. You must support your points by reference to, or quotation from, the poems that are on your course.

Here are some reasons you might give for liking Wordsworth's poetry:

- His poems are wonderfully descriptive.
- The poems convey Wordsworth's deep feeling for the natural world.
- His poems make the beauty of the world alive for the reader.
- His poems give us a vivid impression of his personality and ideas.
- Wordsworth conveys his meaning in a language that is not difficult to understand.

Here are some reasons you might give for not liking Wordsworth's poetry:

- His poems can have little appeal for modern readers living in towns and cities.
- His poems are too focused on himself.
- Wordsworth's poems lack either wit or humour and are too solemn and serious.
- Wordsworth's poems have too little to say about the problems affecting modern human beings.

Sample Essay

The bond between the poet and nature is at the heart of Wordsworth's poetry. Discuss.

We could not speak of a bond between the poet and nature if we thought of nature simply as trees, flowers, streams, waterfalls and mountains, as Wordsworth puts it in 'Tintern Abbey': 'all that we behold'. For Wordsworth, nature is a larger and more universal force than a collection of beautiful sights. 'The mighty world / Of eye, and ear' is sustained by a force capable of restoring the distracted mind of the poet to tranquillity and harmony, of making him feel at one with the whole universe. It puts him in tune with 'the still, sad music of humanity'. Nature is 'a motion and a spirit' that 'rolls through all things'. Above all, communion with the spirit of nature has a strong moral influence on Wordsworth and, he suggests, on all good people who love nature as he does. He recognises in nature, as he puts it so memorably in 'Tintern Abbey':

> The anchor of my purest thoughts, the nurse,
> The guide, the guardian of my heart, and soul
> Of all my moral being.

[Answer addresses the point straight away by coming to terms with the question and introducing the first poem to be discussed]

Nature thus influences conduct in a fundamental way. It acts on that 'best portion of a good man's life' to bring forth 'His little, nameless, unremembered acts / Of kindness and of love.'

All of these benign effects are brought about by the contemplation of the 'beauteous forms' of external nature, the landscape surrounding the River Wye, and the recollection of these years later 'in lonely rooms, and 'mid the din / Of towns and cities'.

[Points are developed through an appropriate use of reference and quotation]

In an important sense the bond between Wordsworth and nature is akin to that between a religious worshipper and the deity he or she worships. In 'Tintern Abbey' he declares himself 'a worshipper of Nature'. This spiritual bond is expressed in specifically religious terms: 'this prayer I make', 'our cheerful faith', 'all which we behold / Is full of blessings', 'unwearied in that service', 'with far deeper zeal / Of holier love'. Nature, like the spirit of a god, unites Wordsworth, through its presence in him, with all of creation. Its 'dwelling is the light of setting suns / And the round ocean and the living air, / And the blue sky'. Above all, it lives 'in the mind of man'.

The spirit that unites Wordsworth, and humankind in general, with all the rest of nature, which 'rolls through all things', is like a god who cannot be separated from any part of his creation, who is everywhere and who cannot be thought of as distinct. Hence Wordsworth's sense of his intimate bond with the natural world.

[Further development of points based on 'Tintern Abbey', which offers the greatest scope for answering the question posed.]

'Tintern Abbey' is the finest expression of this idea. However, it is also at the heart of 'The Stolen Boat' episode of *The Prelude*. Here Wordsworth develops the idea that even in youth he could not break the bond uniting him to nature. The aspect of nature considered in this context is its powerful moral influence, its role as the conscience of the individual. The incident on which this episode is based is simple, even commonplace. The young Wordsworth steals a boat in a mood of 'troubled pleasure'. It is not long before nature asserts its influence as his guide and conscience. The point made by the episode is that to break the moral law, in this case by stealing a boat, is to break the bond with nature. This point is dramatically enforced when nature impresses on his mind, emotions and imagination a sense of the wrong he has done. As he rows along:

> . . . a huge peak, black and huge,
> As with voluntary power instinct,
> Upreared its head

[Discussion now moves to providing evidence from a second poem in support of the answer]

His fear intensifies as the peak, 'with measured motion like a living thing', seems to follow him. In 'Tintern Abbey' nature operates to inspire people to perform deeds 'of kindness and of love'. In 'The Stolen Boat' its function is to chastise those who perform evil deeds, and to deepen their sense of right and wrong. The bond between the young Wordsworth and nature in this poem is like that between a teacher and an erring pupil who is forced to learn a lesson. His experience of the sinister peak leaves a deep impression on his mind and imagination, as 'huge and mighty forms': 'moved slowly through the mind / By day, and were a trouble to my dreams'.

[Notice the use of brief quotations and how these are integrated with the discussion]

Wordsworth's sense of his intimate bond with nature convinces him that what happened as he rowed the stolen boat had a meaning for him: whether as a message, a revelation or a warning. In 'Skating' Wordsworth describes a parallel experience, a sense that the solitary cliffs wheeled by him, as if the earth had rolled 'with visible motion her diurnal round'. Again, he experiences living nature. To him, the earth is not a ball of matter moving mechanically through space, but a living being with feeling and sense, a mysterious presence of which he is aware and to which he is linked or bonded.

[Brief reference to a third poem]

Wordsworth's intimate relationship with the natural world is conveyed in the poem 'To My Sister', the theme of which is the happiness to be derived from experiencing this relationship at first hand. Wordsworth invites his sister to abandon the indoors and spend the day with him in the open air. In this, as in his other nature poems, he sees his bond with nature in all its forms as if it were one between two living beings, nature being the kind giver of gifts, and he the one who benefits from them. He experiences the 'blessing in the air', which also gives joy to 'the bare trees, and mountains bare'. The bond between nature and himself, the lover of nature, is best described in terms of a universal relationship of love:

Love, now a universal birth,
From heart to heart is stealing,
From earth to man, from man to earth:
– It is the hour of feeling.

[Discussion moves to a fourth poem, with appropriate quotation]

The bond Wordsworth has in mind is a totally happy one for the poet, and a totally beneficial one. It enables his sister and himself to 'drink at every pore / The spirit of the season'. Those in communion with nature are in tune with 'the blessed power that rolls / About, below, above'. The bond between such people and nature, as Wordsworth recognises, is one of love. It impresses on his mind feelings of quietness and beauty, and, as he puts it in 'Tintern Abbey', is the foundation of a 'cheerful faith' that 'all which we behold / Is full of blessings'.

[Notice the continuous reference to 'the bond' throughout the entire discussion; this ensures that the answer remains relevant to the terms of the question]

In the sonnet written on Calais beach ('It Is a Beauteous Evening, Calm and Free') the sense of the bond between the poet and nature is particularly strong. Again, as in 'Tintern Abbey', the bond has a strong religious character. The beauty and tranquillity of the scene fill Wordsworth with a sense that nature, 'the mighty Being', is to be worshipped. This idea is conveyed in the image of a praying nun: 'The holy time is as quiet as a Nun / Breathless with adoration'.

[A fifth poem is used to complete the discussion, again with reference and quotation to illustrate the main point]

Wordsworth is in communication with a kindly being as he contemplates nature, which, as the final line in this poem suggests ('God being with thee'), is a reflection of a divine power, whose essence is everlasting beauty: 'The gentleness of heaven broods o'er the Sea'.

[Always bear in mind that the essence of a good answer is to keep the terms of the question constantly in mind, and not to stray from these]

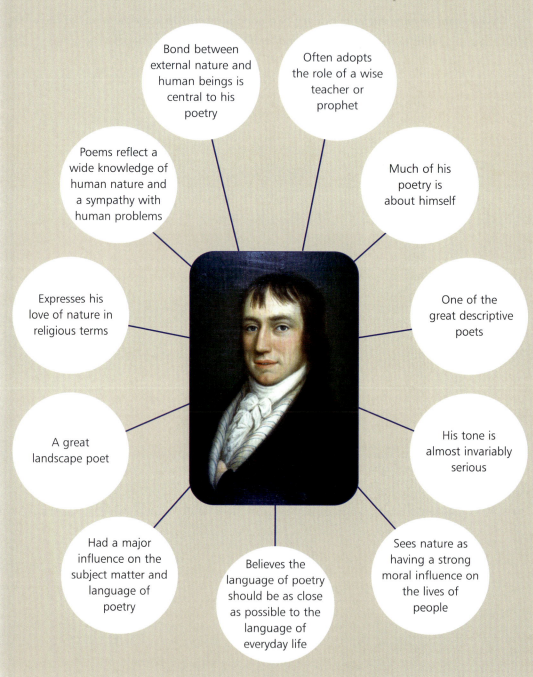

Bond between external nature and human beings is central to his poetry

Often adopts the role of a wise teacher or prophet

Poems reflect a wide knowledge of human nature and a sympathy with human problems

Much of his poetry is about himself

Expresses his love of nature in religious terms

One of the great descriptive poets

A great landscape poet

His tone is almost invariably serious

Had a major influence on the subject matter and language of poetry

Believes the language of poetry should be as close as possible to the language of everyday life

Sees nature as having a strong moral influence on the lives of people

Fleur Adcock

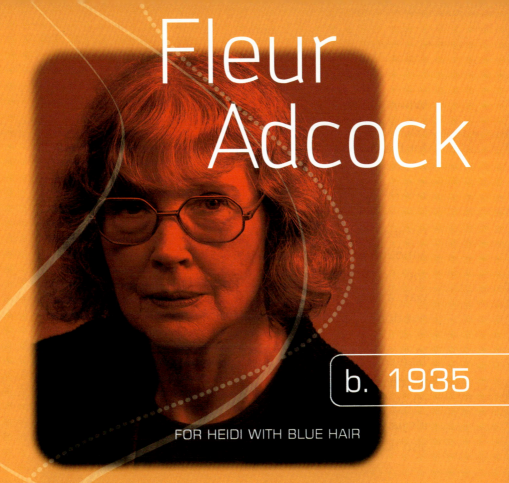

b. 1935

FOR HEIDI WITH BLUE HAIR

Biography

Fleur Adcock was born near Auckland in New Zealand in 1934. Much of her childhood was spent in wartime England. She and her family returned to New Zealand in 1947. She completed her studies at Victoria University in Wellington. Later she returned to England and worked there as a librarian and arts administrator.

Adcock has published several collections of poetry, amongst them *The Incident Book* (1986), which contains 'For Heidi with Blue Hair'. *Selected Poems* was published in 1983 and *Poems 1960–2000* in 2000. She is also a regular contributor to, and editor of, poetry anthologies.

Adcock's work has been awarded many prizes, and she is one of the most popular women poets of recent years. She received an OBE (Officer of the Order of the British Empire) in 1986 and was awarded an the Queen's Gold Medal for Poetry in 2006.

For Heidi with Blue Hair

When you dyed your hair blue
(or, at least, ultramarine
for the clipped sides, with a crest
of jet-black spikes on top)
you were sent home from school   5

because, as the headmistress put it,
although dyed hair was not
specifically forbidden, yours
was, apart from anything else,
not done in the school colours.   10

Tears in the kitchen, telephone-calls
to school from your freedom-loving father:
'She's not a punk in her behaviour;
it's just a style.' (You wiped your eyes,
also not in a school colour.)   15

'She discussed it with me first –
we checked the rules.' 'And anyway, Dad,
it cost twenty-five dollars.
Tell them it won't wash out –
not even if I wanted to try.'   20

It would have been unfair to mention
your mother's death, but that
shimmered behind the arguments.
The school had nothing else against you;
the teachers twittered and gave in.   25

Next day your black friend had hers done
in grey, white and flaxen yellow –
the school colours precisely:
an act of solidarity, a witty
tease. The battle was already won.   30

Glossary

2	*ultramarine*: a deep blue
13	*punk:* a follower of punk rock, a style of music with rather aggressive lyrics, which was popular in the 1970s; punks were thought to be anti-Establishment and in favour of lawlessness and disorder
27	*flaxen yellow*: a pale or soft shade of yellow
29	*solidarity*: joining together, support

Guidelines

Adcock has told us that this poem was written in response to a real incident experienced by her god-daughter, Heidi, who had moved with her father (after the death of her mother) to live in Australia.
Heidi has dyed her hair and the poem deals with the reactions of her school, father and friends.

Commentary

Stanzas 1 and 2

The poem speaks directly to Heidi. Her hairstyle is described in the first stanza. It seems to be a typical 1970s 'punk' style, short on the sides and spiked on top, dyed dark blue and black. Next the poem tells of the reaction of the headmistress. She objects to Heidi's hair for the rather absurd reason that it is not dyed in the school colours. We can hear the voice of the headmistress behind the seemingly casual phrase, 'apart from anything else' (line 9). What else? Perhaps this suggests that she is not being completely open about the reasons why she objects to the hairstyle.

Stanzas 3 and 4

The third stanza continues the story from the point of view of Heidi and her father. We see that they do not share the headmistress's opinion. By using direct conversation (like dialogue in a play), Adcock makes the situation more realistic for the reader. The relationship between Heidi and her father seems to be a supportive one. There is no suggestion that he wants her to break the school rules, though he is described as 'freedom-loving' (line 12).

Stanza 5

By referring to the death of Heidi's mother in the fifth stanza, **the poet shifts our sympathy to Heidi and away from the school**. It has the effect of making us look at Heidi's small act of rebellion in a new way. We now see it as a means of reacting to the stress of bereavement. In this stanza the poet makes her own feelings clear. The attitude of the school is seen as rather negative, as suggested also by the phrase 'the teachers twittered' (line 25), an unflattering description.

Final stanza

In this stanza there is an amusing comment on the whole affair. Heidi's friend's hairstyle is intended as an act of support for Heidi but it is also a challenge to the authority of the school. They will now have to find another reason for disapproving of the hairstyle, since it is now done in 'the school colours precisely' (line 28).

The poem ends with the 'battle' metaphor. It suggests that Heidi and her friends have been the winners here. **Individuality has won out over conformity.**

Thinking about the poem

1. What impression of the headmistress and the school does the poem give?
2. What sort of people are Heidi and her father? Support your answer by reference to the poem.
3. From your reading of the poem do you think Heidi and her father have a good relationship? Explain your answer.
4. What does the poet think of the school rule? How do we know her opinion from the poem?
5. How would you describe the language used in the poem?
6. Does the poem give a realistic picture of teenagers and their attitudes? Explain your answer.
7. In the fifth stanza the death of Heidi's mother is mentioned. How does this affect your attitude to Heidi?
8. What do you think of the action taken by Heidi's friend in the last stanza?
9. With which of these statements would you most agree:

    The poem is quite amusing.

    The poem is quite sad.

    The poem makes an important point about people's rights.

    Give a reason for your opinion.

Taking a closer look

1 'You wiped your eyes, / also not in a school colour' (lines 14–15). Comment on the tone of these lines.

2 'the teachers twittered and gave in' (line 25). What impression of the teachers do you get from the word 'twittered'?

Imagining

1 Write the letter Heidi might have written to her godmother telling her about the incident at school.

2 Imagine the conversation that takes place between the headmistress and Heidi's father on the phone, and write it in a short dialogue.

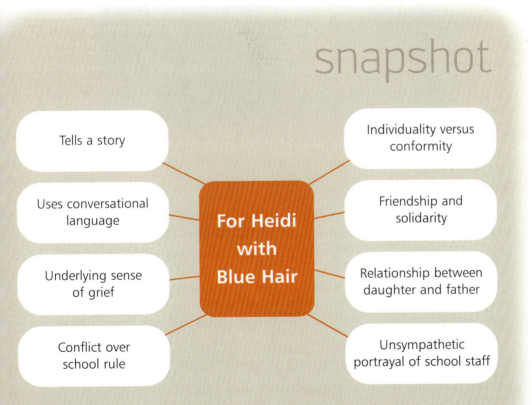

snapshot

Tells a story

Uses conversational language

Underlying sense of grief

Conflict over school rule

For Heidi with Blue Hair

Individuality versus conformity

Friendship and solidarity

Relationship between daughter and father

Unsympathetic portrayal of school staff

Tess Gallagher

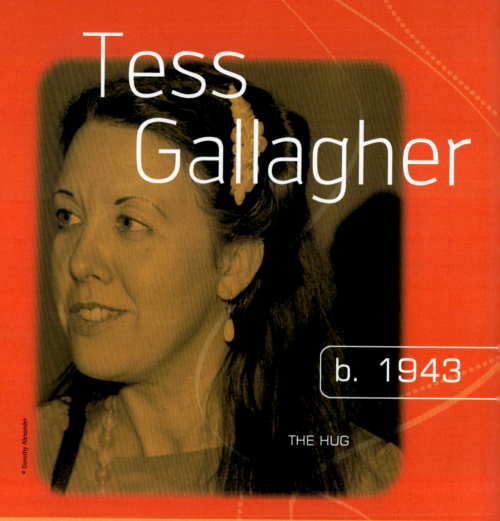

© Dorothy Alexander

b. 1943

THE HUG

Biography

Tess Gallagher was born in 1943 in Port Angeles, a small port town in the Pacific state of Washington on the north-west coast of the United States. She is a poet and a short story writer and was married to Ray Carver one of America's greatest short story writers.

Gallagher's childhood was marred by her father's alcoholism. For the young woman, words and writing were a means of escape from poverty and gave her the power to 'direct and make meaning' in her life. She attended university where she studied creative writing with the celebrated poet Theodore Roethke.

Her 1992 collection, *Moon Crossing Bridge*, was written after Carver's death from cancer in 1988 and is considered among her finest work. Since his death, Gallagher has edited and written introductions to collections of Carver's work. She also worked with Robert Altman on the 1993 film *Short Cuts*, which was based on nine of Carver's short stories.

The Hug

A woman is reading a poem on the street
and another woman stops to listen. We stop too,
with our arms around each other. The poem
is being read and listened to out here
in the open. Behind us   5
no one is entering or leaving the houses.

Suddenly a hug comes over me and I'm
giving it to you, like a variable star shooting light
off to make itself comfortable, then
subsiding. I finish but keep on holding   10
you. A man walks up to us and we know he hasn't
come out of nowhere, but if he could, he
would have. He looks homeless because of how
he needs. 'Can I have one of those?' he asks you,
and I feel you nod. I'm surprised,   15
surprised you don't tell him how
it is – that I'm yours, only
yours, etc., exclusive as a nose to
its face. Love – that's what we're talking about, love
that nabs you with 'for me   20
only' and holds on.

So I walk over to him and put my
arms around him and try to
hug him like I mean it. He's got an overcoat on
so thick I can't feel   25
him past it. I'm starting the hug
and thinking, 'How big a hug is this supposed to be?
How long shall I hold this hug?' Already
we could be eternal, his arms falling over my
shoulders, my hands not   30
meeting behind his back, he is so big!

I put my head into his chest and snuggle
in. I lean into him. I lean my blood and my wishes
into him. He stands for it. This is his
and he's starting to give it back so well I know he's   35
getting it. This hug. So truly, so tenderly
we stop having arms and I don't know if
my lover has walked away or what, or
if the woman is still reading the poem, or the houses –
what about them? – the houses.   40

Clearly, a little permission is a dangerous thing.
But when you hug someone you want it
to be a masterpiece of connection, the way the button
on his coat will leave the imprint of
a planet in my cheek   45
when I walk away. When I try to find some place
to go back to.

Glossary

| 8 | a *variable star*: a pulsating star, its brightness varies considerably |

Guidelines

The poem tells a story. The female narrator of the poem recalls an incident when she and her lover stopped on the street to listen to a woman reading a poem. On an impulse the woman hugged her lover and continued to hold him. Out of nowhere a homeless man approached and asked the lover if he, too, could have a hug. To the woman's surprise, the lover nodded his assent. So the woman walked over to the man and put her arms around him. She gave him a hug and he hugged her back and the woman lost herself in the hug and the connection between them. **Out of this story the poet creates a meditation on love, possession, connection, presence, tenderness and commitment.**

Commentary

Stanza 1

The first stanza sets up the situation. A woman is reading on the street; another woman stops to listen and the narrator and her lover stop, too. There seems no apparent connection between the four people. They are strangers to each other who meet by accident. In this open public place, the narrator and her lover stand with their arms around each other. It is as if the normal activity of the world is suspended, as they listen to the woman reading.

Stanza 2

The narrator describes being possessed by the desire to give her lover a hug. She gives the hug and then continues to hold on to her lover. **The image of the hug and holding suggests an exclusive love shared between the two of them.** The narrator then describes a man, possibly a homeless man, approaching them. **Audaciously, speaking man to man, he asks the lover if he, too, can have a hug. To the surprise of the narrator, her lover gives his permission** and does not insist that their love is exclusive and that the woman (the narrator) is his alone. It is hard to decide if the narrator's surprise is born of anger or disappointment or if it is simply surprise.

Stanza 3

The narrator describes going over to the man, the stranger, and preparing to give the hug. She is uncertain, wondering how hard she should hug the man and for how long. The man is so big that when she puts her hands around his back, they do not meet.

Stanza 4

In the fourth stanza the narrator describes how she settles into the hug, putting her head on the man's chest and leaning into him. The gesture is one of trust and tenderness. The gesture is not only physical. The narrator declares that she leans her blood and her wishes into him. This is an arresting statement. 'Blood' suggests something warm and heart-felt. 'Wishes' suggest that the woman wishes the stranger well. The man, we are told, 'stands for it' (line 34). In other words, he is not overcome by her gesture but accepts it. And then he returns the hug to her so that they meet now not as donor and recipient but as equals.

The phrase 'This hug' (line 36) concentrates all the power of the poem on the moment of contact between the two strangers. Lines 36 to 40 describe the trance-like state the narrator enters in surrendering herself to this hug and the feelings of tenderness and truth. In this state, she has almost no consciousness of her lover, or the woman reading the poem, or the houses on the street.

Stanza 5

The final stanza contains both narrative and reflective elements and moves between the particular hug given to the stranger and all hugs. The statement, 'Clearly, a little permission is a dangerous thing' (line 41) has a sly humour about it. The word 'permission' is interesting. In one sense the permission for the hug has been given by the lover to the stranger. However, it is also the narrator and the stranger who give permission to themselves and to each other. Lines 42 and 43 read as the narrator justifying the kind of hug she gave the man and explaining the motivation behind all hugs: 'But when you hug someone you want it / to be a masterpiece of connection'. If connection is the aim of all hugs, even those given to strangers, what implication does this have on the idea of love as something exclusive and proprietorial?

The image of the button leaving the imprint of a planet in her cheek is beautiful and rich and will repay thinking about. The imprint is like a sign or a seal of the connection that has been made between the man and the woman. Because the hug is a masterpiece, the connection is intense, absorbing and brief.

The future tense 'will' (line 44) and the phrase 'when I walk away' (line 46) suggest that the narrator is still lost in the hug and has not yet found the place to which she will return. At this point in the poem the lover of the earlier stanzas seems absent. This element of disorientation and loss creates a sense of mystery. Will the woman return to her lover, the 'you' of the first two stanzas, or has the hug broken the bond between them? In surrendering herself to the hug, has everything else been left behind?

A love poem

The poem begins as a conventional love poem, based on the exclusive love of a man and a woman, but then the nature of the love described in the poem changes, and the woman reaches out to a stranger in a spirit of loving tenderness. Ironically, it is the lover, the one who gave 'permission' for the hug, who now seems excluded. Overall, the poem conveys a sense of accident, grace and giftedness about the situation. This is a small but good thing that takes place between strangers and it makes the world a more human and tender place.

Style of the poem

The poem has no rhymes and uses irregular stanzas. The voice of the narrator is natural and close to everyday speech. It is a gentle, thoughtful voice. The careful phrasing, the choice of words, the run-on lines and the absence of harsh sounds give the poem a smooth, flowing rhythm. The poem tells its story in a cinematic way with a strong emphasis on the visual. It has a number of arresting images, images of love and moments of pause. Gallagher says that rhythm and the image are important elements in her poetry, as well as mystery.

Tess Gallagher

Thinking about the poem

1 From the first stanza what is your impression of the relationship between the narrator and her lover?
2 Explain the image of the star in stanza 2. Is it effective?
3 What is the reason for the woman's surprise in stanza 2? What surprises you about the events related in stanza 2?
4 As outlined in stanza 3, what kind of thoughts are going through the narrator's head as she prepares to hug the man?
5 What effect does the hug have on the narrator, based on the evidence of stanzas 4 and 5?
6 Many people admire the button imagery of the final stanza. Why, do you think, is this so?
7 The poem is written in the present tense. What is the effect of this? Explain your answer.

8   'The poem explores a moment of loving tenderness that is all the more powerful because the man and woman are strangers to each other.' Give your view of this reading of the poem. Support the points you make with quotations from the poem.

9   From the list, select **three** words which, in your view, capture the mood of the poem: gentle, thoughtful, tender, mysterious, confused, sad. Explain your choice.

10   The woman hugs the man because:

        She has no choice.

        She wants to spite her lover.

        She pities the man.

        She is generous.

Which of these explanations is closest to your reading of the poem? Explain your choice.

Taking a closer look

1   'He looks homeless because of how / he needs' (lines 13–14). Write a note on this statement teasing out its full implications.

2   A 'masterpiece of connection' (line 43). Write a short piece giving your definition of this phrase.

3   'When I try to find some place / to go back to' (lines 46–47) Do you think that the narrator goes back to the place from where she started? Explain your answer.

4   How are the personal pronouns (I, you and we) used in this poem? Do they change over the course of the poem?

5   'The moral of the poem is that no human being ever belongs to another.' Discuss.

6   Choose your favourite image from the poem and say why you chose it.

Imagining

1   If the poem were a film, then stanza 4 would be where the camera zooms in on the couple who are embracing. Using the details in the stanza, describe how you would portray this scene on film.

2   Turn the events described in the poem into a short story written from the perspective of the man who asked for the hug.

3   Write **two** diary entries in the voice of the narrator's lover describing the day of the hug and the impact of the incident on you.

snapshot

A narrative poem – told in the first person

No rhymes or fixed stanza structure

Tells the story of a chance encounter

Smooth flowing rhythm

The Hug

Narrator gets lost in the moment

Voice is gentle and thoughtful

Themes of love, tenderness and connection

Arresting images

Tess Gallagher

Kerry Hardie

b. 1951

DANIEL'S DUCK

Biography

Kerry Hardie was born in 1951 in Singapore and grew up in Co. Down. She studied English at York University in England and then came back to Ireland to work as a researcher and radio interviewer for the BBC in Belfast and Derry:

> This period coincided with the most violent years of the Troubles, and through my job I had access to situations and people I might not otherwise have known. I became fascinated with people who found themselves in a hard place and with how they reacted to this place. Some people adapted astonishingly fast to their new realities, but others spent their energies resisting and could only change to meet them when they had in some way been broken by them.

Hardie has published several collections of poetry. Her first novel, *A Winter Marriage*, was published in 2002, and her second novel, *The Bird Woman*, was published in 2006.

A *Furious Place* (1996) includes poems that record people in their own landscapes and explores the way in which landscape permeates their lives. Other poems dwell on the hardships and lessons of a chronic illness. Hardie suffers from ME (Chronic Fatigue Syndrome):

> Being chronically sick makes you an observer rather than a participant. Before I was sick, I lived very hard and my life was very outgoing; now my life is quiet and disciplined and reflective. . . . It took me a long time to come to terms with the change, but now I find my life immensely rich and rewarding.

Many of the poems in *The Sky Didn't Fall* (2003), from which 'Daniel's Duck' is taken, deal with grief and loss and the contrast between the outside world and our inner feelings.

Hardie has won major literary awards and she is a member of Aosdána, the national arts organisation. She lives in Kilkenny with her husband, Sean Hardie, who is also a writer.

Kerry Haride

Daniel's Duck

(for Frances)

I held out the shot mallard, she took it from me,
looped its neck-string over a drawer of the dresser.
The children were looking on, half-caught.
Then the kitchen life – warm, lit, glowing –
moved forward, taking in the dead bird,   5
and its coldness, its wildness, were leaching away.

The children were sitting to their dinners.
Us too – drinking tea, hardly noticing
the child's quiet slide from his chair,
his small absorbed body before the duck's body,   10
the duck changing – feral, live –
arrowing up out of black sloblands
with the gleam of a river
falling away below.

Then the duck – dead again – hanging from the drawer-knob   15
the green head, brown neck running into the breast,

the intricate silvery-greyness of the back;
the wings, their white bars and blue flashes,
the feet, their snakey, orange scaliness, small claws, piteous webbing,
the yellow beak, blooded,   20
the whole like a weighted sack –
all that downward-dragginess of death.

He hovered, took a step forward, a step back,
something appeared in his face, some knowledge
of a place where he stood, the world stilled,   25
the lit streaks of sunrise running off red
into the high bowl of the morning.

She watched him, moving to touch, his hand out:
What is it, Daniel, do you like the duck?
He turned as though caught in the act,   30
saw the gentleness in her face and his body loosened.
I thought there was water on it –
he was finding the words, one by one,
holding them out, to see would they do us –
But there isn't.   35
He added this on, going small with relief
that his wind-drag of sound was enough.

Glossary		
1	*mallard*: a wild duck (the male or drake has the markings described in the poem)	
6	*leaching away*: seeping or draining away; disappearing	
11	*feral*: wild; not tame or domesticated but fending for itself	
12	*arrowing up*: flying upwards with wings outstretched the duck resembles an arrow shape	
12	*sloblands*: mudflats or land reclaimed from the sea	
19	*scaliness*: the quality of being covered in scales or scab-like, thin plates that provide protection on the legs of birds and the skin of fish and reptiles	
19	*piteous*: deserving or giving rise to pity; heartrending; pathetic	
37	*wind-drag*: when birds fly they use their wings to push the air out of the way and the sound made by their wings is the result of the drag or resistance of the wind	

Guidelines

The poem tells a story, a little drama from daily life. In a kitchen, where the children sit down to their dinner and the adults drink tea, **a young boy encounters death in the form of a shot mallard and tries to make sense of his experience.** The poem focuses on the moment when the boy begins to understand something, though he has not the words to express his new knowledge. Standing absorbed before the bird, he enters a private world and feels something like guilt when he becomes aware of the attention of the adults. To his relief, the adults are satisfied by the words he finds to explain his fascination for the duck.

Within the narrative, the poem encompasses many ideas and contrasting themes: the contrast between the living wild duck and the dead bird hanging in the kitchen; the contrast between the duck 'arrowing up out of black sloblands' and the force of death dragging the body down; the dawning of knowledge in the child; the private, interior world of the child; the contrast between things we can describe and those experiences for which we struggle to find words.

Commentary

Stanzas 1 and 2
The narrator tells us that the handing over of the duck to the woman of the house and the hanging of the bird on the dresser was something that 'half-caught' (line 3) the attention of the children before the life of the kitchen, the warm domestic life of the household, moved on and the duck began to lose its 'wildness' (line 6).

We learn that one child, the Daniel of the title, has slid from the chair and is standing in front of the duck. Reading between the lines, the poem suggests that Daniel is seeing the duck as though it was alive in its wild or feral state.

Stanzas 3 and 4
There is a detailed description of the duck as he is now, hanging dead on the drawer-knob. The description emphasises its intricate colouring, including the blood on its 'yellow beak' (line 20), and the way in which the duck is weighed down and dragged down by death.

The young boy tries to make sense of what he sees. The verb 'hovers' suggest that his thought is moving back and forth and he is absorbed in the moment, so much so that the world is 'stilled' (line 25). **The idea that he understands something for the first time is suggested in the imagery of the dawn and the sun rising.**

Stanza 5

As he reaches out his hand to touch the dead duck, the boy is interrupted by a woman's voice. He seems almost guilty: 'as though caught in the act' (line 30), but he relaxes when he sees 'the gentleness in her face' (line 31). **He tries to find the words to explain himself and is relieved when no more questions are asked.**

Form and style of the poem

The story is narrated by an adult, possibly the person who shot the duck. Clearly the narrator's account is sympathetic to Daniel and, arguably, parts of the poem are written as if seen through the child's eyes. **'Daniel's Duck' brings us into the middle of a small drama, but intriguingly it leaves a number of questions unanswered.** Who speaks the words: the poet or a persona like a narrator in a novel? Is it a man or a woman? What is the speaker's relationship to the 'she' of the poem and to Daniel? Is the 'she' Daniel's mother?

Although the poem is written in irregular stanzas with no rhyme scheme, Hardie pays great attention to sound and rhythm and there are many examples of alliteration as well as consonance and assonance. Look, for example, at how the 'l' sound is repeated throughout the first stanza, or how 'b' and 'd' sounds echo through the second stanza and into the first lines of stanza 3. You will also notice the words which end with '-ness'. Note, too, the succession of noun phrases that are used to great effect in stanza 3 to describe the duck.

Thinking about the poem

1   According to the speaker of the poem in the first stanza, what happened to the duck once it was hung from the door-knob of the dresser?

2   There is a reference in stanza 2 to 'the duck changing' (line 11). Where and how does the duck change?

3   The third stanza is a detailed description of the appearance of the shot duck. Comment on each detail and its significance.

4   The fourth stanza focuses on the young boy. In your own words explain what happens to the boy and the 'something' that 'appeared in his face' (line 24).

5   In the final stanza, what was Daniel's initial reaction when the woman called out to him?

6   Think about the meaning of the last word of the poem 'enough'. In what sense was Daniel's answer 'enough'?

7   There are many contrasts in the poem. Identify as many of them as you can and comment on each.

8   Having read the poem, what age is Daniel, in your opinion?

9   Here are three views of what the poem is about. Which **one** of them is closest to your view?

> A child's first encounter with death.
>
> The difference between the things we can describe and those which are beyond words.
>
> The difference between the private world of children and the world of adults.

Explain your choice.

10 'Good poetry creates vivid pictures in our minds.' In your opinion, is this true of 'Daniel's Duck'? Support your view by reference to the poem.

Taking a closer look

1   Give your view of the effectiveness of the phrase 'that downward-dragginess of death' (line 22).

2   'the lit streaks of sunrise running off red / into the high bowl of the morning' (lines 26–27). In your view, why has the poet included these lines at this point in the poem?

3   Comment on the phrase 'his wind-drag of sound' in the last line of the poem.

4   There are many interesting uses of words in the poem. Select **two** which you like and say why you like them.

Imagining

1   Imagine you are Daniel. You are now a young man. Write a diary entry in which you record your experiences and feelings on the day described in the poem.

2   If you were to make a film that interprets the poem, what images would you include and what kind of music would you select as a musical score?

Kerry Haride

snapshot

Poem tells a story

It is set in a family kitchen

Focuses on a little boy

Describes a first encounter with death

Daniel's Duck

Little boy struggles to find words to describe his experience

Poem uses contrasts

Some questions left unanswered

Emphasis on sounds and rhythm

Brendan Kennelly

b. 1936

NIGHT DRIVE

Biography

Brendan Kennelly was born in 1936 in Ballylongford, Co. Kerry. He was educated at St Ita's College, Tarbert, Co. Kerry, and Trinity College, Dublin. He also studied at Leeds University in England.

He has lectured at the University of Antwerp, at Barnard College, New York, and at Swarthmore College, Pennsylvania. He was Professor of Modern Literature at Trinity College, Dublin, for over thirty years, and retired from that post in 2005. He now teaches part-time in the United States and lives in Dublin.

Kennelly has published over thirty books of poetry, among them *My Dark Fathers* (1964), *Cromwell* (1983), *Breathing Spaces: Early Poems* (1992), *Poetry Me Arse* (1995), *Familiar Strangers: New and Selected Poems 1960–2004* (2004) and *Now* (2006).

He has also translated poems from Irish, and these are collected in the volume *Love of Ireland* (1989). He edited *The Penguin Book of Irish Verse* (1981) and published two novels. He is a well-known dramatist whose plays include versions of the Greek plays *Antigone* and *Medea*, and a stage version of his poem *Cromwell*. He is a renowned and popular broadcaster on radio and television where he has done a great deal to bring poetry to a wider audience.

Night Drive

I
The rain hammered as we drove
Along the road to Limerick
'Jesus what a night!' Alan breathed
And – 'I wonder how he is, the last account
Was poor.'   5
I couldn't speak.

The windscreen fumed and blurred, the rain's spit
Lashing the glass. Once or twice
The wind's fist seemed to lift the car
And pitch it hard against the ditch.   10
Alan straightened out in time,
Silent. Glimpses of the Shannon –
A boiling madhouse roaring for its life
Or any life too near its gaping maw,
White shreds flaring in the waste   15
Of insane murderous black;
Trees bending in grotesque humility,
Branches scattered on the road, smashed
Beneath the wheels.
Then, ghastly under the headlights,   20
Frogs bellied everywhere, driven
From the swampy fields and meadows,
Bewildered refugees, gorged with terror.
We killed them because we had to,
Their fatness crunched and flattened in the dark.   25
'How is he now?' Alan whispered
To himself. Behind us,
Carnage of broken frogs.

II

His head
Sweated on the pillow of the white hospital bed.   30
He spoke a little, said
Outrageously, 'I think I'll make it.'
Another time, he'd rail against the weather,
(Such a night would make him eloquent)
But now, quiet, he gathered his fierce will   35
To live.

III

Coming home
Alan saw the frogs.
'Look at them, they're everywhere,
Dozens of the bastards dead.'   40

Minutes later –
'I think he might pull through now.'
Alan, thoughtful at the wheel, was picking out
The homeroad in the flailing rain
Nighthedges closed on either side   45
In the suffocating darkness
I heard the heavy breathing
Of my father's pain.

Glossary	
14	*gaping maw*: a stomach that devours its prey
17	*grotesque*: bizarre
23	*gorged*: made fat
28	*carnage*: slaughter
33	*rail*: to scold or curse
34	*eloquent*: expressive
44	*flailing*: striking out in all directions

Guidelines

'Night Drive' is from *Breathing Spaces* (1992). **In this poem, Kennelly describes his feelings as he travels with his brother, Alan, to visit their dying father.**

Commentary

Part 1

The dreadful weather is described in a series of powerful images, as if it has a life of its own: the rain can 'spit' (line 7), the wind has a 'fist' (line 9). Strong verbs reinforce the violence of the weather: the rain that 'hammered' (line 1), the wind that seemed to 'pitch' (line 10) the car against the ditch.

It is as if nature is in tune with the turmoil of the two brothers' feelings, although it is Alan who is given the direct speech. The poet himself says simply in line 5: 'I couldn't speak.'

The River Shannon, which they pass on their journey to Co. Kerry, is compared to a 'boiling madhouse' (line 13) with a 'gaping maw' (line 14) or stomach that would devour all in its path. The metaphors prepare us for the images of destruction that follow: the stark white and black of the water is 'murderous' (line 16), the branches of the trees are 'smashed' (line 18) beneath the wheels of the car. The trees themselves are 'bending in grotesque humility' (line 17), helpless before the strength of the storm.

Another 'ghastly' (line 20) sight is that of the frogs, driven out of the flooded fields like 'refugees' (line 23) searching for safety but being killed underneath the wheels of the car. 'Crunched and flattened' (line 25) expresses the sound and sight of what the poet describes as 'carnage of broken frogs' (line 28).

Again, it is Alan who voices his concern about their father. **The sights and sounds of death and destruction in the world outside the car are subconsciously related to the father's struggle for life.**

Part II

There is a moving description of their dying father as he lies in his hospital bed. He is struggling against the inevitable end. His fierce will to live is reflected in what he says, 'I think I'll make it' (line 32) but the poet seems to know that he speaks 'outrageously' – there is little hope that he will survive. We get a glimpse of him as having been a strong man who would once have cursed such weather, but now he needs all his energy to stay alive.

Part III

As the poet and his brother make their way home after the hospital visit, their attitudes to their father's illness seem to differ. Alan appears quite hopeful about his recovery, in contrast to the lifeless frogs that are strewn on the roadway. But the poet does not appear to share his optimism. As he describes his brother driving carefully home, words such as 'flailing', 'closed' and 'suffocating' (lines 44 to 46) remind us that the poem is about the struggle with death that is part of nature, for the frogs as well as human beings.

The poem ends with an image that does not flinch from the hopelessness of this struggle: the 'heavy breathing' of their 'father's pain' (lines 47 and 48). His desire to survive will end with the 'suffocating darkness' (line 46) of the grave.

Thinking about the poem

1   In what way does the weather reflect the human situation that is described in the poem?

2   Do you think that the image of the frogs is significant in the poem? Explain your answer.

3   Why does the poet describe the journey in more detail than the actual visit to his father do you think? Give a reason for your answer.

4   What impression of the poet's father do you get when you read the poem?

5   Did the father have a good relationship with his sons? Explain your answer.

6   How do the images of death and destruction contribute to the mood of the poem?

7   Choose the word which in your opinion most closely describes the atmosphere created in 'Night Drive': tense, depressing, sad, hopeful or confused. Explain your choice.

8   'The poem deals with the theme of death in a powerful and moving way.' Write a paragraph in which you agree or disagree with this statement.

Taking a closer look

1   Comment on the effect of the following phrases in the poem:

'the Shannon – / A boiling madhouse roaring for its life' (lines 12–13)

'Trees bending in grotesque humility' (line 17)

'Carnage of broken frogs' (line 28).

2   Suggest a new title for the poem, giving a reason for your choice.

Imagining

1   You have been asked to make a short film of the first part of the poem. Describe the sort of atmosphere you would like to create, and say what music, sound effects and images you would use.

2   A collection of poems called *Last Memories* is being put together. Explain why you would or would not recommend the inclusion of 'Night Drive' in the collection.

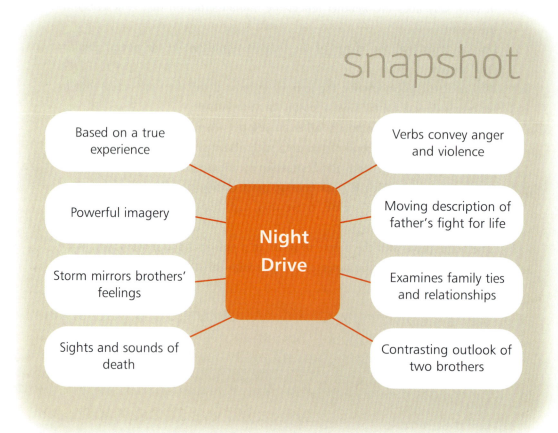

snapshot

Based on a true experience

Powerful imagery

Storm mirrors brothers' feelings

Sights and sounds of death

Night Drive

Verbs convey anger and violence

Moving description of father's fight for life

Examines family ties and relationships

Contrasting outlook of two brothers

Michael Longley

b. 1939

BADGER

Biography

Michael Longley was born in Belfast in 1939. He was educated at the Royal Belfast Academical Institution and later studied Classics at Trinity College, Dublin. At Trinity he met his wife-to-be, the distinguished scholar Edna Broderick. The couple returned to Belfast, where Edna Longley became a professor of literature at the Queen's University, Belfast. Michael Longley has worked as a teacher in London, Dublin and in Northern Ireland. Until 1991 he was combined arts director of the Arts Council of Northern Ireland.

His first poetry collection, *No Continuing City*, was published in 1960. It was followed by *An Exploded View* (1973), *Man Lying on a Wall* (1976) and *The Echo Gate* (1979). After a gap of twelve years, a new collection, *Gorse Fires*, was published in 1991, and this won the Whitbread Poetry Award. *The Weather in Japan* won the Irish Literature Prize for Poetry in 2001. *Collected Poems* was published in 2006.

Longley is a Fellow of the Royal Society of Literature and a member of Aosdána. He is also a founder member of the Cultural Traditions Group, which aims to foster acceptance of the diversity of cultural traditions within Northern Ireland.

Badger

for Raymond Piper

I
Pushing the wedge of his body
Beneath cromlech and stone circle,
He excavates down mine shafts
And back into the depths of the hill.

His path straight and narrow   5
And not like the fox's zig-zags,
The arc of the hare who leaves
A silhouette on the sky line.

Night's silence around his shoulders,
His face lit by the moon, he   10
Manages the earth with his paws,
Returns underground to die.

II
An intestine taking in
patches of dog's-mercury,
brambles, the bluebell wood;   15
a heel removing acorns;
a head with a price on it
brushing cuckoo-spit, goose-grass;
a name that parishes borrow.

III
For the digger, the earth-dog   20
It is a difficult delivery
Once the tongs take hold,

Vulnerable his pig's snout
That lifted cow-pats for beetles,
Hedgehogs for the soft meat,   25

His limbs dragging after them
So many stones turned over,
The trees they tilted.

Glossary

Dedication	*Raymond Piper*: a painter and botanist, friend of Longley
2	*cromlech and a stone circle*: archaeological relics of ancient Ireland
3	*excavates*: digs out
7	*arc*: circular shape
8	*silhouette*: shadow
13	*intestine*: part of the digestive system
14	*dog's mercury*: a herbaceous plant
18	*cuckoo-spit*: froth secreted by frog-hoppers on plants
18	*goose-grass*: silverweed, a roadside plant with silky underside leaves
19	*a name that parishes borrow*: there are numerous place names containing the word 'badger' e.g. Badgerstown, as well as the Irish word 'broc'
22	*tongs*: an implement used to pull the badger out of the earth

Guidelines

'Badger' is from the collection *An Exploded View* (1973). It was written, the poet tells us, after a conversation with his friend, the artist and botanist Raymond Piper. The three sections into which the poem is divided each focus on different aspects of the life and death of a badger.

Commentary

Part 1

This first section describes the badger's movements, emphasising his strength and determination. He is seen as 'Pushing the wedge of his body' (line 1) as far as he can into the depths of the hill. He is unique in his natural environment. His straight, narrow movements are like neither those of the fox (who moves in a zig-zag manner) nor the hare (whose movements are circular). He moves deliberately and carefully, 'back' and 'down' and 'into the depths'. He 'excavates' as a miner or archaeologist would (lines 3 and 4). A nocturnal creature, he is at one with the night and the moon. He controls his own habitat: 'Manages the earth with his paws' (line 11). But the last line of the third stanza jolts us with a sense of the badger's mortality: he 'returns underground to die'.

Part II

The poet looks at the badger from a slightly different perspective in the second section. The food he eats is precisely named, with a botanist's love of accuracy. The imagery is still physical, like that in the first section: his 'intestine' (line 13) that can digest many different plants, his 'heel' that moves acorns around (line 16). But he is also a hunted animal, 'a head with a price on it' (line 17). His capture will be rewarded. His name can be found in many place names in Ireland, which suggests how significant an animal the badger is.

Part III

The third part of the poem focuses on the badger's death. It is a cruel death in a badger hunt. Longley describes his death in terms of a birth. The 'tongs' used by the people to pull the badger out of his sett resemble the forceps used to deliver a child in a difficult birth. This is a disturbing image, suggesting pain and cruelty. The badger is pulled violently out of his place in the earth, which we have previously seen him make in the peace and quiet of the moonlight.

The last six lines give a sense of the badger's vulnerability but also suggest his strength and power. Although human beings will destroy him, he does not go quietly in an easy death. In his last struggle he drags stones with him and the stumps of trees he has upturned. Our final impression of the badger is as a force to be reckoned with. He is an animal that commands respect.

Tone of the poem

Although the poet does not directly express his feelings about the badger, his description of the animal as a creature of grace and strength and how he associates him with the night and the moon suggests admiration and respect. But the poem is not sentimental about the badger. He is not seen as a cuddly creature. He preys on other species such as beetles and hedgehogs. Nevertheless, the way he meets his death at the hands of human beings leaves us with a sense of pointless cruelty.

Thinking about the poem

1   What impression of the life of the badger do you get from Part I of the poem?
2   How does the language used by the poet contribute to that impression?
3   What is the poet's attitude to the badger in Parts II and III of the poem, do you think?

4 Choose **two** images from the poem that appeal most to you and give a reason for your choice.

5 Would you share the poet's feelings about the animal? Give a reason for your answer.

6 What impression of human beings does the poem create? Explain your answer.

7 'The poem conveys Longley's love and knowledge of nature.' Write a short paragraph in response to this statement.

Taking a closer look

1 The badger 'Manages the earth with his paws' (line 11). What do you think the poet is suggesting here?

2 'For the digger, the earth-dog / It is a difficult delivery / Once the tongs take hold' (lines 20–22). Comment on the images in these lines.

Imagining

1 Write a paragraph in which you give your view for or against the hunting of animals, making reference to the poem.

2 Suggest a different title for the above poem. Explain your choice.

snapshot

Nature poem

Describes life and death of a badger

Images are precise and detailed

Badger is strong and determined

Badger

Elemental creature in tune with his environment

Poem shows respect and admiration for animal

Hints at human cruelty

Tone is not sentimental

John Milton

1608–74

WHEN I CONSIDER HOW MY LIGHT IS SPENT

Biography

John Milton, the son of a scrivener (moneylender), was born in London in 1608. He had an excellent academic education at St Paul's School and at Christ's College, Cambridge. He then lived the life of a leisured gentleman with his parents, first in Hammersmith, London, and later in Buckinghamshire. He devoted his time to an ambitious programme of private study. In 1638 and 1639 he travelled in Italy. When he returned to England he became a schoolteacher in his own home. An accomplished Latin and Greek scholar, as well as a biblical scholar, a theologian and a historian, he was one of the most learned of all the English poets.

Milton supported the cause of Parliament against the King during the English Civil War, and was an admirer of Oliver Cromwell. In 1649 – the year King Charles I was beheaded (an act which Milton supported) – he was appointed Secretary for Foreign

Tongues by the Parliamentary Council of State. By then he was blind in one eye. He lost the sight of his other eye in 1652. Milton retired from public life after the restoration of the monarchy in 1660. For a time he was in danger of imprisonment, perhaps death, for his earlier opposition to the monarchy.

Milton wrote most of his early poems in Latin. His first major English poem, celebrating Christ's birth, was written in 1629, when he was twenty-one years old. He composed his three greatest works – *Paradise Lost, Paradise Regained* and *Samson Agonistes* – after his enforced retirement. He dictated these long poems to friends and family members.

He died peacefully in 1674, at the age of sixty-six. His reputation as the supreme English non-dramatic poet was established within a few decades of his death.

When I Consider How My Light Is Spent

When I consider how my light is spent
Ere half my days, in this dark world and wide,
And that one Talent which is death to hide
Lodged with me useless, though my Soul more bent
To serve therewith my Maker, and present   5
My true account, lest he returning chide;
'Doth God exact day-labour, light denied?'
I fondly ask; but Patience to prevent
That murmur, soon replies, 'God doth not need
Either man's work or his own gifts; who best   10
Bear his mild yoke, they serve him best. His State
Is kingly. Thousands at his bidding speed
And post o'er Land and Ocean without rest:
They also serve who only stand and wait.'

Glossary

2	*Ere*: before
3	*talent*: a unit of money in biblical times, as well as a skill or ability of mind
4	*bent*: determined
6	*lest*: for fear that
6	*chide*: rebuke, scold
7	*Doth*: does
7	*exact*: demand
8	*fondly*: foolishly
9	*murmur*: complaint
10	*mild yoke*: light burden
12	*Thousands at his bidding speed*: thousands of angels hasten to carry out God's commands
13	*post o'er*: travel with speed over

Guidelines

A hundred years after this sonnet was written, one of Milton's editors, Bishop Newton, gave it the title 'On his Blindness', which has been in frequent use ever since. This title is misleading. Although Milton was blind when he composed the sonnet, the main issue is not his blindness but the loss of his poetic inspiration and his guilt at having wasted time writing political pamphlets instead of poetry. The real emphasis of the sonnet, however, is on the two contrasting ways – active and passive – in which God can be served.

The first eight lines of the sonnet set the scene and ask a question. This question is answered in the final six lines.

Commentary

The question
'Light' in this sonnet does not have a single meaning. When Milton writes 'my light is spent' (line 1), this may literally mean: I have lost my eyesight (as Milton was blind by the time he dictated this sonnet) or it may be a reference to the inward light of poetic inspiration. Some commentators suggest that it is the loss of this inward light that is the main theme of the sonnet.

The expression 'Ere half my days' (line 2) is puzzling. Milton lost his sight in the early 1650s, when he was in his early forties, and the sonnet is usually dated to about 1652. One conclusion is that Milton expected to live into his eighties, given that his father lived to the great age of eighty-four, and therefore felt he was at the halfway point in his life.

The sonnet is inspired by the parable of the talents (Matthew, chapter 25, verses 14–30), in which a master gives five talents (sums of money) to one servant, two to another and one to a third. The servants are expected to develop these talents and two of them succeed in doubling their value through wise investments. The servant who has been given only one talent, who is lazy and inactive, buries it in the earth and is later rebuked and cast into outer darkness by his master (this is the 'death to hide' in line 3).

Milton identifies with the servant with the single talent. As he sees it, his single talent is his God-given ability to compose great poetry. Milton fears that, having neglected this poetic gift, he faces God's punishment. This is the question he seeks an answer to.

Has Milton been cast into outer darkness (blindness) like the servant in the parable because he was neglecting to use his single talent (as a poet)? Has his inward light (poetic inspiration) disappeared with the external light of his physical vision? If that is the case, what does God now expect of him?

The answer

The answer to this question is supplied from line 8 onwards. There is something more important than making good use of God's gifts. Milton realises that God does 'not need / Either man's work or his own gifts' (lines 9–10); in other words, God does not need either what we do by our own will and effort or what God's gifts enable us to do.

Milton realises that he must be patient. He should not think of himself as a man for whom God has a special plan. Rather, he must adjust himself to a humbler idea of service to God. This will mean submitting himself to God's will, and patiently enduring the 'mild yoke' (line 11) of his blindness.

Milton recognises God as a powerful monarch, 'His state / Is Kingly (lines 11–12), and identifies two groups of angels: those who busy themselves travelling far and wide to serve God, and those who remain constantly in God's presence and offer the service of worship (lines 12 to 14). This suggests to him that God does not demand a return of his talent, but asks only for a spirit of patient endurance. Milton should not give up hope of being used further, he need not sit in despair, but should stand ready to receive God's commands, and wait patiently, as angels do, for God's guidance. The use of the word 'wait' is probably a pun: to 'wait' is to serve as an attendant at table, a humble role.

John Milton

Thinking about the poem

1   This poem tells us a number of things about Milton. Mention **three** of these. Support your answer with reference to the poem.

2   The poem suggests that the burden God expects us to bear is light. Do you think that this is true in Milton's case? Explain your answer.

3   How does Milton respond to his problem? Do you admire his response?

4   God is at the heart of this sonnet. What impression of God does Milton convey?

5   How does Milton see his relationship with God?

6   Explain the reference to 'that one talent which is death to hide' (line 3).

7   How does Milton suggest God's great power?

8   According to Milton, what is the best way of serving God?

9   Is there a lesson to be learned from this poem? If so, what is that lesson?

10 How would you interpret the final line of the poem?

Taking a closer look

1   How would you describe the language of this sonnet? Does it contain any lines which might be heard in everyday ordinary speech?

2   The following four elements are to be found in this sonnet: humility, patience, deep religious faith, and trust. Give **one** example of **each** of these.

3   Choose **two** images from the poem that you find impressive, and give reasons for your choice.

4   Many people think that this is a poem about loss of sight. Can it be about something else? Explain your answer.

5   As a result of reading this poem, do you feel pity for Milton? Give reasons for your answer.

6   How does Milton feel about himself and his problem? Refer to the poem in support of your answer.

7   On the evidence of this poem, what kind of life does Milton lead?

Imagining

1   Imagine you are Milton. Write a letter to a friend giving reasons for writing this sonnet.

2   Suggest a suitable title for this sonnet, to convey what the poem is telling you.

A sonnet

Poet's sense of duty to make proper use of his talent

Faith in God

Poet has an optimistic outlook

When I Consider How My Light Is Spent

A deeply religious poem

Poem based on a parable in the Bible

Need for patience

Reflection on the meaning of suffering and loss

John Milton

Paul Muldoon

b. 1951

ANSEO

Biography

Paul Muldoon was born in 1951 in Portadown, Co. Armagh. His mother was a teacher, his father a labourer and market gardener. He was educated at St Patrick's College, Armagh, and the Queen's University, Belfast, where the poet Seamus Heaney was his tutor. Muldoon's first collection of poems, *New Weather*, was published in 1973 while he was aged twenty-two and still at university.

He has worked as a radio and television producer for BBC Northern Ireland and has held writing fellowships at various universities, including Cambridge University, Columbia University in New York and the University of California at Berkeley. He has edited a number of poetry anthologies, among them *The Faber Book of Contemporary Irish Poetry* (1986), and has written a play for television, *Monkeys* (1989). Since 1990 he has been a professor of the humanities and creative writing at Princeton University in New Jersey. In 2007 he became poetry editor of *New Yorker* magazine.

Muldoon has received many awards for his poetry, including the Sir Geoffrey Faber Memorial Award in 1991, the T.S. Eliot Memorial Prize in 1994 for *The Annals of Chile* and the American Academy of Arts and Letters Award for Literature in 1996. In May 1999 he was appointed professor of poetry at Oxford University. His *New Selected Poems 1968–1994* (1996) won the prestigious Irish Times Irish Literature Prize for Poetry in 1997. His collection *Moy Sand and Gravel* (2002) was awarded the Pulitzer Prize in 2003.

Muldoon's tenth poetry collection, *Horse Latitudes*, was published in 2006. He lives in the United States with his novelist wife, Jean Hanff Korelitz, and their daughter.

Anseo

When the Master was calling the roll
At the primary school in Collegelands,
You were meant to call back *Anseo*
And raise your hand
As your name occurred. 5
Anseo, meaning here, here and now,
All present and correct,
Was the first word of Irish I spoke.
The last name on the ledger
Belonged to Joseph Mary Plunkett Ward 10
And was followed, as often as not,
By silence, knowing looks,
A nod and a wink, the Master's droll
'And where's our little Ward-of-court?'

I remember the first time he came back 15
The Master had sent him out
Along the hedges
To weigh up for himself and cut
A stick with which he would be beaten.
After a while, nothing was spoken; 20
He would arrive as a matter of course

With an ash-plant, a salley-rod.
Or finally, the hazel-wand
He had whittled down to a whip-lash,
Its twist of red and yellow lacquers   25
Sanded and polished,
And altogether so delicately wrought
That he had engraved his initials on it.

I last met Joseph Mary Plunkett Ward
In a pub just over the Irish border.   30
He was living in the open,
In a secret camp
On the other side of the mountain.
He was fighting for Ireland,
Making things happen.   35
And he told me, Joe Ward,
Of how he had risen through the ranks
To Quartermaster, Commandant:
How every morning at parade
His volunteers would call back *Anseo*   40
And raise their hands
As their names occurred.

Glossary

title	*Anseo*: the Irish word for 'present', in answer to a roll call
2	*Collegelands*: an area in Co. Armagh near where the poet was brought up
9	*ledger*: register, roll
13	*droll*: amusing
14	*Ward-of-court*: a play on the phrase 'ward of court', which means to be in the care of the courts
22	*salley-rod*: a type of stick cut from the salley tree
24	*whittled down to a whip-lash*: pared down until it became like a whip
25	*lacquers*: varnishes
27	*wrought*: made
38	*Quartermaster*: a staff officer in the army (here, the IRA)

'Anseo' is from the collection *Why Brownlee Left* (1980). It was written when the Northern Ireland conflict, known as the Troubles, seemed to have no solution. It recounts the experience of a boy at school and the path he took as an adult.

Commentary

Stanza 1

Irish children have often used the Irish word *anseo*, meaning 'present', during roll call at school, as the speaker and his classmates did at primary school in Collegelands, Co. Armagh. One of the boys in the class, Joseph Mary Plunkett Ward, was often absent, a fact remarked on quite sarcastically by the Master (teacher).

The boy's name is significant in the context of Irish history as he was clearly called after the republican leader Joseph Mary Plunkett, who was executed after the Easter Rising of 1916. As the poem is set in Northern Ireland it suggests that his parents' political views were those of the Irish republicans. The reasons why Ward was absent from school are not explained. Nor are we given any explanation why the Master reacted as he did, with his rather feeble pun on the boy's last name. The impression we get of the Master is of a sarcastic, insensitive man.

Stanza 2

The speaker remembers how the Master would send Ward out to cut a stick with which the teacher would then beat him. He describes in an unemotional way how the boy became so used to being beaten that he would arrive at school with the stick already cut. The sticks are depicted as beautiful objects, 'sanded and polished' (line 26). Ward seems immune to being punished, as indicated by the fact that he has carved his initials on the stick. It is as if he is proud of being punished, which, as we know, is not a normal reaction.

When you read these lines it is easy to gloss over the fact that corporal punishment was an accepted part of school life. Not only that, but it seems incredible to our modern minds that a child would be asked to prepare his own instrument of punishment, as Ward was. The speaker does not make any comment, just as generations of children did not question the treatment they sometimes got at school.

Stanza 3

It is suggested that his treatment at school had a profound effect on Joe Ward's later career. We see Ward as an adult, as a member of the Irish Republican Army, involved in the Northern Ireland conflict known as the Troubles. He lives 'in the open'

Paul Muldoon

469

(line 31) and is a kind of outlaw from ordinary life. He is now in a position of power over others, as the teacher had once been over him. Ironically, he calls the roll in exactly the same way as the Master did in school, so that the volunteers must answer 'Anseo'.

Theme of the poem

The speaker, or the poet, makes no direct comment on Joe Ward, the adult, or on his situation. The connection is clear, though, between the boy's treatment at school and his later life of violence. His experience had made him insensitive to the pain of others or the damage his actions may cause. He had been brutalised by the Master. Perhaps this is one of the themes of the poem: what happens to us in childhood affects the way we live later on and what we do. Joe Ward seems unaware of this and thinks merely that he is 'fighting for Ireland' (line 34). Is this the worst irony of all?

Thinking about the poem

1   What impression of primary school life does this poem give us?

2   Do you think the experience of primary school has changed from the time in which the poem was set (in the 1950s)? Explain your answer.

3   What aspect of the story do you find most disturbing? Give reasons for your view.

4   Why do you think the poet describes the hazel-wand in such detail in the second stanza?

5   Do you think there is a connection between Ward's early experiences at school and his activities in the IRA? Or is there a more complex reason for his activities? Might it have any connection with his personal circumstances, including the name given to him by his parents? Look again at the first stanza. Give reasons for your view.

6   Which one of these words would come closest to describing the tone of the poem, in your opinion: angry, disappointed, bitter, disgusted or detached? Refer to the poem in support of your views.

7   What, in your opinion, is the main point the poem makes? Do you agree with it?

8   What is the speaker of the poem's attitude to Joe Ward? Choose the lines that best suggest this attitude.

Taking a closer look

1   What do these lines reveal to you about the teacher in the poem?

> And was followed, as often as not,
> By silence, knowing looks,
> A nod and a wink, the Master's droll
> 'And where's our little Ward-of-court?' (lines 11–14)

Explain your answer.

2   Choose **two** images from the poem that had the most impact on you and give a reason for your choice.

Imagining

1   Imagine you are the young Joseph Mary Plunkett Ward. Write an entry from your diary describing your life at home and at school.

2   Imagine you are one of Joe Ward's 'volunteers'. Write a short account of your leader.

snapshot

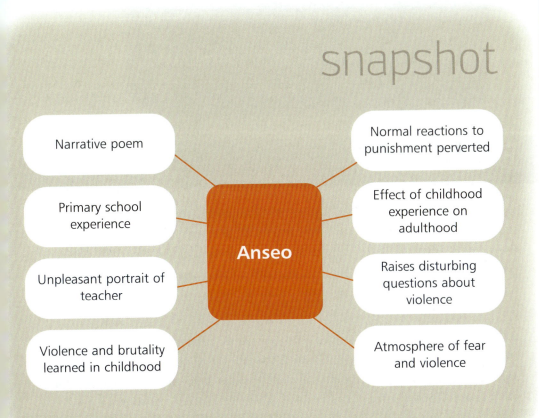

Narrative poem

Primary school experience

Unpleasant portrait of teacher

Violence and brutality learned in childhood

Anseo

Normal reactions to punishment perverted

Effect of childhood experience on adulthood

Raises disturbing questions about violence

Atmosphere of fear and violence

Julie O'Callaghan

b. 1954

PROBLEMS

Biography

Julie O'Callaghan was born in Chicago in 1954 into an Irish-American family. She was the eldest daughter and the second child in a family of seven children. The family lived five minutes from the beach at Lake Michigan and the children spent the summer swimming and playing in the sand. She attended a Catholic primary school and, later, Sullivan High School. English was her favourite subject and she enjoyed writing stories, articles and poetry.

O'Callaghan has lived in Ireland since 1974. She works in the library in Trinity College, Dublin and is married to the poet Denis O'Driscoll. On being a poet in Ireland, she says: 'Poetry in Ireland comes from an ancient tradition and is part of the culture. You don't have to apologise for it. I can't think of a better place to be writing.'

She has published several collections of poetry for children and young adults as well as her work for an adult audience, including *The Book of Whispers* (2006) for children, and *Tell Me This Is Normal* (2008). She is known for her humorous and sly approach to the absurdities of ordinary life.

O'Callaghan has earned numerous distinctions and awards for her work, including a number of Arts Council bursaries. She is a member of Aosdána, the national arts organisation.

Problems

Take weeds for example.
Like how they will overrun
your garden and your life
if you don't obliterate them.
But forget about weeds   5
– what about leaves?
Snails use them as handy
bridges to your flowers
and hordes of thuggish slugs
will invade – ever thought about *that*?   10
We won't even go into
how leaves block up the gutters.
I sure hope you aren't neglecting
any puddles of water in your bathtub
– discoloration will set in.   15
There is the wasp problem,
the storms problem, the grass
growing-between-the bricks-in-the-driveway problem.
Then there's the remembering to
lock-all-the-windows problem.   20
Hey, knuckleheads!
I guess you just don't appreciate
how many problems there are.

Julie O'Callaghan

Glossary

4	*obliterate*: wipe out, eradicate
15	*discoloration*: staining, fading
21	*knuckleheads*: idiots, fools

Guidelines

O'Callaghan got the idea for this poem when she and her husband moved house in the 1990s and each had a different attitude to the minor problems that go with settling into a new home, with one wanting to solve all the problems and the other happy to ignore them.

Commentary

Problem 1: weeds

The poem is written as a dramatic monologue. The opening line brings the reader right into the middle of the action, 'Take weeds for example'. It seems we are eavesdropping on a casual conversation on gardening. The conversation could be between a couple of friends or neighbours.

The tone seems easy-going, colloquial: 'Like how they will overrun / your garden' (lines 2–3). We can imagine the speaker of the poem as a reasonable person making the kind of observation that people make all the time on subjects such as gardening or the weather, the kind of everyday subjects that allow people to connect with each other without anything being at stake or in dispute. However, when the speaker says that the weeds will overrun 'your life' (line 3) the alarm bells begin to sound.

The suspicion that the speaker might lack a sense of proportion or reasonableness is confirmed in line 4 by the use of the verb 'obliterate'. When reading the poem, it is as if we take a step back from the speaker at that point, not wanting to be drawn into an unbalanced and negative view of the world, even if we are fascinated to know why the speaker is getting so worked up.

Problem 2: leaves

The speaker is on a roll now. There is energy in line 5 – 'But forget about weeds' – and the speaker turns to another 'problem', that of leaves and how they act as bridges to allow 'hordes of thuggish slugs' (line 9) to invade the garden and attack 'your flowers' (line 8). The language is striking, the speaker feeling the need to warn 'you' to be vigilant against attack from snails and slugs in the garden. However, the tone seems aggressive, even accusatory: 'ever thought about *that*?' (line 10). This tone implies that the listener (the 'you' of the poem) is not paying enough attention to these problems, or that the speaker has been left to face them alone.

Lines 11 and 12 refer to another 'problem' caused by leaves: that of blocking gutters. Up to this point, we can see a logical progression in the ideas of the speaker: weeds, garden, snails, slugs, flowers, leaves, gutters. The next movement of thought is less predictable.

Problem 3: puddles

The reference to gutters may account for the sudden mention of the problem of 'puddles of water', however, the reader has not been prepared for the location of these puddles 'in your bathtub' (line 14). As in the earlier part of the poem, the tone seems accusatory or suspicious: 'I sure hope you aren't neglecting' (line 13). This is another point in the poem where the person addressed and/or the reader may feel alienated from the speaker.

Four more problems

Lines 16 to 20 present a list of 'problems' delivered in quick-fire succession. The use of hyphenated adjectives, such as 'the grass / growing-between-the bricks-in-the-driveway problem' (lines 17–18), creates a sense of energy and momentum. The run-on lines contribute to the sense of motion. The 'problems' mentioned by the speaker (the wasps, the storms, the grass growing in the driveway, remembering to lock the windows) suggest someone who sees nothing but problems. It is hard to decide whether the speaker is simply obsessed with order or is completely overwhelmed by the small 'problems' of everyday living.

Problem 8: knuckleheads

Having worked him or herself up into an agitated state, the speaker now turns to the biggest problem of all: all the 'knuckleheads' (line 21) who do not 'appreciate' all the problems there are, and who, by implication don't appreciate the speaker who has tried to make 'you' aware of them. The last two lines can be read as the speaker dismissing 'you'; or they may signify that the speaker has expended all his or her energy and is now overcome by the 'many problems there are' (line 23).

Energy of the poem

The poem is dramatic and captures the voice of a persona or character. It uses many of the words and phrases of everyday speech to shape the thought: 'Like how'; 'I sure hope'; 'Hey'; 'I guess'. The use of run-on lines helps generate the energy of the poem. It is not rhymed and is written in lines of varying length. The tone is negative, with the speaker expressing varying degrees of animation, alarm, accusation, frustration and contempt.

A notable feature of the poem is its vigorous language and sounds, as in the phrase 'thuggish slugs'. If you read the poem aloud you will hear many guttural (throaty) and plosive (breathy) sounds that require a physical effort to create them. These add to the energy and expressiveness of the speaker's address and capture tones of disgust, anger or fear.

There are many examples of repetition in the poems, both of words and sounds. Look, for example, at the alliteration in 'thuggish', 'thought', 'that' or how the sounds echo across words as in 'gutters', 'puddles', 'bathtub'. Contributing to the sense of an energetic speaker is the imagery of war in the words: 'overrun', 'obliterate', 'hordes', 'invade'.

Perspective of the speaker

The poem portrays a single individual having 'a rant'. The speaker sees many problems but is frustrated that 'you' (the person he or she is speaking to) does not share those concerns. In the speaker's world the glass is always half empty. The perspective of the speaker may be a source of amusement to 'you' or 'you' might feel exhausted by the relentlessness of the speaker. On the other hand, the indifference of 'you' might be what drives the speaker mad. Reading the monologue, we might feel sympathy for the speaker; we might think the speaker exaggerates; or we might be offended by the way the speaker dismisses as 'knuckleheads' everyone who does not share his or her point of view.

Themes of the poem

One theme that emerges from the poem is that of perspective. Of course, one person's problem is often another person's delight (Gerard Manley Hopkins, for example, speaks of the beauty of spring 'when weeds . . . shoot long and lovely and lush').

Another theme that emerges is that of intolerance – the speaker is so certain that his or her perspective is correct that everyone else is dismissed with contempt.

Thinking about the poem

1. In lines 1 to 5, how are weeds portrayed by the speaker? How does the speaker suggest they should be dealt with?
2. In lines 6 to 12, what charges are laid against leaves by the speaker?
3. In lines 13 to 15, why does the speaker switch his or her attention to the bathtub, do you think?
4. If you were to list the biggest problems in your life, would you include any of those mentioned by the speaker in lines 16 to 20? Explain your answer.
5. In line 21 the speaker calls his or her listeners 'knuckleheads'. What does this name tell you about the speaker?
6. Choose three words from the following list which best describe the tone of the poem: urgent, frustrated, unreasonable, fearful, aggressive, alarmed, accusatory, anxious. Explain your choice.
7. 'The theme of the poem is that of perspective and tolerance.' Give your view of this assessment of the poem.
8. Which of these two statements is closer to your reading of the poem?

    The speaker of the poem is more pitiful than scary.

    The speaker of the poem is frustrated because people do not take things seriously.

    Explain your choice.
9. Based on your reading of 'Problems', suggest an alternative title for the poem.
10. "Problems' is not a poem that we should take too seriously. It's just a humorous representation of a person having a rant.' Give your opinion of this view of the poem.

Taking a closer look

1. Comment on the effectiveness of the description 'hordes of thuggish slugs' (line 9).
2. In your view, what is the effect of the verb 'obliterate' in line 4?
3. Select two examples of interesting sounds in the poem and say why you chose them.

Imagining

1   Imagine you are the 'you' of the poem. Write a monologue in which you have your say. You can begin the monologue with the words, 'Now, wait a minute'.

2   The poem is being dramatised as part of a television series entitled, *I'm as Mad as Hell*. You are the director. Write notes to the actor on how you want him or her to play the part of the speaker.

3   Imagine the scenario in which the monologue might have been spoken. Write a short paragraph describing the scene.

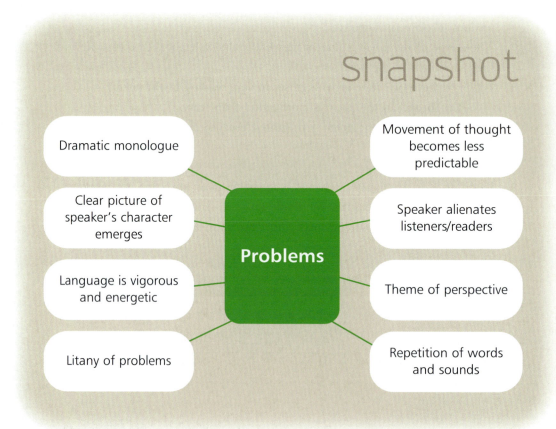

snapshot

Dramatic monologue

Clear picture of speaker's character emerges

Language is vigorous and energetic

Litany of problems

Problems

Movement of thought becomes less predictable

Speaker alienates listeners/readers

Theme of perspective

Repetition of words and sounds

Mary Oliver

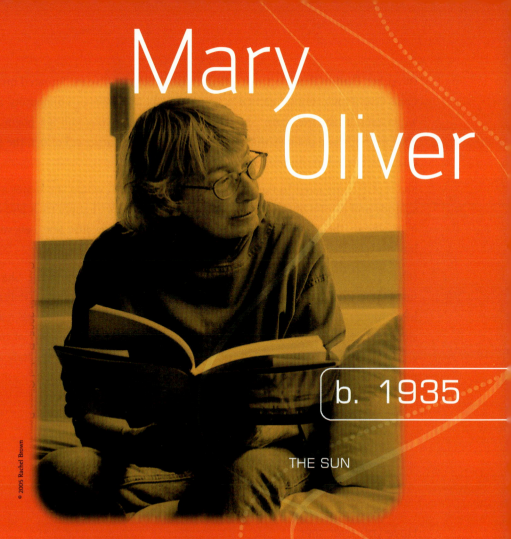

b. 1935

THE SUN

Biography

Mary Oliver was born in 1935 in a small town in Cleveland, Ohio. The farms, fields and woodland that surrounded her home were a source of attraction and she spent long hours in the countryside, frequently playing truant from school. From an early age she was determined to be a writer. She attended Ohio State University but did not obtain a degree. For a time she worked as a secretary to the sister of the poet Edna St Vincent Millay and lived in the poet's home.

Oliver has had a long career, publishing thirty books. Her first collection *No Voyage and Other Poems* appeared in 1963. It contains many nature poems that celebrate the Ohio countryside. Indeed, all her collections show a deep love for the natural world and the connections between humans, animals and plants. Apart from writing, she has taught writing at various colleges and universities in the United States.

Oliver has lived in Provincetown, Massachusetts for many years. Situated on the tip of Cape Cod, Provincetown earned a reputation as a bohemian community and many writers and artists live there. She takes long walks every day and her poems are filled with the birds and animals that she observes on her excursions. For her, the process of poetry is related to the process of walking.

She is often compared to the poet Emily Dickinson, with whom she shares a liking for solitude and careful observation of nature. Like Dickinson, her poetry is also interested in exploring the nature of the self. Oliver lives a simple life. She believes that an interest in material things hinders the curiosity of the spirit.

Oliver is one of the most popular poets in the United States today. She has won numerous awards including the National Book Award and the Pulitzer Prize. Interestingly, critics have praised and criticised her poetry for the same reasons: the simplicity of her language and her focus on nature. One reviewer said of her: 'She is a poet of wisdom and generosity whose vision allows us to look intimately at a world not of our making.'

The Sun

Have you ever seen
anything
in your life
more wonderful

than the way the sun,   5
every evening,
relaxed and easy,
floats toward the horizon

and into the clouds or the hills,
or the rumpled sea,   10
and is gone –
and how it slides again

out of the blackness,
every morning,
on the other side of the world,   15
like a red flower

streaming upward on its heavenly oils,
say, on a morning in early summer,
at its perfect imperial distance –
and have you ever felt for anything   20

such wild love –
do you think there is anywhere, in any language,
a word billowing enough
for the pleasure

that fills you,   25
as the sun
reaches out,
as it warms you

as you stand there,
empty-handed –   30
or have you too
turned from this world –

or have you too
gone crazy
for power,   35
for things?

Glossary	
10	*rumpled*: wrinkled, dishevelled
17	*streaming*: flowing directly
19	*imperial*: commanding, majestic
23	*billowing*: rising up, flowing, swelling out, surging, rolling in great waves

Guidelines

'The Sun' is written as one long sentence and contains four questions. The first two questions challenge us to admire and appreciate the beauty of the sun as it sinks and rises. The third and fourth questions contain a rebuke for those who have turned from the sun and its gifts. The speaker remains anonymous. There is no 'I' or 'We' pronoun in the poem so the emphasis falls on 'You'. 'You' is given neither a name nor a gender so that the poem addresses everyone who reads it.

Commentary

The first question

The first line of the poem, 'Have you ever seen' asks a question on observing the movement of the sun. What makes this line interesting is that its meaning changes depending on which word you place the emphasis on: 'you', 'ever' or 'seen'. The emphasis on 'you', for example, gives the line an accusatory tone, compared with the joyful effect of emphasising 'ever'.

A sense of joy, admiration and wonder is expressed in stanzas 2, 3 and 4 and into stanza 5 as the poem describes the setting and rising of the sun. The speaker clearly admires the sun's 'relaxed and easy' (line 7) attitude as it 'floats' (line 8) without any sense of hurry or anxiety, 'toward the horizon'. Its return is described as sliding 'out of the blackness' (line 13) while keeping its 'perfect imperial distance' (line 19). 'Imperial' suggests the stately majesty of the sun. The visual imagery of these stanzas is now replaced by the image of the sun's warmth, as the speaker asks a second question.

The second question

The language of the second question, 'Have you ever felt for anything . . .' (line 20), is more intense and more passionate than the first as the perspective shifts from observing the sun to experiencing its warmth. The move towards feeling intensifies the language so that the speaker refers to 'wild love' (line 21) and searches for a word that is 'billowing enough' (line 23) to express the pleasure of feeling the sun 'as it warms you' (line 28).

Throughout the first six stanzas of the poem the focus is more on the sun than on the person ('you') to whom the poem is addressed. However, from stanza 7, 'you' comes more into focus. We are given an image of 'you': standing 'empty-handed' (line 30) as the sun 'reaches out' and 'warms you' (lines 27 and 28). 'You', the reader, is almost made to feel mean or unappreciative.

Disappointment and the third and fourth questions

The word 'or' indicates a change in tone and mood. Gone now is the ecstasy and admiration for the sun. They are replaced by the accusatory, disappointed tone of 'or have you too / turned from this world? / or have you too / gone crazy / for power / for things?' (lines 31–36). **The implication is clear: those who turn from nature ('from this world') lose their ability to admire and appreciate the natural world and become obsessed with lesser things such as power and material wealth.** The emphasis in the poem is less on the spiritual gain to be had from encountering nature and more on the spiritual loss in turning your back on it. In an era of global warming, the relationship between humans and nature is more important than ever.

The mystery of nature, the fall and rise of the sun and the daily repetition of that miracle, is miracle enough for Oliver. There is no appeal to a higher power, just a delight in nature itself.

Form and style of the poem

The poem is written in nine four-line stanzas. The layout of the short lines on the page directs us in our reading of the poem, drawing attention to individual words and the feelings and ideas the poet wishes to emphasise. In stanza 7, for example, the emphasis falls on the word 'you' by placing it at the end of the line. The tone of the poem and the rhetorical questions that give it shape do not allow for contradiction.

Thinking about the poem

1 What does the poet describe and celebrate in the first question of the poem (lines 1–19)? Do you share the poet's enthusiasm?

2 What is the 'wild love' that the poet speaks of in the poem's second question (lines 20–30)?

3 What are the two questions that the poet asks in the last six lines of the poem?

4 Which two of the following statements is closest to your view of the speaker's mood in the last six lines of the poem?

> She is disappointed.
>
> She is disgusted.
>
> She is sad.
>
> She is angry.

Explain your answer.

5   Which of the following statements is closest to your own response to the poem?

The appeal of 'The Sun' is that it is easy to read and to understand.

The problem with 'The Sun' is that it is easy to read and to understand.

Explain your choice.

6   'The poem celebrates the daily miracle of the sun and attacks humans for ignoring it.' Is this a fair assessment of the poem? Explain your answer.

7   There is an absence of any clue to the gender of either the speaker or the addressee of the poem. What, in your view, is the effect of this?

8   Oliver has described herself as 'married to amazement'. Is this quality evident in 'The Sun'?

9   Oliver entitles the poem, 'The Sun'. Suggest another title and explain the reason for your choice.

Taking a closer look

1   Comment on the poet's choice and use of the following words and describe their impact upon you:

the rumpled sea (line 10)

slides (line 12)

its perfect imperial distance (line 19)

wild love (line 21)

a word billowing enough (line 23)

2   What are the implications of the description 'empty-handed' in line 30?

3   Do you think that the word 'crazy' is well-chosen in the final stanza (line 34)? Explain your answer.

Imagining

1   'That's not fair.' Write a short letter to Mary Oliver in which you challenge her on the accusations she makes against her fellow humans at the end of the poem.

OR

'Wild love.' Write a letter to Mary Oliver in which you tell her why you like her poem so much.

2   Imagine you were asked to turn the poem into a short film. Describe the kind of film you would make.

snapshot

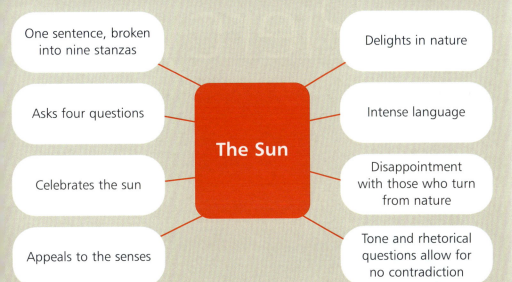

One sentence, broken into nine stanzas

Asks four questions

Celebrates the sun

Appeals to the senses

The Sun

Delights in nature

Intense language

Disappointment with those who turn from nature

Tone and rhetorical questions allow for no contradiction

Mary Oliver

Marge Piercy

b. 1936

WILL WE WORK TOGETHER?

Biography

Marge Piercy was born in 1936 in Detroit, Michigan. The Piercy family lived in a working-class neighbourhood in Detroit. Her childhood was affected by the Great Depression, during which her father struggled to find employment. He eventually found a job installing and repairing machinery. Although Piercy's father was not Jewish, her mother and maternal grandmother raised her in their Jewish faith.

Piercy was educated at public school in Detroit and later won a scholarship to the University of Michigan; she was the first person in her family to go to college. During her career Piercy has been involved in the feminist movement and other political issues such as the protests against US involvement in the war in Vietnam. She has lived in France, Chicago and New York. She now lives in Cape Cod, Massachusetts, with her third husband, writer Ira Wood.

She has written plays and novels as well as poetry. She has also edited anthologies. Along with her husband, she founded a small literary publishing company. Among her many publications are *The Moon Is Always Female* (1977), *Circles on the Water: Selected Poems of Marge Piercy* (1982) and *Colors Passing through Us* (2003).

Will we work together?

You wake in the early grey
morning in bed alone and curse
me, that I am only
sometimes there. But when
I am with you, I light   5
up the corners, I am bright
as a fireplace roaring
with love, every bone in my back
and my fingers is singing
like a tea kettle on the boil.   10
My heart wags me, a big dog
With a bigger tail. I am
a new coin printed with
your face. My body wears
sore before I can express   15
on yours the smallest part
of what moves me. Words
shred and splinter.
I want to make with you
some bold new thing   20
to stand in the marketplace,
the statue of a goddess
laughing, armed and wearing
flowers and feathers, like sheep
of whose hair is made   25
blankets and coats. I want
to force from this fierce sturdy
rampant love some useful thing.

Glossary

20	*bold*: daring, brave
27	*sturdy*: strong
28	*rampant*: out of control

Guidelines

'Will we work together?' is from the collection *The Moon Is Always Female*, published in 1977. In the poem the speaker expresses her strong feelings for her beloved and her desire to love him as best she can.

Commentary

Lines 1–18

The speaker says that her beloved 'curses' her when he finds she is not there in bed with him in the morning (lines 1 to 4), but the rest of the poem leaves him in no doubt as to the strength of her feelings for him. The tone of the poem is highly emotional.

Similes and metaphors of light and heat, as well as of loud sound, convey how passionately she loves him. She is 'bright / as a fireplace roaring / with love' (line 6–8), her bones are 'singing / like a tea kettle on the boil' (line 10). Physical images – 'bone', 'back', 'fingers', 'heart', 'body' – combine with the senses of sight and touch to express her passion for this man.

Piercy uses some interesting and original metaphors in seeking to express her strong feelings in lines 11 to 18. Her heart is compared to a 'big dog / with a bigger tail' (lines 11–12), generous with his affection. She is 'a new coin printed with / your face' (lines 13–14), an image that surely suggests the close relationship between them – and perhaps the newness of their relationship too. She goes on to say that she can scarcely find the words to express 'the smallest part / of what moves me' (lines 16–17), as words seem to 'shred and splinter' (line 18) in the attempt to convey how she feels for him. Again, we get an indication of the explosive nature of these feelings.

Lines 19–28

Moving beyond her immediate feelings, **the speaker describes the kind of relationship she wishes to create with her beloved.** Two unusual images suggest the creative possibilities of their love. The first is that of a 'statue of a goddess / laughing, armed and wearing / flowers and feathers' (lines 22–24). This, she says, will 'stand in the marketplace' (line 21).

As we know from history, statues are objects of respect, erected to commemorate or symbolise some great person or event. A statue represents public recognition and endurance. Goddesses were powerful, respected figures. Piercy wants to 'make' such a statue: a relationship that will be publicly acknowledged and that will last. It will also be beautiful, 'wearing flowers and feathers' (line 24), and happy, 'laughing' (line 23).

The second image that she creates is more unexpected. She hopes that their love will produce 'some useful thing' (line 28), as useful as woollen 'blankets and coats' (line 26). This cosy domestic image contrasts greatly with the public nature of the statue image. The suggestion is that both aspects of their love – the public and the intimate – are essential to her. The three adjectives she uses in the final two lines – 'fierce sturdy / rampant' each emphasise how fiery and passionate this love is, but there is also a sense in these lines that it is greater than them both. From its energy can spring something good and lasting.

Title

At this stage we can see why the poem is called 'Will we work together?' **She is asking her lover to 'work' with her to produce this beautiful, lasting, creative relationship.**

Thinking about the poem

1   What sort of relationship does the poet have with her beloved?
2   How does the language she uses (similes, metaphors, images) convey her feelings?
3   Do you think that the relationship is a new one, or has it existed for some time? Give a reason for your opinion.
4   How would you describe the relationship that the poet hopes to have with her beloved in the future?
5   With which of the following statements would you agree most?
    The speaker is too much in love for her own good.
    The relationship seems to be too one-sided.
    The relationship has great potential for both the man and woman.
    Explain your choice.
6   Do you like the way in which the speaker expresses her feelings in the poem? Give a reason for your answer.
7   From your reading of the poem, describe the personality of the speaker.

8   Do you think the title of the poem is appropriate? Give a reason for your view.

9   'I think 'Will we work together?' is a wonderful love poem.' Write a paragraph in which you agree or disagree with this view.

Taking a closer look

1   Choose **two** images from the poem that you find most effective in expressing love. Explain your choice.

2   What do lines 22 to 24 – 'the statue of a goddess / laughing, armed and wearing / flowers and feathers' – suggest to you about the kind of relationship the speaker would like to have with her beloved?

Imagining

1   Imagine someone (male or female) has written the above poem for you. In your diary, say how you felt when you received the poem.

2   Your class is compiling a selection of love poems and songs. You wish to include the above poem. Say why you think it is suitable for the collection.

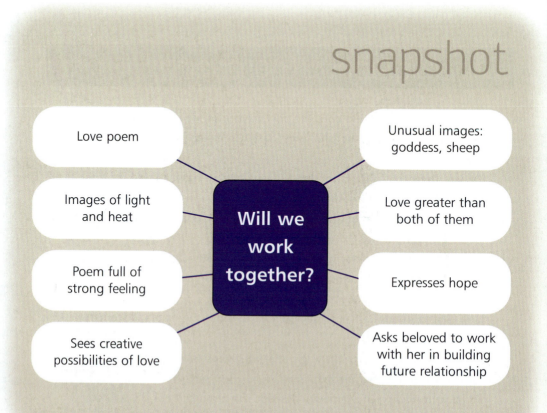

snapshot

Love poem

Images of light and heat

Poem full of strong feeling

Sees creative possibilities of love

Will we work together?

Unusual images: goddess, sheep

Love greater than both of them

Expresses hope

Asks beloved to work with her in building future relationship

Penelope Shuttle

b. 1947

JUNGIAN COWS

Biography

Penelope Shuttle was born in Middlesex, England, in 1947. Since 1970 she has lived by the sea in Falmouth, Cornwall, in south-west England. The weather, the landscape and the history of Cornwall have inspired her work and, in her own words, enlarged her imagination. She was married to the poet Peter Redgrove, who died in 2003. With her late husband she wrote two books on women's menstrual cycles, which combine anthropology, poetry and Jungian psychology.

Since 1980 Shuttle has published six collections of poems to date, all of which have been highly regarded. In an interview she said:

I follow my dreams as a poet, and draw from the deep reservoir of the images I find there and the places of the collective unconscious to which dreams lead. I always like that quote of Freud's – the craziest dreams are the most profound.

'Jungian Cows' is taken from her 1988 collection, *Adventures with My Horse*. *Redgrove's Wife* (2006) is a book of laments on the deaths of her husband and her father, as well as a celebration of her husband's life and work.

She has a keen interest in yoga and has remarked on the importance of breath in determining the shape and form of a poem: 'For me it is the way the poem breathes that gives it form.' On the importance of writing in her life, Shuttle says:

> With writing (and reading) active in my life, I can concentrate on the chaos, hold experience steady. I can explore, enjoy, mourn, comprehend within my own limits, and keep pushing them as far as I can.

Jungian Cows

In Switzerland, the people call their cows
Venus, Eve, Salome, or Fraulein Alberta,
beautiful names
to yodel across the pastures at Bollingen.

If the woman is busy with child or book,   5
the farmer wears his wife's skirt
to milk the most sensitive cows.

When the electric milking-machine arrives,
the stalled cows rebel and sulk
for the woman's impatient skilful fingers   10
on their blowzy tough rosy udders,
will not give their milk;

so the man who works the machine
dons cotton skirt, all floral delicate flounces
to hide his denim overalls and big old muddy boots,   15
he fastens the cool soft folds carefully,
wraps his head in his sweetheart's Sunday-best fringed scarf,
and walks smelling feminine and shy among the cows,

till the milk spurts hot, slippery and steamy
into the churns,   20
Venus, Salome, Eve, and Fraulein Alberta,
lowing, half-asleep
accepting the disguised man as an echo of the woman,
their breath smelling of green, of milk's sweet traditional climax.

Glossary	
title	*Jungian*: relating to the theories of Carl Gustav Jung (1875–1961), the Swiss psychologist who developed the concept of the collective unconscious and its archetypes. The collective unconscious is that part of the unconscious mind which stores memories, instincts and experiences common to all humans and inherited from our ancestors. These are organised in archetypes and influence dreams and behaviour
1	*Switzerland*: European country that is the birthplace of Jung and where there is a strong tradition of farming and herding
2	*Venus, Eve, Salome*: all three names are associated with female power. Eve exercised her power over Adam; Salome persuaded her stepfather, Herod, to give her the head of John the Baptist; Venus was the Roman Goddess of love
2	*Fraulein*: German word for an unmarried woman, used as a form of address or a title similar to 'Miss' in English
2	*Alberta*: a common girl's name.
4	*yodel*: a style of singing or vocalisation that was developed in the Swiss Alps as a way of communicating between one mountain valley and another
4	*Bollingen*: a small village on the northern shore of Lake Zurich in Switzerland, where Jung built a country retreat and completed much of his writing
11	*blowzy*: flushed and full with milk
14	*dons*: puts on, wears
14	*flounces*: frills
20	*churns*: containers for collecting milk
22	*lowing*: mooing
24	*climax*: the high point or culmination of an experience or sequence of events

Penelope Shuttle

Guidelines

A recurring feature of Shuttle's poetry is her humour and playfulness. Many of her poems deal with the extraordinary (myth, magic or fantasy) as it is found in ordinary life. The narrative of a Shuttle poem often has a fantastical or surreal quality but it is delivered in a dead-pan tone.

'Jungian Cows' may be read as a playful suggestion that the physical process of milking is linked to a feminine principle that is deeply rooted in the unconscious of the cows. In order that the cows respond to 'the man who works the machine' he has to take on the feminine persona of a milkmaid. Once the cows accept the man as an 'echo' (line 23) of the traditional milkmaid, they are content and give their milk happily.

This is a humorous version of an idea that occurs in different guises in Shuttle's work, namely, that **various forms of healing come not from masculine solutions but from an openness to feminine experience, know-how and wisdom.**

Together with her late husband, Peter Redgrove, Shuttle has pursued her interest in Jungian psychology. 'Jungian Cows', which is set in Bollingen where Jung did most of his writing, is a humorous application of his ideas to that most Swiss of Swiss animals, the dairy cow.

Commentary

Stanzas 1 and 2

The poem has a gentle, conversational tone with the speaker offering us some information on Switzerland. The speaker says the Swiss give names to their cows and remarks that the names are beautiful ones to call across the mountain pastures.

In the second stanza the speaker tells us that a Swiss farmer will put on his wife's skirt to milk the most sensitive cows if his wife is busy. **This information is given as fact, though we are not sure how seriously we are to take it.**

Stanzas 3 and 4

The speaker tells us that the cows are not happy when the milking machine replaces milking by hand. The cows sulk for a woman's touch and will not give their milk. So the man who works the machine dresses in his 'sweetheart's' good scarf (line 17) and wears her cotton skirt and walks 'smelling feminine' (line 18) among the cows until the milk comes because the cows accept the man 'as an echo of the woman' (line 23) and are content.

Form and style of the poem

The poem is written in irregular, unrhymed stanzas. The whole poem flows, aided by the run-on lines, the soft sounds and the long vowels. The poem is written in the present tense, which gives the impression of unhurried timelessness. The humour in the poem comes from the straight-faced recounting of stories that sound like tall tales.

Thinking about the poem

1   What do you think of the names that the speaker says are given to cows in Switzerland? What kinds of personalities are suggested by the names?

2   What is your reaction to the information that the farmer puts on a skirt if his wife is busy 'with child or book' (line 5)?

3   What is the cows' reaction to the arrival of the milking machine?

4   How does 'the man who works the machine' (line 13) make himself feminine so that he is accepted by the cows 'as an echo of the woman' (line 23)?

5   The man 'walks smelling feminine and shy among the cows' (line 18). What is your reaction to this image?

6   What happens when the cows accept the man 'as an echo of the woman' (line 23)?

7   Which two of the following statements best describe your view of the poem?

It is a poem about cows.

It is a poem about getting in touch with one's feminine side.

It is a poem about the ingenuity of farmers.

It is a poem about modern and traditional ways of farming.

It is a poem about the importance of the feminine.

Explain your choice using reference to the text.

8   In your view, what is the connection between the title of the poem and the men dressing as women?

9   'Jungian Cows' has been described as 'an amusing and humorous poem'. Discuss this statement. Support the points you make with reference to the poem.

10   'Behind the humour, the poem reminds us of the need for openness to the feminine in life.' Give your response to this reading of the poem.

Taking a closer look

1   How, in the context of the poem, do you understand the phrase 'the most sensitive cows' (line 7)? What, in your opinion, is a Jungian cow?

2   Comment on the phrase 'the woman's impatient skilful fingers' (line 10).

3   Do you think the adjectives are well-chosen in 'blowzy tough rosy udders' (line 11)?

4   In the last line of the poem the breath of the cows is described as 'smelling of green, of milk's sweet traditional climax'. How do you interpret this line?

5   Shuttle has written on the relationship between breath and the shape and form of a poem. Read 'Jungian Cows' aloud. How would you describe the relationship between breath and the shape of the poem on the page.

Imagining

1   Imagine you are to make a video of 'Jungian Cows' to show to your class. What visual and sound effects would you use in the production? Explain your choices by reference to the poem.

2   Write a short letter to Penelope Shuttle, telling her about your thoughts and feelings on the poem. Refer to the text of the poem in your letter.

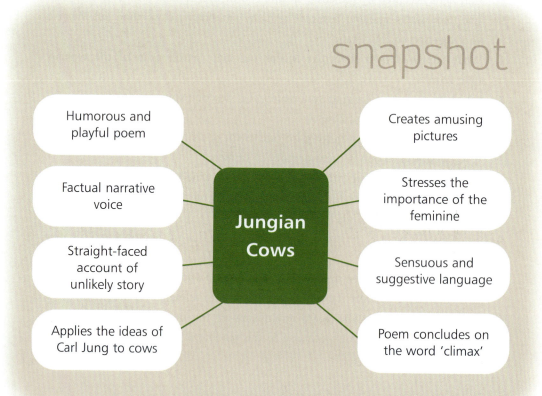

snapshot

Humorous and playful poem

Creates amusing pictures

Factual narrative voice

Stresses the importance of the feminine

Jungian Cows

Straight-faced account of unlikely story

Sensuous and suggestive language

Applies the ideas of Carl Jung to cows

Poem concludes on the word 'climax'

Peter Sirr

b. 1960

MADLY SINGING IN THE CITY

Biography

Peter Sirr was born in Waterford in 1960. He lives in Dublin, where he is a freelance writer and translator. He is project manager of the Liffey Project, a multilingual literature site. He is also a part-time lecturer at Trinity College, Dublin. He is a former director of the Irish Writers' Centre and a former editor of *Poetry Ireland Review*. He lived in Holland and Italy for a number of years before returning to settle in Dublin. He is married to the poet Enda Wyley.

His collections of poetry are *Marginal Zones* (1984), *Talk, Talk* (1987), *Ways of Falling* (1995), *The Ledger of Fruitful Exchange* (1995), *Bring Everything* (2000), *Nonetheless* (2004), *Selected Poems 1982–2004* (2004), *The Thing Is* (2009). The poem 'Madly Singing in the City' is from *Bring Everything*, a collection in which several of the poems are inspired by Sirr's reading of poetry from many countries and historical periods.

He is a member of Aosdána. In 1982 he won the Patrick Kavanagh Award for his poetry and in 1998 the O'Shaughnessy Award of the Irish-American Cultural Institute.

Madly Singing in the City

after Po-Chii-i

And often, when I have finished a new poem,
I climb to the dark roof garden
and lean on a rail over an ocean of streets.
What news I have for the sleeping citizens
and these restless ones, still shouting their tune   5
in the small hours. Fumes rise from the chip-shop
and I am back at the counter, waiting my turn.
Cod, haddock, plaice, whiting.
The long queue moves closer;
men in white coats paint fish with batter,   10
chips leap in the drying tray.
There's a table reserved for salt and vinegar
where the hot package is unswaddled,
salted, drenched, wrapped again
and borne out into the darkness   15
In darkness I lean out, the new words ready,
the spires attentive, St Werburgh's, St Patrick's, Nicholas
of Myra. Nearby, the Myra Glass Company
from where we carried the glass table-top.
In a second I will sing, it will be as if   20
a god has leaned with me, having strolled over
from either of the two cathedrals, or from the green
and godly domes of Iveagh Buildings.
Ever since I was banished from the mountains
I have lived here in the roar of the streets.   25
Each year more of it enters me, I am grown
populous and tangled. The thousand ties of life
I thought I had escaped have multiplied
I stand in the dark roof garden, my lungs swelling
with the new poem, my eyes filled with buildings   30
and people. I let them fill, then,
without saying a word, I go back down.

Glossary

Dedication	*Po-Chii-i*: a Chinese poet
13	*unswaddled*: unwrapped, opened
17	*St Werburgh's*: a church on Werburgh Street, backing on to Dublin Castle; the chip-shop mentioned in line 6 is also on Werburgh Street
17	*St Patrick's*: St Patrick's Cathedral on Patrick Street
17–18	*Nicholas of Myra*: a church on Francis Street
22	*two cathedrals*: Christchurch Cathedral is close to St Patrick's Cathedral and the other places mentioned in the poem
23	*Iveagh Buildings*: blocks of flats on Patrick Street
27	*populous*: abundantly populated, full of people

Guidelines

'Madly Singing in the City' is a narrative poem (it tells a story). The story is an unusual one. It is about a poem composed but not shared with an audience. It is short on incident. **A poet, having composed a poem, stands on a roof garden looking down on the streets of Dublin, ready to read his poem. Attracted by the fumes of a chip-shop in a street below him, he visits the shop. He returns to his roof garden and thinks about the disadvantages of living in a city. He abandons the idea of reading the poem aloud. We are left to guess why.**

Commentary

Dedication

The dedication, 'after Po-Chii-i', indicates that Sirr's poem is written in imitation of, or was inspired by, a Chinese poet named Po-Chii-i who lived from 772 to 846 AD. Po-Chii-i believed that poetry should be understood by the common people. His poems were notable for their simple diction, natural style and social content. These influences can be seen in Sirr's poem. For example, 'I climb to the dark roof garden' (line 2), 'The long queue moves closer' (line 9), 'In darkness I lean out' (line 16).

Po-Chii-i used his poems to attack government corruption, heavy taxation and abuse by powerful officials of the common people. He favoured the simple life. 'In Madly Singing in the City', the speaker associates a new poem he has completed with news he has for the citizens. Since Sirr's model for this poem is Po-Chii-i, we may guess that the new poem contains a political message for the citizens of Dublin, perhaps some social comment or criticism of life in the city, a place that the speaker claims has made him 'populous and tangled' (line 27).

The speaker tells us that he was 'banished from the mountains' (line 24). Po-Chii-i was banished from the capital city of his country for taking a stand against dishonest people in power. One of his beliefs was that poems and songs should be written 'to influence public affairs'. Is this the poet's purpose in Sirr's poem?

Sense of mystery

The poem retains a sense of mystery throughout. We do not know what the speaker's newly finished poem is about. We do not know why the speaker does not recite his poem. Particularly since he seems ready and even eager to do so at a number of points: 'In darkness I lean out, the new words ready, / the spires attentive' (lines 16–17); 'In a second I will sing' (line 20); 'I stand in the dark roof garden, my lungs swelling / with the new poem' (lines 29–30).

The final lines may give a clue to his failure to speak his poem. His lungs may be swelling with his new poem, but his eyes are 'filled with buildings / and people' (lines 30–31). We already know that city life does not appeal to him. Are we to understand that he is so overcome by dislike for what the city stands for that his enthusiasm for communicating his 'news' to its people quickly fades?

Form and style of the poem

Notice that the lines do not rhyme, and that they are of uneven length. There is no fixed rhythm. If the poem is read aloud, it can be made to sound like a passage of prose. It might even have been composed as prose, and simply broken up to resemble a poem. It would be interesting to rewrite it as a series of prose sentences, and to read it aloud in that form.

The tone of the poem is matter-of-fact. The diction is that of everyday speech. The poem has little in the way of poetic ornament such as imagery or sound patterns.

Thinking about the poem

1 Why, do you think, did the poet choose 'Madly Singing in the City' as the title for this poem?

2 The speaker mentions two groups of citizens: the sleeping ones and the restless ones, and the news he has for each kind. What kind of news do you think he might have?

3 Who are 'these restless ones' (line 5)? What tune are they shouting in the small hours?

4 Who are the 'men in white coats' (line 10)?

5 Halfway through the poem (lines 16–17) the speaker says: 'In darkness I lean out, the new words ready, / the spires attentive'. What are 'the new words'? Have they been mentioned already in the poem? What does the expression 'the spires attentive' suggest?

6 What does the speaker mean when he says, 'In a second I will sing' (line 20)? What will he sing?

7 From line 24 on, the speaker is conscious of two contrasting phases in his life. What are these? Which one would he prefer? Explain your answer.

8 What does the speaker mean when he says he has grown 'populous and tangled' (line 27)? What has caused him to be like this, do you think?

9 Why, do you think, does the speaker go 'back down' 'without saying a word' (line 32)?

Taking a closer look

1 Do you think this poem has a single theme? Explain your answer.

2 More than one-quarter of the poem is devoted to events in a chip-shop. What has this to do with the rest of the poem?

3 The speaker tells us that when he sings, 'it will be as if / a god has leaned with me' (lines 20–21). Why does the speaker introduce a god here?

4 The god the speaker mentions is imagined as strolling over to join him from 'either of the two cathedrals' (line 22). What do you think this image signifies?

5 What are the 'thousand ties of life' (line 27) the speaker thought he had escaped but which have now multiplied?

6 Does the poem suggest that the speaker is happy with his present life? Base your answer on details from the poem.

7 Choose **two** images from the poem that you find appealing. Explain your choice.

8 Based on your reading of the poem, give your overall impression of the kind of person the speaker is.

9 Did you find this poem difficult? Explain your answer.

Imagining

1 The speaker does not tell us why he 'was banished from the mountains' (line 24). Write a paragraph setting out one or more reasons why he might have been banished.

2 Choose an alternative title for the poem, and explain your choice.

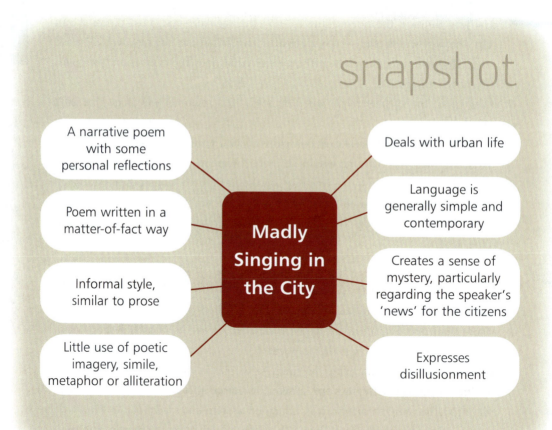

snapshot

A narrative poem with some personal reflections

Poem written in a matter-of-fact way

Informal style, similar to prose

Little use of poetic imagery, simile, metaphor or alliteration

Madly Singing in the City

Deals with urban life

Language is generally simple and contemporary

Creates a sense of mystery, particularly regarding the speaker's 'news' for the citizens

Expresses disillusionment

William Stafford

1914–93

TRAVELING THROUGH THE DARK

Biography

William Edgar Stafford was born in 1914 in Hutchinson, Kansas, the first of four children of well-educated parents. The Stafford family, like millions of others, became victims of the Great Depression. In search of employment, the family travelled from place to place. William played his part by helping to support his parents and siblings. He took a variety of odd jobs, but still completed his high school education in 1933. He graduated from the University of Kansas in 1937.

Stafford was drafted into the United States army in 1941, but became a conscientious objector and registered as a pacifist. He was allowed to perform public service duties as an alternative to military service. This involved doing forestry and soil conservation work in a number of states for nominal wages. During this period he married Dorothy Hope Frantz, whom he met while working in California. Later, after being awarded a PhD by the University of Iowa, he held a variety of academic posts.

His writing career did not begin until 1960, when he was forty-six years old. *Traveling Through the Dark*, his first major collection of poetry, was published in 1962; it won the National Book Award in 1963. Between 1962 and his death, he published over fifty volumes of poetry. In all, he wrote over 20,000 poems, 3,000 of which were published.

He died of a heart attack in 1993, having written a poem earlier in the day containing the advice 'just be ready for what God sends'.

Traveling Through the Dark

Traveling through the dark I found a deer
dead on the edge of the Wilson River road.
It is usually best to roll them into the canyon;
that road is narrow; to swerve might make more dead.

By glow of the tail-light I stumbled back of the car   5
and stood by the heap, a doe, a recent killing;
She had stiffened already, almost cold.
I dragged her off, she was large in the belly.

My fingers touching her side brought me the reason –
her side was warm; her fawn lay there waiting,   10
alive, still, never to be born.
Beside that mountain road I hesitated.

The car aimed ahead its lowered parking lights;
under the hood purred the steady engine.
I stood in the glare of the warm exhaust turning red;   15
around our group I could hear the wilderness listen.

I thought hard for us all – my only swerving –
then pushed her over the edge into the river.

Glossary

2	*Wilson River road*: a popular destination for drivers of four-wheel-drive vehicles along Wilson River in north-west Oregon, on the Pacific coast of the United States. Stafford worked in the area during the Second World War
3	*canyon*: a deep gorge or valley, with sheer sides, often with a river or stream at its bottom
5	*tail-light*: red light at the rear of the car
5	*back of the car*: to the back of the car
6	*doe*: female deer
10	*fawn*: young deer, in this case an unborn deer
14	*hood*: bonnet of the car

Guidelines

'Traveling Through the Dark' is the opening poem of a collection with the same title. Encountering a dead deer, the speaker feels obliged to remove it from the road as it might be the cause of a further accident. However, his decision to push the deer into the river at the bottom of the canyon becomes complicated when he discovers that the deer is pregnant with a still-living fawn.

Commentary

The speaker's dilemma

The speaker is faced with an ethical problem (set out in the first three stanzas), which causes him to hesitate before acting. He knows that if he rolls the dead dear away to clear the road, this will inevitably kill the still-living fawn. He also knows that he does not have the means to deliver the fawn alive.

There is a conflict between the speaker's sentiment, which favours preserving an unborn life, and his duty to act against his sentiments because a decision not to roll the deer over ('to swerve') might result in another accident ('make more dead') and this time the victims may be human beings (line 4). Thus, doing his duty is an unfortunate task: whatever he does, he will feel either guilty or unhappy: guilty if he does not dispose of the deer and unhappy if he does because it will mean the certain death of its fawn. It is a harsh dilemma.

Stanza 4

The speaker's car takes on a human aspect: 'aimed ahead' (line 13), while its engine purrs like a cat. The suggestion here is that the car is awaiting the speaker's decision. The surrounding wilderness also seems to listen, holding its breath, waiting for his decision, which is announced only in the final line of the poem. We imagine that the listening wilderness, in sympathy with the doomed fawn, is wishing for a particular outcome.

Final two lines

The speaker must make a difficult decision. When he says that he 'thought hard for us all' (line 17), he is including the unborn fawn as well as other drivers.

Before he acts, he hesitates for a final moment. He calls this hesitation 'my only swerving' (line 17), a phrase which looks back to 'swerve' in line 4. The word suggests that by swerving away from his duty to push the deer into the canyon, he could cause future drivers to swerve to their deaths.

Notice how abruptly the poem ends. The deed is done. The speaker makes no apology for his painful decision, nor does he try to lessen its effect.

Influence of Robert Frost

This poem addresses a man's lonely struggle to deal with a challenging situation. It resembles some of Robert Frost's most celebrated poems in its treatment of the themes of obligation and choice. It also resembles Frost's poems in its first-person narration (the speaker presenting the situation in his own voice), in its natural imagery, its focus on ordinary and everyday things, its simplicity of style and diction, its understated approach to its subject-matter, and its exploitation of small, local details. Both Frost and Stafford deal with the nature and consequences of choice. In both, images of nature reflect the concerns of human beings. In 'The Road Not Taken', Frost uses his rural road imagery to illustrate the difficulty of choosing between alternative courses of action, lamenting that he cannot travel both roads, and knowing that in future time he will be wondering about the possibility that he would have done better to have chosen the road he did not travel. Stafford wonders about conflicting duties and obligations, as Frost does in 'Stopping by Woods on a Snowy Evening'.

Thinking about the poem

1. Write out the line or phrase that, in your opinion, best expresses the writer's feelings. Explain why you have chosen that line or phrase.
2. Choose one or more of the following words to describe the poem: serious, worried, concerned, honest, foolish. Explain your choice.
3. Do you sympathise with the speaker of the poem, or not sympathise with him? Give reasons for your answer.
4. The poem gives a vivid picture of a sad event. Would you agree? Support your answer by referring to the poem.
5. This is a poem about a painful and difficult choice. What makes it so?
6. Discuss the ways in which this poem captures the emotions felt by the poet.
7. Which of the following statements is closest to your view of the poet's mood as revealed in this poem?

   > He is unhappy.
   >
   > He is calm.
   >
   > He is worried.

   Explain your choice by reference to the poem.

Taking a closer look

1. Without changing any of the words, could the poem be rewritten as prose? This would work for the first two lines, but would it work for the rest?
2. Comment on the rhythm of the poem, and the absence of rhymes.
3. Select a word or a phrase that you think is really well-chosen and explain your choice.
4. In line 12, the speaker says, 'Beside that mountain road 1 hesitated.' Can you explain why he hesitates? Does he have more than one reason for doing so?

Imagining

1. Imagine that this is a scene from a film. Describe how you would use setting, lights, music and commentary to convey the atmosphere to the audience.
2. The poem is called 'Traveling Through the Dark'. Can you suggest a better title to express the main theme of the poem? Explain your choice of alternative title.
3. Imagine that you are the person who found the deer. Write a diary entry in which you describe your experience of finding the dead deer on Wilson River road and what you did in that situation.
4. You have been asked to choose a poem to be included in a collection of poems for people of your own age. You have chosen 'Traveling Through the Dark'. Write a comment on the poem explaining why you have chosen it.

William Stafford

snapshot

Narrative poem

A poet with a
conscience

Understated
approach to a
serious ethical issue

Language close to
everyday speech

**Traveling
Through
the Dark**

Language plain and
without ornament

Presents painful and
difficult moral choice

Strong presence
of nature

Quiet, matter-of-fact
tone

Dylan Thomas

1914–53

DO NOT GO GENTLE INTO THAT GOOD NIGHT

Biography

Born in 1914, Dylan Thomas was the son of a senior English teacher at Swansea Grammar School in Wales, where Thomas completed his formal education before he was seventeen. He was not interested in academic studies. He became a newspaper reporter for a year, and did some acting. His main occupation from the age of sixteen was the writing of poems.

By 1923 his poems were being published in reputable journals. His first collection, *Eighteen Poems*, was published when he was twenty, and his second, *Twenty-Five Poems*, followed a couple of years later. The response of reviewers to these poems was enthusiastic. His admirers found his work obscure, and acknowledged that much of it did not make much sense, but they were taken by the force and energy of his language.

Thomas became a 'character' and a cult figure, embodying the predominant idea of what a poet should be: wild, disorderly, eccentric. One hostile critic remarked that 'he relied on beer and genius'. His behaviour generated valuable publicity for his poetry, which was extremely popular and still attracts attention. Thomas was also in demand as a broadcaster and his readings of his poems on radio attracted large and appreciative audiences.

His addiction to alcohol helped to bring about his early death, which occurred in the United States in 1953, at the age of thirty-nine, during a lecture tour.

Do Not Go Gentle into that Good Night

Do not go gentle into that good night,
Old age should burn and rave at close of day;
Rage, rage against the dying of the light.

Though wise men at their end know dark is right,
Because their words had forked no lightning they   5
Do not go gentle into that good night.

Good men, the last wave by, crying how bright
Their frail deeds might have danced in a green bay,
Rage, rage against the dying of the light.

Wild men who caught and sang the sun in flight,   10
And learn, too late, they grieved it on its way,
Do not go gentle into that good night.

Grave men, near death, who see with blinding sight
Blind eyes could blaze like meteors and be gay,
Rage, rage against the dying of the light.   15

And you, my father, there on the sad height,
Curse, bless, me now with your fierce tears, I pray.
Do not go gentle into that good night.
Rage, rage against the dying of the light.

Glossary

1	*gentle*: meekly, without a fight	
1	*that good night*: death	
3	*light*: soul, hope, will to live	
4	*at their end*: immediately before their death	
4	*dark*: death	
4	*right*: natural, inevitable	
5	*forked no lightning*: failed to shake or astound the world (with spectacular ideas or creativity)	
7	*last wave*: final farewell	
10	*sun in flight*: passage of time	
13	*Grave men*: serious men (who are also soon to be in their graves)	

Guidelines

The subject, as we learn from the final stanza, is the speaker's father, who is close to death. **The poem is a passionate appeal to the dying man to resist death with all his might.** Although the theme of the poem is straightforward, the language is not, with Thomas preferring to locate meaning in images rather than in statements.

Commentary

Stanza 1

The poem opens with a strong command to the listener: do not submit to death, older people must work hard to retain their passions and strength in order to resist fading away or losing the will to live.

Stanza 2

The second stanza tells of 'Wise men' who recognise that death must come, but still fight to live 'Because their words had forked no lightning' (line 5). When a stroke of lightning divides into different branches it is described, metaphorically, as forked lightning. Forked lightning is a powerful and dramatic spectacle. The suggestion in the poem is therefore that the men's words have failed to make a strong impact.

Stanza 3

The third stanza tells of 'Good men' who resist death because they recognise that they should have achieved more with their lives, that 'Their frail deeds might have danced' (line 8).

Stanza 4

The fourth stanza tells of 'Wild men' who resist death because they recognise that they allowed time to pass without making the most of it.

Stanza 5

The fifth stanza tells of 'Grave men' who resist death because they recognise they have been too serious and that, even if they have now lost their sight, they can still light up the world with joy.

Stanza 6

The final stanza is a direct address to the poet's father. Thomas wants his father to curse him with 'fierce tears' (line 17). If he did, the curse would be a blessing because it would demonstrate that he still has the strength to fight.

Secondary theme

The meaning of the poem becomes clearer when we learn that the poet's father was blind when he died (line 14), that he was a serious man (line 13) and that he had an ambition to be a poet, although his efforts in that direction were not notably successful (line 5).

His father's qualities and characteristics reveal the poem's secondary theme, which might be described as 'talent frustrated'. Underlying the poem is the sad contrast between the life lived by the father and the life he might have lived, had fate given him the means or the drive to exploit his talents. This gives the poem a sense of regret and loss.

Form of the poem

This poem is a villanelle. The standard form of the villanelle was fixed in the sixteenth century. A few modern poets, including W. H. Auden and Derek Mahon, have experimented with it, but this is the best-known example.

The rules for the villanelle are strict. The first and third lines of the first tercet (group of three lines) recur alternately in the following stanzas as a refrain, and come together at the end to form a rhyming couplet (in a quatrain).

Thinking about the poem

1   In this poem, Thomas deals with death and with individual lives. How does he connect the two themes?

2   Why does Thomas refer to death as 'that good night'?

3   Why should old age 'burn and rave at close of day' (line 2)? What does 'close of day' mean here?

4   What impression of the poet do you get from this poem?

5   Is this an entirely sad poem? Give reasons for your answer.

6   Does the poem suggest that the father's fate is a tragic one?

7   Choose two images that you find appealing from the poem. Explain your choice.

8   Which of the following statements would best describe your view of the poem?

   It is a poem about failure.

   It is a poem about human endurance.

   It is a poem about pity.

   Refer to the text of the poem in support of your choice.

9   What is this poem about?

Taking a closer look

1   One critic remarked that in the poetry of Dylan Thomas, words are 'hurled around in a way which does not make much sense'. Does this remark apply to 'Do Not Go Gentle into that Good Night'?

2   Thomas conveys his meanings through images rather than logical statements. Does this mean that the reader is not sure of precisely what he is trying to say? Can you give examples?

3   It is often said that the success of poems such as this comes mainly from brilliant sound effects and exciting rhythms rather than from the expression of ideas. Would you agree in the case of this poem?

4   Many readers find Thomas's poems extremely difficult. Why do you think this might be so? Describe your own experience of reading this one.

5   In this poem, Thomas balances positive words and images against negative ones, as part of a pattern of plusses and minuses. Consider this idea, giving examples.

Dylan Thomas

6   Thomas thinks of joy and grief, birth and death, as necessary to each other, and this is why he weaves them together in this poem. Consider how he does this.

7   Does this poem suggest that Thomas had an optimistic view of life and death? Does he give the impression that he considers life worth living?

Imagining

1   Try to compose a prose paraphrase of the poem.

2   Compose a short speech that the poet might have made at his father's graveside.

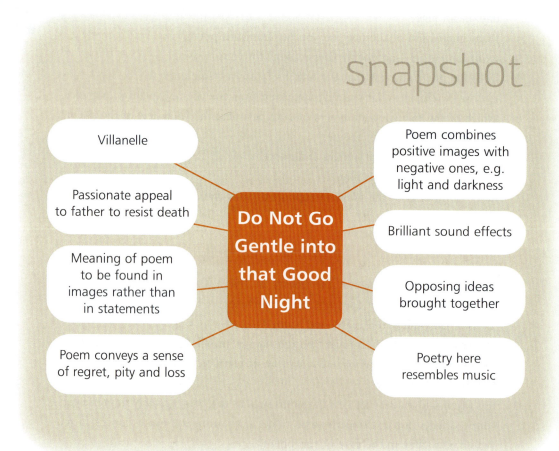

snapshot

Villanelle

Passionate appeal to father to resist death

Meaning of poem to be found in images rather than in statements

Poem conveys a sense of regret, pity and loss

Do Not Go Gentle into that Good Night

Poem combines positive images with negative ones, e.g. light and darkness

Brilliant sound effects

Opposing ideas brought together

Poetry here resembles music

David Wheatley

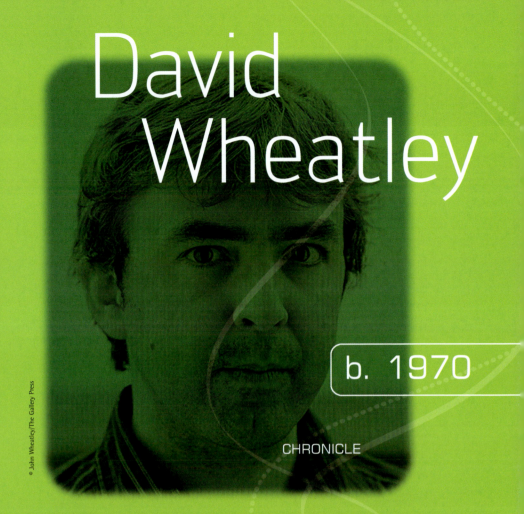

b. 1970

CHRONICLE

Biography

David Wheatley was born in Dublin in 1970 and grew up in the seaside town of Bray, Co. Wicklow. He was educated at Trinity College, Dublin, where he wrote a PhD on the poetry of Samuel Beckett. He edited the student magazine *Icarus* and was co-founder, with fellow poet Justin Quinn, of the literary magazine *Metre*.

Wheatley's first collection, *Thirst* (1997), was awarded the Rooney Prize for Irish Literature and was also shortlisted for the Forward Prize. His second collection, *Misery Hill*, was published in 2000. *Mocker* appeared in 2006, and in 2010 he published *A Nest on the Waves*. He has been writer-in-residence in Co. Wicklow, during which time he edited *Stream and Gliding Sun: A Wicklow Anthology*, and *I am the Crocus*, a volume of children's verse. He has also translated a number of poems from medieval and early-modern Irish for *The Penguin Book of Irish Verse*.

A distinguished reviewer and critic, Wheatley is a lecturer at the University of Hull, England.

Chronicle

My grandfather is chugging along the back roads
between Kilcoole and Newtown in his van,
the first wood-panelled Morris Minor in Wicklow.
Evening is draped lazily over the mountains;
one hapless midnight, mistaking the garage door   5
for open, he drove right through it, waking my father.

The old man never did get to farm like his father,
Preferring to trundle his taxi along the back roads.
Visiting, I stand in his workshop door
and try to engage him in small talk, always in vain,   10
then climb the uncarpeted stairs to look at the mountains
hulking over soggy, up-and-down Wicklow.

Cattle, accents and muck: I don't have a clue,
I need everything explained to me by my father.
Clannish great-uncles somewhere nearer the mountains   15
are vaguer still, farming their few poor roods,
encountered at Christmas with wives who serve me oven-
baked bread and come to wave us off at the door.

My grandfather pacing the garden, benignly dour,
a whiskey or a Woodbine stuck in his claw,   20
a compost of newsprint in the back of his van.
You're mad to go live in Bray, he told my father,
somewhere he'd visit on rare and timorous raids,
too close to 'town' to be properly *Cill Mhantáin*.

All this coming back to me in the mountains   25
early one morning, crossing the windy corridor
to the Glen of Imaal, where schoolchildren read
acrostics to me of 'wet and wonderful Wicklow',
and driving on down to Hacketstown with my father
we find grandfather's grandfather under an even   30

gravestone gone to his Church of Ireland heaven,
and his grandfather too, my father maintains,
all turned, long since turned to graveyard fodder
just over the county line from their own dear Wicklow,
the dirt tracks, twisting lanes and third-class roads   35
they would have hauled themselves round while they endured,

before my father and I ever followed the roads
or my mountainy cousins first picked up a loy
or my grandfather's van ever hit that garage door.

Glossary	
Title	*Chronicle*: a history of events
2	*Kilcoole and Newtown*: villages in Co. Wicklow. Newtown is short for Newtownmountkennedy
3	*Morris Minor*: a popular vehicle in the 1950s and 1960s
5	*hapless*: unfortunate
12	*hulking*: towering
15	*Clannish*: closely united through family ties
16	*roods*: an old measurement of land, about 400 square metres
19	*benignly*: kindly
19	*dour*: sullen, grim
20	*Woodbine*: a brand of cigarette
21	*compost*: decaying mixture
21	*newsprint*: the type of paper on which newspapers are printed
22	*Bray*: a seaside town in Co. Wicklow
23	*timorous*: timid
24	*Cill Mhantáin*: the Irish name for Wicklow
27	*Glen of Imaal*: a scenic valley in west Co. Wicklow
28	*acrostics*: poems or puzzles in which the first letters of each line spell a word or sentence
29	*Hacketstown*: town in east Co. Carlow
33	*fodder*: food, usually for livestock
34	*line*: border
38	*loy*: long, narrow spade

David Wheatley

Guidelines

'Chronicle' is from the collection *Misery Hill* (2000). The poet's experience of working as writer-in-residence in Co. Wicklow summons up history and memories of his family, long established in the mountains of Wicklow. Like most family histories or 'chronicles' the poem is made up of personal memories, anecdotes and hearsay.

Commentary

Stanza 1

The poet remembers his grandfather as he drove along the Wicklow roads in his van, the 'first wood-panelled Morris Minor' in the county. 'Chugging' is an expressive word that suggests the actual sound of the van, and by using this and writing in the present tense ('is') the poet makes us feel as if it is still happening rather than being a memory of a time gone by (line 1). A sense of remembered family pride in the car and a story of how his grandfather had driven it one night through the garage door bring his family history to life for us even more. The figures of grandfather, father and son (the poet) are closely linked.

Stanza 2

The poet's grandfather is seen in relation to his own father, a farmer, which brings the family chronicle back further in time. We are reminded of time passing as the poet remembers himself as a child 'visiting' (line 9) – he is not really a part of the life that is lived here – and trying in vain to communicate with his grandfather. For the poet as a child, it was the mountains and landscape of Wicklow, always in the background, that held his interest.

Stanza 3

Once more the poet describes himself as somewhat of an outsider in Wicklow, not understanding about cattle or how people talked unless his father explained it to him. Other relatives too (great-uncles and their wives) are remembered as the 'clannish' people (line 15) he met only at Christmas and who were vaguely kind and welcoming to him. It may be significant that he remembers them as they waved him 'off at the door' (line 18), the word echoing his sense of being an outsider as he stood at the 'door' of his grandfather's workshop in line 9.

Stanza 4

The focus is once again on the grandfather, remembered as he walked in the garden with his whiskey or his cigarette in hand, while newspapers rotted in the back of his van. He is 'benignly dour', a contradictory phrase that nevertheless conveys a kindly personality behind his silence. We get another glimpse of him as a somewhat reclusive man, set in his ways. To him, even a small town like Bray seemed an intimidating place, not 'properly *Cill Mhantáin*' (the original Irish name for Co. Wicklow) and therefore to be avoided (line 24). It is the poet's father who must have told him of the grandfather's opinion that he would be 'mad' to go and live there (line 22). (Wheatley was brought up in Bray.)

Stanza 5

In this stanza the poet is remembering 'all this' (line 25) as he crosses the mountains in his car, in the course of his work as writer-in-residence in Wicklow. Part of his duties would have been to visit schools and listen to the children's poems about 'wet and wonderful Wicklow' (line 28), poems which echo the love his father and grandfather have for their native county.

Stanza 6

The poet goes further back again into his family history as he describes finding the graves of his forebears (his grandfather's grandfather and 'his grandfather too', line 32). Once they may have 'turned' to their Church of Ireland faith (perhaps from Catholicism), now they have 'turned' to graveyard soil (what he calls 'fodder' in line 33) in the neighbouring county (Carlow), just beyond where they lived and travelled during their lifetimes.

Stanza 7

There are only three lines in this final stanza, but in them the poet evokes the sense of time long past. He imagines his long-dead relatives, who existed before any of things he remembers had happened. The word 'ever' in line 37 seems to suggest a long span of time. By ending the poem with the word 'door', might the poet suggest the barrier between the living and the dead that can only be opened to a certain extent, and that we can never fully understand those who lived in the past?

Theme of the poem

Genealogy has become a very popular pastime The poet's interest in his family history clearly inspired him to write the poem. In doing so he succeeds in conveying a sense of the connections and also the distances between the generations. These distances may not have been solely caused by time, they are also due to temperament and circumstances. But throughout the poem he makes us aware of the landscape of Co. Wicklow as a backdrop to the lives of everyone he mentions, including himself, which gives a great sense of the continuity of generations of the Wheatley family.

Form of the poem

Wheatley has chosen to write 'Chronicle' in the form of a sestina. A sestina is a rather old form of poem in which there are six stanzas of six lines each, followed by a three-line seventh stanza. This means there are thirty-nine lines in the poem.

The main feature of a sestina is that the poet uses six particular words throughout the poem as end words of each line, but in a different order each time. Finally, in the 'triplet', he uses all six words, in no particular order and not necessarily as end words. The six main words in this poem are: roads, van, Wicklow, mountains, door, father. (These are all established as the end words of each line in the first stanza.)

However, Wheatley has cleverly played around with the form by sometimes changing the words in a subtle way, making use of how sounds of words echo each other. For instance, whereas 'roads' is one of the key words, it becomes 'roods' (line 16), 'raids' (line 23), 'read' (line 27). 'Van' becomes 'vain' (line 10), 'oven' (line 17), 'even' (line 30), 'heaven' (line 31). 'Mountains' becomes 'Cill Mhantáin' (a witty pun that depends on how you look at the word) in line 24, 'maintains' in line 32, and 'mountainy' in line 37. 'Wicklow' is also echoed in a clever manner: 'clue' (line 13), 'claw' (line 20), 'loy' (line 38). The sound of the word 'door' is echoed in 'dour' (line 19), 'corridor' (line 26) and 'endured' (line 36). The word 'father' remains the same, however, with the one exception of 'fodder' in line 33.

It is possible to enjoy the poem without looking too closely at how the effects are achieved, but in the case of a sestina the form is usually so rigid that it is interesting to see how Wheatley varies it. In the poem he refers to the schoolchildren writing their 'acrostics' or word-puzzles – he has done a similar thing in writing this sestina.

Repetition is an important part of a sestina, so it is an appropriate form in which to write of family connections and continuity.

Thinking about the poem

1   What impression of the poet's grandfather do you get from reading the poem?
2   From your reading of the poem, how would you describe Co. Wicklow?
3   What sort of people are the poet's relations? Explain your answer.
4   How do the place names contribute to the atmosphere of the poem?
5   Images of roads and journeys occur throughout the poem. Do you think they are effective? Give a reason for your opinion.
6   What, in your opinion, does the poem say about families and where they live?

7   Would you agree that the word 'father' is a significant one in the poem? Can you say why this might be?

8   'The poem gives a great sense of how the past and the present are linked.' Would you agree with this view? Give reasons for your opinion.

Taking a closer look

1   Choose two details that appealed most to you from the poem and say why you chose them.

2   'Clannish great-uncles somewhere nearer the mountains / are vaguer still, farming their few poor roods' (lines 15–16). What do these lines suggest to you about the poet's relatives and their lives in Co. Wicklow?

Imagining

1   You have discovered a long-lost relative who emigrated to Australia fifty years ago. Write a letter asking him or her about the life they have led abroad, and giving them some (fictional) news about the family as it is at present.

2   Write out the conversation that might have taken place between the grandfather and his son (the poet's father) when he said that he'd be 'mad to go live in Bray (line 22)'.

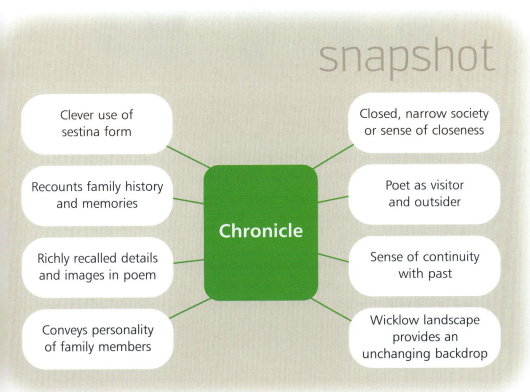

snapshot

Clever use of sestina form

Recounts family history and memories

Richly recalled details and images in poem

Conveys personality of family members

Chronicle

Closed, narrow society or sense of closeness

Poet as visitor and outsider

Sense of continuity with past

Wicklow landscape provides an unchanging backdrop

Richard Wilbur

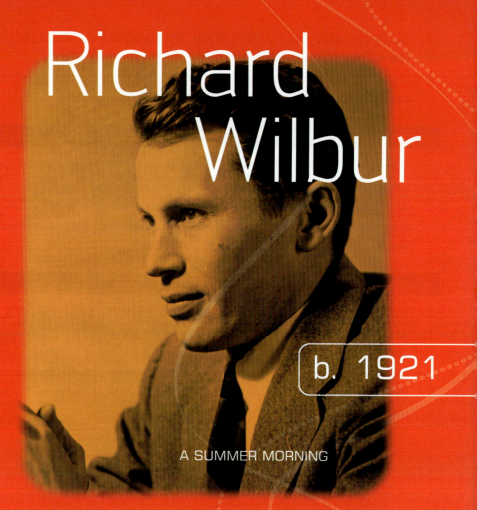

b. 1921

A SUMMER MORNING

Biography

Richard Wilbur was born in New York in 1921. He was educated at Amherst College and Harvard University. He has been a lecturer, professor of English and writer-in-residence at a number of universities in the United States, including Harvard, Wellesley College and Smith College in Massachusetts. In 1961 he was the US cultural exchange representative in the then USSR.

The son of a commercial artist, Wilbur was interested in painting in his youth, but he eventually chose to become a writer, possibly because of the strong literary influence of his maternal grandfather and great-grandfather, both of whom were editors. His writing career began after he had served in the United States army during the Second World War.

Themes in his poetry include nature, political issues, childhood innocence and love. His translations of French classical plays, in particular those of Racine and Molière, are highly regarded and have been successfully produced in New York. A distinguished critic, he has won numerous awards for his poetry, including the Pulitzer Prize. In 1987/8 he was named Poet Laureate of the United States. His *Collected Poems* was published in 1989.

A Summer Morning

Her young employers, having got in late
From seeing friends in town
And scraped the right front fender on the gate,
Will not, the cook expects, be coming down.

She makes a quiet breakfast for herself.   5
The coffee-pot is bright,
The jelly where it should be on the shelf.
She breaks an egg into the morning light,

Then, with the bread-knife lifted, stands and hears
The sweet efficient sounds   10
Of thrush and catbird, and the snip of shears
Where, in the terraced backward of the grounds,

A gardener works before the heat of day.
He straightens for a view
Of the big house ascending stony-gray   15
Out of his beds mosaic with the dew.

His young employers having got in late,
He and the cook alone
Receive the morning on their old estate,
Possessing what the owners can but own.   20

Glossary

3	*fender*: bumper of a car
7	*jelly*: jam
11	*catbird*: member of the thrush family of birds
16	*mosaic*: design made up of small different-coloured pieces of stone or glass

Guidelines

The poem is written from the points of view of a cook and a gardener, who work in what seems to be a big house set in its own grounds. Their employers are a young couple who had been out late the night before and are still in bed.

Commentary

Stanzas 1 to 3

We learn that the cook's employers are young and that they scraped the bumper of their car on the gate last night when they returned home late from a social night out in town.

Knowing that her employers are likely to sleep late, the cook prepares a 'quiet breakfast for herself' (line 5). She enjoys her coffee, jam, egg and bread in the 'morning light' (line 8), listening to the 'sweet efficient sounds' (line 10) of the birds and of the gardener's shears as he works outside. The lines appeal to our senses and create a simple but pleasant image of someone appreciating the surroundings in which she works.

Stanzas 4 and 5

The second image is that of the gardener, trying to get work done early on this summer's day, before it gets too hot. He also appreciates his surroundings: the view of the house he can get from his flower-beds, still covered in a 'mosaic' (line 16) of morning dew (we can imagine the pattern of drops forming an intricate design on the earth and plants).

In the final stanza the poet reminds us that the cook and the gardener are employees: they do not own the house or the garden. However, only they are able to truly 'receive the morning' (line 19). The image suggests welcome, honour and celebration.

The poem is highlighting a distinction between 'possessing' and 'owning' property. Ownership seems to be pointless; those who 'own' it, the young employers, are indifferent to it, but the cook and gardener who 'possess' it (if only temporarily) by working in it, truly appreciate the beauty of their environment and care for it. What, then, does 'ownership' mean? This is the issue that concerns the poet here.

Tone of the poem

Although the poem raises an important question concerning ownership, the tone of the poem is bright and light-hearted throughout. This easy-going atmosphere is created by the title, the images and the harmonious sound patterns of alliteration (e.g. 'snip of shears') and of end-rhyme.

Other interpretations

On a wider note, we could interpret the poem as relating to debates about ownership of land that have taken place in many modern societies in respect of the indigenous population, for example Native Americans in the United States and the Aboriginal peoples in Australia. Does the land belong to those who have worked it and are closest to it, like these early inhabitants, or to those who 'own' it through legal transactions, money or power?

Thinking about the poem

1   What contrast does the poet make between the employers and their employees?
2   How does the poet convey the atmosphere of early morning in the poem?
3   How do we know from the poem that the cook and gardener like where they work?
4   What sort of life do the young employers lead, as described in the poem?
5   Which **one** of the following statements best describes the poet's attitude to the young employers?

> He thinks they do not deserve what they have.
>
> He thinks they are careless and selfish.
>
> He feels a bit sorry for them.

Explain your choice.
6   What is your own attitude to the employers?
7   Do you like the picture of working life given in the poem? Give a reason for your answer.

Richard Wilbur

8 'The poem raises a lot of questions about ownership of land and care of the environment.' Would you agree with this statement? Give reasons for your answer based on the poem.

Taking a closer look

1 The poem is full of pleasant images. Choose the two that especially appeal to you and explain why you chose them.
2 'He and the cook alone / Receive the morning on their old estate' (lines 18–19). What do these lines suggest to you? Explain your answer.

Imagining

1 Write the diary entry for the cook or gardener for the day described in the poem. Then write the diary entry for one of the young people who own the estate. Try to show the different attitudes each of them has to where they live.
2 Suggest a new title for this poem. Give reasons for your choice.
3 A collection of poems called *Summer* is being put together. Explain why you would or would not recommend this poem for inclusion in the collection.

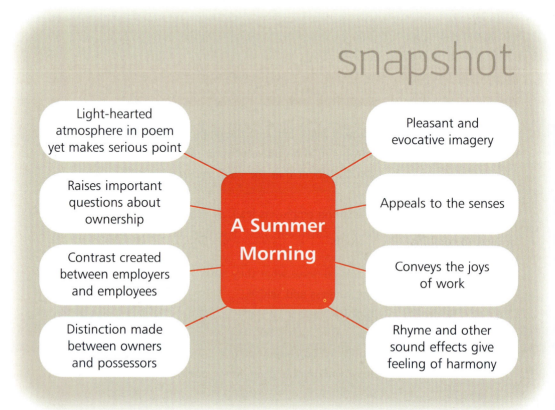

snapshot

Light-hearted atmosphere in poem yet makes serious point

Pleasant and evocative imagery

Raises important questions about ownership

Appeals to the senses

A Summer Morning

Contrast created between employers and employees

Conveys the joys of work

Distinction made between owners and possessors

Rhyme and other sound effects give feeling of harmony

Reading Unseen Poetry

Reading the Unseen Poem

Reading a poem is an activity in which your mind, your beliefs and your feelings are called into play. As you read, you work to create the poem's meaning from the words and images offered to you by the poet. This process takes a little time, so be patient. However, the fact that poems are generally short – much shorter than most stories, for example – allows you to read and re-read a poem many times over.

As you read a poem, jot down your responses. These notes may take the form of words or phrases from the poem that you feel are important, although you may not be able to say at first why this is so. Write questions, teasing out the literal meaning of a word or a phrase. Write notes or commentaries as you go, expressing your understanding. Record your feelings. Record your resistance to, or your approval of, any aspect of the poem – its statements, the choice of words, the imagery, the tone, the values it expresses.

Begin with the title. What expectations does it set up in you? What does it remind you of? Consider the different expectations set up by Gerard Manley Hopkins' 'Spring' and Adrienne Rich's 'Diving into the Wreck'.

Next, read the poem and jot down any ideas or associations brought to mind by any element of the poem, such as a word, a phrase, an image, the rhythm or the tone.

Be alert to combinations of words and patterns of repetition. Look for those words or images that carry emotional or symbolic force. Try to understand their effect.

Note other poems that are called to mind as you read the unseen poem. In this way, you create a territory in which the poem can be read and understood.

Poems frequently work by way of hints, suggestions or associations. The unstated may be as important as the stated. Learn to live with ambiguity. Learn to enjoy the uncertainty of poetry. Don't be impatient if a poem does not 'make sense' to you. Most readers interpret and work on poems with more success than they know or admit! Learning to recognise your own competence, and trusting in it, is an important part of reading poems in a fruitful way. Remember that reading is an active process and that your readings are provisional and open to reconsideration.

Do not feel that you have to supply all the answers asked of you by a poem. In a class situation, confer with your fellow students. Words and images will resonate in different ways for different readers. Readers bring their own style, ideas and experiences to every encounter with a poem. Sharing ideas and adopting a collaborative approach to the reading of a new poem will open out the poem's possibilities beyond what you, or any individual, will achieve alone.

In an examination situation, of course, you will not be able to talk with your fellow students or return to the poem many times over a couple of days. **Trust yourself.** The poem may be new to you, but you are not new to the reading of poems. Draw on your experience of creating meaning.

Poetry works to reveal the world in new ways. D. H. Lawrence said, 'The essential quality of poetry is that it makes a new effort of attention and "discovers" a new world within the known world.' In an examination answer, you are looking to show how a poem, and your reading of it, presents a new view of the world. Read the poem over, noting and jotting as you do so, and then focus on different aspects of the poem. **The questions set on the poem will help direct your attention.**

Possible Ways into a Poem

There are many ways to approach a poem, here are some suggestions.

The words of the poem

Remember that every word chosen by a poet suggests that another word was rejected. In poetry some words are so charged with meaning that everyday meaning gives way to poetic meaning. Often there are one or two words in a poem that carry a weight of meaning – these words can be read in a variety of ways that open up the poem for you. Think, for example, of how the words 'rocks' and 'sea' come to signify fixed forms and formlessness in Sylvia Plath's poem 'Finisterre'.

Here are some questions you might ask yourself:

- Are the words in the poem simple or complex, concrete or abstract?
- Are there any obvious patterns of word usage, for example words that refer to colours, or verbs that suggest energy and force?

- Is there a pattern in the descriptive words used by the poet?
- Are there key words – words that carry a symbolic or emotional force, or a clear set of associations? Does the poet play with these associations by calling them into question or subverting them?
- Do patterns of words establish any contrasts or oppositions, for example night and day, winter and summer, joy and sorrow, love and death?

The music and movement of the poem

In relation to the sounds and rhythms of the poem, note such characteristics as punctuation, the length of the lines, or the presence or absence of rhyme. A short line can create a feeling of compressed energy; a long line can create an impression of unhurried thought.

Look carefully at the punctuation in a poem and the way in which it affects your reading. Think of Gerard Manley Hopkins' 'Spring' and the way in which the punctuation works with the line endings and the alliteration to influence the flow and energy of the poem.

Consider how sound patterns add to the poem's texture and meaning. For example, do the sound patterns create a sense of hushed stillness, or an effect of forceful energy?

Ask yourself the following questions:
- What is the pattern of line length in the poem?
- What is the pattern of rhyme?
- Is there a pattern to vowel sounds and length? What influence might this have on the rhythm of the poem or the feelings conveyed by the poem?
- Are there patterns of consonant sounds, including alliteration? What is their effect?
- Are there changes in the poem's rhythm? Where and why do these occur?
- What part does punctuation play in controlling or influencing the movement of the poem?

The voice of the poem

Each poem has its own voice. When you read a poet's work, you can often recognise a distinctive, poetic voice. This may be in the poetry's rhythms or in the viewpoint the poems express. Sometimes it is most evident in the tone of voice. Sometimes you are taken by the warmth of a poetic voice, or its coldness and detachment, or its tone of amused surprise.

Try to catch the distinctive characteristic of the voice of the poem, as you read. Decide if it is a man's voice or a woman's voice and what this might mean. Try to place the voice in a context; for example, is it the voice of a child or an adult? This may help you to understand the assumptions in the poem's statements, or the emotional force of those statements.

The imagery of the poem

Images are the descriptive words and phrases used by poets to speak to our senses. They are mostly visual in quality (word pictures) but they can also appeal to our sense of touch, smell, taste or hearing.

Images and patterns of imagery are key elements in the way that poems convey meanings. They create moods, capture emotions and suggest or provoke feelings in the readers.

Ask yourself these questions:

- Are there patterns of images in the poem?
- What kind of world is suggested by the images of the poem – familiar or strange; fertile or barren; secure or threatening; private or public; calm or stormy; generous or mean? (Images often suggest contrasts or opposites.)
- What emotions are associated with the images of the poem?
- What emotions might have inspired the choice of images?
- What emotions do the images provoke in me?
- If there are images that are particularly powerful, why do they carry the force they do?
- Do any of the images have the force of a symbol? What is the usual meaning of the symbol? What is its meaning in the poem?

The structure of the poem

There are endless possibilities for structuring a poem, for example:

- The obvious structures of a poem are the lines and stanzas. Short lines give a sense of tautness to a poem. Long lines can create a conversational feel and allow for shifts and changes in rhythm.
- Rhyme and the pattern of rhyme influence the structure of a poem.
- The poem is also structured by the movement of thought. This may or may not coincide with line and stanza divisions. Words such as 'while', 'then', 'and', 'or' and 'but' may help you to trace the line of thought or argument as it develops through the poem.
- In narrative poems, a simple form of structure is provided by the story itself and the sequence of events it describes.
- Another simple structure is one in which the poet describes a scene and then records his or her response to it.

- A poem may be built on a comparison or a contrast.
- A poem may be structured around a question and an answer, or a dilemma and a decision.
- The structure may also come from a series of parallel statements, or a series of linked reflections.

The structure of a poem can be quite subtle, perhaps depending on such things as word association or changes in emotions. Be alert to a change of focus or a shift of thought or emotion in the poem.

Quite often there is a creative tension between the stanza structure (the visual form of the poem) and the emotional or imaginative structure of the poem. Think, for example, of the three-line stanza form of Sylvia Plath's 'Elm', which gives an impression of neat tidiness, and the alarming changes of tone that occur within this structure. For this reason, look out for turning points in poems – these may be marked by a pause, a change in imagery or a variation in rhythm.

If the poem is in a conventional form such as a sonnet or a villanelle, consider why the poet chose that structure for the subject matter of the poem. Also note any departures from the traditional structure and consider why the poet has deviated from the convention. For example, Derek Mahon's sonnet 'Grandfather' does not conform to the strict rhyming patterns and structure of the sonnet form, however, these breaks with convention seem appropriate for a poem that describes an unusual and eccentric individual.

Five Poems for You to Try

In each case, answer **either** Question 1 **or** Question 2

Thistles by Ted Hughes

Thistles

Against the rubber tongues of cows and the hoeing hands of men
Thistles spike the summer air
Or crackle open under a blue-black pressure.

Every one a revengeful burst
Of resurrection, a grasped fistful   5
Of splintered weapons and Icelandic frost thrust up

From the underground stain of a decayed Viking.
They are like pale hair and the gutturals of dialect.
Every one manages a plume of blood.

Then they grow grey, like men.   10
Mown down, it is a feud. Their sons appear,
Stiff with weapons, fighting back over the same ground.

1   (a)   What in your view is the poet's attitude to thistles and where is it most
          evident? Refer to the text in support of your answer.

    (b)   Choose one image in the poem that appealed to you. Explain your choice.

OR

2   Give your personal response to the poem, highlighting the impact it made upon
    you. Support your answer with close reference to the text of the poem.

Eating Poetry

Ink runs from the corners of my mouth.
There is no happiness like mine.
I have been eating poetry.

The librarian does not believe what she sees.
Her eyes are sad   5
and she walks with her hands in her dress.

The poems are gone.
The light is dim.
The dogs are on the basement stairs and coming up.

Their eyeballs roll,   10
their blond legs burn like brush.
The poor librarian begins to stamp her feet and weep.

She does not understand.
When I get on my knees and lick her hand,
she screams.   15

I am a new man.
I snarl at her and bark.
I romp with joy in the bookish dark.

1   (a)   What in your view is the mood of the poem and how is it conveyed by the
          poet?
    (b)   Choose an image or idea from the poem that appealed to you and explain
          your choice.

OR

2   Write a response to the poem, explaining the impact it made on you. Support
    your answer with reference to the poem.

Lay Back the Darkness by Edward Hirsch

Lay Back the Darkness

My father in the night shuffling from room to room
on an obscure mission through the hallway.

Help me, spirits, to penetrate his dream
and ease his restless passage.

Lay back the darkness for a salesman   5
who could charm everything but the shadows,

an immigrant who stands on the threshold
of a vast night

without his walker or his cane
and cannot remember what he meant to say,   10

though his right arm is raised, as if in prophecy,
while his left shakes uselessly in warning.

My father in the night shuffling from room to room
is no longer a father or a husband or a son,

but a boy standing on the edge of a forest   15
listening to the distant cry of wolves,

to wild dogs,
to primitive wingbeats shuddering in the treetops.

1   (a)   What impression of the father–son relationship do you get from reading
          the poem?
    (b)   Briefly describe the mood or feeling you get from reading the poem.

OR

2   Write a personal response to the poem. Support your answer with close reference
    to the poem.

Dreams

Hold fast to dreams
For if dreams die
Life is a broken-winged bird
That cannot fly.

Hold fast to dreams   5
For when dreams go
Life is a barren field
Frozen with snow.

1   (a)   Give your response to the imagery in lines 3–4 and 7–8.

   (b)   In your view, does the poem create a mood of optimism or pessimism?

OR

2   Describe the impact that the poem makes on you. Refer to the poem in your answer.

A Blessing by James Wright

A Blessing

Just off the highway to Rochester, Minnesota,
Twilight bounds softly forth on the grass.
And the eyes of those two Indian ponies
Darken with kindness.
They have come gladly out of the willows   5
To welcome my friend and me.
We step over the barbed wire into the pasture
Where they have been grazing all day, alone.
They ripple tensely, they can hardly contain their happiness
That we have come.   10
They bow shyly as wet swans. They love each other.
There is no loneliness like theirs.
At home once more,
They begin munching the young tufts of spring in the darkness.
I would like to hold the slenderer one in my arms,   15
For she has walked over to me
And nuzzled my left hand.
She is black and white,
Her mane falls wild on her forehead,
And the light breeze moves me to caress her long ear   20
That is delicate as the skin over a girl's wrist.
Suddenly I realize
That if I stepped out of my body I would break
Into blossom.

1   (a)   Do you think that the poem describes an interesting experience? Explain
          your answer.
    (b)   Comment on the image that most appeals to you in the poem.

OR

2   Give your personal response to the poem.

Exam Advice from the Department of Education and Skills

The Department of Education and Skills published this advice to students on answering on the unseen poem in the Leaving Certificate Examination.

> As the Unseen Poem on the paper will more than likely be unfamiliar to you, you should read it a number of times (at least twice) before attempting your answer. You should pay careful attention to the introductory note printed above the text of the poem.

It has also issued an explanation of the following phrases, which may be used in the exam questions on poetry:

'Do you agree with this statement?'

You are free to agree in full or in part with the statement offered. But you must deal with the statement in question – you cannot simply dismiss the statement and write about a different topic of your choice.

'Write a response to this statement.'

As above, your answer can show the degree to which you agree/disagree with a statement or point of view. You can also deal with the impact the text made on you as a reader.

'What does the poem say to you about . . . ?'

What is being asked for here is your understanding/reading of the poem. It is important that you show how your understanding comes from the text of the poem, its language and imagery.

Last Word

The really essential part in reading a poem is that you try to meet the poet halfway. Bring your intelligence and your emotions to the encounter with a poem and match the openness of the poet with an equal openness of your mind and heart. And when you write about a poem, give your honest assessment.

In responding to the unseen poem in the exam, never lose sight of the question you have been asked. Make sure you support every point you make with clear references to the poem. Your answers do not have to be very long, but they must be clearly structured in a coherent way. For this reason, write in paragraphs. Write as clearly and accurately as you can.

Guidelines for Answering Questions on Poetry

Phrasing of Examination Questions

Questions may be phrased in different ways in the Leaving Certificate English examination. In the earlier years of the examination questions were usually phrased in a general way. Some examples include:

- Poet V: a personal response.
- What impact did the poetry of Poet W have on you as a reader?
- Write an introduction to the poetry of Poet X.

However, in recent years students have been presented with more specific statements about a poet, to which they are then invited to respond. Some examples include:

- 'The poetry of Sylvia Plath is intense, deeply personal, and quite disturbing.' Do you agree with this assessment of her poetry? Write a response, supporting your points with the aid of suitable reference to the poems you have studied. (2007)
- 'Elizabeth Bishop poses interesting questions delivered by means of a unique style.' Do you agree with this assessment of her poetry? Your answer should focus on both themes and stylistic features. Support your points with the aid of suitable reference to the poems you have studied. (2009)
- 'Derek Mahon explores people and places in his own distinctive style.' Write your response to this statement supporting your points with the aid of suitable reference to the poems you have studied. (2008)

Answering the full question

You will notice that these questions refer to more than one aspect of the poet's work. For example, one asks you to consider Bishop's 'interesting questions' (i.e. the issues that concern her, her themes) as well as her 'unique style'.

Pay special attention to the guidelines for answering that follow the opening statement. For example, 'Your answer should focus on both themes and stylistic features.' Examiners will expect discussion of both aspects of the question, although it is not necessary to give both equal attention.

Do not neglect the final aspect of the questions asked. 'Support your points with suitable reference to the poems you have studied.' This may take the form of direct quotation or paraphrasing of the appropriate lines.

Whatever way the question is phrased, you will need to show that you have engaged fully with the work of the poet under discussion.

Marking criteria

As in all of the questions in the examination, you will be marked using the following criteria:

- *Clarity of purpose* (30% of marks available). This is explained by the Department of Education and Skills as 'engagement with the set task' – in other words, are you answering the question you have been asked? Is your answer relevant and focused?

- *Coherence of delivery* (30% of marks available). Here you are assessed on your 'ability to sustain the response over the entire answer'. Is there coherence and continuity in the points you are making? Are the references you choose to illustrate your points appropriate?

- *Efficiency of language use* (30% of marks available). This concerns your 'management and control of language to achieve clear communication'. Aspects of your writing such as vocabulary, use of phrasing and fluency will be taken into account – in other words, your writing style.

- *Accuracy of mechanics* (10% of marks available). Your levels of accuracy in spelling and grammar are what count here. Always leave some time available to read over your work – you are bound to spot some errors.

Preparing for the Examination

In order to prepare well for specific questions such as those above, it is necessary to examine different aspects of the work of each poet on your course.

The poet's choice of themes

Be familiar with the issues and preoccupations of each poet on your course. In writing about themes in the examination, you will need to know how the poet develops the themes, what questions are raised in the poems and how they may or may not be resolved. Bear in mind that the themes may be complex and open to more than one interpretation.

Write about how you responded to the poet's themes. In forming your response, questions you should ask yourself include:

- Do the poet's themes appeal to me because they enrich my understanding of universal human concerns such as love or death?
- Do the themes offer me an insight into the life of the poet?
- Do I respond to the themes because they are unusual or unfamiliar?
- Do the themes appeal to me because they reflect my personal concerns and interests?
- Do I respond to themes that appeal to my intellect as well as to my emotions, for example politics, religion or history?

The poet's style or use of language

Any discussion of a poet's work will involve his or her style or use of language. In preparing for the examination you should study carefully the individual images or patterns of imagery used by each of the poets on your course.

When you write about imagery, try to analyse how the particular poet you are dealing with creates the effects he or she does (i.e. what the poet's unique or distinctive style is). Ask yourself the following questions:

- Do the images appeal to my senses – my visual, tactile and aural senses, and my sense of taste and of smell? How do I respond? Do I find the images effective in conveying theme or emotion?
- Are the images clear and vivid, or puzzling in an unusual or exciting way?
- Are the images created by the use of simile and metaphor? Can I say why these particular comparisons were chosen by the poet? Do I find them surprising, precise, fresh, painterly . . . ?

- Has the poet made use of symbol or personification? How have these devices added to the poem's richness?
- Does the poet blend poetic and conversational language? Has language been used to denote (to signify) and/or to connote (to suggest)?
- Does the poet use simple expression to convey his or her ideas or complex language to express complex ideas?

An exploration of language may include style, manner, phraseology and vocabulary, as well as imagery and the techniques mentioned above.

The sounds of poetry

Many people find that it is the sound of poetry that they respond to most. It is an ancient human characteristic to respond to word patterns like rhyme or musical effects such as rhythm. This may be one of the aspects of a poet's work that makes it unique or distinctive.

Sound effects such as alliteration, assonance, consonance and onomatopoeia may be used for many reasons – some thematic, some for emotive effect, some merely because of the sheer pleasure of creating pleasant musical word patterns.

Look carefully at how each of the poets you have studied makes use of sound. Your response will be much richer if it is based on close reading and attention to sound patterns and effects.

The poet's life, personality or outlook

Since poems are often written out of a poet's inner urgency, they can reveal a great deal about the personality of the poet. An examination question may ask you to discuss this aspect of a poet's work. (See, for example, the question on Sylvia Plath mentioned earlier.)

Poems can be as revealing as an autobiography. Read the work of each of the poets carefully with this in mind. Ask yourself the following questions:

- Can I build up a profile of the poet from what he or she has written, from his or her personal voice?
- Is this voice honest, convincing, suggesting an original or perceptive view of the world?
- Do I find the personal issues revealed to be moving, intense, disturbing? What reasons can I give for my opinion?

It may also be that you like the work of a particular poet for a contrasting reason: that he or she goes beyond personal revelation to create other voices, other lives. Many poets adopt a different persona to explore a particular experience. Might this enrich our understanding of the world? Your response may also take this aspect into account.

Poetry and the emotions

At their best, poems celebrate what it is to be human, with all that being human suggests, including confronting our deepest fears and anxieties. Very often it is the emotional intensity of a poem that enables us to engage with it most fully.

Questions to consider include:

- What is the tone of the poem? Tone conveys the emotions that lie behind the poem. All of the elements in a poem may be used to convey tone and emotion. Each stylistic feature – such as the poet's choice of imagery, language and sound patterns – contributes to the tone of the poem. Look at the work of the different poets with this in mind.
- What corresponding emotions does the work of each poet on the course create in you as a reader? Do you feel consoled, uplifted, disturbed, perhaps even alienated?
- Does the poet succeed in conveying his or her feelings effectively, in your view?

These are issues you should consider in preparing to form your response to a specific question in the examination.

Conclusion

It is worth remembering that you will be rewarded for your attempts to come to terms with the work of the poets you have studied in a personal and responsive way. This may entail a heartfelt negative response, too. But even a negative response must display close reading and should pay attention to specific aspects of the poems mentioned in the question. Do not feel that you have to conform to the opinions of others – even the opinions expressed in this book!

Read the question carefully. Some questions may direct your attention to specific aspects of a poet's work – make sure you deal with these aspects in your answer.

Some questions may simply invite you to include some aspects of a poet's work in your response. It would be unwise to ignore any hints as to how to proceed!

You will be required to support your answer by reference to or quotation from the poems chosen. The Department of Education and Skills has published the following advice to students on answering the question on poetry:

> It is a matter of judgement as to which of the poems will best suit the question under discussion and candidates should not feel a necessity to refer to all of the poems they have studied.

Remember that long quotations are hardly ever necessary.

Good luck!

Glossary
of Terms

Allegory

A story with a second symbolic meaning hidden or partially hidden behind its literal meaning. Poems such as Elizabeth Bishop's 'Filling Station' or Thomas Kinsella's 'Littlebody' may be considered allegorical.

Alliteration

Alliteration is a figure of speech in which consonants, especially at the beginning of words, are repeated. The term itself means 'repeating and playing upon the same letter'. Alliteration is a common feature of poetry in every period of literary history. It is used mainly for emphasis, to reinforce a point. A good example is found in Gerard Manley Hopkins' sonnet 'Spring': 'When weeds, in wheels, shoot long and lovely and lush'.

Allusion

An allusion is a reference to a person, place or event or to another work of art or literature. The purpose of allusion is to get the reader to share an experience that has significant meaning for the writer. When a writer makes use of allusion, he or she takes it for granted that the reader will possess the background knowledge necessary to understand its significance in the context of the work. In many cases, the significance of the allusion becomes clearer as the poem evolves. The title of Elizabeth Bishop's poem 'The Prodigal' is an allusion to Christ's parable of the prodigal son told in the gospel of St Luke. The poem alludes to some of the themes of that parable.

Ambiguity

Ambiguous words, phrases or sentences are capable of being understood in two or more possible senses. In many poems, ambiguity is part of the poet's method and is essential to the meaning of the poem. The tile of Philip Larkin's celebrated poem 'Church Going' involves a suggestive ambiguity. It means both 'going to church' and 'the church going' (i.e. disappearing, going out of use, or becoming decayed).

Assonance

Assonance is the repetition of identical or similar vowel sounds, especially in stressed syllables, in a sequence of nearby words. Assonance can contribute significantly to the meaning of a poem. An example is 'with tiny white sea-lice' from Elizabeth Bishop's 'The Fish'.

Ballad

Ballads were originally songs, transmitted orally. They commented on life by telling stories in a popular style. In ballads, the attention of the reader is concentrated on the story and the characters. Every ballad must have a meaning that can easily be grasped by the reader. They are usually composed in quatrains with the second and fourth lines rhyming. The second part of Thomas Kinsella's 'Dick King' exhibits ballad-like features.

Colloquialism

A colloquial word or phrase is one that is used in everyday speech and writing. The colloquial style is plain and relaxed. At the end of the eighteenth century, William Wordsworth declared that his aim was to imitate, as far as possible, what he called 'the very language of men'. In much poetry of the twentieth and twenty-first centuries, there is an acceptance of colloquialism, even slang, as a medium of poetic expression. Fleur Adcock's 'To Heidi with Blue Hair' is an example of a poem that uses a number of colloquial words and phrases.

Conceit

The term 'conceit' is generally used for figures of speech that establish arresting parallels between objects or situations that, at first glance, seem to have little or nothing in common. All comparisons discover a likeness in things unalike. A comparison becomes a conceit when the poet forces us to concede likeness, while at the same time we are strongly conscious of unlikeness.

Consonance

Consonance is the name given to the repetition of consonant sounds that are not confined to the initial sounds of words, as in alliteration, though they may support and echo an alliterative pattern. In William Shakespeare's Sonnet 18, the sound of the consonant 'l' features throughout the poem in words such as 'lovely', 'darling', 'lease', 'gold', 'complexion', 'declines' and 'eternal'.

Convention

This is the name given to any aspect of a literary work that author and readers accept as normal and to be expected in that kind of writing. For example, it is a convention that a sonnet has fourteen lines that rhyme in a certain pattern. Sometimes conventions are abandoned or replaced. Eighteenth-century poetic diction, for example, gave way to a more 'natural' form of expression.

Diction

Diction is the vocabulary used by a writer – his or her selection of words. Until the beginning of the nineteenth century, poets wrote in accordance with the principle that the diction of poetry had to differ, often significantly, from that of current speech. There was, in other words, a certain sort of 'poetic' diction, which, by avoiding commonplace words and expressions, was supposed to lend dignity to the poem and its subject. This is entirely contrary to modern practice.

Genre

The term is used to signify a particular literary species or form. Traditionally, the important genres were epic, tragedy, comedy, elegy, satire, lyric and pastoral. Until modern times, critics tended to distinguish carefully between the various genres and writers were expected to follow the rules prescribed for each. For example, if a poet wrote an epic, it was assumed that his or her language would be dignified, in keeping with the heroic nature of the subject, and that he or she would use epic similes and long descriptive passages.

Imagery

This is a term with a very wide application. When we speak of the imagery of a poem, we refer to all its images taken collectively. The poet Cecil Day Lewis puts the matter well when he describes an image as 'a picture made out of words'. If we consider imagery in its narrow and popular sense, it signifies descriptions of visible objects and scenes, as, for example, in Derek Mahon's 'After the Titanic': 'Where the tide leaves broken toys and hat-boxes / Silently at my door'. In its wider sense, imagery signifies figurative language, especially metaphor and simile.

Lyric

Originally a lyric was a song performed to the accompaniment of a lyre. The term is now used to signify any relatively short poem in which a single speaker, not necessarily representing the poet, expresses feelings and thoughts in a personal and subjective fashion. Most poems are either lyrics or feature lyrical elements.

Metaphor and simile

Metaphor and simile are the two commonest figures of speech in poetry. A simile contains two parts – a subject that is the focus of attention, and another element that is introduced for the sake of emphasising some quality in the subject. In a simile, the poet uses a word such as 'like' or 'as' to show that a comparison is being made.

Metaphor differs from simile only in omitting the comparative word ('like' or 'as'). If in a simile someone's teeth are like pearls, in a metaphor they *are* pearls. While in the case of a simile the comparison is openly proclaimed as such, in the case of a metaphor the comparison is implied. A metaphor is capable of a greater range of suggestiveness than a simile and its implications are wider and richer. The simile, by its very nature (with the 'like' or 'as' formula), is limited to a comparatively small area of suggestion. One advantage of metaphor is its tendency to establish numerous relationships between the two things being compared. In Sylvia Plath's 'Poppies in July', the poet compares the red flowers to 'little hell flames'.

Metre

Metre is the rhythm or pattern of sounds in a line of verse. The metrical scheme is determined by the number and length of feet in a line. A foot is a unit of poetic metre that has one unstressed syllable followed by one stressed syllable. The number of feet in a line determines the description of its length, for example a line of five feet (or five stresses) is described as a pentameter.

Onomatopoeia

Onomatopoeia involves the use of words that resemble, or enact, the very sounds they imitate. If a poet tries to make the sound reflect the meaning, he or she is using onomatopoeia. In Thomas Kinsella's 'Mirror in February' the phrase 'hacked clean' captures the sound of the axe cutting into the wood of the tree.

Paradox

A paradox is an apparently self-contradictory statement, which, on further consideration, is found to contain an essential truth. Paradox is so intrinsic to human nature that poetry rich in paradox is valued as a reflection of the central truths of human experience. Derek Mahon's 'Antarctica' explores the paradox that the ridiculous can contain the sublime.

Personification

Personification involves the attribution of human qualities to an animal, concept or object. For example, time and beauty are personified in many of William Shakespeare's sonnets, where time is depicted as the destroyer, delving furrows in fragile beauty's brow (see Sonnet 60).

Sestina

A sestina is a form of poem in which there are six stanzas of six lines each, followed by a three-line seventh stanza (known as an envoy). The main feature of a sestina is that the poet uses six particular words throughout the poem as the end words of each line, but in a different order in each stanza. Elizabeth Bishop's 'Sestina' and David Wheatley's 'Chronicle' are in the form of a sestina.

Sibilance

Sibilance is the hissing sound associated with certain letters such as 's' and 'sh'. The sound is used to good effect by the poet Mary Oliver when she tells us how the sun 'slides again / out of the blackness' in her poem 'The Sun'.

Simile

See 'metaphor and simile'.

Sonnet

A sonnet is a single-stanza lyric, consisting of fourteen lines. These fourteen lines are long enough to make possible the fairly complex development of a single theme, and short enough to test the poet's gift for concentrated expression. The poet's freedom is further restricted by a demanding rhyme scheme and a conventional metrical form (five strong stresses in each line). The greatest sonnets are those in which the poet has overcome the limitations of the form and achieved the great aim of reconciling freedom of expression, variety of rhythm, mood and tone and richness of imagery with adherence to a rigid set of conventions.

English poets have traditionally written one of two kinds of sonnet – the Petrarchan and the Shakespearean. The Petrarchan sonnet, favoured by William Wordsworth, falls into two divisions – the octave (eight lines rhyming *abba*, *abba*) and the sestet (six lines generally rhyming *cde*, *cde*). The octave generally presents a problem, situation or incident; the sestet resolves the problem or comments on the situation or incident. The Shakespearean sonnet consists of three quatrains (groups of four lines rhyming *abab*, *cdcd*, *efef*) and a rhyming couplet (*gg*).

Style

Style may be defined as the manner of expression characteristic of a writer – that is, his or her particular way of saying things. Consideration of style involves an examination of the writer's diction, use of figures of speech, order of words, tone and feeling, rhythm and movement.

Traditionally, styles were classified according to three categories: high (formal or learned), middle and low (plain). Convention required that the level of style be appropriate to the speaker, the subject matter, the occasion that inspired the poem and the literary genre. The critic Northrop Frye suggests that styles could be classified under two broad headings: demotic style, modelled on the language, rhythms and associations of everyday speech, and hieratic style, involving formal, elaborate expression, with the aim of separating literary language from ordinary speech.

Symbol

A symbol is anything that stands for something else. In this sense, all words are symbols because they signify things other than themselves. Literary symbolism, however, comes about when the *objects* signified by the words stand in turn for things other than themselves. At a simple level, symbolism is familiar to almost everybody because certain conventional symbols are universally popular. Objects commonly associated with fixed ideas or qualities have come to symbolise these: for example, the cross is the primary Christian symbol, and the dove is a symbol of peace. Colour symbols have no fixed meaning, but derive their significance from a context: green may signify innocence or Irish patriotism or envy.

The literary symbol is not a token with a precise meaning to be pinned down and accurately described, and many derive from the private experience of the poet. In William Stafford's 'Traveling Through the Dark', for example, the journey is symbolic of the lonely choices individuals have to make in moments of crisis.

Tone

When one is trying to describe the tone of a poem, it is best to think of every poem as a spoken, rather than a written, exercise. A poem has at least one speaker who is addressing somebody or something. In some poems, the speaker can be thought of as meditating aloud, talking to himself or herself. We, the readers, catch him or her in the act and overhear the words.

Every speaker must inevitably have an attitude to the person or object being addressed or talked about, and must also see himself or herself in some relationship with that person or object. This attitude or relationship will determine the tone of the utterance. Tone may thus be defined as the expression of a literary speaker's attitude to, and relationship with, the listener or the subject. In real life, a person's attitude to another is often revealed in the tone of voice of that person and in the words chosen. A sensitive reading aloud of most poems will soon reveal the tone of a speaker's utterance. Adrienne Rich's poems present an interesting study in tone. The language of her poetry is clear and direct and reveals a range of tones from bitterness to hope.

Villanelle

A villanelle is a highly stylised formal poem. It has five stanzas of three lines (tercets) and a final stanza of four lines (quatrain). In the tercets the rhyme scheme is *aba*. Each of these three-line stanzas ends in a refrain and there are two refrains that alternate throughout the poem. In the quatrain the two refrains come together. The villanelle is often used for poems that deal with death and grief. Derek Mahon's 'Antarctica' is an example of a villanelle.

Poets Examined at Higher Level in Previous Years

2010
T. S. Eliot
Patrick Kavanagh
Adrienne Rich
W. B. Yeats

2009
Derek Walcott
John Keats
John Montague
Elizabeth Bishop

2008
Philip Larkin
John Donne
Derek Mahon
Adrienne Rich

2007
Robert Frost
T.S. Eliot
John Montague
Sylvia Plath

2006
John Donne
Thomas Hardy
Elizabeth Bishop
Michael Longley

2005
Eavan Boland
Emily Dickinson
T.S. Eliot
W.B. Yeats

2004
G.M. Hopkins
Patrick Kavanagh
Derek Mahon
Sylvia Plath

2003
John Donne
Robert Frost
Sylvia Plath
Seamus Heaney

2002
Elizabeth Bishop
Eavan Boland
Michael Longley
William Shakespeare

2001
Elizabeth Bishop
John Keats
Philip Larkin
Michael Longley

Notes

22669498

i22669528

Notes